HOMER'S LIVING LANGUAGE

What if formularity, meter, and *Kunstsprache* in Homer weren't abstract, mechanical systems that constrained the poet's freedom, but rather adaptive technologies that helped poets to sustain feats of great creativity? This book explores this hypothesis by reassessing the key formal features of Homer's poetic technique through the lenses of contemporary linguistics and the cognitive sciences, as well as by drawing some unexpected parallels with the contemporary world (from the dialects of English used in popular music, to the prosodic strategies employed in live sports commentary, to the neuroscience of jazz improvisation). Aimed at Classics students and specialists alike, this book provides thorough and accessible introductions to the main debates in Homeric poetics, along with new and thought-provoking ways of understanding Homeric creativity.

CHIARA BOZZONE is currently Privatdozentin at the Institute for Indo-European and Historical Linguistics at the Ludwig-Maximilians-Universität München.

HOMER'S LIVING LANGUAGE

Formularity, Dialect, and Creativity in Oral-Traditional Poetry

CHIARA BOZZONE

Ludwig-Maximilians-Universität München

Shaftesbury Road, Cambridge CB2 8EA, United Kingdom

One Liberty Plaza, 20th Floor, New York, NY 10006, USA

477 Williamstown Road, Port Melbourne, VIC 3207, Australia

314–321, 3rd Floor, Plot 3, Splendor Forum, Jasola District Centre, New Delhi – 110025, India

103 Penang Road, #05–06/07, Visioncrest Commercial, Singapore 238467

Cambridge University Press is part of Cambridge University Press & Assessment, a department of the University of Cambridge.

We share the University's mission to contribute to society through the pursuit of education, learning and research at the highest international levels of excellence.

www.cambridge.org
Information on this title: www.cambridge.org/9781009065887

DOI: 10.1017/9781009067157

© Chiara Bozzone 2024

This publication is in copyright. Subject to statutory exception and to the provisions of relevant collective licensing agreements, no reproduction of any part may take place without the written permission of Cambridge University Press & Assessment.

First published 2024
First paperback edition 2025

A catalogue record for this publication is available from the British Library

Library of Congress Cataloging-in-Publication data
NAMES: Bozzone, Chiara, author.
TITLE: Homer's living language : formularity, dialect, and creativity in oral-traditional poetry / Chiara Bozzone, Ludwig-Maximilians-Universität München.
DESCRIPTION: Cambridge ; New York, NY : Cambridge University Press, 2024. | Includes bibliographical references and index.
IDENTIFIERS: LCCN 2023030523 (print) | LCCN 2023030524 (ebook) | ISBN 9781316512418 (hardback) | ISBN 9781009065887 (paperback) | ISBN 9781009067157 (ebook)
SUBJECTS: LCSH: Homer – Literary style. | Homer – Language. | LCGFT: Literary criticism.
CLASSIFICATION: LCC PA4175 .B69 2024 (print) | LCC PA4175 (ebook) | DDC 883/.01–dc23/eng/ 20230816
LC record available at https://lccn.loc.gov/2023030523
LC ebook record available at https://lccn.loc.gov/2023030524

ISBN 978-1-316-51241-8 Hardback
ISBN 978-1-009-06588-7 Paperback

Cambridge University Press & Assessment has no responsibility for the persistence or accuracy of URLs for external or third-party internet websites referred to in this publication and does not guarantee that any content on such websites is, or will remain, accurate or appropriate.

*A Ryan e Leone,
i miei amori*

Contents

List of Figures	*page* x
List of Tables	xi
Acknowledgments	xii
Note on the Transliteration	xv
List of Abbreviations	xvi

Introduction: The Paradox of Homeric Creativity	1
1 Formularity	**5**
1.1 The History of Homeric Formularity	6
1.1.1 Parry: Homer's Style as Traditional	6
1.1.2 Homer's Orality and the Quantitative Study of Formulas	11
1.1.3 Formulas and Their Flexibility	13
1.1.4 The Disappearance of the Formula	17
1.2 Formularity in Language	20
1.2.1 The Disadvantage of the Early Start	20
1.2.2 Formularity in Corpus Linguistics, Psycholinguistics, and Historical Linguistics	22
1.2.3 Measuring the Idiom Principle	25
1.3 Formularity in Cognition	27
1.3.1 Working Memory, Chunking, and Automation	27
1.3.2 Formularity, Mastery, and Genre	30
1.3.3 Collocational Measures in Homer and Other Corpora	33
1.4 A General Theory of Formularity	44
1.4.1 The Memory of the Poet	44
1.4.2 From Themes, to Conceptual Associations, to Collocations	48
1.4.3 Enter Meter and Syntax: From Collocations to Constructions	50
1.4.4 From Phrase Constructions to Sentence Constructions	52
1.4.5 Constructions and the Poet's Mind	55
1.4.6 Formulas and Diachrony	58
1.5 Conclusion: What Are Formulas and What Can We Do with Them?	61

2 Meter 64

- 2.1 The Dactylic Hexameter 66
  - 2.1.1 Syllables, Moras, and Feet 66
  - 2.1.2 Scanning the Hexameter 72
  - 2.1.3 Incisions and Bridges 80
- 2.2 The Colometry of the Hexameter and the Prosodic Hierarchy 86
  - 2.2.1 The Colometry of the Hexameter 86
  - 2.2.2 What Are the Constituents of the Hexameter? 87
  - 2.2.3 The Prosodic Hierarchy 88
  - 2.2.4 Mapping Prosody onto Meter: The Hexameter and Its Prosodic Constituents 92
  - 2.2.5 Homeric Enjambement from a Prosodic Perspective 103
- 2.3 Historical Approaches to the Hexameter 107
  - 2.3.1 The Antiquity of the Tradition 107
  - 2.3.2 The Tichy–Berg Theory of the Proto-hexameter 111
  - 2.3.3 Kiparsky (2018) on the Indo-European Origin of the Hexameter 113
- 2.4 Meter and Cognition 115
  - 2.4.1 Meter and Language 115
  - 2.4.2 Prosodic Regularization in Hyperfluent Speech 117
  - 2.4.3 Prosodic Regularization in Ancient Greek 124
- 2.5 Conclusion: Meter as Prosodic Optimization and the Poet's Freedom 126

3 Dialect 130

- 3.1 Introduction: Words and Forms Archaic and Dialectal 130
- 3.2 Archaic and Dialectal Features in Homer 136
- 3.3 Greek Dialects and Identity 145
  - 3.3.1 The Maiden Choir at Delos, and Faking Others' Dialects 145
  - 3.3.2 Dialect and Identity 147
  - 3.3.3 Dialects in Performance 150
- 3.4 Interpreting Homer's Dialect 151
  - 3.4.1 Ancient Critics 151
  - 3.4.2 Modern Critics 153
- 3.5 Interlude: Open Questions and Big-Picture Questions 162
- 3.6 *Kunstsprachen* in Popular Music Today 162
  - 3.6.1 Adele and the Motivation of the Singer 162
  - 3.6.2 Bob Dylan and the Biographic Temptation 169
  - 3.6.3 The Beatles: Between Synchronic and Diachronic Variation 173
  - 3.6.4 Green Day and the Punk Rock Phase Theory 178
  - 3.6.5 Alesha Dixon and the Conflict between Topic and Genre 182
  - 3.6.6 Arctic Monkeys, Stage Persona, and the Perception of Dialect 183
  - 3.6.7 Iggy Azalea, Realness, and Overshooting 185
- 3.7 Conclusion: Style between Tradition and Identity 190

4	Creativity	194
	4.1 The Poet as a Craftsman	195
	4.2 The Poet as Divinely Inspired	197
	4.2.1 Divine Inspiration Before Plato	197
	4.2.2 Divine Inspiration in Plato's *Ion*	200
	4.3 Creative Improvisation	205
	4.3.1 The Cognitive Science of Creativity	205
	4.3.2 The Study of Jazz Improvisation	206
	4.3.3 Improvisation, Creativity, and Flow	210
	4.4 The Neuroscience of Improvisation	213
	4.4.1 The Neural Substrate for Creativity and Flow	213
	4.4.2 Experimental Studies of Improvisation	217
	4.5 Conclusion: Hypofrontality, *Tékhnē*, and *Enthousiasmós*	220

Conclusion: Creativity, Memory, and the Muses   223

Glossary of Linguistic Terms   227
References   239
Index Locorum   266
General Index   267
Index of Homeric forms   271
Index of PIE forms   272
Index of Homeric phraseology   273

Figures

1.1	Two pages of Schmidt's *Parallel Homer* (1885: 186–87)	page 21
1.2	Type and token counts of two-, three-, four-, and five-word collocations in the LOB corpus of written English	36
1.3	Type and token counts of two-, three-, four-, and five-word collocations in Herodotus	37
1.4	Type and token counts of two-, three-, four-, and five-word collocations in Homer	38
1.5	Type and token counts of two-, three-, four-, and five-word collocations in Homer vs. Herodotus	38
1.6	Type and token counts of two-, three-, four-, and five-word collocations in Homer vs. Quintus Smyrnaeus	41
1.7	Type and token counts of two-, three-, four-, and five-word collocations in Herodotus vs. Quintus Smyrnaeus	42
2.1	The inscription on Nestor's Cup (Pithēkoûssai, eighth century BCE)	67
2.2	Syllable structure for the word *cat* [kæt]	70
2.3	Syllable structure for the word *sphinx* [sfɪŋks]	71
2.4	Statistics on incisions and bridges in the *Iliad* (from Hagel 1994: 90)	83
2.5	A simple syntactic tree of the sentence "the cat eats the fish"	89
2.6	The preferred "melody" of the hexameter in the *Iliad* (after Hagel 1994: 100)	99
3.1	Greek dialects in the first millennium	149
4.1	The lobes of the brain	215
4.2	The dorsolateral prefrontal cortex	216

Tables

1.1	Parry's noun–epithet formulas for Odysseus and Achilles in the nominative (after Parry 1971: 39)	*page* 10
1.2	Some definitions of formula	19
1.3	Proportion of prefabs in the analyzed texts (after Erman and Warren 2000: 37)	26
1.4	Distribution of prefab types (after Erman and Warren 2000: 37)	27
1.5	The ten most frequent two-word, three-word, four-word, and five-word collocations in the LOB corpus	34
1.6	The ten most frequent two-word, three-word, four-word, and five-word collocations in Homer	40
1.7	The ten most frequent two-word, three-word, four-word, and five-word collocations in Herodotus	41
1.8	The ten most frequent two-word, three-word, four-word, and five-word collocations in Quintus Smyrnaeus	42
1.9	From conceptual association to collocations	48
1.10	From themes to formulas	52
2.1	Common incisions and bridges in the Homeric hexameter	82
2.2	Incisions in the two hexameters from Nestor's Cup	84
2.3	The prosodic hierarchy in Ancient Greek	92
2.4	Prosodic constituents and their metrical equivalents	93
2.5	A Pear Story, recorded at the University of California, Los Angeles, on April 16, 2014	94
2.6	Bakker's division of the hexameter in intonation units (after Bakker 1997: 66–67)	96
2.7	Comparing Vedic and Greek lyric meters: the eleven-syllable line	109
3.1	Three versions of "Man of Constant Sorrow"	172
3.2	Two versions of "Hey Jude"	174

Acknowledgments

In many ways, this is the book I wanted to write the morning I was standing in the sunny kitchen of my rental apartment in Milan, sometime in the spring or fall of 2006, and I suddenly felt the exhilarating, uncontainable urgency to run out of the door, jump on the first bus, and – just barely – make it to Mario Cantilena's office hours, so that I could ask him to supervise my BA thesis (he said yes). It is fair to say that if I hadn't taken Mario's classes, if I hadn't read his work, and if I hadn't joined his Homeric seminar, I would not have become a Homerist, and this book would not exist.

That first thesis was supposedly about the means of textual cohesion and coherence in some books of the *Iliad*, but I was already set on my quest to understand Homeric composition and creativity. The first two books that I read back then (and apparently not in the order Mario had suggested) were Elizabeth Minchin's *Homer and the Resources of Memory* and Albert Lord's *The Singer of Tales*. It will be clear to anybody reading this volume that they both left an indelible mark. A major realization that I had while writing that thesis was that, if I really wanted to understand Homer's poetic technique, I had to first become a linguist (or at least a classicist in linguist's clothes). Which is why, over the following decade, I moved first to Leiden and then to the University of California, Los Angeles (UCLA), pursuing degrees in Indo-European and historical linguistics.

Many teachers and mentors who crossed my path during my graduate years had an impact on my work – so many that it would be impractical to list them all. But the first names that come to mind (in geographical order) are José Luis García Ramón, Alexander Lubotsky, Brent Vine (the best *Doktorvater* one could ask for), Stephanie Jamison, Craig Melchert, Joseph Nagy, and the late Calvert Watkins. I cannot overstate how joyful and formative the years at UCLA were, and how they turned me into the scholar that I am today.

Acknowledgments

I owe special thanks to Egbert Bakker, whom I met at a conference in London in 2008 (which I had attended in the hope of meeting the author of *Poetry in Speech*!), and who has been following my career ever since, offering steady encouragement and unwavering support. In more recent years, Albio Cesare Cassio has provided feedback and advice on many of the materials that ended up in this book. I could not be more thankful for his generosity, and my (admittedly impossible) wish is to maybe one day know as much about Ancient Greek as he does. I am also grateful to Lowell Edmunds for encouragement and advice on the very first ideas for this manuscript. Finally, I must thank Olav Hackstein, who welcomed me to the Ludwig-Maximilians-Universität (LMU) in Munich and agreed to supervise this book project as my Habilitation thesis. The feedback that he and the other members of my Habilitation committee have provided has saved me from many a pitfall.

Over the last few years, early versions of some of the chapters in this book have been presented at conferences and invited lectures in Boston, Milan, London, Venice, L'Aquila, Tartu, Vienna, and Princeton. I am deeply grateful for the audience questions and comments at those events and to the lovely organizers who made those events possible. The conference in L'Aquila was particularly memorable because I met Sonja Zeman there, and it's fair to say that I would not have survived the postdoc years and the process of writing a Habilitation thesis without our weekly coffee and research meetings.

I am fortunate to have colleagues and friends who are willing to answer random requests for me at the drop of a hat. The people I pestered at different times for this book include Tony Yates, Dieter Gunkel, Adam Gitner, John Gluckman, and Margit Bowler. Special thanks to Marta Cota for mailing me a copy of her work on quantitative metathesis, and to Stefan Hagel for letting me reprint his figures on the hexameter in Chapter 2.

My students at UCLA and the LMU have been exposed to some of the materials in this book from early on (some of them multiple times!) and have helped me to talk and think more clearly about them. If it sounds like I am teaching when I am writing, it's because I am thinking of them.

I am particularly grateful to the good people at Cambridge University Press who have helped to turn my Habilitation manuscript into a book, and especially my editor, Michael Sharp, whom I first contacted about publishing a book back in 2015 (!), and who has been nothing but efficient and encouraging ever since. I am in his debt for finding the nicest reviewers with whom I have ever worked, who have provided countless constructive and useful suggestions (one of them is clearly far more knowledgeable about contemporary music than I am).

While the original book proposal for this volume was composed during LA's endless summer, sitting out at the Pan Pacific Park, most of this volume was written in Munich, in the office at the LMU which I share with Ryan Sandell, in the short hours between dropping off Leone, our toddler, at childcare in the morning and picking him up again in the early afternoon. There isn't a sentence in this book that Ryan hasn't read and proofread at least twice, and there isn't an idea I haven't run by him over the fifteen years (!) during which we have studied and worked side by side (it is some bizarre form of *contrappasso* that I, who never paid enough attention to accents and diacritics, should be married to a phonologist who works on accent systems). I cannot come close to expressing the love and gratitude that he deserves.

It goes without saying that any factual errors, wobbly arguments, and typos that might remain are entirely mine.

Because this book is the culmination of many years of thinking, learning, and writing about Homer's language, a few early, condensed, and partial versions of some topics treated in this volume have appeared in previous articles. My early thinking on formularity appears in Bozzone (2010, 2014). A first kernel of the ideas for what will become Chapter 4 appeared in Bozzone (2016). Bozzone (2022) is a short preview of topics that are now organized and developed throughout the book.

Note on the Transliteration

In transliterating Greek terms and names, my goal is to reproduce the Greek form as faithfully as possible (including accents and vowel lengths), unless a well-established English form for it already exists. For some Homeric characters, this is sometimes a hard line to draw, and I have tried to err on the side of caution. Thus I will use the personal name Alkínoos (for Gk. Ἀλκίνοος) and the place name Pithēkoûssai (Gk. Πιθηκοῦσσαι), but I will write Achilles (instead of Akhilleús) and Homer (instead of Hómēros). This also means that terms like τέχνη will be transliterated as *tékhnē*, as opposed to *techne*. The rationale here is to convey all of the phonological distinctions that would have been meaningful for an Ancient Greek speaker (which would have included accents and vowel lengths), while at the same time not having the undesirable effect of "exoticizing" names and terms that are already known to the general audience.

In particular, I use the digraph <kh> to transliterate <χ> (as opposed to <ch>, which is used in latinizations of Greek terms); <kh> is used here as a reminder that this segment is an aspirated counterpart of the sound [k] <κ> (in post-classical times, it would develop into a fricative). I use <u> (as opposed to <y>) to transcribe <υ>, since this reflects more closely the original pronunciation of this sound in most dialects outside of Attic-Ionic. The sound change that caused Attic-Ionic [u] to become fronted to [y], which underlies the transcription practice with <y>, is post-Homeric (note that all sounds given within square brackets use the International Phonetic Alphabet). For readers curious about matters of Ancient Greek pronunciation (and how we know about them), a thorough discussion is provided in Allen (1968).

Abbreviations

Grammatical Terms

1	First person
2	Second person
3	Third person
nom	Nominative
acc	Accusative
gen	Genitive
dat	Dative
voc	Vocative
sg	Singular
pl	Plural
act	Active
mid	Middle
ind	Indicative
imp	Imperative
impf	Imperfect
pres	Present
N	Noun
NP	Noun phrase
S	Sentence
V	Verb
VP	Verb phrase

Languages and Dialects

AAE	African American English
Aeol	Aeolic
AG	Ancient Greek
Av	Avestan

Dor	Doric
Gk	(Ancient) Greek
Hitt	Hittite
IE	Indo-European
Lat	Latin
Myc	Mycenaean (Greek)
PDE	Present-Day English
PIE	Proto-Indo-European
Skt	Sanskrit
Ved	Vedic

Metrical Symbols

–	Heavy syllable (or position in a metrical scheme for a heavy syllable)
⌣	Light syllable (or position in a metrical scheme for a light syllable)
×	Position in a metrical scheme for either a heavy or a light syllable
|	Metrical incision (i.e., word-end within a verse)
||	End of a metrical period

Phonological Notation

[a]	Sound
/a/	Phoneme
<a>	Grapheme
*a	Reconstructed segment
C	Consonant
R	Resonant
V	Vowel
V:	Long vowel
QM	Quantitative metathesis
μ	Mora
σ	Syllable
φ	Phonological phrase
ω	Phonological word
C	Clitic group
I	Intonational phrase

INTRODUCTION

The Paradox of Homeric Creativity

Dixeris egregie, notum si callida verbum
reddiderit iunctura novum

(Horace, *Ars Poetica* 47–48)

You will speak outstandingly, if a skilled combination
will make a familiar word new

Οὐδὲ γὰρ ῥᾷστον
ἀρρήτων ἐπέων πύλας
ἐξευρεῖν

(Bacchylides, *Paean* 5)

For it is not easy
to find the doors of things unsaid

Human language, is, by definition, creative. Anyone, even a child, can easily come up with a sentence that has never been uttered before, and we get the impression that this may be true for most of what we say in our everyday lives.[1] When it comes to anything longer than a sentence or a phrase, creating new language from scratch strikes us as easier and more natural than reproducing a pre-existing text exactly: anybody can speak for several hours without previous planning, while exactly remembering and reproducing a text of similar length would require significantly more effort. Without any special training, our capacity to create language seems to easily outstrip our capacity to remember it.[2]

When it comes to poetry and literature, we regard creativity as even more essential. While of course we recognize that originality can be hard to achieve (as Bacchylides reminds us), we have come to understand

---

[1] This is claimed by, among others, Pinker (1994: 9): "Virtually every sentence that a person utters or understands is a brand-new combination of words, appearing for the first time in the history of the universe." Data from corpus linguistics may belie this impression (more on this in Chapter 1 below).
[2] The topic of how oral traditions exploit the resources of human memory has attracted considerable attention on the part of cognitive psychologists. For oral traditions in general, see Rubin (1995); for an application of cognitive psychology to Homer, see Minchin (2001).

creativity as the poet's main task and defining feature (as Horace, and the Hellenistic tradition he inherits, reminds us as well). It is on this basis that poets are judged and praised. And we would not call somebody a poet for memorizing and reciting somebody else's words: reproduction, in other words, is seen as a means of last resort – or as the purview of the lesser artist.

Within this frame of thinking, Homer[3] presents us with a paradox. As we comb through the poems, as Milman Parry and Albert Lord (and many before and after them) did, we find layer upon layer of tradition and automation. Many of Homer's expressions are, in a sense, not original creations: they are traditional formulas, passed down for what could be generations; and neither are his stories: they are traditional themes, stretching back hundreds of years. At close inspection, a complex machinery emerges, with precise laws regulating the placement of words in the line or motifs in an episode, and the very choice of vocabulary and dialectal inflections. How do we reconcile all of this mechanicity with Homer's standing as the first great poet in the Western tradition?

There are two ways of reacting to this discovery, each reflecting a different conception of how human creativity works. The first is to investigate how Homer could have exercised his creativity *despite* the mechanicity involved. Following this line of inquiry, we study the machinery in order to filter out its effects, so that we can focus on what made Homer unique and original. True, the machinery is there, but Homer *transcended* the machinery, exploiting it to create something new – and this, the reasoning goes, is why Homer's works survived, while others did not. Much research in this vein has been produced since Parry's demonstration of the traditionality of Homer's technique, in the attempt to

---

[3] The word "Homer" is used in many ways by scholars, depending on their own beliefs and convictions with respect to the Homeric question (i.e., the problem of how the texts of the *Iliad* and the *Odyssey* as we have them came to be). In the most traditional sense, scholars use "Homer" as they would "Shakespeare" or "Dante" – real poets who lived at a given point in time and whose lives and insights are reflected in their art. Sometimes scholars continue this usage even when they believe that two distinct poets (at a minimum) should be responsible for the *Iliad* and the *Odyssey* respectively (in this sense, the term is used to mean "the poet of the *Iliad* and/or the *Odyssey*"). Of course, the realization that Homer's art is oral complicates matters considerably: if scholars of the oralist persuasion (such as myself) use the term "Homer," they often intend it as a shortcut, either to mean "the *text* of the *Iliad* and *Odyssey* as we have them" (e.g., this word is found three times in Homer), or as a personification of archaic Greek oral epic tradition as reflected in the *Iliad* and the *Odyssey* as we have them (e.g., Homer's art, technique, creativity, greatness, etc.). A useful terminological discussion is offered in Ready (2019: vii–viii).

salvage Homer from the lower ranks of oral-traditional poets and to vindicate his poetic greatness.[4]

The second route is to investigate the machinery itself, in order to understand it not as an obstacle to the poet's work, but as what *enabled* Homer's creativity and greatness. Perhaps Homer did not achieve greatness despite the machinery, but *because* of it. Perhaps he did not *transcend* the machinery: he simply used it, masterfully, to achieve precisely what it was designed to do – to create great poetry. Could it be, in other words, that we have misjudged the machinery and its effects?

For one thing, machineries of this kind are more common than we sometimes recognize. Oral-traditional poetry is a near-universal phenomenon,[5] and while many different kinds of oral traditions exist, and each tradition's methods are unique, the hypothesis that this book pursues is that these traditions are *adaptive*. They develop systems that complement and boost the poet's cognitive skills and help poets achieve their goals, and do not detract from them. And they do so in ways that are subtler and smarter than we may have realized so far, and which may illuminate some hidden features of human creativity and cognition.

My overall goal in this book is to pursue this second route, specifically by taking three defining features of Homer's poetry (formularity, meter, and *Kunstsprache*) and reassessing them as aids, not obstacles, to the poet's creativity. In doing so, we shall be assisted by several contemporary disciplines (particularly linguistics and the cognitive sciences), and we shall explore many everyday, contemporary parallels for the aforementioned features, in order to gain a more concrete understanding of how Homer's traditional machinery contributes to his poetry. What is at stake, ultimately, is our understanding of creativity, artistry, and the conditions that enable poetic greatness.

Even though I aim to contribute to many ongoing debates on the topic of Homer's language and poetic technique, I wrote this book with the beginner in mind, hoping that even a non-specialist could pick it up and find useful introductions to the main formal features of Homer's poetry, along with new ways to understand them. I assume familiarity with the

---

[4] The trouble with this type of reasoning is that, since Homer is pretty much all that we have left of archaic heroic poetry (the cycle survives in very few fragments, though much work has been done to reconstruct its themes: see Burgess 2001), establishing what is traditional vs. what *must* have been Homer's innovation is often a circular matter (what we like and find striking must be Homer's, and the rest must be the tradition).

[5] For an overview, see Finnegan (1977), and more recently, Foley (2002).

Greek alphabet (and ideally some basic knowledge of Greek language and literature), but beyond that, I try to provide explanations, examples, and translations for all matters under discussion. A glossary at the end of the book provides short definitions for technical linguistic terms, and copious footnotes throughout serve the same purpose.

CHAPTER I

Formularity

Our starting point in the investigation of Homer's machinery is *formularity*, which we can broadly define as the poet's reliance on prefabricated linguistic sequences in the composition of his verses. Few introductions to Homer will fail to mention the frequent recurrence of phrases like *long-suffering divine Odysseus* (42x in the poems) or *swift-footed Achilles* (30x),[1] and most (if not all) modern language translations of the epics will try to convey some of this repetitiveness as they render Homer's verses. Any reader of Homer will soon discover that this repetitiveness does not affect short phrases alone: whole clauses recur unchanged, from the atmospherically evocative *When early-born, rosy-fingered Dawn appeared* (22x) to the entertainingly irate "*What words escaped the fence of your teeth?*" (8x). And there are entire scenes, like duels or banquets, which often appear to be composed entirely, or almost entirely, of slight variations of the same handful of expressions.

Over the last century, formularity has acquired the status of perhaps the most notorious feature of Homer's style, and it has played a fundamental role in revealing the oral-traditional background of Homer's art. Formularity is also the feature of Homer's style on which the field is most divided, with scholars variously disagreeing on its definition, its function, and the extent to which it appears in the poems (50 percent? 90 percent?), and whether it can be used to demonstrate the orality of a text.

Because of the complex history of the term, I shall first give an overview of how the concept has evolved within Homeric studies, and the many issues it comprises (for a history of oral-formulaic theory outside of Homeric studies, see now Frog and Lamb 2022). Next, we will turn to

---

[1] These repeated expressions consisting of a proper name (e.g., Odysseus) and some "epithetic words" (e.g., *long-suffering, divine*) modifying it have been called *noun–epithet formulae* in Homeric scholarship since Parry's (1971: 17) seminal study.

linguistics and cognitive studies in order to find parallels for Homeric formularity in everyday language and cognition, and to establish whether there are any qualitative or quantitative differences between formularity in Homer and formularity in natural languages. Finally, we will tackle the practical questions of how best to describe Homeric formularity, and how to evaluate its meaning and antiquity.

1.1 The History of Homeric Formularity

1.1.1 Parry: Homer's Style as Traditional

Few scholars nowadays would doubt that formularity played a substantial role in the poet's technique. After all, formularity is very *visible* in the *Iliad* and the *Odyssey* as we have them. As Parry explained:

> The easiest and best way of showing the place the formula holds in Homeric style will be to point out all of the expressions occurring in a given passage which are found elsewhere in the *Iliad* or the *Odyssey*, in such a way that, as one reads, one may see how the poet has used them to express his thought. (Parry 1971: 301)

Below, I reproduce the first twenty-five lines of *Iliad* 1 as given in Parry's *Homer and Homeric Style* (1971: 301–2), minus the heavy apparatus (the added translation is mine).[2] For several decades, this type of illustration was the only available evidence of the density of formulas in Homer, and played an important role in shaping the debate on Homeric style. Here, solid underlining identifies expressions that are found, unchanged, elsewhere in the poems (what Parry would call *formulas*). Broken underlining identifies expressions that appear to be slight variations of expressions found elsewhere in the poems (what Parry would call *formulaic expressions*).[3]

---

[2] Unless specified otherwise, the Greek text reproduced in this book reflects the *Thesaurus Linguae Graecae* (http://stephanus.tlg.uci.edu). For Homer, this means the editions of Allen (1931) for the *Iliad* and Von der Mühll (1962) for the *Odyssey*.

[3] Note that, in theory, both criteria can be true at the same time, and thus an expression might appear to be a slight variation of an already-known formula *and* it might be repeated elsewhere in the poems. While this is not captured in Parry's analysis, it is captured in Lord's analysis of the first fifteen lines of the same passage (Lord 1960: 143), where almost every line is shown with a thorough broken underlining – suggesting that close to everything about the phraseology is traditional, even when expressions are not repeated verbatim.

(1)

Μῆνιν ἄειδε θεὰ Πηληϊάδεω Ἀχιλῆος (1)	The wrath sing, o goddess, of Peleus' son, Achilles, (1)
οὐλομένην, ἣ μυρί' Ἀχαιοῖς ἄλγε' ἔθηκε,	ruinous, which brought countless sufferings upon the Achaeans,
πολλὰς δ' ἰφθίμους ψυχὰς Ἄϊδι προΐαψεν	and hurled down to Hades many excellent souls
ἡρώων, αὐτοὺς δὲ ἑλώρια τεῦχε κύνεσσιν	of heroes, and their bodies, it left them prey to the dogs
οἰωνοῖσί τε πᾶσι, Διὸς δ' ἐτελείετο βουλή, (5)	and birds of all kinds, and so the will of Zeus was done, (5)
ἐξ οὗ δὴ τὰ πρῶτα διαστήτην ἐρίσαντε	from the time the two first began their stand-off,
Ἀτρεΐδης τε ἄναξ ἀνδρῶν καὶ δῖος Ἀχιλλεύς.	the son of Atreus, lord of men, and divine Achilles.
Τίς τάρ σφωε θεῶν ἔριδι ξυνέηκε μάχεσθαι;	But who was it among the gods who set them up to fight?
Λητοῦς καὶ Διὸς υἱός· ὃ γὰρ βασιλῆϊ χολωθεὶς	It was the son of Zeus and Leto: for he was angry with the king,
νοῦσον ἀνὰ στρατὸν ὄρσε κακήν, ὀλέκοντο δὲ λαοί, (10)	and he awoke a plague among the army, a terrible one, and the people were dying, (10)
οὕνεκα τὸν Χρύσην ἠτίμασεν ἀρητῆρα	because the son of Atreus had disrespected his priest, Khrúsēs.
Ἀτρεΐδης· ὃ γὰρ ἦλθε θοὰς ἐπὶ νῆας Ἀχαιῶν	He had come to the fast ships of the Achaeans,
λυσόμενός τε θύγατρα φέρων τ' ἀπερείσι' ἄποινα,	wanting to free his daughter, bringing infinite gifts,
στέμματ' ἔχων ἐν χερσὶν ἑκηβόλου Ἀπόλλωνος	holding in his hands the insignia of apollo the far-shooter,
χρυσέῳ ἀνὰ σκήπτρῳ, καὶ λίσσετο πάντας Ἀχαιούς, (15)	on his golden staff, and he implored all of the Achaeans, (15)
Ἀτρεΐδα δὲ μάλιστα δύω, κοσμήτορε λαῶν·	and especially the two sons of Atreus, leaders of men:
Ἀτρεΐδαι τε καὶ ἄλλοι ἐϋκνήμιδες Ἀχαιοί,	"Sons of Atreus and all other strong-greaved Achaeans,
ὑμῖν μὲν θεοὶ δοῖεν Ὀλύμπια δώματ' ἔχοντες	may the gods, who inhabit the houses of Olympus, grant you
ἐκπέρσαι Πριάμοιο πόλιν, εὖ δ' οἴκαδ' ἱκέσθαι·	to take the city of Priam, and to return home unscathed.
παῖδα δ' ἐμοὶ λύσαιτε φίλην, τὰ δ' ἄποινα δέχεσθαι, (20)	But free my daughter, and accept my gifts,
ἁζόμενοι Διὸς υἱὸν ἑκηβόλον Ἀπόλλωνα.	appeasing the son of Zeus, Apollo the far-shooter."

Ἔνθ' ἄλλοι μὲν πάντες ἐπευφήμησαν Ἀχαιοὶ	And then all of the other Achaeans called out in approval,
αἰδεῖσθαί θ' ἱερῆα καὶ ἀγλαὰ δέχθαι ἄποινα·	to show respect to the priest and to accept the splendid gifts:
ἀλλ' οὐκ Ἀτρεΐδῃ Ἀγαμέμνονι ἥνδανε θυμῷ,	But this did not please the *thūmós* of Agamemnon, the son of Atreus;
ἀλλὰ κακῶς ἀφίει, κρατερὸν δ' ἐπὶ μῦθον ἔτελλε. (25)	instead, he sent him away badly, and he gave him a harsh command: (25)

In this sample, there is hardly a line without underlining, which means that there is hardly a line whose component expressions do not also appear somewhere else in our corpus. The message here is that the poet does not seem to be striving for originality. Rather, he seems to be putting verses together the way a child assembles a Lego castle: by snapping together prefabricated bricks (i.e., the underlined parts).

As confirmation of this theory, metrical blemishes may often be found at the junctures between bricks: sometimes, the poet will try to snap together pieces that don't perfectly fit (something that, admittedly, the Lego simile does not allow), and a small metrical bump will result. The classical study is Parry (1971: 201–21): for instance, in order to mention Telemachus in the second half of the line, the poet relied on the noun–epithet formula Ὀδυσσῆος φίλος υἱός "Odysseus' dear son," which is isometric (i.e., metrically equivalent) to many other famous noun–epithet formulas (βοὴν ἀγαθὸς Διομήδης "Diomedes good at the war-cry," βοὴν ἀγαθὸς Μενέλαος "Menelaus, good at the war-cry," πολύτλας δῖος Ὀδυσσεύς "much-suffering divine Odysseus," etc.), but begins with a vowel. While the latter formulas can happily follow a formulaic expression containing the verb ἠρᾶτο "s/he prayed," the former cannot: when the poet, used to combining ἠρᾶτο with noun–epithet formulas of that shape, tries to snap the pieces together, a metrical bump (in this case, hiatus, i.e., the meeting of two vowels at a word boundary) results:[4]

(2) δὴ τότ' ἔπειτ' ἠρᾶτο βοὴν ἀγαθὸς Διομήδης (*Il.* 5.114)

and then Diomedes good at the war-cry prayed.

(3) ὣς δ' αὔτως ἠρᾶτο Ὀδυσσῆος φίλος υἱός. (*Od.* 3.64)

thus in this manner Odysseus' dear son prayed.

---

[4] For an introduction to Homeric metrics (and metrical bumps therein), see Chapter 2.

These small bumps are a strong indication that the poet is composing by juxtaposing the bricks, and that he has come to rely on this strategy so much that, sometimes, he will disregard the meter to continue composing in this way.

But who made the bricks? Are they the poet's invention? And how could one go about establishing this either way? Parry observed that, in Homer, noun–epithet formulas, when considered together, appear to form a system which displays both *extension* and *economy* (or *thrift*). For each task, the poet has just as many different-sized bricks as they need (*extension*), and virtually nothing more (*economy*). Extension and economy are exemplified in Parry's charts for noun–epithet formulas, one of which I partially reproduce in Table 1.1.[5]

Next, Parry turned to poets who wrote in the epic tradition and who attempted to imitate Homer's style, such as Virgil and Apollonius Rhodius. He showed that these poets behaved differently from Homer. While they did rely on some premade expressions (akin to Homer's noun–epithet formulas), there appeared to be no system in place: there were too many bricks for some tasks, and none for others, with no regard for economy or extension (Parry 1971: 24–36).

Parry argued that this difference could be explained by tradition: while Virgil and Apollonius made their own bricks (and just for a few tasks), Homer inherited them, in very large numbers, from the poets before him. It was the force of tradition which, over generations, and through a process similar to natural selection, strategically shaped the bricks into the elegant interlocking system that Homer had at his disposal.[6] In other words, Parry concluded, Homer's technique was (mostly) traditional, while that of Virgil or Apollonius was (mostly) individual.[7]

---

[5] One should notice how, even in Parry's formulation, economy is a strong tendency rather than an absolute law: even among noun–epithet formulas for main heroes, one finds equivalent formulas, though usually one of the variants is overwhelmingly more common than the other.

[6] An attempt to more fully articulate this process of evolution and renewal in the technique is seen in Hainsworth (1978). Gray (1947) studies the system of epithets for metal weapons in an attempt to uncover how the tradition develops new phraseology for technological innovations.

[7] Sale (1996) extends Parry's study by comparing extension and economy of formulas (as well as other criteria) in Homer and Quintus Smyrnaeus, demonstrating how even a very good literary imitator of Homer such as Quintus could not match the formal properties of Homer's formularity.

Table 1.1 *Parry's noun–epithet formulas for Odysseus and Achilles in the nominative (after Parry 1971: 39)*

	Between the feminine caesura and the end of the line	Between the hephthemimeral caesura and the end of the line	Between the bucolic diaeresis and end of the line
Odysseus	πολύτλας δῖος Ὀδυσσεύς "long-suffering divine Odysseus" (38)	πολύμητις Ὀδυσσεύς "Odysseus of many counsels" (81) πτολίπορθος Ὀδυσσεύς "Odysseus conqueror of cities" (4)	δῖος Ὀδυσσεύς "divine Odysseus" (60) ἐσθλός Ὀδυσσεύς "good Odysseus" (3)
Achilles	ποδάρκης δῖος Ἀχιλλεύς "divine Achilles who runs to the rescue" (21)	πόδας ὠκύς Ἀχιλλεύς "swift-footed Achilles" (31) μεγάθυμος Ἀχιλλεύς "Achilles of the great *thūmós*" (1)	δῖος Ἀχιλλεύς "divine Achilles" (34) ὠκύς Ἀχιλλεύς "swift Achilles" (5)

1.1.2 Homer's Orality and the Quantitative Study of Formulas

The type of tradition that Parry had in mind came into focus in his later work, thanks to his experiences in the field. Between 1933 and 1935, Parry, accompanied by his student Albert Lord, traveled to then-Yugoslavia to record the performances of singers in the Islamic tradition of oral epic.[8] There, he recognized many parallels between the technique of the poets he encountered (who were composing their songs *in performance*, and not simply reciting them from memory) and the formal features he had observed in Homer's diction (here, too, singers relied on formulas and formulaic expressions). He concluded that Homer's technique must also have been developed in the context of an oral tradition, and with the specific goal of supporting oral composition in performance.

Naturally, these observations raised several additional questions about Homer and his poems, which continued the centuries-old tradition of the Homeric question: was Homer (whatever we mean by the term) an oral poet or did he simply behave like one? If he was an oral poet, and he composed his poems orally, how did the poems come to be written down?[9] Or was Homer perhaps an exceptional figure who used his training as an oral poet to compose his poems in writing, thus allowing them to survive?[10]

Answers to these questions were pursued, at first, empirically: Parry and Lord sought to prove that a skilled oral poet could compose a work of the length of a Homeric epic without the aid of writing.[11] They found Avdo Međedović, who, over the course of several days, could dictate a poem of the length and complexity of a Homeric epic.[12] They named him the Homer of the Balkans.

But a typological parallel was not enough: the next step was to identify a measurable feature in the Homeric poems that could speak to their oral composition. At this point, many scholars turned to *quantitative formula*

---

[8] The series *Serbo-Croatian Heroic Songs* (Harvard University Press) presents some of the materials collected by Parry and Lord. The online portion of *The Milman Parry Collection of Oral Literature* is available at https://library.harvard.edu/collections/milman-parry-collection-oral-literature.
[9] For the process of textualization in oral traditions, see Honko (2000).
[10] Recent and specific attempts to answer all of these questions have been made by Skafte Jensen (2011), who envisions the epics as oral-dictated texts, and Martin West (2011 and 2014), who envisions the authors of the *Iliad* and *Odyssey* as writing poets. An important recent contribution is Ready (2019).
[11] I.e., by relying on a traditional technique of oral composition in which poems are put together in performance by relying on traditional story patterns (*themes*) and linguistic expressions (*formulas*). For an introduction, see Lord (1960).
[12] The poem in question is *The Wedding of Smailagić Meho*, edited and translated by Lord in 1974.

analysis – that is, counting the density of formulas in the *Iliad* and the *Odyssey*. Thus, Lord argued:

> There are ways of determining whether a style is oral or not, and I believe that quantitative formula analysis is one of them, perhaps the most reliable. (Lord 1968: 16)

The logic was appealingly simple: if prefabricated expressions (i.e., expressions that are not invented at the moment of performance, but that are arguably stored in the memory of the poet) are indicative of oral composition in performance, then a poem made overwhelmingly of prefabricated expressions ought to be considered an orally composed poem.[13]

Crucially, for many years, there were no automated ways of obtaining such counts, and there were no similar studies looking at prefabricated expressions in natural language. As a result, the few counts that were made were partial (such as example (1) above, comprising only twenty-five verses of the *Iliad*), and did not look at natural language for comparison. This led to a systematic overestimation of the portion of formularity in Homer (up to 90 percent, according to Parry and Lord – and based on example (1) above), and to a systematic underestimation of the extent of formularity in natural language (which was not usually discussed). Years after the beginning of the debate, Lord writes:

> What is clearly needed most desperately is a moratorium on baseless speculation about formula quantity and in its stead active research in formula incidence and density, both in Homer and in oral poetry. (Lord 1968: 19)

Lord's wish was fulfilled when formulaic counts finally started to appear, either through painstaking hand-counting (e.g., Cantilena 1982), or, much later on, through computerized concordances (Pavese and Boschetti 2003).[14]

Yet, the question of the orality of Homer remained far from settled. In the absence of comparison with a wider selection of texts, and most of all

---

[13] Naturally, actual practice (as we shall see below) was more complicated, since one had to grapple with many methodological questions: what expressions should one count, and how can we definitely tell that they are prefabricated? Some expressions are identical to some others (thus likely to be prefabricated), but others are only almost, not precisely, identical. Where to draw the line? And finally, are prefabricated expressions all that matters in establishing the orality of a text? An extensive attempt to answer this last question was made by Peabody (1975).

[14] Existing quantitative formular analyses for the Greek epics include (partial analyses in italics): *Iliad* and *Odyssey* (Parry 1971, Lord 1960, 1968, Hainsworth 1968, *Danek 1998*, Pavese and Boschetti 2003), *Homeric Hymns* (Cantilena 1982), *Scutum* (Venti 1991), *Batrachomyomachia* (Camerotto 1992), Hesiod (*Minton 1975*, Pavese and Venti 2000).

with natural language, the counts were often interpreted in a circular fashion: whatever amounts of prefabricated expressions Homer showed (set at around 50 percent in Pavese and Boschetti 2003) were argued to be indicative of oral composition, and whatever smaller amounts later texts showed were argued to be indicative of a transition to writing.[15] Few scholars hailed these results as conclusive – unsupported by agreement on a larger theory of formularity, the empirical findings largely fell by the wayside. Scholars could not agree, in fact, on what they had been measuring in the first place.

1.1.3 Formulas and Their Flexibility

For several decades, the exact definition of formula had been an arena of constant battle.[16] To this day, most Homerists agree to disagree on the matter, or are content to adopt the term in a generic manner (i.e., to refer to any phraseology in Homer that appears to be repeated, and thus traditional). In practice, formulas proved hard to pin down for two main reasons: they are a hybrid phenomenon (in that they can be defined at the textual or at the psychological level) and a gradient one (in that each expression in Homer can be arranged on a scale from more formulaic to less formulaic).

Parry famously defined formula as follows:

> An expression regularly used under the same metrical conditions to express an essential idea. (Parry 1971: 13)

The definition combines two very different elements: a textual entity (an expression found regularly under the same metrical conditions) and a psychological entity (the essential idea). Over the next few decades, and depending on the specific nature of their inquiry, scholars often ended up privileging one side of the definition or the other. Those interested in quantitative analysis needed a text-based definition of what could count as a formula or not, and were not in a position to focus on the *psychological reality* of the formula. Repetition in a text was considered a sufficient criterion for establishing the formulaic status of a sequence.[17] Scholars

---

[15] Never mind that, when measuring the formularity of a small corpus using Homer as reference, we are measuring how similar that corpus is to Homer (i.e., how much phraseology it shares with the *Iliad* and the *Odyssey*) more than anything else.

[16] Edwards (1986, 1988) gives an impressively detailed account of the debate.

[17] When dealing with living speakers, one can rely on a series of established psycholinguistic tests to verify whether a linguistic sequence (expression) is stored as a whole in memory or generated on the spot. This possibility is, of course, absent when discussing closed corpus languages. Schmitt et al. (2004) argue that corpus data on its own is a poor indicator of whether a linguistic sequence is stored

who were more interested in the process of oral composition and understanding the poet's technique were instead naturally drawn to a psychologically based understanding of the formula, which emphasized the gradience of formulaic phenomena and the remarkable flexibility of the system.

Already in *Homer and Homeric Style*, Parry was well aware that formulas exist along a continuum going from fixity to flexibility. Commenting on the *Iliad* passage quoted above in example (1), he noted:

> I have put a solid line beneath those word-groups which are found elsewhere in the poems unchanged, and a broken line under phrases which are of the same type as others. In this case I have limited the type to include only those in which not only the metre and the parts of speech are the same, but in which also one important word or group of words is identical, as in the first example: μῆνιν ... Πηληιάδεω Ἀχιλῆος and μῆνιν ... ἑκατηβόλου Ἀπόλλωνος. (Parry 1971: 301)

In other words, there are *formulas* (expressions that are found elsewhere in the poems unchanged), and there are *formulaic expressions* (expressions which are of the same type as others). This last category is left somewhat vague by Parry, but it seems like it could be easily extended to describe a vast amount of data.

In this direction, Russo (1966) coined the concept of the *structural formula* – a pattern of expression where the meter and the parts of speech (i.e., noun, verb, etc.) are the same, but no words or word groups are shared. Importantly, a structural formula has no essential idea: it is pure structure. As an example, the structural formula $[-\smile]_{Verb}$ $[\smile--]_{Noun}$ can be used to describe the two expressions τεῦχε κύνεσσιν "threw to the dogs" and δῶκεν ἑταίρῳ "gave to his/her companion," where the only "idea" shared is that of having a finite verb followed by a noun in the dative (in this particular case, one could speak of a shared *argument structure* – i.e., a similarity at the level of syntax). While many scholars would agree that such patterns are to be found in our texts, many regard them as too generic and abstract to meaningfully qualify as formulas (see Kiparsky (1976: 89–90), who suggests that these phenomena are common in written poetry as well).

Even with respect to the canonical Parrian formula, the flexibility and creativity of Homeric diction was gradually vindicated. Hoekstra (1964) illustrated how poets could renew their hoard of formulas in order to accommodate linguistic innovations; specifically, he studied how recent

---

in the mind as a whole (i.e., whether it is a "psychological" formula), though the study is very limited in its scope and methods, and more research is needed to verify its results.

sound changes in the Ionic dialects may have had an impact on (and forced restructuring of) some formulaic systems, also trying to use this phenomenon as a way of dating the composition of the poems (which, in his view, would have to have happened shortly after these changes took place).

Going further, Bryan Hainsworth demonstrated how poets could adapt formulaic sequences to the needs of composition: formulas could be moved to other parts of the line, expanded, separated, or morphologically inflected (these modifications are illustrated in his 1968 monograph *The Flexibility of the Homeric Formula*). Hainsworth understood formularity as a living synchronic and diachronic system, in which *frequency of usage* determined what was fixed and what was flexible:

> Highly schematized formula-types are then the consequence of ossification of more flexible systems at points of frequent use. (Hainsworth 1968: 113)

That is, the more a poet has to use a given expression, the more that expression is likely to become fixed.[18] Hainsworth (1962, 1978) argued that frequency also played a role in establishing which formulas would stand the test of time, and which would be replaced by other, newer creations. We will see that this attention to frequency puts Hainsworth in tune with many contemporary approaches to formularity in language in general.

Kiparsky (1976) was a substantial theoretical step forward, in that it marked the introduction of tools from linguistic theory (namely, generative syntax) into the study of formularity.[19] Kiparsky compares Homeric formulas to *bound phrases* in natural language – that is, idioms, such as *kick the bucket*, and fixed collocations, such as *foreseeable future*.[20] He further distinguishes between *fixed bound phrases* (which are effectively retrieved from memory, not generated, and can thus have odd syntactic behavior and noncompositional semantics) and *flexible bound phrases* (which are generated anew and should thus be syntactically and semantically well behaved). These would correspond, respectively, to fixed formulas and flexible formulas in Homer.[21] In Kiparsky's model, flexible formulas in Homer ought to

---

[18] One is reminded here of the famous dictum by John Du Bois, "grammars code best what speakers do most" (Du Bois 1985: 363).

[19] Admittedly, some terminology inspired by generative grammar had already been introduced by Nagler 1967 (see below in section 1.1.4), but this did not amount to a true linguistic approach to the issue.

[20] The main difference between idioms and fixed collocations is that idioms are *non-compositional* in their meaning (i.e., their meaning does not transparently arise from the sum of their parts).

[21] In replying to a comment by Calvert Watkins, Kiparsky admits that this strong bipartition is stipulative: "I cannot prove that they are exactly two categories. It might be that there is a continuum, for example: fixed formulas, flexible formulas, and all kinds of gradations of flexibility in between. And I don't see any way of settling the matter" (Kiparsky 1976: 114).

correspond to well-formed syntactic constituents (this restriction does not apply to fixed formulas). Kiparsky does away with any metrical requirements in his definition. As he puts it, the true essence of the formula is the *abstract bond* between the formula's components: for instance, the bond between ἄλγος "pain" and παθ- "suffer" (Kiparsky 1976: 86),[22] or τεύχεα "weapons" and καλά "beautiful" (Kiparsky 1976: 87); it is not, then, surprising that a flexible formula would be split across multiple lines, as happens to τεύχεα καλά in *Iliad* 22.322–23, 19.10–11, and 18.82–84. One could summarize Kiparsky's flexible formula as a syntactic constituent that is filled by lexical items that have a strong tendency to co-occur with each other (i.e., lexical items which are collocates of each other), and Kiparsky's fixed formula as any linguistic sequence which is entirely retrieved from memory.

But the zenith of flexibility within the concept of formula was arguably reached by scholars operating within a historical perspective. Here, Watkins (1995), working on Indo-European poetics, argued that very ancient formulas, encapsulating important cultural *themes*, can be preserved over centuries while continually undergoing *lexical renewal*.[23] In Watkins' diachronic approach, everything that identifies a formula as such is its essential idea (its *theme* – e.g., the idea HERO SLAYS DRAGON), while the specific lexical items chosen to express this idea might change over time and space.[24]

This stance has radical consequences: if we look back at Parry's definition, where a formula was intended as (1) a recurring fixed expression, (2) occurring under the same metrical conditions, and (3) expressing a given essential idea, we see how meter and fixity of expression have been

---

[22] For these examples, see discussion in section 1.4.2 below.

[23] Note that, in Lord's *Singer of Tales*, formulas and themes were objects of radically different size and nature: formulas pertained to the diction, and themes to the narrative structure (Lord 1960: Chapter 4 fn. 1 recognized that themes in this sense corresponded to *motifs* as classified in the field of folklore studies). So a formula could be "swift-footed Achilles" (which does not correspond to any theme, unless we want to elevate the idea of a hero being fast to a theme in itself), while a theme (which Lord 1960: 68 defines as "a grouping of ideas regularly used in telling a tale in the formulaic style of traditional song") could be "the assembly," or "the recognition," or even "the return of the hero." In his definition, Watkins erases the distinction in scale between theme and formula, effectively focusing on some themes that can be expressed by a single formula (these are normally formulas centered on a finite verb).

[24] In a recent contribution, Kiparsky (2017: 156) embraced the idea that themes (in Watkins' sense), rather than formulas, should be seen as central to creativity in oral-traditional poetry. Themes allow for great flexibility; they can be exchanged and borrowed between traditions, and leave room for individual expression. In this definition, a theme can be as abstract as the idea of "magical growth or paradoxical disproportion" as it appears in several episodes of the *Kalevala*. Next to themes, Kiparsky recognizes the existence of structural formulas (à la Russo) as a means of formal organization of the diction.

essentially done away with, leaving the "essential idea" as the only peg on which to hang the entirety of oral-formulaic theory.

1.1.4 The Disappearance of the Formula

One risk of proceeding in this direction (i.e., taking the essential idea as the only defining element for a formula) is that of doing away with formularity entirely, either by denying that formularity is different from nonformularity, or by arguing that everything in Homer is formulaic by virtue of being there. At one extreme, those wishing to do away with formulas could cast them as an epiphenomenon: Nagler's "generative" approach (1967) to the formula insisted that formulas were generated anew every time, and that they only appeared identical in every iteration because they satisfied identical constraints, in the way a calculator will always produce the same result for the same arithmetical operation. According to Nagler, formulas only existed as a *preverbal Gestalt* (i.e., Parry's essential idea) in the poet's mind: for instance, every time a poet tried to express the idea of Achilles after the hephthemimeral caesura, the string "swift-footed Achilles" was the only possible combination he could come up with. While Nagler's explanation is a logical possibility (and might even be true for some repeated expressions in the poems), we now know, from the point of view of linguistic processing, that generating the same sequence anew over and over instead of simply retrieving it from memory is a very poor strategy for language production, and not the way human brains generally operate. This view also fails to explain how some formulas may preserve older linguistic features that are not part of the poet's active grammar (if a poet generates each expression anew every time, wouldn't those expressions always be linguistically up to date?).

Several decades later, Visser's (1987, 1988) study of battle scenes argued that Homer's process of composition proceeded by words, not formulas: core words (the *nucleus*) were placed in the line first, and the formulaic system only supplied metrical filling (the *periphery*), which was semantically vacuous, in order to help the poet complete his lines. According to Visser, this would make Homer similar to any "writing" poet wrestling with the strict demands of the hexametric line. There are several issues with Visser's argument, which cannot be fully explored here; some basic limitations seem to stem from approaching language production without making reference to some foundational concepts of syntactic theory.[25] For instance, the idea that a writing poet (or a normal speaker) would "compose" by single words is in itself

---

[25] For an introduction to syntactic theory, see Adger (2003) or Carnie (2013).

problematic: language is organized and produced by *constituents* (e.g., noun phrases, verb phrases, etc.), not single words.[26] Visser's own concept of nucleus and periphery, moreover, largely overlaps with the basic syntactic concept of *headedness* – that is, the fact that constituents have heads (what Visser would call *nucleus*), as well as complements and adjuncts (what Visser would call *periphery*). But there are issues on the Greek side as well: Visser's study is limited to battle scenes where the poet is trying to express the idea "X killed Y" by fitting every element of the sentence (including the full names of the killer and the victim) in a single hexameter line. This is only one of the many possible options, and not even the most frequent (some killings are recounted over several lines, some in half a line; characters can be referred to by pronouns or ellipsis, and these options are actually the most frequent for subjects, largely because of discourse considerations). Most importantly, Visser overstates the freedom of word order in Greek, and assumes that the poet could arrange their words in any linear order needed to satisfy the meter without changing the meaning of the sentence. This is not the case: in the first place, as we have known for a long time, word order *within constituents* is not free in Greek (e.g., in a prepositional phrase, a preposition should come before its complement; definite articles do not follow the noun they modify, etc.); second, as we now know, after decades of research on syntax and information structure in Ancient Greek, different constituent orders (e.g., whether the subject and object precede or follow the finite verb) reflect different discourse configurations and result in different meanings.[27] Bozzone (2014: 219–22), for instance, shows that among the supposedly synonymous verbs of killing ἔπεφνε and ἐνήρατο (both "s/he killed"), the former is used when the discourse is centered on the victims ("Who was killed next?"), while the latter is used when the discourse is centered on the attackers ("Who killed whom next?"). In other words, constituent orders in Greek are not freely interchangeable.

---

[26] The concept of syntactic constituent has been established in syntactic theory at least since the work of Bloomfield (1933). For a history of the issue, see Seuren (2015).

[27] In simple terms, Ancient Greek is one of the many *discourse-configurational languages* in which the status of a given referent as new vs. already known to the listener (in more technical terms, whether something is a *focus* or a *topic* respectively) will affect where in the sentence that referent will surface. A known pattern in Ancient Greek is, for instance, for the new information (*focus*) to be placed immediately before the finite verb. This pattern can be observed in the first line of the *Iliad*, where the most important piece of new information (the *focus*), is placed in the preverbal position: thus μῆνιν ἄειδε "THE WRATH sing." For recent work on word order in Ancient Greek, see Dik (1995, 2007), Matić (2003), Goldstein (2014); see Bozzone (2014) for an application of these insights to the problem of word order in Homer's battle scenes.

At the other extreme, the definition of formularity was stretched to accommodate whatever blocks would fit in the system (prefabricated or not). While Russo's concept of structural formula was a step in this direction, Nagy's conception, whereby everything that is part of the tradition is formulaic (and vice versa: see, for instance, Nagy 2010), is perhaps now the most often quoted contribution. Nevertheless, erasing the difference between formularity and nonformularity has struck many as unhelpful: many scholars still feel that a well-worn and widespread formula like *swift-footed Achilles* is not quite the same as an isometric expression that only occurs once in our corpus, and might have been the lone invention of a single poet.

Among recent contributions, Bakker (1997: 186–87) argued that formulas are routinized bits of speech;[28] while this illuminates the process that creates the formula, it does not contribute to the question of how we can identify one in a text.

The main contributions summarized so far are presented in Table 1.2.

Table 1.2 *Some definitions of formula*

Parry (1971)	1.	Group of words: πόδας ὠκὺς Ἀχιλλεύς "swift-footed Achilles"
	2.	Metrical conditions: ‿ ‿ – ‿ ‿ – –
	3.	Essential idea: Achilles
Russo (1963, 1966)		Structural formula: [– ‿]V [‿ – –]N
		e.g.: τεῦχε κύνεσσιν "threw to the dogs," δῶκεν ἑταίρῳ "gave to his companion"
Nagler (1967)	1.	Preverbal Gestalt (true formula): idea of Achilles
	2.	Surface realization (not really a formula): πόδας ὠκὺς Ἀχιλλεύς
Hainsworth (1968)	1.	Basic Formula: καρτερὰ δεσμά "strong chains" (the mutual expectation between the two words)
	2.	Modifications: (a) dislocation, (b) modification (i.e., inflection), (c) expansion, (d) separation
		e.g.: expansion + modification: κρατερῷ ἐνὶ δεσμῷ "in strong chains" (*Il.* 5.386)
		separation + modification: δεσμοῖο ‿ – κρατεροῦ. "strong [. . .] chain" (*Od.* 8.360)
Kiparsky (1976)	1.	Fixed formula (a linguistic sequence stored in memory): Ἦμος δ' ἠριγένεια φάνη ῥοδοδάκτυλος Ἠώς "As soon as early-born rose-fingered Dawn appeared"
	2.	Flexible formula (a well-formed syntactic constituent): [[ἄλγος]NP παθ-]VP "pain [. . .] suffer"

---

[28] More recently, Bakker (2013: 159) defines formula as "a phrase that has been created in order to be uttered repeatedly or routinely." This is part of a discussion on the theme of *interformularity* – i.e., whether we can take Homeric formulas as textually referential, to which we will return below.

Table 1.2 *(cont.)*

Visser (1987, 1988)	[πόδας ὠκὺς]ₚₑᵣᵢₚₕₑᵣᵧ [Ἀχιλλεύς]ɴᵤᴄʟᴇᵤs
Watkins (1995: 302)	Theme: HERO SLAY (*$g^{wh}en$-) SERPENT (with WEAPON/with COMPANION)
	Conventionally, the word order is English. Some syntax is implied, though not expressed notationally (e.g., the sentence often exhibits the marked word order Verb-Object). The boxed portion constitutes the basic formula (the HERO is typically not realized overtly).

Pulled in these opposite directions, the debate exhausted itself by failing to agree on its basic unit of measurement. Many felt that formularity was getting in the way of understanding the poetry, making Homer mechanical and abstract instead of clarifying his art. In what follows, I argue that the study of formularity in Homer was, in fact, suffering from what we can call "the disadvantage of the early start."

1.2 Formularity in Language

1.2.1 The Disadvantage of the Early Start

We know now that formularity, or *idiomaticity* (i.e., relying on prefabricated expressions which might have conventionalized meaning, whatever their precise length or shape), is not at all a rare phenomenon in human language. On the contrary: it permeates many aspects of language usage and acquisition, and it has in fact attracted extensive study in many areas of linguistics over the past several decades.[29] But why, we might ask, did it take us so long to come to this realization?

The perceived exoticism of Homer's traditional language is, in large part, a historical accident. The fact is that we are rather blind to the occurrence of formularity (i.e., repetition) in our daily lives. We notice it at the extremes (a memorized quote, a cliché, a plagiarized speech at a public event), but we don't see it or look for it otherwise. In this respect, formularity in language is akin to the many other automatic behaviors that fill our everyday experience and assist us in completing any cognitively demanding task (as we shall see below): it runs quietly in the background, unnoticed.

---

[29] For an overview, see Bozzone (2010), with references.

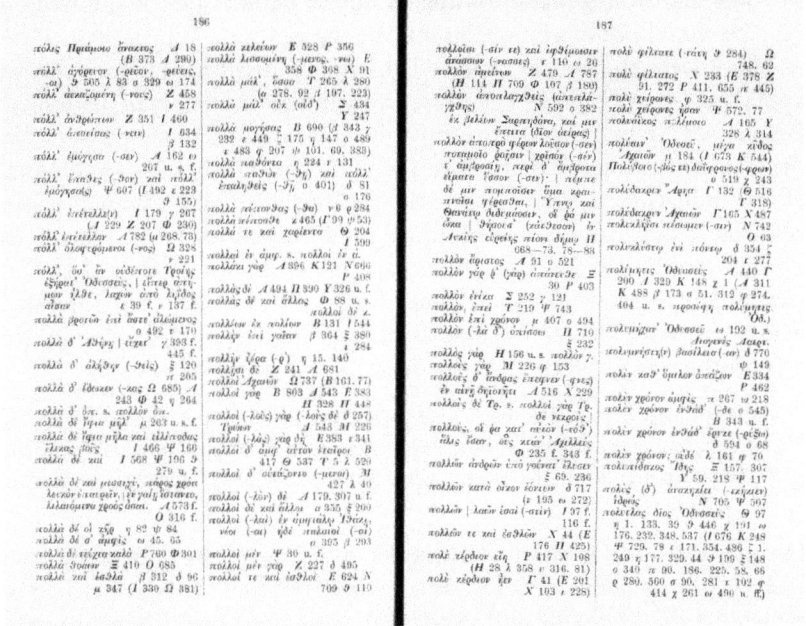

Figure 1.1 Two pages of Schmidt's *Parallel Homer* (1885: 186–87)

In order to see formularity in language (i.e., to spot recurring, conventionalized expressions), we need special tools, such as searchable digital corpora or, more mundanely, paper concordances. And both of these tools were in short supply for most literary texts until relatively recently. In particular, given the time-consuming nature of compiling a concordance by hand, only a few religious texts like the Hebrew Bible, the Septuagint, and the Koran had paper concordances made in predigital times – with a notable addition: Homer.[30] When working on his master's thesis (entitled "A comparative study of diction as one of the elements of style in early Greek poetry"), which he would later expand in his dissertation work at La Sorbonne, Parry could consult Schmidt's *Parallel Homer* (1885) in order to find patterns in Homer's diction: this allowed him to quickly recognize the repetitive structures that pervade our poems.

---

[30] For a history of the concordance, see Haeselin (2019), with references. Other literary authors for which concordances had already been made in the nineteenth century are Shakespeare, Milton, and Pope (Higdon 2003: 57).

Tools that would enable a similar study of natural spoken and written English would not be compiled until the 1970s.[31]

There were theoretical reasons behind this disadvantage as well: for a good part of the twentieth century, a very influential theory in linguistics, Generative Grammar (as inaugurated by the work of Noam Chomsky in the 1950s), was concerned principally with the generative, creative potential of the human language faculty – not its formulaic bits. Idiomaticity in language was perceived as exceptional, and pushed to the margins.[32] As a result, studies of Homeric formularity and studies of formularity in natural languages were "out of sync" for several decades. Paul Kiparsky, who (as we have seen above) was the first to attempt to reconcile the two areas within the generative framework, was well aware of this fact:

> Formulaic diction has been extensively studied, but for the most part as a phenomenon *sui generis*. Noone has attempted to compare systematically the phrase patterns of oral poetry with those of ordinary language. (Kiparsky 1976: 1)

Decades later, we are in a much better position to carry out Kiparsky's wish. Within generative theory, much more attention has been devoted to explaining the idiomatic and selectional restrictions that affect otherwise productive rules, and the role of the lexicon has been steadily expanded. Generative theory is not alone in this regard: other areas of linguistics have in fact also been busy exploring formularity for the past several decades, and providing us with theoretical insights and practical frameworks that can now be usefully applied to Homer. These areas are corpus linguistics, language acquisition studies, and usage-based linguistics – and it is into these areas that we shall venture next.

1.2.2 Formularity in Corpus Linguistics, Psycholinguistics, and Historical Linguistics

One of the first results of the development of corpus linguistics, since its beginnings in the 1970s, was the realization that idiomaticity was a much

---

[31] For a history of corpus linguistics, see Facchinetti (2007).
[32] "How is bound phraseology to be accounted for in the framework of a formal generative grammar? This is a question which has received regrettably little attention in linguistics recently. As might be expected, most of the excitement has for some time been around the new ways of investigating productive syntactic (and phonological) processes which generative grammar has opened up. The less productive regularities of language, notably morphology and phraseology, on which generative grammar does not throw nearly so much light, have been treated as sideshows, though interest in them is clearly beginning to revive" (Kiparsky 1976: 77).

broader phenomenon than previously acknowledged. Fixed linguistic expressions (termed *collocations*[33] in the field) seemed to account for a substantial percentage of the corpora, far from being relegated to the periphery. At the level of language production, scholars in this field started to doubt that syntax was as free as generative approaches assumed.[34] There was the so-called *puzzle of native-like selection*:

> Native speakers do not exercise the creative potential of syntactic rules to anything like their full extent [...] indeed, if they did so they would not be accepted as exhibiting nativelike control of language. The fact is that only a small proportion of the total set of grammatical sentences are nativelike in form [...] in contrast to expressions that are grammatical but are judged to be "unidiomatic", "odd" or "foreignisms". (Pawley and Syder 1983: 193)

Language production seemed to involve large amounts of simple retrieval of stored sequences:

> Speakers do at least as much remembering as they do putting together [...]. We are now in a position to recognize that idiomaticity is a vastly more pervasive phenomenon than we ever imagined, and vastly harder to separate from the pure freedom of syntax, if indeed any such fiery zone as pure syntax exists. (Bolinger 1976: 2–3)[35]

What the field of psycholinguistics has established is that, while the brain does much that is creative, it also does a lot of simple retrieval. In fact, retrieval is often cheaper (i.e., less demanding) from the processing viewpoint:[36]

> The indications from neurophysiology and psychology are that, instead of storing a small number of primitives and organizing them in terms of

---

[33] "[Collocation] is a *psychological association* between words (rather than lemmas) up to four words apart and is *evidenced by their occurrence together* in corpora more often than is explicable in terms of random distribution" (Hoey 2005: 5, emphasis mine). Note the striking similarity to Parry's definition of formula.

[34] A very readable history of the scholarship is Partington (1998), from which I derive many of the following quotations.

[35] In fact, in contemporary generative theories of syntax, pretty much every lexical item is specified for selectionality (in simple terms, almost every lexical item has preferences or requirements for what types of other elements it can combine with) – which puts a heavy burden on the lexicon and notably diminishes the realm of the "fiery zones of syntax" that Bolinger talks about.

[36] The amount to which our conceptions of human processing capacities are shaped by the development of information technology is instructive. In the early days of computers, storage was indeed expensive. Bill Gates is quoted as saying in the 1970s that computers in the future will need *little* storage capacity (and that would be a form of progress). The quote is allegedly: "No one will need more than 637 kb of memory for a personal computer" (http://en.wikiquote.org/wiki/Talk:Bill_Gates). The exact opposite has in fact occurred. Similarly, research on brain processing has moved from the view that processing is cheap and storage is expensive, to the view that storage is cheap and processing is expensive.

a (relatively) large number of rules, we store a large number of complex items which we manipulate with comparatively simple operations. The central nervous system is like a special kind of computer which has rapid access to items in a very large memory, but comparatively little ability to process these items when they have been taken out of memory. (Ladefoged 1972: 282)

The field of morphology has perhaps explored these topics to the greatest extent, especially when it comes to determining whether a speaker is generating a morphologically complex word anew (using a productive process in their language) or merely pulling it from memory. Let us take the English word *happiness*, for instance: is the speaker pulling it from memory, or deriving it from its base form, *happy*? And what about the word *bookishness* (memorized or generated)? This question can be tested in the psycholinguistic lab using *lexical decision tasks*, in which speakers are shown morphologically complex words and asked to decide whether they are real words in their language. These types of experiments consistently show that frequent words are more quickly recognized than infrequent ones; a widespread interpretation of this fact is that frequent words are stored, rather than assembled using grammatical processes (so, to answer our question, *happiness* is likely stored, and *bookishness* is likely generated).[37] In other words, frequency seems to decide, for each speaker, whether a linguistic string is more likely to be retrieved from memory or generated anew.

Frequency effects go beyond morphology, and can be observed in syntax as well. The process of *chunking*, for instance, happens when speakers begin to store a sequence of words (e.g., a phrase) as a single item, given its frequency of occurrence, and no longer generate it from scratch.[38] Everyday examples of chunked sequences include standardized greetings like *Thank you*, *How are you?* and *Bless you*, or frequent replies like *I don't know* (compare the informal spelling *dunno*).

Evidence for chunking can easily be found in the historical record, where chunked items can effectively become a single word, and lose any internal structure; often, erosion of phonetic material accompanies the fusion (see *dunno* above), as well as a semantic shift. A well-known example is the English collocation *going to*, which has now largely developed in the spoken language into *gonna* or even *'ma*[39] (along with the phonetic erosion, the meaning has shifted too, from an expression of physical movement to an expression of

---

[37] For one model, see Baayen and Schreuder (1995).
[38] For an introduction to chunking, see Bybee (2010: Chapter 3).
[39] For instance, the expression *I'ma let you finish* (where the first word can also be spelled as *I'mma*) can be used in some dialects of spoken American English as a more colloquial form of *I'm gonna let you finish*. For a short history of *I'ma*, see Whitman (2010).

tense), or, more simply, the development of the Old English expression *on slǽpe* (Middle English *on sleep*) into Present-Day English (PDE) *asleep*. Chunking is in fact the first step in the process of *grammaticalization*, which is a way in which languages create new morphological material out of syntactic units.[40] According to Bybee (2002), chunking might even be at the root of the hierarchical organization that is pervasive in human language.

1.2.3 Measuring the Idiom Principle

To sum up, speakers seem to operate in at least two ways when producing language: they create some expressions from scratch (following the rules of their grammar), and they retrieve some from memory. The last strategy seems preferable with high-frequency items, so that a speaker can avoid computing the same task repeatedly. John Sinclair captured this duality in language processing – that is, computation vs. retrieval – in the principles of *idiom* and *open choice*:

> The principle of idiom is that a language user has available to him a large number of preconstructed or semi-preconstructed phrases that constitute single choices, *even though they appear to be analyzable into segments*. (Sinclair 1991: 110, emphasis mine)[41]

The principle of open choice, on the other hand, entails that "at each point where a unit is completed (a word, phrase, clause), a large range of choice opens up and the only restraint is grammaticalness" (Sinclair 1991: 109).

A 2000 study by Erman and Warren sought to measure the extent to which the idiom principle was responsible for the creation of everyday spoken and written texts.[42] To do this, the authors introduced the concept of the prefabricated unit, or *prefab*:

> A prefab is a combination of at least two words favored by native speakers in preference to an alternative combination which could have been equivalent had there been no conventionalization. (Erman and Warren 2000: 31)

---

[40] See Bybee (2015: 117–39).
[41] This last point touches on what Langacker has termed the *rule/list fallacy* (Langacker 1987): just because something can be rule-generated, it does not mean that it cannot be stored (i.e., listed) as well. In the framework of *Emergent Grammar* (Hopper 1987), rules "emerge" from storage, and are thus epiphenomenal.
[42] Composition of the (admittedly small) corpus: seven extracts of 600 to 800 words from *The London–Lund Corpus of Spoken English* plus ten extracts of 100 to 400 words from the *Lancaster–Oslo–Bergen Corpus* (written English) plus two 400-word extracts from two versions of *Goldilocks*.

Note that prefabs are not just repeated word sequences: they are *conventionalized sequences*, in that they display restricted modificability (e.g., they cannot be negated, or pluralized, or undergo gradation, without losing in idiomaticity). Thus, the procedure for finding prefabs in a text has two steps: (1) finding all repeated sequences in a corpus, (2) running a restricted modificability test, to verify which sequences are conventionalized. For instance, a sequence like *black cat* (if repeated) would meet requirement (1), but not requirement (2), since it is not idiomatic and can be freely modified. A sequence like *black box* would meet both (1) and (2), since it is idiomatic, and cannot be modified (a *very black box* is something different entirely). Our definitions of Homeric formularity, which are simply based on repetition (and do not test for conventionalization), are thus less restrictive than the definition of prefab.[43] Still, the results of the study (as reported in Table 1.3) were rather striking: more than 50 percent of both spoken and written texts in the sample proved to be made up of prefabricated units, and while a difference was discernible in the amount of prefabs between spoken and written texts, it was rather narrow (a mere six percentage points).

The true difference between spoken and written corpora seemed to lie in the distribution of prefab types rather than in their quantity. For instance, Table 1.4 highlights the different proportions of *lexical prefabs* and *pragmatic prefabs* in written vs. spoken texts. As per Erman and Warren (2000: 38), "Lexical prefabs are semantic units in that they have reference and denote entities, properties, states, events, and situations of different kinds" (e.g., *intensive care, all over the place, here and there, a waste of time, on a clear night*). These appear to be nearly twice as frequent in written texts as in spoken ones. Pragmatic prefabs, on the other hand, "are functional in that they do not directly partake in the propositional content of the

Table 1.3 *Proportion of prefabs in the analyzed texts (after Erman and Warren 2000: 37)*

	Word slots	Filled with prefabs
Spoken	5,000	2,930 (58.6%)
Written	5,246	2,745 (52.3%)
	10,246	5,675 (55.4%)

---

[43] To be fair, it would be much harder to run a restricted modificability test on a repeated expression in a dead language, since we cannot rely on native-speaker intuition.

Table 1.4 *Distribution of prefab types (after Erman and Warren 2000: 37)*

	Lexical	Grammatical	Pragmatic	Reducible
Spoken	38.8%	20.5%	16.7%	24.0%
Written	71.5%	16.9%	2.4%	9.2%

utterance in question [. . .] Most of them are restricted to spoken language and some have functions which could be indicated by punctuation, paragraphing, or in other graphic ways in written texts" (Erman and Warren 2000: 43); examples include *and then, and finally, and of course, but anyway, the thing is that . . . you know, I mean, and so on, well I thought, as I said*. These, unsurprisingly, are decidedly rare in written texts (2.4 percent), and almost seven times more frequent (16.7 percent) in spoken ones.

These results[44] should cause any supporter of a quantitative formula analysis to question many of their basic assumptions. If formularity is caused by oral composition in performance and the strictness of the meter, why do we find it in natural language? And what causes it, then? Why is it so extensive in both writing and speaking? And why is writing apparently even more formulaic than speaking in some categories? Is Homer, then, not any more formulaic than natural language, and should we give up hope of demonstrating Homer's orality?

In order to answer these questions, we need to develop a *general* account of formularity, one that combines insights from linguistics and oral-formulaic theory, and is grounded in what we know about human cognition. It is to this goal that we turn in the next section.

1.3 Formularity in Cognition

1.3.1 *Working Memory, Chunking, and Automation*

While we might pride ourselves on the complex achievements of the human brain, researchers in the cognitive fields have long known that human memory is, in many ways, heavily limited. This is especially true of

---

[44] Of course, Erman and Warren (2000) is just one study, on a limited corpus. Subsequent studies have also reported substantial numbers of formulaic sequences in natural-language corpora, if somewhat less than what was reported by Erman and Warren (a recent survey can be found in Read and Nation 2004). Additional research is certainly desirable.

the type of memory that we rely on, constantly, for all of our conscious endeavors: our working memory.[45] A long tradition in the field of cognitive psychology limits its capacity to just a handful of items, the exact number spanning from four to nine at the most (Miller 1956, Cowan 2001), and of course depending on the nature of the items. In fact, working memory functions as a bottleneck for much of what we do. The reason we are not particularly good at multitasking (despite what we might like to believe) lies precisely in our limited personal RAM.[46,47]

Yet, this limitation does not stop us from achieving some rather complicated and impressive feats of attention management, like driving a car along a busy freeway, playing a musical instrument, and, perhaps most impressively of all, using human language. How can it be the case that we can carry out all of these resource-intensive activities (and sometimes even two of them at the same time), if our working memory is so limited?

All of the aforementioned complex activities have something in common: no one is able to do them well right away. They all require a long period of training, during which a lot of the component behaviors are performed over and over, until they become entirely automatic (one might say, second nature). Automation really is the key here: what is automatic can run in the background, without taking up space in our working memory. In other words, we can bypass the limitations of our working memory by bypassing working memory entirely.

We already mentioned the notion of *chunking* with regard to linguistic units. The same notion applies to all sorts of cognitive units, including units of human motor activities (*action units*: see Fenk-Oczlon and Fenk 2002: 221).[48]

---

[45] Current models of human memory posit, at minimum, three components: sensory memory, working memory, and long-term memory (Baddeley, Eysenck, and Anderson 2009: 6). For further subdivisions of working memory, see Baddeley et al. (2009: Chapter 3).

[46] RAM, or *random access memory*, is a form of computer memory that is typically used to temporarily store working data, as opposed to a computer's hard drive, which is typically used for long-term data storage.

[47] There are many classic experiments that illustrate the limitations of our working memory; some of these may involve remembering word lists, or sequences of digits (the classic study is Miller 1956). Perhaps most memorably, the famous "invisible gorilla" experiment (Simons and Chabris 1999) illustrates how, when our working memory is busy with one task, we are effectively blind to much else that happens. In this type of experiment, participants are asked to keep track of some events (like how many times the ball was passed by the members of one team) while watching a short video (originally, this featured a ball game). Because they were busy with this task, participants typically completely missed an otherwise remarkable event in the video (in the original study, this entailed a person wearing a gorilla suit walking across the frame).

[48] Chunking can also be applied as a mnemonic strategy: it is well known that dividing information into small chunks makes it easier to remember. Everyday examples include the way in which the sixteen-digit sequences on credit cards are written out as four chunks of four digits each. Or the way telephone numbers are written out (and read out loud), which typically involves creating smaller

In fact, we might see linguistic units (especially units of speech like *intonation units* or *prosodic phrases*)[49] as a special case of more general action units in which all of our behaviors are broken down. While performing each of these units might be effortful, training and chunking can alleviate much of the cognitive load involved. When learning to play an instrument, then, we are building up our repertoire of chunked action units, just as oral poets build up their repertoire of chunked formulaic units, and just as speakers build up their repertoire of chunked linguistic units (see Wray and Perkins 2000). These chunks support the fluent execution of complex behaviors.

In fact, experiments have shown that *mastery* in many fields relies on the capacity to organize information into large chunks, both perceptually and in terms of recall. A classic study of chess players (Chase and Simon 1973) revealed that experienced players are able to handle much larger chunks of information (in this case, the details of a chess position) than novice players, resulting in more accurate recall and faster processing. When shown a chess position for just five seconds, experienced players were able to reconstruct it to a great level of accuracy, while novice players could not.[50] When looking at the chess board, experienced players did not see isolated pieces: they combined the information into large chunks, which they could then easily hold in their working memory. The same chunking ability assisted experienced players when making quick decisions about the next move: "What was once accomplished by slow, conscious deductive reasoning is now arrived at by fast, unconscious perceptual processing"(Chase and Simon 1973: 56). Any complex, repeated activity will come to rely on chunking.

Chunking similarly assists experienced oral-traditional singers in the impressive feat of being able to "faithfully" reproduce an unknown song that they have heard just once before.[51] While for the untrained listener a song is made up of hundreds of unchunked details (and thus almost

---

sequences of two to four digits each. A recent popular introduction to mnemonic techniques is Foer (2011).

[49] In oral-traditional poetry, the basic unit of production is the *traditional word* (Greek ἔπος, Serbo-Croatian *reč*), which often corresponds to an entire line or half-line (see discussion in Foley 2002: Chapter 2).

[50] The difference between the two groups disappeared when an impossible position was shown (i.e., a random arrangement of pieces on a chess board): experienced chess players were good at chunking meaningful chess positions – not just anything.

[51] Of course, *verbatim* reproduction is not the standard by which we measure such tasks. A song will count as "faithfully" reproduced when all the plot points are there, and when it is narrated in the same traditional style. See discussion in Lord (1960: Chapter 5). If these conditions are met, traditional singers will insist that two songs are the same even when their transcripts are quite different.

impossible to remember faithfully), a masterful singer will perceive the song as a combination of large, well-known chunks (provided the song belongs to a tradition with which they are familiar, of course), and will thus be able to easily reproduce it and make it their own.

What is interesting here is the link with creativity: one might think that automatic behaviors resulting from chunking are detrimental to the creative endeavor, but in fact the opposite is true. Just as it does for the experienced chess players, a greater reliance on chunking allows us to engage in more complex tasks more quickly. Freed from the low-level concern of verse-making, oral poets can focus on more complex narrative tasks. Formulas and prefabs in language corpora are just that: an (imprecise) measure of the automatic behaviors (chunks) poets and speakers have come to rely on when producing language. They are the trace of mastery.

1.3.2 Formulary, Mastery, and Genre

Of course, mastery might look different depending on the task you are trying to complete, and different circumstances can affect our reliance on automation (acting as dials, in a way, decreasing or increasing the amount of automation required for a given task). It is fully expected that we will find many formulaic sequences in both spoken and written language, since people tend to develop automatic behaviors for what they frequently do (and in our day and age, some of us write perhaps just as much as we speak).

At the same time, the *nature* of the formulary (e.g., the types of prefabs) that we find for each task will depend on the nature of the task itself: thus, in Erman and Warren's terminology, spoken language has more pragmatic prefabs (automatic behaviors for regulating interpersonal communication, like greetings) and written language has more lexical prefabs (automatic behaviors for describing objects and situations). This, of course, is simply a reflection of the types of linguistic tasks that speakers of PDE tend to do more often in one medium than another.

Different genres of language (whether spoken or written) are also likely to develop different types of prefabs: when it comes to professional language, waiters will develop different linguistic habits from lawyers, and might not recognize the prefabs used by the other group as such. The language of oral poetry is really just a specific type of professional language, with its own special types of prefabs, which may happen to be metrical. Within any linguistic community, speakers will share a large number of prefabs, but many others will be limited to given individuals or groups thereof.

In any given text, the amount of formularity will also depend on the individual and their experience: as an academic, I have come to rely on many automatic behaviors that support teaching and academic writing in English, but I am a lot less knowledgeable about verbal chunks that would be useful for describing a football game, or a ballet (or, sadly, for carrying out similar academic tasks in my native Italian or decidedly non-native German). Doing tasks in which we have relatively less training will result in fewer chunks (less mastery, fewer chunks).

Levels of formularity might also change for the same individual depending on the overall challenge of the task at hand: the higher the pressure on our cognitive resources (e.g., having to speak particularly quickly, or when particularly tired), the higher the likelihood of reliance on chunks. For instance, sportscasters tend to rely more on formulaic language when responding to events that are fast, unexpected, or important: "announcers tended to use more clichés when the game deviated from the expected outcome. Announcers also tended to use more clichés in games involving teams that were highly ranked" (Wanta and Meggett 1988: 87). Following this logic, a singer performing for a big audience, or in a high-stakes competition, might be more formulaic than when performing for a small, intimate crowd.

Finally, some genres might explicitly require verbal originality, and might thus encourage us to reduce our reliance on chunks. This is really what Horace is getting at in his *Ars Poetica*, as quoted in the Introduction: we expect originality (though not absurdity) from poets (even though, of course, the poets Horace is referring to are quite different from Homer), and known language chunks can sound weathered and worn; by creating new and effective word combinations, a poet can make language sound fresh again.

At the other end of the spectrum, genres in which *exact wording* is needed to obtain a given result might force us to rely extensively on chunks; we can think of the language of law, or the language of ritual, in which practitioners would be very wary of innovative wording even if they had the time to come up with it (*I proclaim you wife and husband* does not have the same effect as *I pronounce you man and wife*).

Is Homer more like Horace or more like a lawyer? This is a good question. In general, one might contrast the task of the epic poet (telling a traditional story in a traditional way) with that of the lyric poet (evoking traditional stories in a nontraditional way). The theory that an oral epic poet, when given more time to compose (by slowing down his delivery for the purposes of dictation or writing), would rely on fewer formulas actually rests on the assumption that verbal originality would be, in this context, a desirable goal.

It is unclear that this would always be the case.⁵² Some formulaic expressions are arguably there to achieve a given effect; they are rich in traditional associations, and the poet would be foolish to give them up.⁵³ At the same time, originality might be desirable for some areas of the tale. This is true for some types of storytelling that we experience today: when telling the story of *Little Red Riding Hood*, the words spoken between the little girl and the wolf dressed as Grandma ("What big eyes you have," etc.) must remain the same – and especially the last crucial exchange: "What a big mouth you have"; "The better to eat you with, my dear!"⁵⁴ Ornamentation and improvisation are allowed (and in some cases even encouraged) in other areas of the story. For Homer, it is commonly observed that similes (certainly part of the ornamentation) are lower in formularity and higher in recent linguistic features (Shipp 1972: Chapter 6).⁵⁵

To sum up, the degree of formularity in a given text may be impacted by a multitude of factors, some having to do with the nature of the task, some with the skill level of the speaker, and some with the conditions of performance. If we find two texts, A and B, and the first is higher in formularity and the second is lower, the reasons could be many:

a. We could be looking at the same speaker under different levels of cognitive strain (higher strain = more formularity), performing familiar vs. unfamiliar tasks (like, paradoxically, dictating a text at an unusually slow pace) or responding to different circumstances which encourage or discourage formularity.

---

⁵² Lord (1991: 43) observes that oral poets who write down their songs produce lower-quality texts because they don't have mastery of the written medium, and yet they are moving away from the technique they know: "They become wordy and stilted to the point of being unconsciously mock heroic. The natural dignity of the traditional expressions is lost and what remains is a caricature. The literary technique takes several generations to mature." With respect to Homer, Lord (1991: 45) makes the argument that the poet of the *Iliad* seems to have all the habits of an oral poet and none of the habits of somebody who is accustomed to writing.

⁵³ Foley (1991) has introduced the concept of *traditional referentiality* to clarify this property of traditional formulas. The expression "swift-footed Achilles" does not simply mean "Achilles": it provides a link for the audience between the present performance and the hundreds of previous epic performances they have witnessed. It reminds them of all the traditional associations that come with Achilles.

⁵⁴ Note the archaic syntax in the wolf's response. This is a case where formularity preserves an earlier stage of the language (see more in section 1.4.6 below).

⁵⁵ The usual interpretation of this fact is that similes (and other ornamentation) are the areas where individual poets feel more free to leave their mark, and thus are more open to linguistic (and thematic) innovation. If similes are conceived as pieces of *bravura*, one can imagine individual oral poets rehearsing them in advance, and perhaps even memorizing them in preparation for a performance. Finkelberg (2012) is an updated look at the appearance of more recent linguistic features in the speeches in the *Iliad*, another area that is generally seen as more open to linguistic innovation.

b. We could be looking at two speakers with different levels of mastery of the same task (higher mastery = more formulary).
c. We could be looking at speakers who have similar levels of mastery but are trying to achieve different goals (traditionality vs. originality, different genre aesthetics).
d. Finally, we could be more informed about the types of formularity in text A than in text B (which might represent a subgenre about which we have little information).

While some of these differences might correlate with the spoken vs. written divide, not all do. The reason why Homer is more formulaic than, say, parts of the *Homeric Hymns* could be (b), (c), or (d). The reason why he is more formulaic than Virgil is arguably a version of (c). For this reason, quantitative formula analysis is far from a perfect tool, and one whose results should not be interpreted simplistically.

1.3.3 Collocational Measures in Homer and Other Corpora

With all this being said, we might still rightly wonder about the amount of formularity in Homer vis-à-vis the amount of "formularity" in natural language (spoken or written). Is there really no difference to be observed there? Is there any way to confirm the general intuition that Homer is more "repetitive" than normal speech? Even though a large number of prefabricated sequences are to be expected in many areas of human language, there might still be something quantitatively different about Homer.

In this section, I will discuss *collocational measures* that can be easily obtained using concordancing software and a digitized corpus, and which help us substantiate some of our intuitions about Homer being more formulaic than the norm. These collocational measures might not amount to a proof of orality, but they might allow us to isolate what exactly it is in Homer that we perceive as more automatic and more repetitive than other authors.

A concept similar to that of the prefab, but a lot more neutral, since it does not presume psychological reality or syntactic constituency (or even semantic contentfulness), is that of *collocation*. Collocations are text-based units formed by two or more orthographic words which tend to occur close to each other in a given corpus.[56] For instance, the words *foreseeable* and *future* constitute a collocation in English, since finding the first one in

---

[56] Words that are *collocates* (i.e., take part in a collocation) do not need to be immediately adjacent to each other, though many of the examples discussed below are. When looking for collocations in a text, one can specify a collocation window span (e.g., 5L 5R, meaning five words to the left

Table 1.5 *The ten most frequent two-word, three-word, four-word, and five-word collocations in the LOB corpus*

	2-word	3-word	4-word	5-word
#1	of the	one of the	the end of the	at the end of the
#2	in the	there was a	at the same time	and at the same time
#3	to the	out of the	in the case of	in the case of the
#4	on the	the end of	on the other hand	on the part of the
#5	and the	some of the	at the end of	the other side of the
#6	it is	part of the	for the first time	there is no doubt that
#7	for the	there is a	per cent of the	in the middle of the
#8	to be	it was a	i don t know	at the same time the
#9	at the	there is no	one of the most	as a result of the
#10	that the	i don t	as a result of	at the top of the

a text considerably increases the likelihood of finding the second one immediately afterwards, while the words *red* and *future* do not (since finding the first one does not make the occurrence of the second one any more likely).

Table 1.5 is a list of the ten most frequent two-word, three-word, four-word, and five-word collocations from the Lancaster–Oslo–Bergen (LOB) corpus of written English (the corpus also used by Erman and Warren 2000). One should note that most of these collocations appear to us to be substantially smaller and less contentful than a formula or a prefab as defined by Erman and Warren (2000). The average length of prefabs studied by Erman and Warren is three words for lexical prefabs, and about two words for grammatical, pragmatic, and reducible prefabs (Erman and Warren 2000: 40). Yet all of these prefab types constitute some kind of recognizable syntactic constituent (e.g., a noun phrase or an adjective phrase: see Erman and Warren 2000: Table 5), while most two-word and three-word collocations in our table do not. Similarly, most of the collocations in our table would not be units that we would recognize as candidates for Homeric formulas, in that many do not seem to express "a single essential idea." In other

and five words to the right) within which the collocates can be sought. This is the case, for instance, for the Proximity text search tool provided by the Thesaurus Linguae Graecae (which was employed to obtain some of the data in section 1.4.2 below). For a short introduction to different approaches to identifying collocations in a text, see Gablasova, Brezina, and McEnery (2017).

words, while all prefabs (or formulas) are collocations, the reverse is not true.

The advantage of using collocations instead of prefabs (or formulas) is that collocations can be easily counted in an automated fashion, while the individuation of prefabs relies on manual analysis of each instance and the application of native speaker judgment, which makes the resulting measurements both more difficult to obtain and harder to replicate. What I hope to show below is that what bare, text-based collocational measures lack in sophistication (they are simple measures of repetitiveness, not of actual formularity), they make up for in efficacy.

For our comparison between Homer and natural language, it is enough to say that two-word collocations are extremely common in spoken and written language, and that they can be seen as prime evidence for the phenomenon of *chunking* mentioned above. On the other hand, what tends to be relatively less common in natural language corpora is an abundance of longer collocations – that is, collocations involving three or more words. Below, for instance, are some collocational data for the LOB corpus of written English, showing type and token frequencies[57] of collocations formed by two words, three words, four words, and five words respectively (see Figure 1.2).

By looking at the token frequency, we can see that two-word collocations are extremely common in the corpus, and that longer collocations are less and less so, as witnessed by the steeply declining slope of our token line. Looking at the relative position of type frequency and token frequency reveals something else: while two-word collocation types are likely to be repeated very frequently in our corpus (e.g., the most frequent two-word collocation type, *of the*, is repeated 9,009 times), this value steeply decreases as our collocations become longer (e.g., the most frequent five-word collocation type, *at the end of the*, is repeated only

---

[57] Within corpus linguistics, an important distinction is made between *tokens* and *types*. When calculating word frequencies for a given corpus, this is the difference between counting how many occurrences of a given word are found in that corpus (i.e., how many tokens of a given word are in that corpus), and how many different words (how many types of words) are found in that corpus. In the sentence *A cat sees another cat*, there are five word tokens, belonging to four word types (*a*, *cat*, *sees*, and *another*); the type *cat* has two tokens (i.e., it occurs twice), while all other types have one token each (they are all, within this short text, *hapax legomena*). In the following section, the type and token counts of collocations (as opposed to single words) will be discussed.

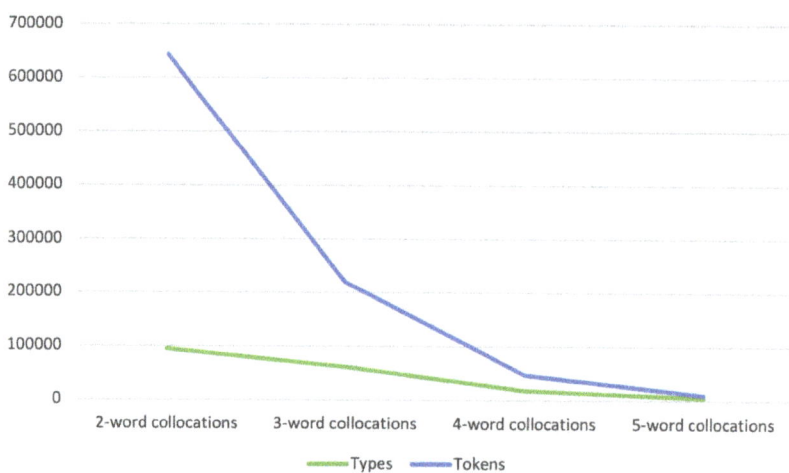

Figure 1.2 Type and token counts of two-, three-, four-, and five-word collocations in the LOB corpus of written English

twenty-eight times).[58] In other words, the longer the collocations become, the less they are repeated, and the more type and token lines tend to converge.

We can also observe this convergence in the sharp decrease in the proportion of collocation tokens of a given length that are repeated more than twice, and the corresponding increase in collocation tokens that are *singula iterata*. For two-word collocations, about 93 percent of all tokens are repeated more than twice – that is, only 7 percent of two-word collocations in our corpus are *singula iterata*. For five-word collocations, only 16 percent of all tokens are repeated more than twice – that is, 83 percent of five-word collocations are *singula iterata*.

While these tendencies could easily be replicated using many other modern corpora, one might object that the LOB corpus is very large (1,033,210 words), and in English, and as such might not provide an ideal comparandum for Homer. To this end, it would be ideal to study an Ancient Greek corpus of a length similar to that of the *Iliad* and the *Odyssey* combined (ca. 199,000 words). An ideal candidate in this sense is Herodotus (ca. 186,000 words), an author whom the ancients, for independent reasons, called ὁμηρικώτατος "the most Homer-like." Figure 1.3

---

[58] Note that this decline is also to be expected because longer collocates can fully contain smaller collocates, just like *at the end of the* contains *of the*.

Figure 1.3 Type and token counts of two-, three-, four-, and five-word collocations in Herodotus

shows the type and token counts of collocations that we find in Herodotus, ranging from two to five words.[59]

Overall, the situation in Herodotus seems to replicate the LOB situation, albeit on a much smaller scale (the *Historiae* are about one-tenth of the size of the LOB). Here, too, the number of collocations steadily diminishes with the length of the sequence, and our lines converge around the five-word collocation point. The fall in the ratio of token to type frequency appears somewhat sharper than what we saw in the LOB corpus: at the five-word collocation level, collocations repeated more than twice make up only 10 percent of our tokens, with *singula iterata* constituting 90 percent of the attested five-word collocations.

If we run the same counts using the Homeric corpus (Figure 1.4), we can see that the overall trend is similar: two-word collocations are the most frequent, and the number steadily decreases as we look at longer sequences. At the same time, the token and type lines gradually draw closer to each other.

---

[59] These counts were obtained by first extracting the complete texts of Herodotus and Homer using the Classical Language Toolkit (http://cltk.org) under Python 3, and feeding them through the software CasualConc (https://sites.google.com/site/casualconc/home), which then generated type and token lists of two-, three-, four-, and five-word collocations as requested (using the Word Count function). These lists were then exported into Microsoft Excel, where type and token counts were made for each list. The results were then visualized by entering the token and type counts in a separate table in Microsoft Excel, and generating a graph from the table. The same procedure was used for the counts below regarding Quintus Smyrnaeus.

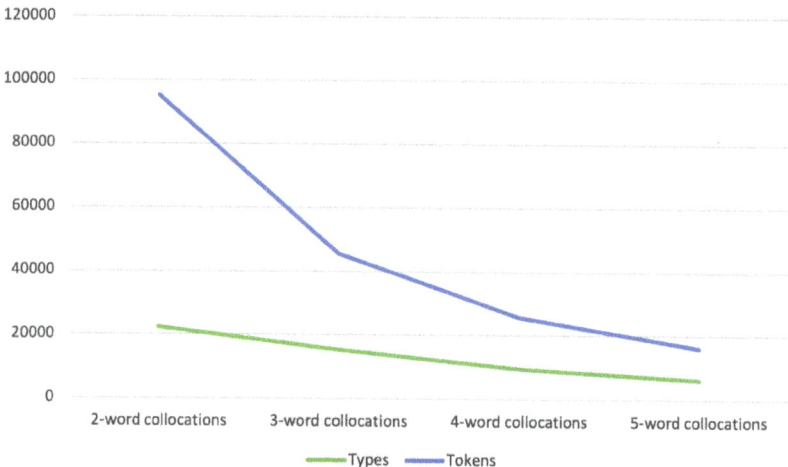

Figure 1.4 Type and token counts of two-, three-, four-, and five-word collocations in Homer

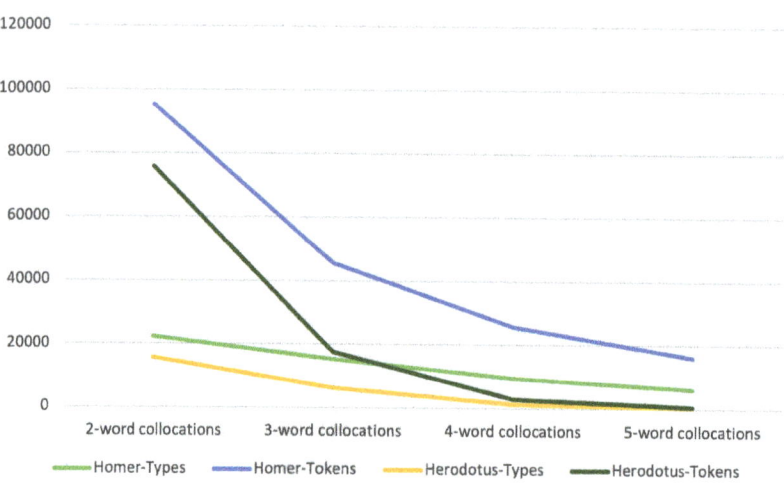

Figure 1.5 Type and token counts of two-, three-, four-, and five-word collocations in Homer vs. Herodotus

Yet, the similarities end here: if we compare Homer and Herodotus, we see that Homer registers significantly more collocations than Herodotus does *at all sizes*, and this is true in terms of both types and tokens (see Figure 1.5 above

Formularity in Cognition

for a direct comparison). Even at a superficial level, Homer does appear to be more repetitive than Herodotus.

A closer look at the data reveals even starker differences. The difference in number of collocations between Homer and Herodotus might seem small at the two-word level, though it is already statistically significant. But starting at the three-word level, it becomes noticeably larger. And remarkably, in Homer the token and type lines never touch: at the five-word stage, collocations repeated more than twice still make up 25 percent of all tokens, with *singula iterata* accounting for only 75 percent of the attested five-word collocations. A list of the ten most frequent two-word, three-word, four-word, and five-word collocations in Homer and Herodotus respectively is given in Tables 1.6 and 1.7. (Note that, for text processing reasons, apostrophe signs were removed from the corpus, and as such they do not appear in the tables.)

The next step is to compare our results concerning Homer and Herodotus with some other Greek hexametric poetry that is not suspected of being composed orally. This is to exclude the possibility that the "repetitiveness" that we observed in Homer might simply be due to the realities of composing hexametric poetry, regardless of orality. As it is traditional within the field of Homeric formularity, we can turn to authors like Apollonius Rhodius and Quintus Smyrnaeus – that is, poets who wrote, and who (to different extents) endeavored to imitate Homer's style and language. Quintus offers a particularly apt comparison here, since several scholars have argued that his technique (while still being markedly distinct from Homer's) comes closest to a genuine approximation of Homer's oral style, including developing his own patterns of formularity.[60]

Figures 1.6 and 1.7 contrast the results from Quintus Smyrnaeus (whose corpus counts ca. 61,000 words) with those from Homer and Herodotus respectively.[61] The comparison is instructive: even at first sight, Quintus appears much more similar to Herodotus than to Homer. In Figure 1.7, the shapes and the slopes of the lines are almost identical for Quintus and Herodotus (the only exception being Herodotus having significantly more tokens of two-word collocations than Quintus; other than that, the figures overlap almost perfectly). If we contrast Quintus with Homer (Figure 1.6), on the other hand, we find the usual discrepancy observed above: the type

---

[60] See the discussion in Sale (1996) and, most recently, Bakker (2019).
[61] The type and token counts for Homer and Herodotus have been scaled down in Figures 1.6 and 1.7 to match the smaller corpus size of Quintus. Specifically, the numbers for Homer have been divided by 3.3, while the numbers for Herodotus have been divided by 3.1.

Table 1.6 *The ten most frequent two-word, three-word, four-word, and five-word collocations in Homer*

	2-word	3-word	4-word	5-word
#1	τε καί	ἔπεα πτερόεντα προσηύδα	τὸν δ αὖτε προσέειπε	δ ἀπαμειβόμενος προσέφη πολύμητις Ὀδυσσεύς (47x)
#2	τὸν δ	δ ἀπαμειβόμενος προσέφη	τὸν δ ἠμείβετ ἔπειτα	αὖ Τηλέμαχος πεπνυμένος ἀντίον ηὔδα (41x)
#3	δ ἄρα	δ αὖτε προσέειπε	τὸν δ ἀπαμειβόμενος προσέφη	δ αὖ Τηλέμαχος πεπνυμένος ἀντίον (41x)
#4	ὁ δ	τὸν δ αὖτε	δ ἀπαμειβόμενος προσέφη πολύμητις	ἔπος τ ἔφατ ἔκ τ (41x)
#5	δ ἄρ	ἀλλ ὅτε δή	ἀπαμειβόμενος προσέφη πολύμητις Ὀδυσσεύς	καί μιν φωνήσας ἔπεα πτερόεντα (35x)
#6	δέ οἱ	δ ἠμείβετ ἔπειτα	τ ἔφατ ἔκ τ	τὸν δ αὖ Τηλέμαχος πεπνυμένος (30x)
#7	οἳ δ	τὸν δ ἀπαμειβόμενος	Τηλέμαχος πεπνυμένος ἀντίον ηὔδα	μιν φωνήσας ἔπεα πτερόεντα προσηύδα (29x)
#8	οἱ δ	προσέφη πολύμητις Ὀδυσσεύς	αὖ Τηλέμαχος πεπνυμένος ἀντίον	ὣς ἔφαθ οἱ δ ἄρα (28x)
#9	δ αὖτε	ἐς πατρίδα γαῖαν	ἔπος τ ἔφατ ἔκ	ὣς ἔφαθ οἳ δ ἄρα (28x)
#10	δ ἐν	τὸν δ ἠμείβετ	δ αὖ Τηλέμαχος πεπνυμένος	τὸν δ ἀπαμειβόμενος προσέφη πολύμητις (27x)

and token lines in Quintus meet at around the four-word collocation mark, while in Homer they never do; and the token line in Homer is significantly higher throughout (i.e., Homer contains a lot more repeated sequences than Quintus, at any length).

To summarize our results, there *is* something measurably different about the text of Homer when it comes to collocational tendencies, especially when looking at longer collocational sequences. These longer collocations are notably more common in the text of Homer than they are in all other corpora

Table 1.7 *The ten most frequent two-word, three-word, four-word, and five-word collocations in Herodotus*

	2-word	3-word	4-word	5-word
#1	τε καί	καὶ δὴ καί	γῆν τε καὶ ὕδωρ	ἐμοὶ μὲν οὐ πιστὰ λέγοντες (5x)
#2	ἐς τήν	Ὁ μὲν δή	ἐν δὲ δὴ καί	ὡς καὶ πρότερόν μοι εἴρηται (5x)
#3	δὲ καί	ἐπὶ τὴν Ἑλλάδα	στρατεύεσθαι ἐπὶ τὴν Ἑλλάδα	ἔτι καὶ ἐς ἐμὲ ἦν (4x)
#4	μὲν δή	Οἱ μὲν δή	ἔτι καὶ ἐς ἐμέ	Ὁ δὲ εἶπε Ὦ βασιλεῦ (4x)
#5	μέν νυν	ἐς τὴν Ἀσίην	ὡς καὶ πρότερόν μοι	ὡς καὶ πρότερόν μοι δεδήλωται (4x)
#6	ἐν τῇ	τοῦτον τὸν χρόνον	περὶ μὲν τῇσι κεφαλῇσι	Μετὰ δὲ οὐ πολλὸν χρόνον (3x)
#7	οἱ δέ	τῶν ἡμεῖς ἴδμεν	τὸ δὲ ἀπὸ τούτου	Ταῦτα ὡς ἀπενειχθέντα ἤκουσαν οἱ (3x)
#8	ἐν τῷ	τῷ οὔνομα ἦν	Ὁ δὲ εἶπε Ὦ	Χρόνου δὲ οὐ πολλοῦ διελθόντος (3x)
#9	ἐκ τῆς	Ταῦτα μέν νυν	καὶ δὴ καὶ ἐς	δι᾿ ἀλλέων δέκα ἡμερέων ὁδοῦ (3x)
#10	ἐς τό	τῶν ἐν τῇ	τά τε ἄλλα καί	δὲ περὶ μὲν τῇσι κεφαλῇσι (3x)

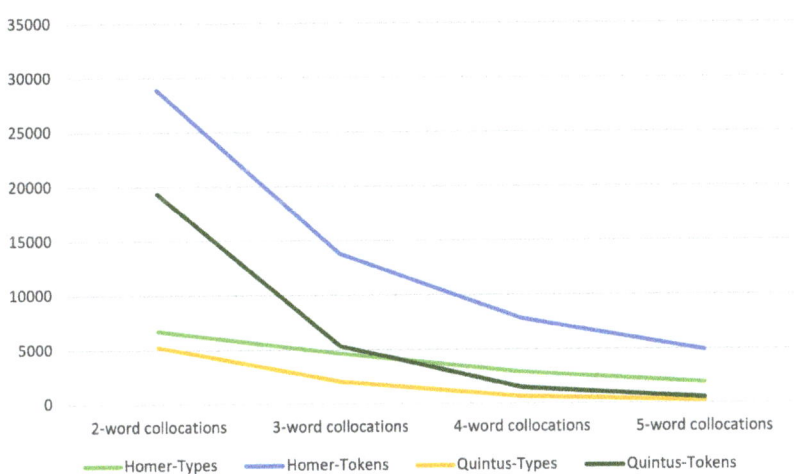

Figure 1.6 Type and token counts of two-, three-, four-, and five-word collocations in Homer (scaled down to match the corpus size of Quintus) vs. Quintus Smyrnaeus

Table 1.8 *The ten most frequent two-word, three-word, four-word, and five-word collocations in Quintus Smyrnaeus*

	2-word	3-word	4-word	5-word
#1	δέ οἱ	Ὣς ἄρ ἔφη	Ὣς φάτο τοὶ δ	φάμενον προσέειπεν Ἀχιλλέος ὄβριμος υἱός (5x)
#2	δ ἄρ	Ὣς δ ὅτ	ἀμφὶ δ ἄρ αὐτῷ	ὁ δ ἄρ οὔ τι (5x)
#3	δ ἄρα	ἀμφὶ δ ἄρ	Ὣς φάτο τὸν δ	Ὣς φάμενον προσέειπεν Ἀχιλλέος ὄβριμος (5x)
#4	τε καὶ	Καὶ τὰ μὲν	Καί ῥ οἱ μὲν	Καὶ τὰ μὲν ὡς ὥρμαινε (4x)
#5	ὁ δ	ὁ δ ἄρ	Καὶ τὰ μὲν ὡς	τότ ἀρήιοι υἷες ἐυσθενέων Ἀργείων (4x)
#6	οὔ τι	ὡς οἵ γ	δ ἄρ οὔ τι	Ὣς ἄρ ἔφη Τρώων τις (4x)
#7	ἀμφὶ δὲ	Ἀλλ ὅτε δή	δέ οἱ οὔ τι	δι ἠέρος ἄλλοτε δ αὖτε (3x)
#8	δέ μιν	δ ἄρ αὐτῷ	τοῖον ποτὶ μῦθον ἔειπε	δὴ τότ ἀρήιοι υἷες ἐυσθενέων (3x)
#9	οἱ δ	Ὣς φάτο τοὶ	ἀλλά μιν οὔ τι	δὴ τότε πυρκαϊὴν οἴνῳ σβέσαν (3x)
#10	δὲ καί	ἄλλοτε δ αὖτε	Καί νύ κε δή	καί ῥ ὀλοφυδνὸν ἄυσε μέγ (3x)

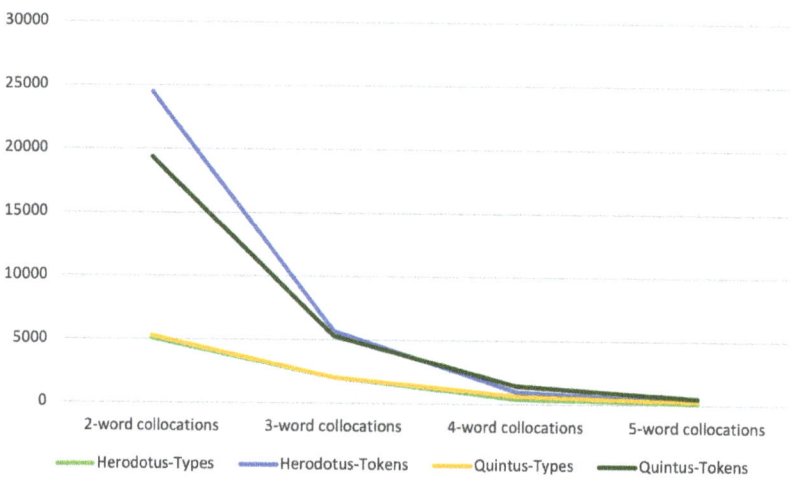

Figure 1.7 Type and token counts of two-, three-, four-, and five-word collocations in Herodotus (scaled down to match the corpus size of Quintus) vs. Quintus Smyrnaeus

under consideration. That is to say, the text of Homer *may* have a similar overall percentage (say, between 50 percent and 60 percent) of prefabricated sequences (as defined by Erman and Warren) or formularity (as defined by Pavese and Boschetti) as spoken and written natural language corpora do (both of these measures would only count a small subset of collocations as valid for their measurements), but we find significantly more *long collocations* in Homer than in other texts.

What does this mean? If we take collocational measures as a sign of *chunking* – that is, as indicating which sequences are likely to be stored vs. generated by speakers – we may say that Homer seems to operate with larger chunks than "normal speakers" do. His reservoir of collocations does not mostly stop at two- or three-word sequences, but keeps providing many options for four- and five-word sequences and beyond. Homer seems to be taking a natural tendency of human language (and cognition in general), and amplifying it. He is like an experienced chess player, who is able to handle much larger chunks (in this case, language chunks) than novice players can.

I would not venture to claim that in these collocational measures we have found a *direct and universal* proof of orality of composition. What we are seeing are the traces of mastery, and the results of extensive, likely years-long training to establish those longer chunks in the poet's memory.[62] Following Parry and Lord, I find persuasive the argument that only within an oral tradition would the conditions have arisen for this type of training to take place, and for this type of mastery to be desirable. But we cannot in principle exclude that types of written composition, under the correct conditions, could also yield similar collocational values; we simply have not come across any so far that do. Within the Greek tradition, the fact that Quintus Smyrnaeus specifically fails this test, is to me a strong indication that even literate poets who

---

[62] An interesting question is whether, when analyzing a poem by a novice vs. expert oral poet, we would find more or fewer fixed runs – i.e., sequences of several lines that appear to be retrieved as a whole from memory, rather than generated anew during composition (note that this would not necessarily mean more formularity, just more verbatim repetition). Lord's (1960: Chapter 2) account of the poet apprenticeship suggests that the capacity to use formulaic materials more flexibly is something that develops over time (this also parallels what children do during language acquisition – see Bozzone 2010), and that the apprentice poet is more reliant on "fixed" materials. My prediction is that an accomplished oral poet will know (and thus potentially employ) more different formulaic sequences, as well as fixed runs, than an apprentice poet, because they have had more years to acquire them. In other words, an accomplished poet will be able to choose whether they want to use more or fewer fixed materials in their compositions, depending on the performance conditions and requirements, while a novice poet might have no choice but to rely more on a smaller set of fixed runs and fixed formulas.

attempted to imitate Homer's style did not end up developing as many automatic behaviors as we find in Homer's oral technique.

1.4 A General Theory of Formularity

We have seen that formularity (in a very wide sense) is a common feature in human language and cognition, rooted in the well-understood psychological phenomenon of chunking.[63] We have also seen that Homer seems indeed to be more formulaic than natural language or other Greek authors; this is not in the sense that Homer necessarily relies on more formulaic sequences overall, but in the sense that he relies on formulaic sequences that are longer than the ones which normal language users employ (i.e., he uses larger chunks).

But how are we to treat formularity in Homer in practice? How are we to classify different "formulaic" sequences and phenomena, and how do we go about uncovering them in the texts? In what follows, I will sketch out a general theory of Homeric formularity and illustrate the different forms that formularity can take in the poet's diction. I will also provide examples of a formal notation that we can employ to describe such formulaic phenomena. To do so, I shall rely on concepts derived from usage-based linguistics, in particular from the frameworks of *Lexical Priming* (Hoey 2005) and *Construction Grammar* (Goldberg 2006). I will refrain from giving a single definition of the Homeric formula. One of the main problems in the formula debate was that scholars were trying to describe many distinct but similar and interrelated phenomena with just one or two terms. We shall go a different way: I will try to guide the reader through the maze of interconnected meanings and words that form the poetic language, using the concept of *collocation* as a heuristic tool to uncover formulaic phenomena.

1.4.1 *The Memory of the Poet*

Before we start mapping the poet's technique, however, we need to pick a basic cognitive model of how we think information is stored and organized in the poet's mind.[64] We will go with *connectionism* – that is, the theory that

---

[63] For more on formularity and chunking, see Pagán Cánovas (2020), which expands on Pagán Cánovas and Antović (2016), and whose outlook on formularity and cognition is largely compatible with mine.
[64] Of course, this is a scientific question that stretches far beyond the limits of this chapter. For our purposes here, we shall proceed with a very simplified model and discussion.

our mind is structured like a massive network which connects simple units working in parallel. The most influential implementation of connectionism in the twentieth century was *parallel distributed processing* (PDP), an approach developed in the 1970s by James L. McClelland, David E. Rumelhart, and the PDP Research Group (Rumelhart and McClelland 1986). Taking the human neural structure as an inspiration, PDP embraced a view of cognition in which complex processes emerged from a large number of simple microprocesses happening throughout the network (distributed vs. localized) at the same time (parallel vs. in sequence). In the 1980s, connectionism was pitted against computationalism (the idea that human cognition proceeds through explicit sequential operations on symbols – like high-level computer programming languages).[65] Today, connectionist models are alive and well in the form of neural networks employed in machine learning (for an introduction, see Graupe 2013). In linguistic theory, the frameworks of *Harmonic Grammar* (Legendre, Miyata, and Smolensky 1990) and *Optimality Theory* (Prince and Smolensky 1993) partly descend from connectionist models, and are still widely employed today.

From a connectionist perspective, different mental states result from different activation patterns of units (*nodes*) within the network, and the strength of connection between two given nodes is increased every time the nodes are activated at the same time. Let us say, then, that we have two words: *foregone* and *conclusion*.[66] The connection between the two words is strengthened each time they occur together. After a while, the activation of the word *foregone* is enough to activate the word *conclusion* as well. In the terminology used above, we can say that the two units have become chunked.[67] Another (more granular) way of expressing a similar concept is that of *priming*: in psycholinguistic experiments, we can see that the word *foregone* primes the word *conclusion* (i.e., showing the word *foregone* to a subject as a *stimulus* makes the subject faster at recognizing the *target*

---

[65] For a recent discussion of such problems, see Legendre and Smolensky (2006). A classic (and much more introductory) read on the architecture of the human mind, which introduces concepts of distributed cognition, is Minsky (1986).
[66] For the purposes of this illustration, we posit that each word would correspond to a node. Of course, a single word might in fact correspond to a given *pattern of activation* of many more nodes.
[67] Note that, of course, the same words can take part in several different chunks/collocations, and genre or context of usage are also a factor: while *foregone conclusion* might be recognized as a more generic (though formal) chunk of English, *foregone income* or *foregone earnings* are English collocations too, but in the specific context of accounting and finances (and, as such, they might be unfamiliar to some speakers).

word *conclusion* immediately after).[68] While chunking applies to units that have become so strongly associated as to work effectively as a single node, priming captures weaker associative effects between nodes.

To be more specific, there are actually two ways in which a given element (word, structure, etc.) can prime another: *absolute frequency* (long-term memory), and *recency* (working memory). Classic priming studies really reflect absolute frequency: the word *foregone* primes the word *conclusion* because the two are associated in a speaker's long-term memory, so that activating one activates the other as well. But recency matters too: several priming studies have focused on *syntactic priming* – that is, the tendency of speakers to reuse syntactic structures that have just been employed.[69] In English, for instance, speakers can choose between two equivalent structures when making a ditransitive clause: they can say *I gave Mary the book* or *I gave the book to Mary*, where the first sentence uses a dative construction, and the second a prepositional construction.[70] Studies have shown that the activation of a given syntactic structure in the working memory of a speaker prompts them to use it again shortly thereafter. This can happen across speakers or for the same speaker: thus, if somebody is asked a question using a prepositional construction (*To whom did you give the book?*), they are more likely to answer that question using a prepositional construction as well (*I gave the book/it to Mary*). Similarly, if somebody has already used a prepositional construction (*I gave one book to Mary*), they are more likely to use it again shortly after (*and I gave another one to Paul*).

More fine-grained studies (e.g., Gries 2005) have shown that the two types of priming can actually interact; for instance, if a given lexical item (e.g., the verb "give") is strongly primed (long-term memory) to prefer a given construction, it is more likely to resist syntactic priming (working memory) for a different construction. This is to say that some primings are stronger than others, and some constructions are more likely to resist contextual adaptation.

---

[68] For a history of the concept of priming in psychological research and corpus linguistics, see Pace-Sigge (2013). Classical references for priming in psychology are Neely (1977, 1991) and Anderson (1983).

[69] See Gries (2005) with references.

[70] The sentence *I gave Mary the book* can also be described as a *double-object construction*. Many English verbs which take an indirect object allow for both a dative construction (i.e., *a double-object construction*) and a prepositional construction, though the conditions of usage might differ, and this is known in the literature as the *English dative alternation* problem or *dative shift*. A similar alternation has been described in many other languages (Indo-European and not). Literature on this problem is immense; an influential study is Hovav and Levin (2008). See most recently Goldberg (2019).

An easy-to-grasp theory of language that builds upon these insights is *Lexical Priming*, a framework developed by Michael Hoey (2005), which argues that linguistic knowledge (lexical *and* grammatical) is really a network of stronger and weaker primings that affect each word, morpheme, and even phonological sequence.[71] What a speaker knows about their language, in other words, is really how likely one element (a word, a morpheme, a phonological sequence) is to co-occur (or not co-occur) with another, based on a lifetime's worth of language exposure (i.e., an ever-updating database that contains all of the speaker's linguistic experiences). When it comes to language production, this approach argues that words (i.e., lexical items) come first, and that grammatical structure emerges from each word's co-occurrence preferences, not vice versa (e.g., in a rule-based approach to language, where one would start from an empty grammatical structure and *then* proceed to fill it with lexical items).[72]

How do these insights translate to the study of Homer? From a Lexical Priming perspective, we can describe the poetic language as a network of associations, in which ideas, word forms, syntactic constructions, and metrical positions can all come to be associated with each other, each association possessing a different strength. When the association is strongest, and when it affects all levels (ideas, word forms, syntactic constructions, and metrical positions), we find prototypical formulaic phenomena. But the technique is really composed by all the other, weaker associations as well. These associations provide the epic text with its texture, its familiar feel, its cohesion, and much of its poetic strength (i.e., the capacity, directly or indirectly, to evoke feelings in its audience). We will keep in mind that primings will exist at the long-term memory level as well as in the working memory level. Working memory primings will explain short-term repetitions. Long-term memory primings will explain long-distance repetitions.

In what follows, we shall look at some examples of such associations, moving from the base of the iceberg (i.e., weaker associations) to its tip (stereotypical formulaic phenomena).

---

[71] A similar approach to understanding linguistic knowledge is fleshed out by Goldberg (2019), who discusses how words (Chapter 2) and syntactic constructions (Chapter 3) are learned and stored in the brain as "clusters of lossy [i.e., not fully specified] memory traces," resulting in a rich network. We will return to Goldberg and *Construction Grammar* in section 1.4.3 below.

[72] This, one might add, is not too far from some aspects of the Minimalist program in generative syntax (Chomsky 1995), whereby each lexical item contains stored syntactic information (called features) which controls and constrains syntactic derivations (i.e., the process by which phrases and sentences are created).

1.4.2 *From Themes, to Conceptual Associations, to Collocations*

In Lord's definition, themes are "the groups of ideas regularly used in telling a tale in the formulaic style of traditional song" (Lord 1960: 68). Even more so than formulas, they are the building blocks of traditional storytelling. Themes exist at different sizes: some are as large as entire plot plans (i.e., the theme of the return song), some are the size of *motifs* (e.g., the ones described in the folkloric literature, such as Thompson's 1955 *Motif-Index of Traditional Folk-Literature*), and some of *type scenes* (a banquet scene, an arming scene). Yet, at the most basic level, a theme can also be the simple association between two ideas (i.e., a *conceptual association*), which a poet picks up as part of their training. Many of these traditional conceptual associations (or *mini-themes*) can be seen as the root of formulaic and non-formulaic diction alike. It is at this microscopic scale that Parry's essential idea and Lord's theme come to coincide, and it is here that our description of formulaic phenomena in Homer begins.

There are many expressions in Homer that express the traditional *conceptual association* (*mini-theme*) PAIN and SUFFER.[73] Most famously, the root παθ- "suffer" tends to occur in the vicinity of the root ἀλγ- "pain," both within and without recognizable formulaic patterns. We can call this the ἀλγ- + παθ- *collocation*.[74] To this family belong the well-established formula ἄλγεα πάσχων "suffering pains" (9x in our poems)[75] as well as the

Table 1.9 *From conceptual association to collocations*

Conceptual association	PAIN + SUFFER
Collocation	ἀλγ- + παθ-
Formula	ἄλγεα πάσχων (9x)
Unique expressions	ἄλγεα πάσχουσιν (*Od.* 9.121), ἵν' ἄλγεα πολλὰ πάθοιμεν (*Od.* 9.53)

---

[73] Much like in Watkins' notation for the inherited formula, I use English words in all capitals to convey a concept (i.e., PAIN, the idea of pain) as opposed to a specific lexical realization thereof (e.g., the Greek root ἀλγ-, the English word *pain*).

[74] Note that Meusel (2020: 25–48), in the context of reconstructing Indo-European phraseology, introduces the distinction between collocations and formulas (along with the categories, which we shall not cover here, of idioms and part idioms).

[75] We designate this expression as a *formula* (*fixed formula*) because it recurs identically more than once in our poems. A *unique expression*, on the other hand, is an expression that occurs only once in our corpus.

unique expressions ἄλγεα πάσχουσιν "they suffer pains" (*Od.* 9.121) and ἵν' ἄλγεα πολλὰ πάθοιμεν "so that we might suffer many pains" (*Od.* 9.53).

Other possible surface realizations of the same *conceptual association* (PAIN + SUFFER) are the *fixed formula* (part of a longer formulaic run) πρίν τι κακὸν παθέειν "before suffering something bad" (*Il.* 17.31–32, *Il.* 20.197–98), as well as the unique expressions αἰνὰ παθοῦσα "suffering pains" (*Il.* 22.431) and παθέειν τ' ἀεικήλια ἔργα "to suffer shameful deeds" (*Il.* 18.77). Even the compound αἰνοπαθής "pain-suffering" (*Od.* 18.201), a *hapax* in the *Odyssey*, belongs to this conceptual association.[76] These last few expressions exemplify how traditional conceptual associations (minithemes) underlie both formulaic and unique phraseology, and remain constant even when the diction changes. This is similar to Watkins' insight, discussed above, that the surface form of an inherited PIE formula could undergo lexical renewal in the daughter languages.

Conceptual associations can give us a glimpse into the process of lexical renewal within the technique. For instance, the *conceptual association* between DARKNESS (=DEATH),[77] COVER, and EYES underlies an entire family of traditional expressions, among which some are clearly older, and some are clearly innovative. Here, while the concept of COVER is always expressed by the verb καλύπτω "conceal," the concepts of DARKNESS (=DEATH) and EYES can be expressed by different lexical items (e.g., νύξ "night" vs. σκότος "darkness," ὀφθαλμούς "eyes" vs. ὄσσε "two eyes"). See, for instance, the formulaic line τὸν δὲ κατ' ὀφθαλμῶν ἐρεβεννὴ νὺξ ἐκάλυψε "a dark night covered his eyes" (*Il.* 5.659, 13.580, 22.466) vs. the unique expression announcing Sarpedon's death, which is split over two lines Ὣς ἄρα μιν εἰπόντα τέλος θανάτοιο κάλυψεν / ὀφθαλμούς ῥῖνάς θ' "The edge of death covered his eyes and nose as he spoke" (*Il.* 16.502–3). The same conceptual association, this time realized with the archaic dual word form ὄσσε "two eyes" (a direct reflex of PIE *$h_3ókʷ-ih_1$ "id."), underlies the more archaic-looking formula τὸν δὲ σκότος ὄσσε κάλυψε(ν) "darkness covered his two eyes" (11x in the *Iliad*, all functioning as standard announcements of death) as well as the rare expressions ἀμφὶ δὲ ὄσσε κελαινὴ νὺξ ἐκάλυψε(ν) "a dark night

---

[76] To be more precise, one could see these all as reflexes of the conceptual association (NEGATIVE EXPERIENCE + SUFFER), since κακόν "something bad" and ἀεικήλια ἔργα "shameful deeds" are not necessarily physical or psychological pain in all of their readings.

[77] Various metaphors of death in the *Iliad* have been treated by Horn (2018), within the framework of conceptual metaphor theory (Lakoff and Johnson 1980, Lakoff and Turner 1989). For DEATH IS DARKNESS specifically, see Horn (2018: 368–71). Other recent applications of conceptual metaphor theory to Homer are Forte (2017) and Zanker (2019).

covered his two eyes" (*Il.* 5.310, 11.356, when Aeneas and Hector respectively are nearly killed by a projectile) and τὼ δέ οἱ ὄσσε / νὺξ ἐκάλυψε μέλαινα "a black night covered his two eyes" (*Il.* 14.438–39, when Hector is nearly killed by a stone thrown by Ajax and rescued by his companions). Interestingly, then, the fixed formula is seemingly used for typical business, while the unique expressions based on the traditional conceptual association are made to fit more atypical circumstances (an important character coming close to death but escaping it).

1.4.3 Enter Meter and Syntax: From Collocations to Constructions

So far, we have seen how *conceptual associations* can be expressed as *collocations* in our poems. In Parry's (1971: 13) terms, we have covered the "repeated group of words" and the "essential idea" in the definition of formula. We haven't, however, talked about meter ("same metrical conditions"), or syntax (à la Kiparsky). These last two criteria are necessary to describe phenomena that have been classified as *flexible formulas* (as per Hainsworth) or *formulaic expressions* in the Homeric literature so far. Let's look at one example.

Another important formulaic complex belonging to the conceptual association PAIN + SUFFER is the *collocation* of the stems πηματ- "misery" and παθ- "suffer," seen in the repeated line δήμῳ ἔνι Τρώων, ὅθι πάσχετε πήματ' Ἀχαιοί "in the land of the Trojans, where you Achaeans suffered misery" (*Od.* 3.100, 4.243, 4.330), as well as, in the *Odyssey*, in the line-final expressions πήματα πάσχων "suffering misery" (*Od.* 5.33, 17.444, 17.524),[78] πήματα πάσχει "he suffers misery" (*Od.* 1.49), πήματα πάσχειν "to suffer misery" (*Od.* 1.190), πήματα πάσχεις "you suffer misery" (*Od.* 8.441), and πήματα πάσχω "I suffer misery" (*Od.* 7.152). These last five expressions clearly belong together, and can be grouped into what Hainsworth would have called a *flexible formula*.

There is a way to notate this more precisely. To do so, we shall make use of the concept of *construction*, loosely derived from Construction Grammar. Within this framework, constructions are defined as "a learned

---

[78] Note that line-final expression πήματα πάσχων "suffering pains" provides a useful metrical alternative to line-final ἄλγεα πάσχων "suffering pains," as discussed above: the former starts with a consonant, the latter with a vowel. It is not true, however, that every expression combining πηματ- "misery" and παθ- "suffer" simply exists as a metrical alternative to expressions combining ἀλγ- "pain" and παθ- "suffer": for one thing, the collocation πηματ- + παθ- appears overall later in attestation (it occurs only once in the *Iliad*, in a unique expression, and is otherwise limited to the *Odyssey*), and is significantly more flexible in usage than the ἀλγ- + παθ- collocation.

pairing of form and function" (Goldberg 2006: 4). Construction Grammar holds that, during language acquisition, children learn constructions as generalizations that emerge from encountering expressions that share similarities in form and meaning (Tomasello 2003, 2009: 75–79).[79] For instance, a child encountering the expressions *more milk*, *more juice*, and *more chocolate*, all sharing the function that they can be employed to ask for more of the item, will make the generalization that one can create expressions to request more food by combining the fixed part *more* + a variable slot containing a noun phrase expressing a food substance. We can notate this generalization as follows:

(4)   **more** [*food substance*]$_{\text{Noun Phrase}}$

This particular construction is made up of a fixed part (bolded) and a variable part (in brackets). Syntactic labels can be added to various parts of the construction as needed. Note that the notation only expresses the form of the construction. The function, here, would be "asking for more food."

Coming back to Homer and to our examples above, a singer in training will figure out that, following the bucolic diaeresis, one can make a (finite or participial) verb phrase meaning "suffering misery" by combining the fixed sequence πήματα πάσχ- with an appropriate morphological ending for the verb (provided this ending corresponds to one heavy syllable). We can notate this generalization, which combines collocational information, syntactic information, and metrical information (something new to the concept of construction, which we need to add for Homer), as follows:

(5) ^{5a}[πήματα πάσχ- –]$_{\text{Verb Phrase}}$

Here the variable slot in the construction is expressed by a metrical symbol (for a heavy syllable), and the brackets are used to encompass the entirety of the verb phrase. Metrical notation (5a) indicates that the construction starts with the first syllable of the fifth foot.[80] This is a *metrical construction*.

We can add even more material to the mix. In the *Odyssey*, in the same position in the line, we find the unique expressions πῆμα παθόντες "having suffered misery" (*Od.* 12.27) and πῆμα πάθῃσι "he will suffer

---

[79] Linguists of different persuasions will accept or deny this characterization of language acquisition. This point is immaterial to our current discussion, in which we simply borrow the concept of construction as a way to notate some generalizations that speakers might make about the linguistic data that they observe, and we apply it to the language of Homer.

[80] For the metrical terminology (after Janse 2003), see discussion in Chapter 2.

Table 1.10 *From themes to formulas*

	same ideas	same lexical item(s)	same syntax	same meter
Conceptual association (mini-theme)	✓			
Collocation	✓	✓		
Construction	✓	✓	✓	
Metrical construction (formula)[81]	✓	✓	✓	✓
Structural formula (à la Russo)			✓	✓

misery" (*Od.* 7.195), which use the singular of the noun to make room for the trisyllabic forms of the verb (here seen in the aorist stem instead of the present stem). We could, as above, write a construction expressing the commonalities between these two expressions. But there is a larger pattern here: it seems like we are looking at a type of metrically localized collocational paradigm, whereby the collocation πημστ- + παθ- is localized to a particular slot in the hexameter (5a–6b), and used in a specific syntactic structure (a verb phrase). All of this can be expressed by the following notation:

(6) $^{5a}[πήματ\text{-} + παθ\text{-}]^{6b}_{\text{Verb Phrase}}$

The possibilities covered so far are summarized in Table 1.10.

1.4.4 *From Phrase Constructions to Sentence Constructions*

Constructions exist at different sizes and levels of abstraction. So far, we have seen some small examples, mostly limited to a single syntactic phrase, and with very little variation allowed. These are the smaller chunks in the poets' repertoire. Poets also had much larger units they could work with, which would help them to structure an entire line, or an even longer run. Many of these types of whole-line constructions exist around the most

---

[81] In this group we put fixed formulas and (most) flexible formulas alike. Fixed formulas are instances of metrical constructions that recur without variation; flexible formulas are metrical constructions that allow for some variation. Admittedly, some of Hainsworth's flexible formulas are independent of meter (e.g., in cases of separation and dislocation). These would better be described as collocations, not formulas.

frequent finite verbs in our poems, and have already been described in the literature, starting with Parry's seminal study of noun–epithet formulas and their usage (Parry 1971: 33–55).

For instance, there are 100+ lines in our poems that show formal and functional similarities to the examples below, all of which feature the verb form προσέφη in position 3b–4a (right after the masculine caesura in the third foot), and serve to introduce direct speech:[82]

(7) Τὸν δ' ἄρ' ὑπόδρα ἰδὼν προσέφη πόδας ὠκὺς Ἀχιλλεύς· (*Il.* 1.148)

To him, looking darkly, replied swift-footed Achilles.

(8) Τὴν δὲ βαρὺ στενάχων προσέφη πόδας ὠκὺς Ἀχιλλεύς (*Il.* 1.364)

To her, sighing deeply, replied swift-footed Achilles.

(9) Τὸν δ' ἐπιμειδήσας προσέφη κρείων Ἀγαμέμνων (*Il.* 4.356)

To him, smiling, replied Lord Agamemnon.

(10) Τὴν δὲ μέγ' ὀχθήσας προσέφη νεφεληγερέτα Ζεύς· (*Il.* 1.517)

To her, greatly enraged, replied cloud-gathering Zeus.

A constructional notation that would capture the similarities shared by these examples would be as follows:[83]

(11)   [–]Object.Pronoun δ' [⏑⏑–⏑⏑–]Subject.Participial Phrase **προσέφη** [⏑⏑–⏑⏑– –]Subject.Noun Phrase

These types of finite verb constructions have been studied by Bozzone (2014, forthcoming), who set out to establish which speech-introduction constructions appear to be gaining vs. losing ground in the technique as we move from the *Iliad* to the *Odyssey* (see section 1.4.6 below). These are only a particular kind of construction. At the most abstract level, the conceptual association they represent is identical to the argument structure of their main verb (e.g., SUBJECT + REPLY + OBJECT + IN A GIVEN MANNER). They are constructions for entire sentences. As such, they can work as a container for smaller constructions and collocations.

For instance, the participial phrase βαρὺ στενάχων "sighing deeply" seen in (8) is in itself a formula (attested 7x in the *Iliad*, in the line position 1c–3a, but not in the *Odyssey*), as well as an instance of the collocation βαρυ- "deep" + στεναχ- "to sigh," which is seen in the line-final formula βαρέα στενάχοντα "sighing deeply" (4x in the *Iliad* and 4x in the *Odyssey*) and in the *singulum iteratum* βαρὺ δὲ στενάχοντος

---

[82] On speech presentation in the Homeric poems (including speech introductions), see Beck (2012).
[83] For the metrical notation, see Chapter 2.

ἄκουσεν "he heard him sighing deeply" (*Od.* 8.95, 534), which is limited to *Odyssey* 8, and always describes Alkínoos heeding Odysseus' crying. Altogether, they represent the conceptual association SIGH + DEEPLY.

The slot following the finite verb in the construction is taken up by a noun–epithet formula of the metrical shape 4b–6b; many of these formulas can be described as collocations and conceptual associations as well. For instance, the well-known formula πόδας ὠκὺς Ἀχιλλεύς "swift-footed Achilles" reflects a more general collocation πεδ- "foot" + ὠκυ- "swift," which is seen in the formulaic epithet for Iris (πόδας ὠκέα "swift-footed"), as well as in a unique epithet for the made-up hero Orsílokhos (πόδας ὠκύν "swift-footed"), part of Odysseus' fanciful tale at *Odyssey* 13.260. The same collocation informs the compound adjective ποδώκης "swift-footed," used mostly for Achilles and horses. Together, these instances represent the conceptual association FEET + FAST, which occasionally can be realized with other lexical items. See, for instance, the epithet πόδας ταχύν "fast-footed," used of Achilles (*Il.* 13.348, 17.709, 18.354, 18.358) and of Aeneas (*Il.* 13.482), as well as the metrical construction ³ᶜ[ποσὶν ταχέεσσι]_Dative.Noun Phrase [διώκ- –]_Verb Phrase "to chase with fast feet," which describes Achilles' chase in *Iliad* 22 (8, 173, 230), as well as a lion's in *Iliad* 8.339. This collocation also appears in *Odyssey* 13, right after the usage of πόδας ὠκύν mentioned above:

(12)   Ὀρσίλοχον πόδας ὠκύν, ὃς ἐν Κρήτῃ εὐρείῃ
       ἀνέρας ἀλφηστὰς νίκα ταχέεσσι πόδεσσιν (*Od.* 13.260–61)

       Swift-footed Orsílokhos, who in vast Crete
       defeated enterprising men with his fast feet.

This appears to be a simple example of *working memory priming* (see section 1.4.1): arguably, the usage of πόδας ὠκύν in the preceding line activated the conceptual association FEET + FAST in the working memory of the poet, who then used this association again (with a slight lexical change from ὠκύς to ταχύς to express the concept FAST) in the phrase ταχέεσσι πόδεσσιν.

We could, of course, try to write constructions for larger units as well. One could write constructions for complex sentences (perhaps specifying some embedded clauses) or even for longer stretches of discourse, taking up multiple verses. We know that poets had chunks of this size, which are visible in type scenes (e.g., banquet scenes or arming scenes). A construction for a larger narrative (or theme) would specify the general direction of events and perhaps some key fixed sentences/keywords that need to be uttered for the tale to be told correctly. For the purposes of this chapter, though, we shall stop at the sentence.

1.4.5 Constructions and the Poet's Mind

A well-meaning reader, looking at the algebraic-style notations in the preceding paragraph, might of course ask: do poets really have such objects in their minds? And how does it help us to write them up in this way? The answer comes in two parts.

First, it should go without saying that these are just notational devices. They are meant to represent a likely generalization that a poet in training might make if they were to use our *Iliad* and *Odyssey* as their learning data (given the nature of our data, this is really all we can hope for). In connectionist terms, these notations represent a given activation pattern resulting from the commonalities of many single instances, namely an abstraction or generalization. Among cognitive researchers, opinions differ as to whether these types of generalizations are stored in long-term memory as separate entities, or whether they are created on the spot based on the needs of the moment (e.g., a poet needs to create a new line containing the conceptual association PAIN + SUFFER, and several possible instances are activated in his mind), and are, as such, never independent from the instances they represent.[84]

Second, as with science in general, the value of these models lies in what they can help us discover or explain that has not been noticed or understood before. We have no living singers belonging to the Homeric tradition, so we cannot directly probe what is in the poet's mind. But our theories can make predictions, and predictions can be tested. For instance, a connectionist view of the poet's mind would predict that we should find some priming effects between the elements that form a construction (or collocation, or conceptual association), testifying to their joint activation in the poet's mind. And we do encounter phenomena in the poems that seem to confirm this prediction.

A well-attested collocation in Homer is the combination of the adjective γλυκύς "sweet" and the noun ἵμερος "desire." This is seen in the unique expression γλυκὺν ἵμερον ἔμβαλε θυμῷ "put a sweet desire in his chest" (*Il.* 3.139), as well as in the formula ὡς σεο νῦν ἔραμαι καί με γλυκὺς ἵμερος αἱρεῖ "like I desire you now and a sweet desire takes me" (*Il.* 3.446, 14.328). The latter line is also an example of a more abstract construction pattern,

---

[84] These are complex topics in human cognition in general, which also come up in the field of morphological processing and in the computational modeling thereof (e.g., to establish whether morphological rules are stored abstractly or generated on the spot based on stored exemplars that can be recalled online). An example of a rule-based approach is found in Albright and Hayes (2003) (on English past tenses); an example of online-generation of patterns based on stored exemplars is Keuleers (2008) (on English past tenses and Dutch noun plurals).

centered on the verb form αἱρεῖ "takes," in which the verb takes a noun phrase containing an adjective + a noun expressing an emotion as its subject. Metrically, the verb is at the end of the line, and the subject immediately precedes it. The expression begins after the 3a caesura. Beyond the half-line καί με γλυκὺς ἵμερος αἱρεῖ "and a sweet desire takes me," examples are μάλα γὰρ χλωρὸν δέος αἱρεῖ "for a green fear took (him/her)" (*Il.* 17.67) and μάλα γὰρ δριμὺς χόλος αἱρεῖ "for a bitter *khólos* took (him/her)" (*Il.* 18.322). A constructional notation would be as follows:

(13)   3b ⏑ ⏑ – [⏑ ⏑ – ⏑ ⏑]Subject.Noun Phrase **αἱρεῖ**V = EMOTION + TAKE.OVER

Now, something interesting seems to happen in the following verse:

(14)   σίτου τε γλυκεροῖο περὶ φρένας ἵμερος αἱρεῖ (*Il.* 11.89 = *Homeric Hymn to Apollo* 461)

a desire for sweet food took over his/their *phrénes*.

There appears to be a sort of modification of the construction above, where the prepositional phrase περὶ φρένας lit. "around the *phrénes*" replaces the adjective γλυκύς that normally modifies the noun ἵμερος. Yet, somehow, the strength of the γλυκ- "sweet" + ἱμερο- "desire" collocation is intact: the displaced root γλυκ- "sweet" appears earlier in the line as a modifier of the noun σῖτος "food." Nowhere else in Homer is this word modified by the adjective "sweet," suggesting that the occurrence of γλυκεροῖο here is likely due to the priming effect of ἵμερος. Thus, the collocation has been preserved, while the syntactic relation between the two items has been changed.

If this is true, it gives us a hint as to how the poet's verse-making proceeded: here, they probably conceived of the end of the line before the beginning (since arguably the occurrence of γλυκεροῖο in the second foot was triggered by the presence of ἵμερος in the fifth foot). Following this model, the poet would start with a given conceptual association (a mini-theme), which would suggest some collocations, which only later would be constrained within a proper syntactic frame. Of course, this might not be the only way for a verse to come together. This model should also be further developed and then tested. But connectionism provides us with a viable starting point.

The concept of joint activation might also help us explain cases of seemingly odd formulaic usages, such as the known puzzle of Penelope's "fat hand" (see Parry (1971: 151), references in Edwards (1988: 31–32), and most recently Vergados (2009)). At the beginning of book 21, Athena inspires Penelope to retrieve Odysseus' bow and put it in front of the suitors (an element that is key to the rest of the plot). As Penelope makes her way to the storage room, she picks up the key for it:

(15)   εἵλετο δὲ κληῗδ' εὐκαμπέα χειρὶ παχείῃ (*Od.* 21.6)

she took a well-curved key with her thick hand.

The usage of the adjective παχείῃ "fat, thick" here has attracted scrutiny, in that it seems like an odd attribute for Penelope. In fact, this verse reflects a formula for the collocation χειρ- "hand" + ἑλ- "take" + παχυ- "fat, thick," which is common in the *Iliad* and the *Odyssey*.

(16)   ἀλλ' ἀναχασσάμενος λίθον εἵλετο χειρὶ παχείῃ (*Il.* 7.264)

but drawing back he picked up a boulder with his thick hand.

(17)   ἣ δ' ἀναχασσαμένη λίθον εἵλετο χειρὶ παχείῃ (*Il.* 21.403)

and, drawing back, she picked up a boulder with her thick hand.

(18)   δόρυ δ' εἵλετο χειρὶ παχείῃ. (*Il.* 10.31)

and he picked up a spear with his thick hand.

(19)   ὣς ἄρα φωνήσας ξίφος εἵλετο χειρὶ παχείῃ (*Od.* 22.326)

thus he spoke, and he picked up a sword with his thick hand.

This formula is normally used with martial connotations, and the subjects tend to be male and strong. Is the usage here in *Odyssey* 21 simply awkward, or consciously humorous? Perhaps. There is, however, one exception to the generalization above: in example (17), the formula refers to Athena, as she picks up a boulder to use as a weapon against Ares. The attribution here seems unobjectionable. So what could explain the odd usage in *Odyssey* 21? In a connectionist model, we could think about which elements in the passage could have conspired to "activate" the expression χειρὶ παχείῃ "with a thick hand" in the poet's mind. We could envision the spread of activation in two ways: the context (the preparation for what will ultimately become a fight) brought up an εἵλετο construction which is normally used for arming scenes (this is in line with Foley's argument that Penelope here is entering a heroic mode). This εἵλετο construction, in turn, combined with the recent mention of Athena, brought up the prepositional phrase χειρὶ παχείῃ. In other words, an attribute that would be appropriate for Athena in this construction was contextually reassigned to Penelope, just like (in example (14) above) an attribute of "desire" was contextually reassigned to "food" (cf. Foley 1999: 202–21, contra Wyatt 1978).

While the last two examples may look like "errors" in the workings of oral composition, the spread of activation through the network actually has the fundamental role of contributing to discourse cohesion: it helps the text hold together, fulfilling the audiences' expectations.

1.4.6 Formulas and Diachrony

A viewpoint that might not interest most readers of Homer directly, but might have an important role in answering the Homeric question, is: to what extent can we use formulas as a window onto the history of the poetic tradition? We have mentioned before the idea that formulas (conceptual associations) can undergo lexical renewal. We are also familiar with the fact that formulas can sometimes preserve very old linguistic features, thus offering us a glance at what could be chunks of poetry that are hundreds of years old (we will discuss this more in Chapters 2 and 3).

Just like our own native language, Homer's trove of expressions is composed of a mixture of very old and very new material. How can we tell archaic expressions apart from innovative ones? The classical method is that of checking whether an expression happens to preserve a clear archaism that is guaranteed by the meter (several examples will be discussed in Chapter 2). This method, however, will only work on a handful of truly old expressions, thus helping us identify only a small subset of everything that is actually old in the language. Another method (Bozzone 2014, 2022) is that of using the *flexibility* of an expression to gauge its antiquity. In general terms, truly archaic expressions tend to survive only in fixed forms, while newer, living expressions tend to display flexibility. This has to do with Kiparsky's dichotomy discussed above in section 1.1.3: what is retrieved from memory as such (e.g., *fixed formulas*) tends to be unchangeable, while what is still actively generated (e.g., *flexible formulas*) can change. If an expression reflects an older stage of the grammar (one that moreover would be at odds with the synchronic grammar of the poet), it is likely to be pulled from memory as a chunk.

Another way to express this concept is that young expressions have company (in the form of other, similar expressions created by the synchronic grammar), while older expressions do not (they are, in other words, the lone survivors of an earlier era). We can thus look at a given expression and its "family" to establish whether it is isolated or not, and then make inferences as to whether it is old or new in the technique. While more precise quantitative measures can be employed to this effect (see discussion in Bozzone 2022 and forthcoming), approximation will often be sufficient. Let us look at some examples.

Bozzone (2010, 2016b) uses the example of two equivalent noun–epithet formulas for Hera, θεὰ λευκώλενος Ἥρη "white-armed goddess Hera" and βοῶπις πότνια Ἥρη "cow-eyed queen Hera," in which the flexibility of each expression and their combinatory possibilities clearly identify one as archaic and fossilized (the latter) and one as more recent and still alive and well in the language (the former).[85] This analysis is confirmed, on the linguistic level, by two archaisms that are preserved in βοῶπις πότνια Ἥρη, namely the hiatus between πότνια and Ἥρη (which would have originated after the lenition of initial *s- in the word for Hera) and the apparent violation of Wernicke's law in the last syllable of βοῶπις (which would have been absent at an earlier stage of the language).[86]

We can use this method in constructions other than noun–epithet formulas, to verify whether an expression was alive in the poet's language or not. For instance, there are two similar ways, in the *Iliad*, to figuratively announce the death of a warrior.[87] The first set of expressions reflects the conceptual association TAKE + EARTH + WITH TEETH, the second reflects the association TAKE + EARTH + WITH PALM. Formulas reflecting these conceptual associations are as follows:

(20)   οἱ μὲν ἔπειθ' ἅμα πάντες ὀδὰξ ἕλον ἄσπετον οὖδας (*Od.* 22.269)

and then they all took the infinite earth with their teeth.

(21)   ὃ δ' ἐν κονίῃσι πεσὼν ἕλε γαῖαν ἀγοστῷ. (*Il.* 13.508)

and falling in the dust he took the earth in his palm.

While, on the surface, these two expressions might appear similar to one another (one seems specialized for the plural, one for the singular), a closer inspection reveals that one is a fossil, and the other one is part of the living language of the poet. The expression ἕλε γαῖαν ἀγοστῷ "s/he took the earth with his/her palm" is relatively high frequency (5x in the *Iliad*), and never displays any flexibility. It also always occurs within the same type of verse construction, with a bisyllabic finite verb starting the line (in enjambement), followed by a syntactic break:

---

[85] These two equivalent noun–epithet formulas have received much attention in the literature. A history of the debate is given in Beck (1986). See also more recently Beck (2005: 129–30).

[86] Wernicke's law is a dispreference for a syllable of the shape Cv̄C in the contracted biceps of the fourth foot (see Chapter 2 for this terminology), when the biceps is filled by the last syllable of a word (conversely, a sequence Cv̄C is preferred). βοῶπις, with short -ι-, violates this law, but an earlier < *βοῶπῑς (with long vowel resulting from PIE *-ih₂-) does not. See Cassio (2016b).

[87] For similar metonymic descriptions of death in the *Iliad*, see Horn (2018: 363–68).

(22) ἤφυσ᾽· ὃ δ᾽ ἐν κονίῃσι πεσὼν ἕλε γαῖαν ἀγοστῷ. (*Il.* 13.508)

[the bronze] pulled out [his innards]. And having fallen in the dust he took the earth with his palm.

(23) ἤφυσ᾽· ὃ δ᾽ ἐν κονίῃσι πεσὼν ἕλε γαῖαν ἀγοστῷ. (*Il.* 17.315)

[the bronze] pulled out [his innards]. And having fallen in the dust he took the earth with his palm.

(24) ἔσχεν· ὃ δ᾽ ἐν κονίῃσι πεσὼν ἕλε γαῖαν ἀγοστῷ. (*Il.* 13.520)

[the heavy spear] pierced him [through his shoulder]. And having fallen in the dust he took the earth with his palm.

(25) ἔσχεν, ὃ δ᾽ ἐν κονίῃσι πεσὼν ἕλε γαῖαν ἀγοστῷ. (*Il.* 14.452)

[the heavy spear] pierced him [through his shoulder]. And having fallen in the dust he took the earth with his palm.

(26) νύξεν· ὃ δ᾽ ἐν κονίῃσι πεσὼν ἕλε γαῖαν ἀγοστῷ (*Il.* 11.425)

[he] hit him. And having fallen in the dust he took the earth with his palm.

There are no other occurrences of the lexical item ἀγοστός in the poems (in fact, its meaning, "palm of the hand," is entirely inferred from these occurrences; in Theocritus, it is used with the meaning "arm"). This conceptual association, in other words, only has one fixed surface realization.

On the other hand, the conceptual association TAKE + EARTH + WITH TEETH knows many incarnations. Next to the more regulated formulaic usages (which are common to the *Iliad* and the *Odyssey*), for example:

(27) οἱ μὲν ἔπειθ᾽ ἅμα πάντες ὀδὰξ ἕλον ἄσπετον οὖδας (*Od.* 22.269)

and then they all took the infinite earth with their teeth.

(28) τώ κ᾽ οὐ τόσσοι Ἀχαιοὶ ὀδὰξ ἕλον ἄσπετον οὖδας (*Il.* 19.61)

then not so many Achaeans would have taken the infinite earth with their teeth.

(29) Ἕκτορος ἐν παλάμῃσιν ὀδὰξ ἕλον ἄσπετον οὖδας. (*Il.* 24.738)

at the hands of Hector they took the infinite earth with their teeth.

one also finds simple collocations (indicated with wavy underlining):

(30) φῶτες ὀδὰξ ἕλον οὖδας ἐμῷ ὑπὸ δουρὶ δαμέντες. (*Il.* 11.749)

the men took the earth with their teeth, tamed by my spear.

as well as combinations in which EARTH and TAKE are expressed by different lexical items:

(31) πρηνέες ἐν κονίῃσιν <u>ὀδὰξ λαζοίατο γαῖαν</u>. (*Il.* 2.418)

  face-first in the dust, they seized the earth with their teeth.

(32) <u>γαῖαν ὀδὰξ εἷλον</u> πρὶν Ἴλιον εἰσαφικέσθαι. (*Il.* 22.17)

  they would have taken the earth with their teeth before ever making it back to Ilion.

From these distributional properties alone, we can safely infer that the conceptual association TAKE + EARTH + WITH TEETH was still lively in the poet's language, while TAKE + EARTH + WITH PALM was an isolated fossil. As confirmation, the expression γαῖαν δ᾽ ὀδὰξ ἑλόντες "having taken the earth with their teeth" is still found in Euripides (*Phoenissae* 1423), while TAKE + EARTH + WITH PALM simply disappears from the later record.

Bozzone (2014, 2022, forthcoming) proposed to use the concept of *linguistic productivity*[88] as a way to assign each formulaic expression in Homer to a different "life stage" within the diction. The idea is that each expression goes through a life cycle that is marked by productivity (i.e., flexibility) changes, and that productivity measures can help us establish the relative "age" of an expression. Furthermore, looking at how the productivity of given expressions changes between two texts (e.g., the *Iliad* and the *Odyssey*) can help us to create a relative chronology of Greek epic. For instance, Bozzone (forthcoming) looks at speech-introduction constructions in the poems, and shows that all constructions seem to "age" between the *Iliad* and the *Odyssey* (while new constructions are introduced as well), which agrees with the general consensus that the *Odyssey* was composed at a later point in time (for a recent discussion, see Andersen and Haug 2012).

1.5 Conclusion: What Are Formulas and What Can We Do with Them?

The discussion above has covered much ground. Following a review of the history of the study of formularity in Homer (section 1.1), sections 1.2 and 1.3 argued that formularity (in the broad sense) is a general and widespread feature of human language and cognition, ultimately rooted in the limitations of our working memory and in the strategies that our mind adopts in order to overcome these limitations. Homeric formularity is, then, just a special case within this general tendency to rely on *chunks* when carrying out a cognitively demanding task.

---

[88] For an introduction to productivity in morphology, see Bauer (2001). For the role of morphological productivity in historical linguistics, see Sandell (2015: 8–32).

While the overall reliance on chunks in Homer is similar to what happens in normal language processing, the extent to which Homer relies on *large linguistic chunks* (i.e., stored verbal sequences that are more than two words long) does seem to set him apart from ancient prose authors like Herodotus, literate hexametric poets like Quintus Smyrnaeus, and modern corpora of spoken and written English. Rather than constituting direct proof of orality of composition, I have argued that this phenomenon points to a high level of *mastery* on the part of the poet, and specifically to the accumulation, likely over the course of a long period of training, of many automated behaviors (i.e., chunks) of increasing size that can support the task of composition. Within the landscape of Archaic Greece, it is persuasive that the conditions that would make such mastery necessary or desirable would only arise within the context of an oral tradition.

Section 1.4 of this chapter has sketched a general theory of formularity in Homer, rooted in cognitive and linguistic frameworks, and has proposed a fine-grained terminology for distinguishing different types of formulaic phenomena in Homer, moving from the very abstract (themes and conceptual associations) to the very concrete (syntactic and metrical constructions – i.e., traditional Parry's formulas). While these definitions have been tailored to the Homeric poems, they should also be applicable to other oral traditions (as well as literary and nonliterary texts in general).

Going forward, one might ask what else can be done after a given formulaic phenomenon has been identified as such – that is, what do we do after we have described a construction, conceptual association, or simple collocation in Homer, and perhaps provided some formal notation for it. For this task, we can take inspiration from the practice of lexicography and literary analysis.

The first step, arguably, would be to establish what the *meaning* and *narrative function* of that phenomenon are. Here, Foley's suggestion that formulas in oral traditions should be regarded as "bigger words" can be employed fruitfully (Foley 2002: 14).[89] In order to establish the meaning of a word (or, in our case, of a formulaic phenomenon) in a closed corpus, one typically starts by collecting and studying all occurrences of that word in the corpus.[90] The same can be done for a formulaic phenomenon in Homer, in order to establish its basic meaning as well as its *traditional referentiality*.[91] Let us say we are studying the word *cat* in a closed corpus: in

---

[89] See Foley (2002: 18): "if the guslar thinks and composes in terms of *reči*, then we must strive to listen and read in terms of *reči*." *Reči* is the plural of Serbo-Croatian *reč* "word, traditional word", discussed in fn. 49.
[90] This is in line with J. R. Firth's (1957: 11) maxim: "You shall know a word by the company it keeps!"
[91] In Foley's (1999) terms, this would mean: what basic traditional associations does the word evoke for an audience that is thoroughly familiar with the specific tradition?

this first step, we would collect all of the occurrences, and describe in general what the basic meaning of the word in the corpus appears to be.

Second, we would study individual usages of our "word"/formulaic phenomenon, in order to see how it works specifically in a given passage. There are at least two aspects to this study: first, we might want to see how the specific context of usage in a given passage selects a specific aspect of the semantic and referential potential of the formulaic phenomenon/"word." In our study of the word *cat*, we might find that the word denotes something different when used in a discussion of house pets vs. in a description of sub-Saharan mammals. Similarly, the same formulaic phenomenon in Homer might express a different meaning when used in different contexts (put another way, the context of usage will select or suggest a specific reading, and a specific referentiality, within all the ones that are possible).

Finally, we might employ some basic techniques of literary analysis in order to ask whether that "word"/formulaic phenomenon is being employed for some special effect (e.g., for intertextual referentiality),[92] or whether it is tied to a specific narrative or stylistic function. Is the word *cat* an important keyword in our text, does it take part in foreshadowing or does it appear to refer to another passage or text? The same can be asked for a formulaic phenomenon.

After these primary facts have been established, we can ask some further questions concerning the status of this item within the poetic technique: is this "word"/formulaic phenomenon traditional or innovative? Does it belong to an archaic or recent layer of the technique? Can we trace its evolution over the course of time? Some examples of how to answer these questions have been sketched in section 1.4.6 above.

---

[92] For the concept of *intraformularity* – i.e., the capacity of formulas to refer to other specific passages in a song or to another song altogether – see Bakker (2013: 157–69).

CHAPTER 2

Meter

<Style> is merely the language itself, running in its natural grooves.

(Sapir 1921: 242)

Meter is not something superimposed on language, a form that exists independently of it; meter emerges from language as part of the process by which special speech emerges from speech.

(Bakker 1997: 146)

While the study of formularity is largely a product of the last two centuries, meter has arguably always been the clearest, most tangible formal feature of Homer's poetry. Each single line in Homer follows the same metrical scheme, and though not every line is perfect (which is to be expected in oral-traditional poetry), a substantial majority of them are.

Hexameters were already recognized as such in antiquity, and they were employed in a variety of occasions and media. Herodotus uses the expression ἐν ἑξαμέτρῳ τόνῳ "in hexametric tone" to refer to both spoken and inscribed verses. This is the case for the response given by the Pythia to the Lydian envoys (*Historiae* 1.47.2), as well as for the prophecy uttered by the χρησμολόγος "soothsayer" Amphílutos to Peisistratus (*Historiae* 1.62.4). When discussing the origin of the alphabet, Herodotus similarly uses the expression ἐν ἑξαμέτρῳ τόνῳ to describe two ancient inscriptions on tripods, written in "Cadmian letters" (*Historiae* 5.60.1). Finally, he uses the expression ἐν ἔπεσι ἑξαμέτροισι "in hexametric verses" to refer to another prophecy by the Pythia to the Spartans (*Historiae* 7.220.3).

In the archaeological record, hexametric lines are also visually set apart: many hexametric inscriptions, starting from some of our earliest attestations, are written out κατὰ στίχον "line by line," and papyri and manuscripts regularly separate out hexameters before they reliably do so for words, or notate accents or punctuation.

Homer's meter has been amply investigated in modern times too, with detailed examinations of how its demands shaped Homer's language,[1] meticulous studies of the various laws and tendencies of the Homeric hexameter (as opposed to the Alexandrinian one), and the development of various competing theories on its origins. Most recently, general theoreticians of meter have attempted to give accounts of the Homeric hexameter that are couched in universal metrical principles (see discussion of Kiparsky (2018) in section 2.3.3 below).

But what does meter actually accomplish for the poet, one might ask? Why would poets agree to obey such a demanding and capricious master? What is gained, for the poets and for their audience, when speech becomes strictly prosodically regulated? This is the path I will attempt to tread in section 2.4, where I revisit the old theory that "meter emerges from language," with some unexpected help from the study of exceptionally fluent speakers (such as professional horse-race callers).

Before we venture there, though, I want to provide (in section 2.1) an overview of the linguistic properties of the Homeric hexameter, starting entirely from scratch – that is, without assuming any previous familiarity with matters of Greek metrics. I believe this is useful for two reasons: (1) Existing treatments of the Homeric hexameter usually fall between two camps: very succinct presentations aimed at students or very technical treatments aimed at metricists, without anything in between. My goal here is to provide a helpful middle way. Beyond offering some up-to-date theoretical foundations to the practice of scanning the Homeric hexameter, I will use this as an opportunity to introduce several concepts from contemporary phonological and metrical theory, which will be relevant for the debate on the colometry of the hexameter and enjambement in Homer, which will be the topics of section 2.2. (2) In the process of describing the hexameter *ab ovo*, I wish to train the reader to see similarities between the properties of natural language and the operation of poetic meter, starting from the small unit of the syllable, and building all the way up to the units

---

[1] This direction of study, often summarized by Kurt Witte's (1913: 2214) dictum that Homer's language is *ein Gebilde des epischen Verses* "a product of the epic verse," took off in the first decades of the twentieth century (Witte 1913, 1972, Meister 1921), and provided a fundamental basis for Parry's work. It rests in turn on an earlier tradition, exemplified by Schulze's (1892) *Quaestiones Epicae* and Solmsen's (1901) *Untersuchungen zur griechischen Laut-und-Verslehre*; see Janko (1992: 8–19).

of the intonational phrase and the metrical line. This will be useful in preparation for section 2.4, where similarities between natural language and metrical language will again come to the fore. This being said, the metrically expert reader might skip to section 2.2, where discussion of the colometry of the hexameter begins in earnest. While the main focus of the first part of this chapter (sections 2.1–2.2) is a synchronic description of the hexameter and its properties, in section 2.3 I will also provide an overview of current theories on the origin of the hexameter.

In section 2.4, finally, I will turn to the question of the function of meter and its ties to human cognition. Specifically, I will argue that meter in oral-traditional poetry should not be seen as a straitjacket imposed on the creativity of a poet, but rather as an adaptive response to the pressure of performance, which enhances fluency and enables innovation precisely by limiting the poet's choices. This view challenges long-held conceptions of meter in oral poetry, and opens further horizons for the investigation of the development and cognitive effects of meter in formulaic speech genres.

2.1 The Dactylic Hexameter

2.1.1 Syllables, Moras, and Feet

Nestor's cup, a small clay drinking vessel found in 1954 on the Italian island of Ischia (ancient Πιθηκοῦσσαι "Monkey Island," a Euboean settlement), bears one of our very oldest Ancient Greek alphabetic inscriptions, and one with important Homeric connections.[2] The inscription consists of three

---

[2] The connections have been drawn at two levels: first, at the level of the phraseology, the last line contains the Homeric collocation ἵμερος "desire" + αἱρέω "seize" (which occurs 3x in the *Iliad*, once in the *Hymn to Apollo*, and once in Hesiod as the line-final formula ἵμερος αἱρεῖ "desire seizes"), as well as the noun-epithet formula καλλιστεφάνου Ἀφροδίτης "of Aphrodite of the beautiful crown," which, while not occurring in Homer, is similar to other genitive expressions such as ἐϋστεφάνου τ' Ἀφροδίτης "of well-crowned Aphrodite" (*Od.* 8.267) and φιλοστεφάνου Ἀφροδίτης "of Aphrodite who loves crowns" (*Hymn to Demeter* 102), and isometric with the nominative formula καλλιστέφανος Δημήτηρ "Demeter of the beautiful crown" (attested 2x in the *Hymn to Demeter*). In other words, the phraseology has an "epic" (if not perfectly Homeric) flavor to it. At the thematic level, scholars have wondered whether the first line, which mentions a "Nestor's cup" is meant to refer to Nestor's famous oversized golden cup (δέπας) in *Iliad* 11.632–37 (brought to its most extreme conclusion, this interpretation would make our cup into a *terminus ante quem* for the *Iliad*). I personally find this second line of reasoning uncompelling, and I believe that the cup from Pithēkoûssai is simply telling us that it belongs to somebody called Nestor (West 1994, Faraone 1996, Pavese 1996), but this is an idea to which scholars keep returning (for a history of the problem, see Gaunt 2017). For a detailed commentary on the inscription, see Pavese 1996. For a historical linguistic commentary, see Watkins (1976). The first edition is Buchner and Russo (1955: 200). A more recent edition is Hansen (1983: 251–52).

Figure 2.1 The inscription on Nestor's Cup (Pithēkoûssai, eighth century BCE)[3]

lines of text, redacted in Euboean alphabet and West Ionic Greek, all running right to left. They read:[4]

(1)   Νεστορος : ε[μ]ι : ευποτ[ον] : ποτεριον
      hος δ'ἀ<ν> τοδε πιεσι : ποτερι[ο] : αυτικα κενον
      hιμερ[ος ℎαιρ]εσει : καλλιστε[φα]νο : Αφροδιτες

In a "normalized spelling" (that is, adding the vowel lengths that are not marked in the original, as well as accent marks and breathings),[5] we can render them as follows:

(2)   Νέστορος : ἐμί[6] : εὔποτον : ποτέριον
      ὃς δ' ἂν τόδε πίεσι : ποτερίō : αὐτίκα κênον
      ἵμερος αἱρέσει : καλλιστεφάνō : Ἀφροδίτēς

If we further "Atticize" the spelling (i.e., by rendering long vowels following the conventions used in the East Ionic alphabet as officially adopted in Athens in 403–402 BCE),[7] we arrive at this text:

---

[3] Image created by Wikipedia user Future Perfect at Sunrise (https://commons.wikimedia.org/wiki/User:Future_Perfect_at_Sunrise). The lighter areas indicate restorations. The only point of the restoration that I do not follow is the introduction of an interpunct after the first word in the third line.

[4] As per the Leiden conventions, angled brackets (<>) indicate letters missing from the text (because of an error or spelling convention) and restored by the editor, square brackets ([]) indicate a lacuna due to physical damage and (when possible) restored by the editor. Interpuncts (:) are used to separate out words and phrases (see more below). For a very brief introduction to Greek epigraphy, see Wachter (2010). For a more extensive treatment, see Guarducci (2017). Note that, following contemporary linguistic convention, I will also use angled brackets in this book to indicate how a sequence is *spelled*, e.g., the sound [s] is spelled as <σ> in the Greek alphabetic script.

[5] For reasons that will become clear later, we will also keep the interpuncts as they appear in the original.

[6] Pavese (1996: 7–8) convincingly argues against restoring εἰμί "(I am)," given both the size of the lacuna and the graphic practice of other inscriptions from Pithēkoûssai and Cuma (Kúmē, Euboea) of spelling εμι for [eːmi] "(I am)." The long [eː] in this word is the result of the first compensatory lengthening, and goes back to Proto-Greek *es-mi < PIE *h₁es-mi "id." The Attic form εἰμί shows the usage of the digraph <ει> for notating a long [eː] arising from relatively recent sound changes (so-called "secondary" [eː]; see also fn. 27 below), as opposed to older (or "original") long [ɛː], which is spelled <η> in Attic. The spelling <ει> was not standard in all dialects, and would be unexpected here. For Attic <ει>, see Allen (1968: 67–69).

[7] This practice, of course, results in an ahistorical text, but one that is easier to read for those who are familiar with classical Attic.

(3)   Νέστορος : εἰμὶ : εὔποτον : ποτήριον
      ὅς δ' ἂν τοῦδε πίησι : ποτηρίου : αὐτίκα κεῖνον
      ἵμερος αἱρήσει : καλλιστεφάνου : Ἀφροδίτης

> I am Nestor's cup, which is good for drinking
> whoever will drink from this cup, immediately that (person)
> will be seized by the desire of Aphrodite of the beautiful crown.

Of these three lines, the last two show the metrical scheme of the dactylic hexameter (we will return to the first line in section 2.3.3 below).

Now, let's imagine we are discovering the hexameter for the first time, taking other metrical traditions as a point of reference. What is regular about these last two lines? What makes them metrical? It is not the total number of syllables in each line, as in meters from the Indo-Iranian tradition (the first line has sixteen syllables, the second fifteen); it's not any pattern of word stresses, rhyme, or alliteration,[8] as in meters from the Romance or Germanic tradition, which sometimes combine all of the features above; it's also not a system of syntactic or semantic parallelisms, as in the Hebrew Bible.[9]

The regularity is slightly more subtle, more abstract: each line consists of the repetition of six smaller metrical units (i.e., *metra*, hence *hexameter*),[10] each consisting of a sequence of two elements: a single heavy syllable plus a sequence of two light syllables. Together, these elements are called a dactyl (or dactylic foot); in traditional metrical notation, they are written as —⏑⏑.[11] Thus the name *dactylic hexameter*. Within the hexametric line, the last foot is "truncated" (*catalectic*), in that it only consists of two syllables (a heavy syllable, plus either a light or a heavy one). There are different conventions for naming each element within the dactylic foot. Maas (1923, 1962) uses *longum* for the first element (the

---

[8] The attentive reader will recognize a little alliteration in the sequences πίησι ποτηρίου (the word-initial [p], here part of a so-called *schema etymologicum*, since both the verb and its object derive from the same verbal root "to drink," PIE *peh_3-) and ἵμερος αἱρήσει (just the word-initial [h]), but this does not seem to play any structural role in the verse, the way it would in a truly alliterative meter like, say, that of *Beowulf*.

[9] For a thorough (and typologically inclusive) discussion of the formal properties of different types of poetry, see Fabb (2015).

[10] In Classical metrics, the term *foot* is used to denote the smallest possible recurring metrical sequence (such as an iamb, dactyl, or spondee), while the term *metron* is used for longer recurring units, formed by feet (e.g., the iambic foot). In the case of the hexameter, the foot and metron coincide in the traditional terminology (thus the hexameter consists of six metra, each consisting of a single dactylic foot).

[11] The reference here, of course, is Gk. δάκτυλος "finger," with one long knuckle followed by two short ones. In metrical notation, – indicates a heavy syllable, and ⏑ a light syllable.

The Dactylic Hexameter

heavy syllable), and *biceps* for the second (the two lights).¹² The first element has also been called *princeps* (West 1982).¹³

The reason this metrical scheme does not result in a fixed number of syllables per line lies in another special feature of the hexameter: the second element of each foot, usually consisting of two light syllables, can optionally be occupied by a single heavy syllable: we call this process *contraction*, and the resulting sequence a *contracted biceps*.¹⁴ Contraction happens very rarely in the fifth foot, and quite rarely all over the line, but it allows for a great amount of variability in the realization of the scheme.¹⁵

But what counts as a light syllable, and what counts as a heavy one? Before going into any further detail, we should take a step back and talk about syllables in general. We shall see that the many phonological concepts we shall introduce here will pay dividends as we venture into a more detailed discussion of Homer's meter, its origin, and its function.

Syllables are basic units of phonology, and they arguably reflect how sounds (i.e., linguistic segments)¹⁶ are grouped together for the purposes of

---

¹² The terminology (*elementum*) *longum* vs. (*elementum*) *breve* is used to refer to the place in a metrical scheme for a heavy and a light syllable respectively; the usage originates in antiquity and conflates two concepts that are now kept apart in contemporary linguistics: length (a property of vowels) and weight (a property of syllables). See discussion in Allen (1968: 97–98), who also addresses the connected and confusing usage of the terms length "by nature" (Lat. *natura*, Gk. φύσει) and length "by position (or convention)" (Lat. *positu/positione*, Gk. θέσει). An updated terminology is accordingly proposed by Pavese (2014: 19), who talks about *elementum leve* and *elementum grave* (and similarly *syllaba brevis* and *syllaba gravis*). In what follows, I will keep the term *longum* for the first element out of tradition (this is also the term that we find in expressions like *brevis in longo*, literally "a short syllable in a long element," more correctly translated as "a light syllable occupying a heavy element," a common type of metrical flaw). I do, however, feel strongly that one should not speak of long and short syllables (or long and short elements), but that one should talk about *vowel length* (a long vowel vs. a short vowel) and *syllable weight* (a heavy syllable vs. a light syllable).

¹³ The ancient terms *arsis* and *thesis* can also be used here, but their long history makes their usage less straightforward (Maas (1923: 6), for instance, recommends avoiding them). Originally, they meant the raising and stamping of a foot in marching or dancing, corresponding to the musical upbeat and downbeat respectively. In metrics, they are used to indicate the two fundamental components of a rhythmical foot. As applied to Homer in antiquity (e.g., by the grammarian Marius Victorinus), the *arsis* was taken to be the first element of the dactyl, the *thesis* the second (for a recent discussion, see Lynch 2016). In modern times, these terms have been used inconsistently: for example, West (1982) regards the first element in a dactylic foot as the *arsis* and the second as the *thesis*, while Devine and Stephens (1994) argue for the opposite interpretation.

¹⁴ The opposite process, whereby two light syllables are allowed to occupy a position for a single heavy syllable in a metrical scheme, is called *resolution*, and is generally not allowed in the hexameter.

¹⁵ West (1982: 37) reports only six entirely spondaic hexameters (i.e., hexameters in which each *biceps* has undergone contraction; Lat. *spondaeus* "spondee," is a metrical term for a foot of the shape – –) in all of the Homeric corpus. One is ψυχὴν κικλήσκων Πατροκλῆος δειλοῖο "calling out the soul of poor Patroclus" (*Il.* 23.221).

¹⁶ A fundamental distinction in phonology is that between *sound* (a concrete, audible unit of speech) and *phoneme* (an abstract psychological entity). Both entities are notated using the International Phonetic Alphabet (IPA, www.internationalphoneticassociation.org/content/ipa-chart), but sounds

speech processing.[17] Syllabification – that is, the language-specific process by which segments are arranged in syllables – can impact many aspects of the grammar, not just poetic meter.

The arrangement of sounds within a syllable is largely determined by *sonority* – that is, a phonological concept that captures how loud a linguistic segment is when pronounced. All segments in a language can be placed along a sonority hierarchy, going from maximally sonorous segments (vowels) to minimally sonorous ones (voiceless stop consonants, like [t], [p], or [k]).[18]

A syllable consists, at minimum, of a syllabic nucleus. The nucleus is occupied by the most sonorous element in the syllable, typically a vowel or a diphthong; in some languages, the more sonorous consonants can act as nuclei as well.[19] The nucleus is (usually) flanked by an onset and (optionally) by a coda; these positions must all be filled by consonants. Nucleus and coda together can be referred to as *rhyme* (also spelled *rime*). A scheme is given in Figures 2.2 and 2.3.

In Figure 2.2, onset and coda are simple – that is, they contain a single segment each. Figure 2.3 is an example of a syllable with complex onset and complex coda (i.e., onsets and codas containing more than one segment).

In general, languages prefer for the sonority of a syllable to gradually increase during the onset, peak in the nucleus, and fade out during the coda

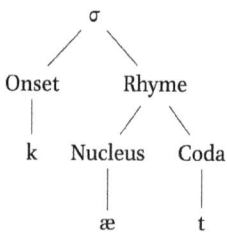

Figure 2.2 Syllable structure for the word *cat* [kæt]

---

are transcribed between square brackets, as in [a], while phonemes are transcribed between slashes, as in /a/. In practice, a notation with square brackets tells us how a linguistic sequence is pronounced (this is also known as *surface realization*), while a notation with slashes tells us how a linguistic sequence is broken down into phonemes in the mind of the speaker (this is also known as *underlying representation*). For more on this distinction, see Hayes (2009a: Chapter 2).

[17] For an introduction to the basic principles of syllabification, see Hayes (2009a: Chapter 13). For more on prosodic structure, see Féry (2017: Chapter 3).

[18] See Hayes (2009a: 75–76).

[19] This is the case for English, which allows /l/, /m/, and /n/ to work as syllable nuclei (notated as [l̩], [m̩], and [n̩] in IPA). Examples are the final syllables of the words *table*, *prism*, and *button*. This was also the case for PIE and Proto-Greek (see section 2.3.1 for the problem of possible traces of syllabic /r/ as a very deep archaism in Homer). See also fn. 106 below.

The Dactylic Hexameter

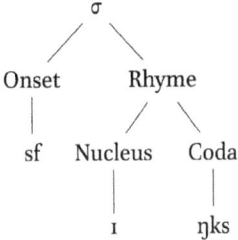

Figure 2.3 Syllable structure for the word *sphinx* [sfɪŋks]

(cf. Hayes 2009a: 77–78). This principle is called *sonority sequencing*, and it makes for syllables that are easy to produce and perceive (children's early speech, for instance, tends to amplify this preference). Many languages will allow for exceptions to this principle (as in the word *sphinx*), but not all the time and everywhere.[20]

Not all syllables are created equal: in each language, syllables with different structural properties can be sorted into different phonological categories. Ancient Greek, for instance, belongs to the count of quantity-sensitive languages – that is, languages which assign different phonological statuses to syllables based on their *weight*. Somewhat simplifying, we can conceptualize phonological weight as a rough approximation of how long it takes, on average, to pronounce a given syllable. The phonological unit of weight is called a *mora* (μ). Syllables containing a single mora are light. Syllables with more than one mora are heavy. Not all segments contribute to syllable weight equally: in general, vowels are always mora-bearing (i.e., they always contribute to syllable weight). Consonants might also be mora-bearing, but that depends on their position in the syllable (i.e., whether they are in the onset or in the coda) and on the language in question.

In Ancient Greek, syllables are sorted into two weight categories: light and heavy. A light syllable is a syllable ending in a short vowel (thus, a syllable with a short vowel in the nucleus and no coda). All other syllables

---

[20] In Ancient Greek and Latin, for instance, you could start a syllable with the sequence [s] + voiceless consonant (i.e., [p], [t], [k], [pʰ], [tʰ],[kʰ]), where the [s] is more sonorous than the following segment. We can see this in Gk. σχολή "free time, leisure," borrowed in Latin as *schola* [ˈskola], and eventually in English as *school*. Spanish and French do not allow for this type of sonority sequencing violation, so they have reshaped the word as *escuela* and *école* respectively. Here, a vowel was added to the beginning of the word (a process called *vowel prothesis*), so that the offending sequence [sk] could be broken up between two syllables; in French, the [s] was further lost to sound change (as marked by the acute accent on the remaining <é>), but is still visible in Old French *escole*.

count as heavy.²¹ Beyond this categorical split into light and heavy syllables, we know that Ancient Greek speakers were sensitive to some further distinctions: for instance, phonological processes in Ancient Greek show that the language dispreferred superheavy syllables – that is, syllables containing more than two moras. Similarly, superheavy syllables are more constrained in the hexameter than regular heavy syllables (Hoenigswald 1991, Cassio 2016b).²²

Languages also have different preferences when it comes to syllable architecture: some won't allow for codas at all (like some Polynesian languages); some will only allow for specific consonants in a coda (like Japanese); some will ban complex onsets or complex codas. In Ancient Greek, some types of complex onsets are accepted, but complex codas are often simplified: in fact, some of the compensatory lengthening processes discussed in Chapter 3 are motivated by precisely this preference.²³

2.1.2 Scanning the Hexameter

Syllables

When scanning a verse into syllables for the purposes of poetic meter, we run all words together: this is called *synapheia* (Gk. συνάφεια "connection, union"). Syllable boundaries (which we mark with a period) can be established according to the following principles, proceeding from left to right:

1. The earliest a syllable can end is with a vowel or diphthong. A syllable will end with a vowel or diphthong if a single consonant (or another separate vowel/diphthong) follows. In that case, the following consonant will serve as the onset of the next syllable.²⁴

---

[21] In most languages (including Ancient Greek), categorical syllable weight depends on rhyme (i.e., nucleus and coda) alone, though onsets too can be shown to contribute to more fine-grained weight distinctions (Topintzi 2010, Ryan 2016).

[22] See Ryan (2011, 2019) for a fine-grained hierarchy of syllable weights in Ancient Greek and other languages.

[23] Often, we can see *sound change* as a solution to some existing problem in the language – though the solution often creates more problems in its turn. In a typical *compensatory lengthening* process, a syllable loses a coda segment (maybe because the language disprefers codas in general); in order for the weight of the syllable to remain constant, the mora (μ) that belonged to the coda segment gets reassigned to the syllable nucleus: a long vowel (2 μ) is thus created. An example taking place in many varieties of English (which we shall discuss further in Chapter 3) is *r-dropping*, where [r] (technically [ɹ]) is lost in a syllable coda, and the preceding vowel is lengthened in compensation. See the British English pronunciation of *card* [kɑːd], vs. Standard American English [kɑɹd]. In Ancient Greek, we usually talk about three compensatory lengthenings, all taking place during the first millennium BCE (Rau 2010: 177–78).

[24] This is true, of course, until we reach the end of the line, and no more syllables can follow.

2. If a vowel or diphthong is followed by two (or more) consonants,[25] the standard practice is to assign the first of those consonants to the coda of the first syllable, and the second to the onset of the second syllable (we shall discuss some special cases below).[26]

Following these rules, a division in syllables of the two lines above (in examples (1), (2), and (3)) is given here, and heavy syllables are underlined. A metrical scheme is given below:

(4) ὅς.δ᾽ ἂν.τοῦ.δε.πί.η.σι.πο.τη.ρί.ου.αὐ.τί.κα.κεῖ.νον
ἵ.με.ρο.ς αἰ.ρή.σει. καλ.λισ.τε.φά.νου.Ἀ.φρο.δί.της

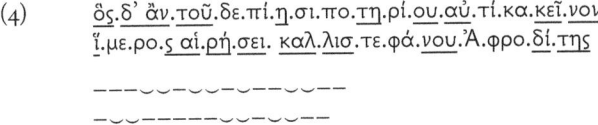

A few notes:

- We can observe many different types of heavy syllables: those ending in a long vowel (η, τη, ἵ. ρή, δί, all 2μ), ending in a diphthong[27] (τοῦ, ου, αὐ, κεῖ, ς αἰ, σει, νου, all 2μ), ending in a short vowel followed by a single consonant (ὅς, δ᾽ ἂν, νον, καλ, λισ, all 2μ), and ending in a long vowel followed by a coda consonant (της, 3μ). The last type is a *superheavy syllable*, as discussed above. Hoenigswald (1991) (building on previous scholarship) showed that superheavy syllables are dispreferred in the last two *longa* of the hexameter.
- The smallest possible syllable in Greek consists of a single short vowel (Ἀ, 1μ). However, such a minimal syllable would not be allowed to work as a standalone word in Ancient Greek, which has a minimal word requirement of two moras.[28] Small words that do not meet the minimal word requirement have to "lean on" other words to receive their accent: they are enclitics and proclitics.

---

[25] Note that the letters <ζ>, <ξ>, and <ψ> all notate double consonants, namely (in the Ionic alphabet) [dz], [ks], and [ps]. For the pronunciation of <ζ>, see Allen (1968: 53–56).
[26] See Hermann (1919) for arguments that this is the usual syllabification practice of Greek.
[27] For simplicity, we will collapse here the distinction between actual diphthongs and *spurious diphthongs* (i.e., the instances, in Attic–Ionic, of the digraphs <ου> and <ει>, which represent the long vowels [eː] and [oː] arising from secondary processes instead of the original diphthongs [ou] and [ei]). Some word-final diphthongs (i.e., αι and οι in some morphological endings) count as forming light syllables for the purposes of the accent. These same diphthongs form heavy syllables for the purposes of the meter, though they can sometimes be elided as well (West 1982: 10).
[28] Note that, in Attic–Ionic, the last consonant of a word is *extrametrical* (i.e., it cannot carry a mora), and as such it does not count towards the computation of the minimal-word requirement (Steriade 1988: 276, Golston 1991: 73–100).

- Word-initial aspiration [h] does not count as a consonant for the purposes of meter. Thus, the beginning of the second line scans ἵ.με. ρο.ς αἰ.ρή.σει and not ἵ.με.ρος. αἰ.ρή.σει, which would be unmetrical.
- When two vowels or diphthongs come into direct contact across a word boundary (i.e., when they are in *hiatus*), several things can happen:
  ○ The first vowel, if short, can be elided (this is always the case for ε, while it is more limited for the other vowels; cf. West 1982: 10).
  ○ The first vowel, if long (or a diphthong), can nonetheless form a light syllable for the purposes of the meter. This is called *hiatus shortening* (or *correptio epica* "epic shortening," or *vocalis ante vocalem corripitur* "a (long) vowel shortens before another vowel"), and can be observed in the sequence πο.τη.ρί.ου. αὐ.τί.κα (– – ⏑ – – ⏑ ⏑), which actually scans as πο.τη.ρί.ου.αὐ.τί.κα (– – ⏑ ⏑ – ⏑ ⏑) in this line. Hiatus shortening is optional, and it does not apply, for instance, in the sequence καλ.λισ.τε. φά.νου.Ἀ.φρο.δί.της, where it would give rise to an unmetrical line.
  ○ In some cases, nothing happens (i.e., hiatus remains without any loss of weight in the first syllable). In many cases in Homer, this type of hiatus results from the loss of word-initial *[w], as in the example below (see discussion in Chapter 3):

(5)   Ἀτρεΐδης τε *[w]ἄναξ ἀνδρῶν καὶ δῖος Ἀχιλλεύς (*Il.* 1.7)[29]

    The lord of men son of Atreus and divine Achilles.

- The word Ἀφροδίτης contains an apparent exception to the scansion rules given above concerning how to deal with a vowel followed by two consonants. Here, both consonants following initial Ἀ are assigned to the onset of the second syllable, resulting in a light first syllable (thus the scansion is Ἀ.φρο and not Ἀφ.ρο). This phenomenon is called *correptio Attica* (since it is standard in Attic verse, especially comedy), and it occurs sometimes in Homer as well, mostly in personal names which would not otherwise fit the meter. *Correptio Attica* does not apply to all two-consonant sequences in Greek, but only to the so-called *muta cum liquida* sequences – that is, consonant clusters formed by an oral stop (no matter whether voiced, voiceless, or aspirated) followed by a consonantal sonorant – i.e., [r], [l], [m], or [n].[30]

---

[29] We know that ἄναξ "lord" used to start with a [w] because the form is attested in Mycenaean as *wa-na-ka*.
[30] For the modern terminology, see Hayes (2009a: Chapter 1); the term *plosive* can also be used instead of stop (as in Allen 1968). In the ancient terminology, Lat. *muta* is a translation of Gk. ἄφωνα "without sound, silent," indicating consonants that cannot be pronounced without a vowel. Lat.

This short survey already covers most of the information necessary to scan Homeric verses. A few more special cases are listed in West (1997: 220–21). The most important are as follows:

- Sometimes, two consecutive vowels or a vowel and a diphthong can be grouped together to form a single heavy syllable. This phenomenon (which is called *synekphonesis*; Gk. συνεκφώνησις "combined pronunciation") is more frequent word-internally (where it's called *synizesis*; Gk. συνίζησις "sitting together") than across word boundaries (where it's called *synalephe*; Gk. συναλοιφή "merging together (of two syllables)"). An example of each is given below:

(6) Μῆνιν ἄειδε θεὰ Πηληϊάδεω Ἀχιλῆος (*Il.* 1.1)

The wrath, sing, o goddess, of Peleus' son, Achilles

(7) μήτε σύ, Πηλείδη, ἔθελ' ἐριζέμεναι βασιλῆϊ (*Il.* 1.277)

Neither you, son of Peleus, should want to antagonize a king

In Chapter 3, we shall discuss a frequent case of synizesis which happens in conjunction with the phenomenon called *quantitative metathesis*, which we see in the word Πηληϊάδεω in example (6).

- Occasionally, a single word-final consonant, when followed by a vowel-initial word, can count as two consonants for the purposes of the meter (i.e., the consonant can be syllabified in the coda of the previous syllable, making it heavy, as well as in the onset of the following syllable). In practice, the affected segments are [n], [s], and [r] (i.e., the only consonants allowed in word-final position in Greek; for mnemonic purposes, these consonants are all contained in the word Nestor).
- Occasionally, word-initial clusters [sk] or [dz] are "treated as a single consonant" for the purposes of the meter.[31] This happens in personal names especially, such as Σκάμανδρος, Σκαμάνδριος, Ζάκυνθος, and so on. These are words that would not otherwise fit the meter.

Some irregular scansions in Homer reflect older stages of the language, in which the scansion would have been correct (just like the cases of word-initial

---

liquida translates Gk. ὑγρά "moist" (perhaps in the sense of "slippery"), a term used by Dionysius Thrax in his *Ars Grammatica*; while Dionysius used the term to describe [r], [l], [m] and [n], in modern linguistic terminology only [r] and [l] are usually referred to as liquids, while [m] and [n] are referred to as nasals (see discussion in Allen 1968: 38). For more details on the treatment of *muta cum liquida* in Homer, see Hackstein (2010: 416–17).

[31] More precisely, the clusters are not split between two consecutive syllables, but both consonants are assigned to the onset of the following syllable, much like the special *muta cum liquida* treatment just discussed.

*[w] mentioned above, and discussed further in Chapter 3). Of these, the most frequent are as follows:

- Single word-initial consonantal sonorants (i.e., liquids and nasals) can occasionally be treated as a sequence of two consonants. This treatment is historically motivated: Proto-Greek used to have several word-initial clusters involving *[s] plus the segments above – that is, *[sn], *[sm], *[sl], and *[sr]. These sequences were first assimilated to *[nn], *[mm], *[ll], and *[rr] respectively, and then degeminated (the geminate outcome is sometimes preserved word-internally). Homer preserves some authentic traces of these clusters – for example, involving reflexes of the Proto-Indo-European (PIE) roots *$snig^{wh}$- "snow," Gk. νιφ- "id." and PIE *sreu- "flow," Gk. ῥόο- "current." In some other cases, the treatment appears to have been extended analogically to words that had no etymological initial cluster.[32]
- The same goes for the Proto-Greek sequence *[wr-], which became [rr] and then [r] in first-millennium Greek. Homer preserves some traces of the cluster, involving for instance reflexes of the PIE root *$wreh_1\acute{g}$- "break" (Present-Day English "wreck"), as in the word ἄρρηκτος "unbreakable" (Il. 2.490), or in the sequence τε ῥήξειν "and to wreck" (Il. 12.198). This treatment, too, was extended analogically to words containing no etymological *[wr-], such as ῥάβδος "stick" in Iliad 24.343.
- Finally, the same applies to the word-initial sequence *[sw-], found in the reflexive personal pronoun *swe-, Homeric accusative singular ἕ, ἑέ. The original *[sw-] prevented hiatus, for instance, in Iliad 2.11 and 20.171 respectively.

Even when taking all of these rules and exceptions into account, some hexameters in Homer do not scan perfectly.[33] This reality is to be expected in poems that result from an oral-traditional context. From other oral traditions, we know that neither poets nor audiences seem to be perturbed by imperfect verses, which might occur as often as once in every ten lines.[34] It is writing poets that are (apparently) held to stricter standards.

---

[32] For "flow," see καλλίρροον in Il. 2.752 and κατὰ ῥόον Il. 21.147. For "snow," see ἀγάννιφον in Il. 1.420 and ἔπεα νιφάδεσσιν in Il. 3.222. For analogical extension to roots without an initial *[s], see Il. 5.358 (initial [l] in λισσομένη, PIE (?) *$le̯it$-), Il. 1.454 (initial [m] in μέγα, PIE *$me\acute{g}h_2$-), and Il. 14.350 (initial [n] in νεφέλην, PIE *neb^h-). For more examples, see Hackstein (2010: 414–16).

[33] The following observations are largely derived from a presentation by Mario Cantilena at the Seminario Omerico in Milan in April 2021, titled Incertezze sull'esametro. An article is in preparation.

[34] This, for instance, was the case for the guslar Ćamil Kulenović, who sang fifty-five eleven-syllable lines (as opposed to the expected ten-syllable lines) in the first 500 lines of a song, as reported by Lord (1960: 282–83).

Antiquity seemingly had two approaches to "bad" verses in Homer: the first approach was to sort them into categories and label them, and not do anything to change the text. We know of a typology of bad hexameters, such as ἀκέφαλοι "headless" (those starting with a light syllable), λαγαροί "hollow" (those containing a light syllable in lieu of a heavy one within the verse), and μύοροι "mouse-tailed" (those containing a light penultimate syllable).

The second approach was to try to conceal the metrical flaws in the Homeric text by tinkering with the spelling; an example of this is arguably *Iliad* 1.2, in which the first word is spelled οὐλομένην instead of the expected – but metrically impossible – ὀλομένην "ruinous."[35] It is hard to tell exactly what the poets themselves would have done in performance – that is, whether they would have artificially lengthened a vowel when needed, or would have maintained the correct – but metrically wrong – pronunciation.[36]

Feet
Let us now return to the two hexameters above. Now that we have scanned each syllable, we can add foot divisions (marked here by commas and spacing) to our lines. This yields the following schema:

(8) ὅς.δ' ἄν.,   τοῦ.δε.πί.,   η.σι.πο.,   τη.ρί.ου.,   αὐ.τί.κα.,   κεῖ.νον
     ἵ.με.ρο.,   ς αἱ.ρῇ.,   σει. καλ., λισ.τε.φά., νου.Ἀ.φρο., δί.της

In the practice of reading the hexameter out loud, we usually stress the first element of each foot (what Maas called *longum*, and West *princeps*), thus artificially translating the quantitative rhythm of the original (which coexisted with the pitch accents of each word) into something more akin to English or German verse.[37] In doing so, we also "delete" the Greek word accents, which we also usually realize conventionally through stress.[38] The result is as follows:

---

[35] These types of examples are separate from the many cases in which the poets appear to have tinkered with the morphology of a word in order to obtain a more suitable metrical shape. For a short overview, see Hackstein (2010: 409–11).

[36] See Cantilena (in preparation) for a discussion.

[37] Verses like these have then been artificially created in various modern European languages, where word accents are aligned with the *longum/princeps*. In the Italian tradition, these attempts are charmingly called *metrica barbara* "barbarous metrics," a term made famous by the poet Giosuè Carducci (1835–1907). They have a notable tradition in English, German, and French literature as well. As recently as 1987, the hip-hop group Public Enemy used dactylic hexameters of this sort in the song "Bring the Noise" (1987).

[38] Unlike languages like English or Italian, where the most prominent syllable in a word (i.e., the *stressed* or *accented* syllable) is marked primarily through increased duration, in Ancient Greek the most prominent syllable in a word is marked primarily through raised pitch. A traditional way of characterizing this difference is to label English and Italian *stress-accent languages*, and Ancient Greek a *pitch-accent language* (or *non-stress accent language*, following the terminology of Beckman 1986);

78   Meter

(9)   /   /   /   /   /   /
    ὃς δ' ἂν τοῦδε πίῃσι ποτηρίου αὐτίκα κεῖνον
      /   /   /   /   /
    ἵμερος αἱρήσει καλλιστεφάνου Ἀφροδίτης

This, of course, is far from an authentic rendition of how a hexameter would have been read (or sung, or chanted) in antiquity, but it is the most straightforward option we have for communicating the metrical structure of each line – and, most importantly, noticing when something is strange, or amiss, in our lines. There have been several interesting attempts to more accurately recreate the authentic pronunciation of the Homeric hexameter (and rhapsodic performance altogether), but they are not always practical for everyday use.[39]

The regularities described so far can be summarized as follows:

(10) $^1\_{-a\smile b\smile c}$, $^2\_{-a\smile b\smile c}$, $^3\_{-a\smile b\smile c}$, $^4\_{-a\smile b\smile c}$, $^5\_{-a\smile b\smile c}$, $^6\_{-a-c}$

In this schema, I follow Janse's (2003) proposal of using a neutral and transparent system for the notation of the hexameter which assigns numbers to the feet and letters to the positions within the feet. So, for each foot, position *a* will be the *longum*, while *b* and *c* will be the first and second units in the *biceps* respectively (a contracted *biceps* will be notated as *c*).

Janse's system is quite different from the traditional metrical practice, which combines numbering systems of disparate origins. On the one hand, the traditional system numbers each half-foot (Gk. μέρος "part") consecutively (so that position 3 is the *longum* of the second foot, position 5 is the *longum* of the third foot, and position 7 is the *longum* of the fourth foot);[40] on the other, it uses a combination of foot number and further metrical terminology to indicate other positions within the feet (e.g., κατὰ τρίτον τροχαῖον "after the third trochaeus," meaning position 3b). As we shall see, Janse's more transparent terminology will be helpful in discussing various word-end phenomena below.[41]

---

the appropriateness of this term is now the object of considerable debate (Hyman 2009). For an introduction to Greek accentuation, see Probert 2003.

[39] For one authoritative attempt (including audio recordings and extensive bibliography), see Danek and Hagel 2002 (www.oeaw.ac.at/kal/sh/).

[40] This is the source of the terms *trithemimeral*, *penthemimeral*, and *hephthemimeral*, which are used to refer to caesuras – see Table 2.1.

[41] Another system that has been used in recent decades (see, for instance, Hagel 1994) is that of numbering moras consecutively, using the sequence 2 3 4 6 7 8 10 11 12 14 15 16 18 19 20 22 24. This system is precise, but less transparent than Janse's. Its legibility can be improved by adding numbered brackets for feet, as in: ^{1}[2 3 4] ^{2}[6 7 8] ^{3}[10 11 12] ^{4}[14 15 16] ^{5}[18 19 20] ^{6}[22 24]. This is the system used, for instance, in Figures 2.4 and 2.6.

Admittedly, we could improve our notation system by adding some indication of which elements can be realized as a single heavy syllable instead of by a sequence of two light syllables: this is accomplished by the sign ⏓ (in hexametric notation, it is usual to use this in feet 1–4, since contraction is uncommon in the fifth foot, and does not apply to the sixth foot).

The last element of the line (which, as we mentioned above, is usually said to be indifferent to quantity) is here conventionally represented by a *longum* (–), though some metricists have rendered it as an *anceps* (×, meaning either – or ⏑), or with the musical sign of the *fermata* (⌒).[42] The different notation here reflects different theoretical considerations: on the one hand, it is a general property of quantitative meters for the last element in the line to be indifferent to categorical weight (in this sense, the term *indifferens* is justified, and the symbol × has been used).[43] On the other hand, there are clear statistical tendencies for given metrical corpora to prefer heavier or lighter syllables at the end of the line (these are termed *finality preferences* by Ryan 2013). For Homer, heavier heavy syllables are strongly favored at the end of the line, and lighter light syllables are strongly dispreferred.[44] Ryan (2019: 152) shows that superheavy syllables are the most favored at the end of the line in both poems (and even slightly more so in the *Iliad* than in the *Odyssey*). From this point of view, it can be justifiable to mark the final element as "–" (as done here), reflecting its most frequent or preferred realization as a heavy syllable.

The musical notation of the *fermata* can be used to convey a general property of the *textsetting*[45] of all quantitative meters, whereby the realization in performance of the last syllable of a line is essentially free in duration – that is, it can be prolonged at will without upsetting the rhythm, and as such it

---

[42] A strong argument for using the *fermata* here instead of the *anceps* is presented by Rossi (1963 [2020]), who suggests using the × (*anceps*) for partially free elements within a line (typically at the beginning of verses, such as various types of bases), the double sign ⏓ for truly free elements within a line (the so-called ἄλογος "irrational," which occurs in trochaic and iambic meters), and the *fermata* (⌒) exclusively for the last element in a line (the real *elementum indifferens*/ἀδιάφορος in ancient terminology).

[43] In other words, the last element in the line "does not care" whether the syllable that occupies it is heavy or light. See the discussion of final indifference in Ryan (2019: 151–53), and Ryan (2013).

[44] Conversely, Catullus' hendecasyllables and the Old Norse *dróttkvætt* are meters that display a preference for lighter final syllables (Ryan 2019: 153).

[45] *Textsetting* is the process by which a speaker/performer "sets a text" to a given rhythm or music. Specifically, it concerns "how lines of linguistic text are arranged in time against a predetermined rhythmic pattern," in the context of sung or chanted verse (Hayes 2009b: 44). When speakers use their native intuition to determine which linguistic units (e.g., syllables, stressed words, phrases) should be matched to which part of the rhythmical and/or musical template, they are engaging in textsetting. On textsetting in general, see Halle and Lerdahl (1993), Hayes and Kaun (1996), Hayes (2009b), and Ryan (2022).

does not have to reflect the usual contrast in duration between light or heavy syllables in the language (see discussion in Ryan 2013).[46] All things considered, it seems to me that the notation that uses "–" would be most informative here, provided that the readers are aware of the phenomenon of final indifference and its typical "*fermata*" realization in textsetting (both of which are general properties of all quantitative meters).

Finally, two vertical lines (||) indicate the end of a metrical period.

(11) ^{1}–a⌣b⌣c, ^{2}–a⌣b⌣c, ^{3}–a⌣b⌣c, ^{4}–a⌣b⌣c, ^{5}–a⌣b⌣c, ^{6}–a–c ||

One word of warning: no metrical scheme will be able to perfectly convey the practice of what poets actually do with their lines. For instance, we might get the impression from the scheme above that contracted *bicipitia*[47] are just as frequent as uncontracted ones in the Homeric hexameter, and that they are just as likely to appear in the first foot (=metron) as in the fifth. This is not the case. In the Homeric corpus, Ryan (2011: 47) found that in the fifth foot well over 90 percent of the *bicipitia* are uncontracted, while in the first foot only a little more than 60 percent are.

Additionally, we might think that any heavy syllable will do in occupying either a *longum* or a contracted *biceps*. This is also not the case. Building on previous observations by many metricists, Ryan (2011: 49–51) has shown that the Homeric hexameter (and thus its poets and audiences) preferred "lighter" heavy syllables[48] when filling a *longum*, and "heavier" heavy syllables[49] when filling a contracted *biceps*. In other words, while, in theory, both the *longum* and the contracted *biceps* should contain the same amount of moras, in practice, their duration was different, and the *biceps* "being of greater duration, requires more stuffing" (West 1982: 39).

2.1.3   Incisions and Bridges

Preferences and Dispreferences for Word Ends

Our metrical scheme above (11) might seem thorough, but it is not complete yet. In fact, we could follow the scheme to the letter, and still

---

[46] One should note, however, that in musical notation, a *fermata* does not *replace* a given note, but is added in order to specify that that note (or rest), which is signaled in the score as having a precise duration, may be sustained indefinitely, after which tempo and rhythm resume as indicated.
[47] (*Elementa*) *bicipitia* is the plural of (*elementum*) *biceps* – i.e., the second element of a dactylic foot, which can be uncontracted (i.e., occupied by a sequence of two light syllables) or contracted (i.e., occupied by a single heavy syllable).
[48] These are heavy syllables whose rhyme contains a short vowel and a consonant (i.e., a VC rhyme).
[49] These are heavy syllables whose rhyme contains a long vowel (i.e., a VV rhyme).

end up with something that is not a well-formed hexameter, as seen in the nonsense example below:

(12)   αἰόλος αἰόλος αἰόλος αἰόλος αἰόλος ἵππος

What is the problem here? While we might have inferred above that word ends do not matter for the purposes of metrical scansion (since all words run together in *synapheia*), this is not entirely true. There are very precise preferences, some amounting to *metrical laws*, which specify where word ends can (and should, and cannot) occur within a line. In part, these preferences are thought to help avoid precisely the situation in the example above, in which feet boundaries and word boundaries coincide.[50]

Positions in the line where word end is very likely to occur are called *incisions*, places where word end is very unlikely to occur are called *bridges*. More specifically, incisions which occur within a metrical foot are called *caesuras*; incisions occurring at foot edges are called *diaereses*.[51] Note that, while each specific hexametric line (each *verse instance*, to use Jakobson's 1960 terminology) will have its unique combination of incisions (i.e., places where word end actually occurs), when we talk about *main incisions* and *bridges* of the hexameter, we are usually talking about statistical tendencies that hold over a given poetic corpus: it is these general statistical tendencies that are captured in our metrical schemes (known as *verse design* in Jakobson's terms).

The main incisions of the Homeric hexameter are undisputed: almost all hexameters (98 percent, according to West (1997: 222–23)) have an incision (caesura) in the third foot, either at 3a or, more frequently, at 3b (i.e., around the middle of the line, though, emphatically, not right at the middle: there is a bridge at 3c). If lines don't have an incision in the third foot (usually because a long word is getting in the way), they will then have an incision (caesura) in the fourth foot (4a). Additionally, very many hexameters (ca. 50 percent) have an incision (diaeresis) at 4c, right before the fifth foot. Hexameters also strictly avoid having an incision at 4b.[52] All of these phenomena have traditional names, sometimes multiple ones, which are given in Table 2.1.

The business of precisely identifying all main incisions and bridges in the Homeric hexameter would be relatively straightforward if everybody

---

[50] For this idea, which goes back to the ancient grammarians (and is attested in Priscian), see Bassett (1919: 366).
[51] This distinction is sometimes collapsed in modern times, and both incisions are called caesuras; see, for instance, West (1982).
[52] Exceptions occur about once in 550 lines, so, say, once in a short book (West 1997: 224).

Table 2.1 *Common incisions and bridges in the Homeric hexameter*

Phenomenon	Traditional terminology
Incision at 2a	Trithemimeral caesura
Incision at 3a	Penthemimeral caesura, Masculine caesura, P[53]
Incision at 3b	Feminine caesura, Caesura κατὰ τρίτον τροχαῖον, T
Bridge at 3c	Varro's bridge
Incision at 4a	Hephthemimeral caesura, H
Bridge at 4b	Hermann's bridge
Incision at 4c	Bucolic diaeresis, B

agreed on what counts as a word in the Homeric corpus. In practice, scholars working on the Homeric hexameter and its laws have used two distinct definitions of "word" in their statistics: the orthographic word (i.e., whatever is spelled between two blanks), and the so-called metrical word (*Wortbild* in German classical scholarship, plural *Wortbilder*).[54] The main difference in these approaches is that the first one considers enclitics and proclitics as their own words, while the second approach considers them parts of the words they rely on for accentual purposes.[55] Unsurprisingly, different definitions yield different statistics.[56] This discrepancy does not really impact the main incisions and bridges (nobody, for instance, doubts the incisions of the third foot, or Hermann's bridge), but it fuels the debate about which of the so-called secondary incisions should be regarded as more salient (to which we will turn in the next section).

Thankfully, Hagel (1994: 90) provides a statistical account of incisions and bridges in the *Iliad* which takes into account both orthographic words and *Wortbilder*. His results are given in Figure 2.4. Based on the data for

---

[53] The notation using capital letters was introduced by White (1912: 152).
[54] The definition of "word" is a complicated problem in linguistic typology. For an overview of the literature and some criteria for defining "word" in different languages, see Dixon and Aikhenvald (2007). In current terminology, one might speak of the *orthographic word*, the *morphological word*, and the *prosodic word*. While these concepts overlap in many cases, they often diverge when it comes to enclitic elements: consider Latin *populusque* "and the people," spelled as a single orthographic word, consisting of two morphological words (the noun *populus* and the conjunction *que*), and pronounced as a single prosodic word [popuˈluskʷe].
[55] As we shall see in the next section, this distinction is a little more complicated than it might seem.
[56] For instance, the famous tables by O'Neill (1942) and Porter (1951) are based on orthographic words, while Fränkel (1926) is based on the *Wortbild* (close to the modern concept of the prosodic word). Hagel (2004) provides new tables following O'Neill's structure, but adding several improvements: among these is a more accurate treatment of appositives.

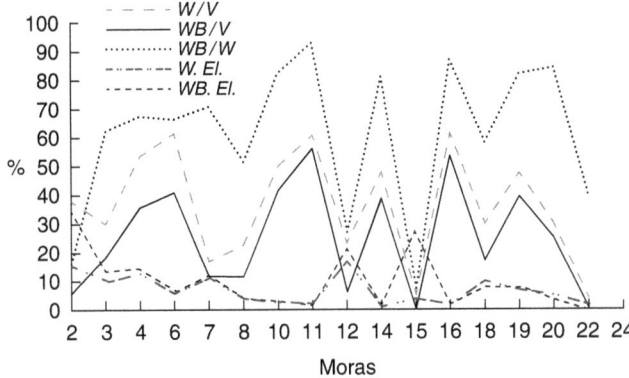

Figure 2.4 Statistics on incisions and bridges in the *Iliad* (from Hagel 1994: 90), showing:
1. The percentage of orthographic word ends at the given position in the line (W/V)
2. The percentage of *Wortbild* ends at the given position in the line (WB/V)
3. The percentage of *Wortbild* ends to orthographic word ends at the given position in the line (WB/W)
4. The percentage of elided words at orthographic word ends at the given position in the line (W.El.)
5. The percentage of elided words at *Wortbild* ends at the given position in the line (WB.El.)

Wortbilder (which, ultimately, is very close to the data on orthographic words), we can set up the following frequency ranking:[57]

- Incisions that occur in over 50 percent of the verses: 3b and 4c
- Incisions that occur in around 40 percent of the verses: 2a, 3a, 4a, and 5b
- Bridges that hold in close to 100 percent of the verses: 4b and 6a
- Bridges that hold in close to 90 percent of the verses: 3c

Hagel's data on elision suggests that bridges are also places in the line where elision (both between words and *Wortbilder*) is particularly likely to occur (and this seems especially to be the case for 4b and 3c). Finally, his data on the coincidence of orthographic word end and *Wortbild* end suggests that in over 90 percent of cases, clitics are not separated from their host word at incisions (and this tendency is particularly sharp at 3b, 4a, and 4c).

---

[57] A very fine-grained discussion of the structure of the hexameter and its incisions, with many interesting observations, is provided by Blanc (2008: Chapter 1).

84   Meter

Table 2.2 *Incisions in the two hexameters from Nestor's Cup*

1	2	3	4	5	6	Positions of word ends
ὅ̱ς.δ' ἄν.,|	τοῦ.δε.|πί.,	η̱.σι.|πο.,	τη̱.ρί.ου.,|	αὐ.τί.κα.,|	κει̱.νον	1c, 2b, **3b**, 4c, 5c
ἴ̱.με.ρο.,|	ς αἰ.ρή́.,	σει.|καλ.,	λισ.τε.φά.,	νου.|Ἀ.φρο.,	δί.τη̱ς	1c, **3a**, 5a

    What is the relationship between incisions and bridges? At least intuitively, it makes sense to regard them as two faces of the same coin – to think of incisions as "being guarded" by bridges. If I am really striving, for instance, to have a word end at either 3a, 3b, or at 4a, it makes sense that I would avoid a word end at 3c and at 4b. Similarly, if I am striving to have a word end at 6b, it makes sense that I would avoid one at 6a.[58] The reverse reasoning can also be applied: if I know I cannot end a word at 3c,[59] my options are to end it at 3a, 3b, or 4a.[60]

    We can now go back to our lines from Nestor's cup and identify where the incisions (i.e., word ends) are located in the line (I mark them in Table 2.2 with a vertical line).

    For the purposes of this exercise, I consider ὅς δ' ἄν and τοῦδε as two metrical words. Of the main incisions discussed so far, the first verse has a so-called feminine caesura (3b), followed by a bucolic diaeresis (4c). Additional incisions occur between the first and the second foot, in the second foot, and between the fifth and sixth foot. The second verse has a masculine caesura (3a) in the third foot, as well as an incision in the first and fifth foot.

    In the second verse, the first foot presents us with an interesting problem: should we say that there is an incision in 1c? While, following from the principles explained above, we might infer that the answer should be no (the word ἵμερος does not end at 1c, since its last consonant, the [s], is serving as an onset for the following syllable in 2a), in the practice of scanning the hexameter, 1c would usually be considered a word end. I have

---

[58] For a discussion of the few exceptions to this bridge, see Blanc (2008: 29–30).
[59] For a discussion of the few exceptions to this bridge, see Blanc (2008: 31–32).
[60] The more philosophical question as to whether any of this intuitive reasoning is true, in the sense of whether incisions or bridges (or both) should be regarded as primary, goes beyond the scope of this chapter.

not found any argument to justify this practice, which might deserve further investigation. It is in fact rather common for main caesuras to depend on this type of phenomenon. See, for instance, *Iliad* 1.7, which we would normally say shows a word end at 3a (as well as one at 4a, for good measure):

(13)   Ἀτρεΐδης τε ἄναξ|³ᵃ ἀνδρῶν|⁴ᵃ καὶ δῖος Ἀχιλλεύς (*Il.* 1.7)

the lord of men son of Atreus and divine Achilles.

Here, the word-final sequence [ks] in ἄναξ is split between the coda of the previous syllable [nak], and the onset of the following [san]. This happens similarly in *Iliad* 1.10, where we would usually say there is a word end at 3b (and again one at 4a), even though the word-final [n] in κακήν ought to be syllabified with the following word. And it happens again in *Iliad* 1.11, where we would say there is a word end at 3a, though the word-final [n] of Χρύσην straddles the word boundary.

(14)   νοῦσον ἀνὰ στρατὸν ὄρσε|³ᵇ κακήν|⁴ᵃ ὀλέκοντο δὲ λαοί
         οὕνεκα τὸν Χρύσην|³ᵃ ἠτίμασεν ἀρητῆρα (*Il.* 1.10–11)

he unleashed a terrible plague among the army, and the people were dying because he had offended Khrúsēs, the priest.

Examples could be multiplied. Additionally, caesuras often happen despite elisions,[61] as the 3b caesura in *Iliad* 1.2 below:

(15)   οὐλομένην, ἣ μυρί'|³ᵇ Ἀχαιοῖς ἄλγε' ἔθηκε (*Il.* 1.2)

ruinous, which brought countless sufferings upon the Achaeans

As seen in the examples above, each individual verse (i.e., each verse instance) has as many incisions as it has word ends, and it can have more than one "main" incision (i.e., incisions that are very frequent in a given corpus). The question as to whether some incisions are structurally or hierarchically more important than others (as opposed to merely more frequent) is a complex one, which we will tackle in the next section.

Reading the Hexameter Out Loud

In the practice of reading the hexameter out loud, we might wonder whether we should mark any of the incisions above with a pause (especially the "main" ones). It seems unlikely that pausing at incisions was part of the Greek practice, since, unlike at the end of the line, there are no systematic

---

[61] This is known as Hermann's law, or *elisio non officit caesurae* "elision does not prevent caesura," from Gottfried Hermann's seminal work on classical metrics (Hermann 1816: 33).

metrical licenses or allowances for hiatus at verse-internal incisions.[62] Similarly, in the recordings of performed oral poetry in the South Slavic epic tradition studied by Parry and Lord, there are no perceptible pauses at line-internal incisions.[63]

In a classroom setting, the practice of pausing might be used in order to signal the location of the main incisions to ourselves or to others. Far from recreating the original conditions of performance, and just like our practice of stressing *elementa longa* (i.e., the first element in a dactylic foot), pausing at incisions may be used as an artificial means of making metrical structures more explicit, and thus more easily perceptible to a modern audience. It might also be a good learning strategy to adopt when becoming familiar with the practice of scanning the line. An equally legitimate choice, which might be indicated for a more expressive reading of the text, is to mark incisions with a pause only when the sense warrants it (for instance, when we find a strong punctuation mark). In the end, there is no one correct way of reading the hexameter today, just different compromises that we can strike for different purposes.

2.2 The Colometry of the Hexameter and the Prosodic Hierarchy

2.2.1 *The Colometry of the Hexameter*

So far, we have seen that the metrical structure of the hexameter cares about syllables (their weight, and how they are grouped into dactylic feet) as well as about words (and more specifically, word ends). Are there any metrical requirements that apply to constituents larger than the word (e.g., the phrase, or the sentence)? This is when things get trickier – and arguably more intriguing.

As we shall see, this question bears directly on the problem of the *colometry* of the hexameter – the much-debated question as to whether we should regard the hexameter as being made up of smaller chunks (i.e., *cola*) stitched together at the main incisions. Depending on the theory, these cola are conceived of as metrical or linguistic units, and their being stitched

---

[62] Presence of word end, tolerance for hiatus, and tolerance for *brevis in longo* (in contemporary terms, a light syllable occupying a heavy element) are the three criteria that August Böckh (1811–21) first developed for establishing the position of line ends in Pindar. According to Böckh's reasoning, these criteria can be taken to indicate the potential presence of a pause (which would in turn indicate the line end). For the history of the scholarship on pauses within the hexameter, see Hagel (1994), fn. 34.

[63] For the caesura in South Slavic epic poetry, see Jakobson (1960: 364–65). Audio recordings for Milman Parry's Collection of Oral Literature are available here: https://curiosity.lib.harvard.edu/milman-parry-collection-of-oral-literature.

together is seen as a synchronic fact or a diachronic process (or both). Beyond getting the synchronic facts about the hexameter right, colometric theories of the hexameter attempt to answer the question as to why incisions and bridges exist at all, what purpose they serve, and how they originate.

Perhaps the most famous colometric theory of the hexameter is that developed by Hermann Fränkel in two influential papers (Fränkel 1926, 1955, which actually present two slightly different accounts of the Homeric hexameter). In a nutshell, Fränkel argues that the main points of incision in the line are to be understood as *Sinnesgliederungen* "sense divisions," and that a poet composing a line is effectively joining together units of meaning at these points.[64] Several contributions have followed, either supporting or rejecting Fränkel's account.[65]

2.2.2 What Are the Constituents of the Hexameter?

The first step on this path is to establish what we mean by "constituents larger than the word," and clarify whether we are thinking about syntactic units (i.e., the phrase, the sentence), semantic units (as often invoked – and not often clearly defined – in various colometric approaches to the hexameter), or something else entirely. A lot of confusion in the discussion of the internal structure of the hexameter is in fact rooted in a lack of clarity in these matters. The main methodological innovation in my treatment is that I will introduce some concepts and theoretical insights from the fields of generative phonology and metrics. These tools, I hope to show, will help make our discussion clearer and, ultimately, more productive.

Recent work in generative metrics has argued that the units that are relevant for metrics are not syntactic or semantic, but *prosodic*.[66] That is to

---

[64] Fränkel's scheme is as follows:

$$^1-|_a\smile|_b\smile_{c} |\qquad ^2-_a|\smile_b\smile_{c},\; ^3-_a|\smile_b|\smile_{c},\qquad ^4-_a|\smile_b\smile_{c}|\; ^5-_a\smile_b\smile_{c},\qquad ^6-_a-_c$$
$$\quad\; 1\; 2\; 3\qquad\qquad\quad 4\qquad\quad 1\; 2\qquad\qquad\quad 1\qquad 2$$
$$\qquad\quad\; A\qquad\qquad\qquad\qquad B\qquad\qquad\qquad\qquad C$$

In Fränkel's system, each incision can be realized either through a "strong" semantic boundary (e.g., the end of a sentence), or, alternatively, through a "weak" boundary (i.e., the end of a word). Perturbations of the system are due to "heavy words" (i.e., words containing six or more moras) stretching over a place of incision. In Homer, the last two incisions (B and C) appear to be more rigidly regulated than the first one (A), and strong semantic boundaries are avoided in the last two feet.

[65] Among these, see O'Neill (1942), Porter (1951), Kirk (1966), Ingalls (1970), Barnes (1986), Higbie (1990), Kahane (1994), and Cantilena (1995). A useful survey of the debate is given in Martinelli (2001).

[66] This was proposed as a general principle of metrics by Hayes (1989), who called it *the Hypothesis of Phonological Metrics*. It states that "meter is essentially a phonological phenomenon" (Hayes 1989:

say, poetic meter can specify where the boundaries of a given prosodic unit should be, but we know of no meters that specify where a given syntactic structure (or semantic unit) should or should not occur in the line. Meter, in other words, is prosodic in nature. In order to answer the question above, then (i.e., what are the constituents of the Homeric hexameter), we need to turn to the prosodic hierarchy.

2.2.3 The Prosodic Hierarchy

Linguistic structure is hierarchical: a sentence, for instance, is not a plain concatenation of words, but rather a sequence of syntactic constituents that are embedded in one another. Thus many of us have learned in school that a simple transitive sentence like "the cat eats the fish" can be diagrammed as follows:

(16) [[the cat]_{Noun Phrase} [eats [the fish]_{Noun Phrase}]_{Verb Phrase}]_{Sentence}

These hierarchical relationships can also be represented by a tree diagram, as in Figure 2.5.[67]

A relatively more recent discovery is that *phonology* works in a similar way. When we speak, we assemble phonetic material into ever-increasing prosodic domains: we group sounds into syllables, syllables into words, words into phrases, and so on – all the way to a complete utterance. And while these categories might remind us of the syntactic structures seen above, they are actually different. An entire subfield of linguistics is in fact dedicated to establishing how syntactic constituents are mapped onto the phonology (i.e., the syntax–phonology interface) and thus "packaged" into prosodic units.[68] In short, the structures are often very similar (mostly because syntactic information is used to decide how to build prosodic domains), but mismatches may arise due to prosodic constraints (we will see some examples below). As mentioned above, it is these prosodic domains, rather than syntactic ones, that are relevant for metrics.

---

224), and that "metrical rules never refer to syntactic bracketing, only to prosodic bracketing" (ibid.). Of course, plenty of poetic traditions exist in which the poetic form is based on syntactic and semantic parallelism (see Fabb 2015: Chapter 6) instead of meter. In this sense, there can be poetry for which prosodic constituency is irrelevant, while semantic and syntactic constituency matter. But this is not the kind of poetry that we find, prototypically, in the Greek and English traditions.

[67] While syntactic trees might be synonymous, for many, with generative linguistics, they originate several decades earlier in American structuralism (for a history of prestructuralist and structuralist approaches to syntax, see Seuren 2015). The first drawn tree diagram in the linguistic literature is found in Nida (1946: 87), for the sentence "Peasants in China work very hard" (Seuren 2015: 144). In current syntactic theories, of course, the tree given below would look rather different in some regards.

[68] A useful recent handbook presentation is Selkirk (2011).

The Colometry of the Hexameter and the Prosodic Hierarchy

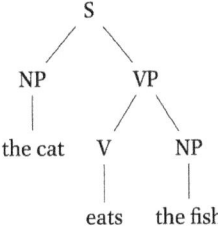

Figure 2.5 A simple syntactic tree of the sentence "the cat eats the fish"

The general repertoire of prosodic domains is called the *prosodic hierarchy*, and has been established as follows by the work of Nespor and Vogel (1986 [2007]):

(17) syllable > foot > phonological word > clitic group > phonological phrase > intonational phrase > phonological utterance.

We are already familiar with some of these concepts, namely the syllable, foot,[69] phonological word, and clitic group (this latter concept is similar to that of the metrical word). What interests us for the current purposes are the domains larger than the clitic group, namely the phonological phrase, the intonational phrase, and the phonological utterance (together, these larger units can be called *prosodic phrases*).

The main way we can tell these domains exist is that different phonological processes apply to different domains within the hierarchy. For instance, some languages have a rule of *final devoicing*[70] that operates at the end of large prosodic phrases (like Icelandic), some at the end of words (like Russian and Polish), and some at the end of syllables (like German and Dutch).

Similarly, there are several phonological changes that apply in connected speech,[71] but only within small groups of closely connected words

---

[69] As we shall see below, it is not just meter that groups syllables into feet. The phonology of (arguably most) languages, including Ancient Greek, does so too. See Bennett (2012) for a survey of the evidence for prosodic feet across languages.

[70] By *final devoicing* we mean a phonological process by which a voiced segment (i.e., a segment pronounced with vibration of the vocal folds), typically a stop, will become voiceless (i.e., pronounced without vibration of the vocal folds) at the end of a given domain. See, for instance, the alternation, in German, between voiceless [k] and voiced [g] in the words *Tag* [tak] "day" and *Tage* [tage] "days".

[71] The general term for these types of phenomena is *sandhi* "putting together" (of sounds), from Sanskrit *sam* "with" and *dhi-* "put." Sandhi phenomena can be broadly thought of as processes that simplify the pronunciation of connected linguistic units, typically, but not exclusively, through various types of *assimilation* (i.e., making two or more linguistic segments more articulatorily similar

(and not, say, across the entire utterance). This is the case for Italian *raddoppiamento fonosintattico* "phonosyntactic gemination," a process which causes some word-initial consonants to geminate when following a word ending in a vowel. This process operates within the *phonological phrase*. In the example below, for instance (adapted from Nespor and Vogel 1986 [2007: 171]), *raddoppiamento* only operates between the underlined segments, and not across the whole sentence.

(18) Ho visto tre colibrí molto belli

I saw three very pretty hummingbirds

The domains within which *raddoppiamento* operates can be notated as follows (where φ stands for phonological phrase):

(19) [Ho visto]$_φ$ [tre colibrí]$_φ$ [molto belli]$_φ$

What is important to note here is that the domains in this example do not constitute separate syntactic constituents (Nespor and Vogel 1986 [2007: 171]). Rather, they are separate *prosodic* domains – that is, domains in which words are grouped for the purposes of pronunciation.[72]

Evidence for phonological phrases can be found in many other languages. In Sanskrit, external *sandhi* mostly operates within phonological phrases,[73] and so do various assimilations of final consonants to following initial consonants in Ancient Greek (Devine and Stephens 1994: 397–98).

The domain larger than the phonological phrase is called the *intonational phrase*. In Ancient Greek, this is the domain in which elision operates. Typically, an intonational phrase will be associated with a specific intonational contour or tune (hence the term intonational

---

to each other). This is, for instance, what happens inside the very word *sandhi*, where the /m/ in the preposition /sam/ has been changed to [n] in order to match the dental place of articulation of the following /d/. Sandhi can happen inside a word (*internal sandhi*) or between words (*external sandhi*). A type of *external sandhi* common in some dialects of British English is the so-called intrusive [r], whereby (under some phonological conditions) a nonetymological sound [r] is inserted in order to prevent hiatus at a word boundary, as in the phrase *law*[r] *and order*.

[72] Examples of the mismatch between syntactic and prosodic domains could be multiplied. Hayes (1989: 239), for instance, discusses the English phrase "the great lakes," which is made up of a clitic element (the definite article) plus two monosyllabic words. Here, while the syntax groups together *great* and *lakes* as complements of the determiner *the* (thus forming a Noun Phrase which is embedded in a Determiner Phrase, headed by *the*), the prosody shows a different bracketing: the need for clitic *the* to find a prosodic host causes it to form a domain with adjacent *great*, and *lakes* is left to form its own domain.
syntax: [the [great lakes]$_{NP}$]$_{DP}$
prosody: [[the great]C [lakes]C]φ

[73] For a description of *sandhi* phenomena in Sanskrit according to prosodic domains (specifically at the level of the utterance, the phrase, and the word), see Selkirk (1980).

phrase). Intonational phrases can sometimes be more tricky to identify, since *speech rate* can affect their formation. In example (20) below, a careful pronunciation like (a) allows for more fine-grained grouping (and pausing), while an allegro pronunciation might collapse more phonetic material into a single domain (c) (Nespor and Vogel 1986 [2007: 58]):

(20) a. [The frog]$_I$ [ate a fly]$_I$ [for lunch]$_I$
      b. [The frog]$_I$ [ate a fly for lunch]$_I$
      c. [The frog ate a fly for lunch]$_I$

We will see that the "stretchiness" of prosodic phrases will provide us with some challenges when it comes to identifying the constituents of the Homeric hexameter.

While we have so far talked about phonological processes as a source of evidence for prosodic constituency, there are other sources too. One is punctuation: in Ancient Greek inscriptions, for instance, interpuncts can be used to mark the edges of different prosodic constituents (Devine and Stephens 1994: 326–30): some inscriptions are (prosodic-)word-marking, some phrase-marking. Nestor's cup above seems to be using interpuncts to mark *phonological phrases*.

Another important source of information on prosodic constituency is clitics. In Ancient Greek (as well as some other old Indo-European languages), some types of clitics are required to always occupy the second position within a given prosodic domain (i.e., they need to immediately follow the first word in that domain).[74] The position of clitics in a sentence can thus give us information as to where given prosodic domains begin and end.

The prosodic domains in Ancient Greek have been discussed in great detail by Devine and Stephens (1994), who use slightly different terminology, as well as, most recently, by Goldstein (2014) (whose specific focus is the behavior of clitics). Table 2.3 gives the relevant terminology (and abbreviations) for the prosodic hierarchy in Ancient Greek, along with examples (adapted from Nestor's cup). Since phenomena similar to these have been discussed within classical rhetoric or metrics, equivalent or near-equivalent terminology is also provided in the table.

---

[74] This phenomenon is traditionally referred to as *Wackernagel's law* (for which now see Goldstein 2014): in the first line of the *Odyssey*, the position of the clitic personal pronoun μοι "to me," immediately following the first word ἄνδρα "man," is an example of Wackernagel's law.

Table 2.3 *The prosodic hierarchy in Ancient Greek*

Nespor and Vogel (1986 [2007]), Hayes (1989)	Devine and Stephens (1994)	Goldstein (2014)	Classical terminology near-equivalent	Examples[75]
		mora (μ)	mora	
syllable (σ)	syllable	syllable (σ)	syllable	.με._σ
foot (Σ)	foot	foot (Σ)	foot (in metrics)	(ἵ)_Σ(με.ρο)_Σ
phonological word (ω)	word	prosodic word (ω)	orthographic word	[ἵμερος]_ω
clitic group (C)	appositive group	recursive prosodic word (ω)	metrical word	[[ἵμερος]_ω τε]_C [[ἵμερος]_{ωmin} τε]_{ωmax}
phonological phrase (φ)	minor phrase	phonological phrase (φ)	comma/colon	[[ἵμερος]_ω [αἱρήσει]_ω]_φ
intonational phrase (I)	major phrase	intonational phrase (ι)	colon	[[[ἵμερος]_ω [αἱρήσει]_ω]_φ [[καλλιστεφάνου]_ω [Ἀφροδίτης]_ω]_φ]_ι
utterance (U)	sentence, utterance	utterance (υ)	sentence/period	

2.2.4 Mapping Prosody onto Meter: The Hexameter and Its Prosodic Constituents

When poets compose a metrical text, then, they take prosodic constituents of different sizes and map them onto metrical structures. They take syllables and map them onto metrical elements, and they also use those syllables to build metrical feet of a given shape;[76] they take phonological phrases made of words and map them onto metrical cola; finally, they take groups of phonological phrases (typically amounting to an intonational phrase) and

---

[75] The standard phonological notation is to separate syllables with periods (.), to use parentheses for feet, and to use square brackets for larger domains.

[76] The regular phonology of the language also builds feet, only of a different shape. Ancient Greek, for instance, built a type of foot called the *moraic trochee* – i.e., a sequence made up of either one heavy syllable (–) or two light syllables (⏑⏑), in which the first syllable is the strong member of the foot. The effects of footing can be seen in derivational morphology (Gunkel 2010, 2011) as well as in the assignment of the recessive accent (Sauzet 1989, Golston 1990). For an introduction to metrical feet and their designations, see Hayes (1995: 62–85). The terminology, which might be confusing for classicists, is based on English metrics, where, for instance, a trochee is not a sequence of a heavy and a light, but a sequence of a strong/stressed position followed by a weak/unstressed one. For an in-depth discussion of Ancient Greek foot structure (and the data used to establish it), see Devine and Stephens (1994: 102–17), and, from a theoretical perspective, Golston (1990).

Table 2.4 *Prosodic constituents and their metrical equivalents*

Prosody	Meter
Syllable	Metrical element
Foot	Metrical foot
Clitic group/recursive prosodic word	Metrical word
Phonological phrase	Metrical colon
Intonational phrase	Line

map them onto a complete line.[77] From this point of view, it can be helpful then to talk about "metrical equivalents" of the prosodic hierarchy, as detailed in Table 2.4.[78]

How does this work in practice for the Homeric hexameter, and how does this help us? Armed with these new categories, we shall look at different efforts of segmenting the hexameter into smaller cola, as well as the decades-long debate on enjambement in Homer.

Intonational Phrases and Intonation Units
Since we have just been discussing the concepts of intonational phrase, it might be useful to introduce the concept of *intonation unit*, which comes from a different tradition of linguistics (namely the study of spoken discourse by Wallace Chafe and his school), and has already been profitably applied to the study of Homer by the work of Egbert Bakker (1997). Bakker (1997: 53) has argued that most Homeric hexameters are made up of several intonation units, and that formulas in themselves are "stylized intonation units."

Intonation units are largely equivalent to the concept of intonational phrase (they can be surrounded by pauses, they have a distinctive intonational contour), and are seen as units of discourse production as well as processing: they are the audible chunks in which spoken language is produced and understood.[79] Syntactically, intonation units tend to correspond to whole grammatical units (Croft 1995). In the transcription of

---

[77] Of course, these processes (like most of a speaker's linguistic competence) are largely unconscious.
[78] See Golston and Riad (2000, 2005) for an application of these principles to several Ancient Greek meters.
[79] Noticing intonation units might require some conscious effort, since they largely blend together in our perception of speech (much like the separate frames in a film blend together in our experience of a movie). Listening to a recorded spoken narrative (like the one in Table 2.5), while paying attention to pauses, hesitations, and intonational tunes, can in this sense be an eye-opening experience.

Table 2.5 *A Pear Story, recorded at the University of California, Los Angeles, on April 16, 2014*[80]

a.	there was A FARMER,	v.	(.39) [laughs] and,
b.	(.1) who was picking	w.	(.6) mmm
c.	(.3) PEARS.	x.	(.57) then then some KIDS came along,
d.	(.3) he put the pears into the basket,	y.	and helped him back up,
e.	.. and then he went up into the tree,	z.	they picked up his PEARS.
f.	(.6) but then A KID came along,	aa.	(.5) for him(?) the pears had fallen over,
g.	(.4) and he took'em,	bb.	(.84) mm
h.	(.88) the kid put'em on his BIKE	cc.	(.16) cause he fell over,
i.	which was also probably stolen,	dd.	(.45) and then the kids kept walking along the way,
j.	(.6) and he was RIDING down –	ee.	(.13) the kid went off into the DISTANCE.
k.	(.4) a path –	ff.	.. and then at the VERY end,
l.	.. and then,	gg.	(.9) the KIDS,
m.	(1.17) he went to,	hh.	(1.44) passed by the,
n.	(.6) past a girl,	ii.	(1.38) farmer,
o.	(.46) he was checking her out –	jj.	(.18) again,
p.	(.1) but WHILE checking her out,	kk.	and the farmer sees them.
q.	(.69) he HIT a rock,	ll.	(.21) with the pears.
r.	(.22) and,	mm.	(1.101) and he,
s.	(.63) fell over.	nn.	(.53) and that's where it ends.
t.	(.72) and then he CRIED.		
u.	(.66) uh no he didn't really cry.		

natural speech corpora, each intonation unit is written as a separate line. Beyond the optional presence of pauses and the presence of a distinct intonational contour, intonation units can also be set apart by changes in voice quality and pace of delivery (Chafe 1994: 69). An example of a short narrative segmented in intonation units is given in Table 2.5.

In spontaneous discourse, intonation units have an average length of two to three seconds, and tend to contain a number of syllables spanning from five to ten, though languages with simpler syllable structures can fit more syllables in each unit (Fenk-Oczlon and Fenk 2002: 223–24). In Chafe's view, each intonation unit usually represents the verbalization of a single *idea unit* (Chafe 1980: 13). Because of the unplanned nature of this type of speech, some units are very short, and some are longer, reflecting the challenges of online discourse processing: some intonation units

---

[80] Notational conventions: each line is an *intonation unit*. A falling intonation (suggesting closure) at the end of a unit is marked by a period. A rising intonation (suggesting continuation), by a comma. A flat intonation (also suggesting continuation), by a dash. The numbers in parenthesis at the beginning of each line are the duration of the pause that preceded it, in seconds. Short pauses, of the duration of less than 0.1 seconds, are marked with two periods. *Capitalized* words carried sentential stress (i.e., they were noticeably louder than their surrounding context).

correspond to a single word (c, ii); some to a phrase (k, ll); in some cases, they correspond to a clause (a, q) or even to a complete sentence (o, z). It is reasonable to assume that many intonation units in this type of unplanned narration will be considerably shorter than they would be in, say, a reading task.

Bakker, starting from the premise that Homeric poetry is, primarily, speech, has attempted to recover the segmentation of intonation units in the Homeric poems. The idea is that this way of segmenting the text might enable us to better appreciate some qualities of Homer's style. Bakker (1997: 147) starts from the assumption that the hexameter itself is too long to contain a single intonation unit, and he uses metrical, syntactic, and phonological criteria (such as the presence of elision and the behavior of clitics) to decide where to divide the text. An example of Bakker's division is given in Table 2.6.

Bakker's divisions largely break the verse into hemistichs, and often encompass a single syntactic clause (sometimes embedded clauses are included, and sometimes they form their own intonation unit, such as in lines e and f below). Like many other previous attempts at segmenting the hexameter into units of meaning, results might be hard to perfectly replicate – since different readers might have different intuitions as to when a unit should end or begin. An updated take on Bakker's methodology is now presented in Janse (2021).

Are Bakker's intonation units actually (and consistently) intonational phrases? This is where things get complicated. Bakker's approach seems to contradict Devine and Stephens (1994: 398), who have argued that *the whole verse* is the prototypical major phrase (intonational phrase) in Ancient Greek, while the hemistich is the prototypical minor phrase (phonological phrase). Can both approaches be right? Verses like 521 and 522 in Table 2.6, where a new clause starts in the middle of the line, can be taken as cases of a line possibly containing two intonational phrases (as Bakker also suggests). On the other hand, a verse like 520 could be analyzed as a single intonational phrase. Thus it might be that Bakker is really segmenting the text into units that are sometimes phonological phrases and sometimes intonational phrases that happen to be shorter than the verse, and not consistently into intonational phrases (note that, in Chafe's framework as adopted by Bakker, these two entities are simply not distinguished).

A further level of complication is added by the speech rate (or *phonostyle*, as defined by Devine and Stephens 1978). The recitation of epic happened at a slower pace than other genres: this can be seen from some metrical evidence related to the behavior of clitics (see Devine and Stephens 1994:

Table 2.6 *Bakker's division of the hexameter in intonation units (after Bakker 1997: 66–67)*

Original (division in hexameter lines)		Bakker's division in intonation units		Bakker's translation
517.	(...) ἀμφὶ δέ μοι χεὶρ	a.	(...) ἀμφὶ δέ μοι χεὶρ	a. And on both sides my arm,
518.	ὀξείῃς ὀδύνῃσιν ἐλήλαται, οὐδέ μοι αἷμα	b.	ὀξείῃς ὀδύνῃσιν ἐλήλαται,	b. By sharp pain it is struck,
519.	τερσῆναι δύναται, βαρύθει δέ μοι ὦμος ὑπ' αὐτοῦ·	c.	οὐδέ μοι αἷμα τερσῆναι δύναται,	c. And my blood, it cannot dry,
		d.	βαρύθει δέ μοι ὦμος ὑπ' αὐτοῦ·	d. And it aches, my shoulder under it,
520.	ἔγχος δ' οὐ δύναμαι σχεῖν ἔμπεδον, οὐδὲ μάχεσθαι	e.	ἔγχος δ' οὐ δύναμαι σχεῖν ἔμπεδον,	e. And my spear I cannot hold fast,
		f.	οὐδὲ μάχεσθαι	f. And not fight either,
521.	ἐλθὼν δυσμενέεσσιν. ἀνὴρ δ' ὤριστος ὄλωλε	g.	ἐλθὼν δυσμενέεσσιν.	g. Going against enemy men,
		h.	ἀνὴρ δ' ὤριστος ὄλωλε	h. And the best man, he is dead,
522.	Σαρπηδών Διὸς υἱός· ὃ δ' οὐ οὗ παιδὸς ἀμύνει.	i.	Σαρπηδών Διὸς υἱός·	i. Sarpedon, Zeus's son,
(*Il.* 16.517–22)		j.	ὃ δ' οὐ οὗ παιδὸς ἀμύνει.	j. And he, he does not even protect his son.

232–34), as well as from typological comparison. For instance, the modern Cretan epic tradition studied by James Notopoulos (1964: 6), has a speech rate of 9.6 fifteen-syllable verses sung per minute (2.4 syllables/second), which is significantly slower than ordinary Modern Greek (8 syllables/second).[81] As seen above, a low speech rate encourages the formation of smaller intonational phrases. In this sense, the small units into which Bakker breaks down the hexameter might (under some performance conditions) be realized as separate intonational phrases after all.

So what is the solution? The key here is to keep in mind that prosodic phrases (such as phonological phrases and intonational phrases) are likely *recursive*,[82] meaning that, for instance, two small phonological phrases can be grouped into a large phonological phrase, which can in turn be grouped into an intonational phrase, which in turn can be grouped into a yet larger intonational phrase. In other words, two levels of analysis (phonological phrase and intonational phrase) are often not enough, and we might be looking at nested domains.

As far as the hexameter is concerned, there is good evidence to suggest that the entire line most often coincides with a complete prosodic unit, and that this prosodic unit was an intonational phrase. Several metrical properties that we observe at the line end can in fact be understood as the "grammaticalization" of prototypical features of the right edge of an intonational phrase. The smaller prosodic units in which the verse can be divided (i.e., the cola of the hexameter in traditional terminology, or Bakker's intonation units) can be labeled as phonological phrases or (occasionally) lower-ranking intonational phrases.[83] In what follows, we'll explore some additional and intriguing data on the prosodic make-up of the hexameter. In particular, we will ask: did the Homeric hexameter have a specific tune, or melodic contour?

Intonational Phrases, Tunes, and the Melodic Contour of the Hexameter
Many modern European languages, including English and Modern Greek, can be defined as *intonation languages*, in that they use "phrase-level pitch

---

[81] Dauer (1980: 24).
[82] See discussion in Féry (2017: 78–93). This is a relatively recent development in the field, where the original assumption was that prosodic domains would follow the *strict layering hypothesis* (cf. Hayes 1989).
[83] Allan (2021) has argued that the cola of the hexameter (which he identifies in Fränkel's tradition) most often match a single discourse act within the framework of Functional Discourse Grammar (Hengeveld and Mackenzie 2008).

patterns to convey abstract meanings of their own, usually related to the structure of the utterance" (Hayes 2009a: 292).[84] These pitch patterns (or *tunes*) can be used, for instance, to distinguish between a statement or a question.[85] Tunes are generally thought to anchor to intonational phrases (Hayes 1989: 219), and are in fact one of the main ways intonational phrases are defined.[86]

In Ancient Greek, these phrase-level tunes[87] had to interact with word-level prominence (i.e., accent or stress), which was also realized primarily through pitch. In other words, strategies were present in the language to avoid clashes between word-level pitches and the phrase-level tunes. It is by studying these strategies that we can reconstruct a picture of the intonational properties of the Homeric hexameter. In particular, Hagel (1994) has gathered statistical evidence showing that the Homeric hexameter had a preferred *melody* – that is, a "prototypical" sequence of higher vs. lower tones. As we shall see, this "melody" can help us shed light on the colometric structure of the hexameter.

A key diagnostic in this sense is the distribution of *oxytone words* (i.e., words that have a high tone on their final syllable)[88] in the line, since the high tone at the end of these words "forces" the phrase-level tune to rise (Hagel 1994: 93); oxytone words, then, are preferred in positions where the phrase-level tune rises and conversely avoided in positions in the line where the phrase-level tune falls. By comparing the frequency of attested oxytones in given positions in the line as opposed to their expected distribution

---

[84] Examples of English tunes are, for instance, the *Declarative Tune* (used in answering an information-seeking question like "Where do you live?"), and the *Emphatic Question Tune* (used for asking a question like "Where do you live?"). Each tune is composed of a sequence of tones: for instance, the Declarative Tune is composed of the sequence MID – HIGH* – LOW, while the Emphatic Question Tune goes MID – LOW* – HIGH. Each tone within a tune has to be anchored to specific syllables within the phonological phrase; tones marked with an asterisk (*starred tones*) need to be anchored to the main word stress of a phrase or utterance (Hayes 2009a: 299).

[85] Try, for instance, uttering the word "Homer" or the phrase "at the end of the hexameter" as statements or as questions. This experiment will also show that the prosodic domains over which tunes are realized are "stretchy" (they can be realized over a single word or over a longer phrase).

[86] Additionally, "the ends of intonational phrases coincide with the positions in which pauses might be introduced in a sentence"; see Nespor and Vogel (1986 [2007: 188]).

[87] See Devine and Stephens (1994: 454–55) for a discussion of the distinction in pronunciation (Gk. ὑποκριτική "recitation") between questions and commands in Aristotle's *Poetics*.

[88] In *Iliad* 1.1–4, for instance, oxytone words include θεά, ἥ, πολλάς, and ψυχάς. Note that, in medieval manuscripts and modern printed editions, the convention is to spell oxytone words with a grave accent (instead of an acute) on the last syllable, unless they are followed by a clitic or punctuation. For an interpretation of this phenomenon, see Devine and Stephens (1994: 180–83), who argue that the grave represents a lowered high tone. See also Probert (2003: 16–18). This distinction does not impact our current discussion. In modern academic convention, the citation form of a Greek oxytone word is printed with an acute.

The Colometry of the Hexameter and the Prosodic Hierarchy 99

(based on the metrical shape of the word alone), Hagel calculates the average "melody" of the hexameter – that is, places where the pitch in the line rises vs. falls. The results of Hagel's study are given in Figure 2.6.

Let us focus on the "melody" line first (i.e., the top, solid line): here, we can roughly identify a sequence of three peaks separated by two troughs. The first two peaks are much more marked than the last, and all peaks decrease in height as we move to the end of the line. The first peak is at mora 8 (2c), followed by a trough which reaches its lowest point at mora 11 (3b); the second peak occupies moras 14 (4a) and 15 (4b), followed by another trough with its lowest point at mora 18 (5a). The last (small) peak is at mora 19 (5b), after which the line falls stepwise to reach its lowest point at mora 24 (6b, the end of the line).

What does this melody tell us? Let's start from the end of the line. It is very common crosslinguistically for the right edges (i.e., the end) of intonational phrases, and especially declarative ones, to be marked by a low tone, properly called a *low boundary tone*. Additionally, most languages show a phenomenon called *downstep* or *downtrend* (Devine and Stephens 1994: 435–55), whereby the pitch of an intonational phrase falls from the beginning to the end, such that, relatively speaking, high tones that come early in an intonational phrase are higher in pitch than subsequent ones. If we assume that the *average hexameter* corresponded to an intonational phrase, we can argue that the downstep, together with the low

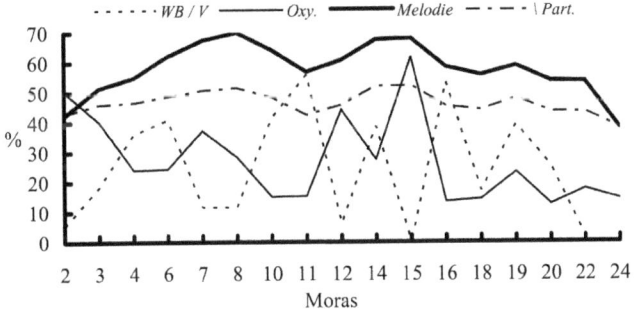

Figure 2.6 The preferred "melody" of the hexameter in the *Iliad* (after Hagel 1994: 100), showing:
1. The percentage of *Wortbild* ends at the given position in the line (WB/V)
2. The percentage of oxytone words to *Wortbild* ends at the given position in the line (Oxy.)
3. An alternative melody line calculated by leaving out postpositive particles (| Part)

boundary tone, is conspiring to inhibit rises in pitch (i.e., the presence of oxytones) in the last two feet of the line. At the same time, the low boundary tone is likely responsible for the sharp drop in pitch in the last syllable.[89]

Crosslinguistically, the ends of intonational phrases can also be marked by final lengthening and by the presence of a pause.[90] The end of the hexameter has metrical evidence for both phenomena: final lengthening can explain why the last element in the line is indifferent to quantity, and the (optional) presence of a pause is arguably what licenses hiatus between lines.[91] In a way, then, the end of the line can be seen as a "grammaticalized" end of intonational phrase.

Looking at the distribution of oxytone words can help us paint a more precise picture of the internal structure of the hexametric line. Figure 2.6 (the thinner, solid line) shows that oxytones are tendentially avoided at main points of incision in the line (such as 3a, 3b, and 4c), as well as in the last two feet. Conversely, oxytones are frequent at bridges (2b, 3c, and 4b). Both of these facts are puzzling if we think of the hexameter as a sequence of words, and bridges and incisions as places where words (orthographic or metrical) are allowed (or not allowed) to end. If that were the case, the accentuation of a given word should not affect whether it can stand at a place of incision or not.

The distribution of oxytones makes a lot more sense if we think of the hexameter as a sequence of *phonological phrases* (or, in general, of prosodic domains larger than the word): in this perspective, incisions are places

---

[89] Of course, not all intonational phrases end in a low boundary tone. Questions, for instance, typically end in a high tone (Devine and Stephens 1994: 453–55); high tone can also be used to indicate incompleteness (i.e., cases in which a sentence or "sense unit" is broken up between more intonational phrases). In Modern Greek, high boundary tones are used for a variety of occasions, including Continuation Rise, Suspicious Calling Contour, Questioning Calling Contour (Arvaniti and Baltazani 2000: 3). Interestingly, Hagel has compiled "melody line" statistics for verses with line-internal punctuation. These, we can extrapolate, are verses where a new clause begins somewhere in the middle of the line, which is then unlikely to be finished by the end of the sixth foot: in other words, these are verses that are likely to show enjambement with the next line. These verses, on average, tend to end with a rising pitch (Hagel 1994: 103), arguably indicating the presence of a high boundary tone (likely as part of a continuation rise) at the end of the line instead.

[90] Concerning intonational phrases (IPs) in Modern Greek, Arvaniti and Baltazani (2000: 3) write: "IPs (even non-final ones) may be followed by a lengthy pause, while pauses are rare after *ips* [i.e., *phonological phrases*] and always very short. It also seems likely that the IP (but not the ip) is the domain of downstep, pitch reset and final lengthening."

[91] In other words, Böckh's criteria of end of word, *brevis in longo*, and hiatus can really be seen as criteria for recovering the boundaries of the metrical equivalent of major intonational phrases in Greek verse.

where phonological phrases tend to end,[92] and bridges are places where the opposite is true.[93]

We know that phonological phrases in Modern Greek are marked by the presence of a phrase accent (H=high or L=low) at their right edge (Arvaniti and Baltazani 2000). The avoidance of oxytones at the main points of incisions might indicate that, in Ancient Greek, phonological phrases that ended at these points tended, on average, to be marked by low phrase accents, which would have clashed with the rise in pitch required by an oxytone. Occasionally, there might be more significant prosodic boundaries here, like the end of a clause (and thus the end of a lower-ranked intonational phrase), which might warrant a proper boundary tone as well (which would also have clashed with an oxytone). In other words, main points of incision repel oxytones, because these points typically host the right edge of phonological phrases, and these are typically marked by a lowering of the phrase-level tune, which is incompatible with realizing a high tone on the last mora of a word.

What about the greater amount of oxytone words (i.e., high tones) at bridges? If low tones, on average, tend to mark phrasal boundaries, high tones, by default, can indicate the absence of one, which is exactly what a bridge stipulates.

What types of constituents tend to end at the main points of incision? The absence of other metrical indications (*brevis in longo*, hiatus tolerance) suggests that we are looking at edges of domains that are less prominent than the end of the line – thus phonological phrases or lower-ranking intonational phrases.

The conclusions drawn so far – that is, that the smaller units within the line are phonological phrases, while the entire hexametric line is, prototypically, an intonational phrase, are confirmed by Hermann's observation that *elisio non officit caesurae* "elision does not prevent caesura" (Hermann 1816: 33). As we mentioned above, in Ancient Greek the intonational

---

[92] This tendency is present at other points of incision too (1c, 2a, 4a), only to a lesser degree, perhaps simply reflecting the lower frequency of word ends here.

[93] Cantilena (1995), for instance, has demonstrated that a ban of word ends in 2b (i.e., Meyer's law, which holds for the Alexandrinian hexameter) is not active in Homer, but that a "metrical-syntactic" bridge seems to be in place instead, banning any "strong syntactic pause." Cantilena names this Nicanor's bridge. In prosodic terms, we can say that Nicanor's bridge bans the end of a prosodic phrase in 2b. By Alexandrinian times, this bridge will have become one that banned the end of any metrical word in 2b – an apparent case of *domain generalization*, a diachronic change in which a process comes to apply to a domain that is more general than it was originally. An example of domain generalization is *final devoicing* in German (already mentioned above), a process which earlier applied to word ends and now applies to the more general domain of syllable ends.

phrase, not just the phonological phrase, is the domain for elision (Devine and Stephens 1994: 262). This means that elision can take place between two words that belong to separate phonological phrases, provided they belong to the same intonational phrase.[94] Elision is thus allowed at caesuras (but not, say, between verses) because the units coming into contact at caesuras are separate phonological phrases that still belong to the same intonational phrase, which in turn corresponds to the entire verse. This means, conversely, that elision should not be taken as evidence for dividing the hexameter into cola (as is often done).

Overall, these findings confirm the main intuition behind some colometric approaches to the hexameter, such as Fränkel's (1926, 1955), which saw main caesuras as stitching points between units of sense (*Sinnesgliederungen*), and not simply as metrical articulations independent of linguistic structure.[95] The only adjustment needed is to understand these units (i.e., cola) as *prosodic* (as opposed to semantic) in nature, and specifically as phonological (and sometimes intonational) phrases (this is in line with Bakker's (1997) argument that the hexameter is made up of intonation units). Given colometric structures, such as those studied by Kirk (1985), are then just particular configurations available to the poets for arranging smaller prosodic constituents in the line. The only caveat, again, is that these constituents are *prosodic* in nature, and their identification should be grounded in prosodic considerations, and not just a vague intuition that some words "belong together."[96]

---

[94] In fact, some elisions are allowed between a main clause and a subordinate clause, where we might have expected a boundary between intonational phrases (as also suggested by the received punctuation). See, for instance, *Od.* 5.1–2, Ἠὼς δ' ἐκ λεχέων παρ' ἀγαυοῦ Τιθωνοῖο / ὤρνυθ', ἵν' ἀθανάτοισι φόως φέροι ἠδὲ βροτοῖσιν "Dawn rose up from her bed by lordly Tithōnós, to bring light to immortals and mortals alike," with an elision (as well as aspiration assimilation, a type of *external sandhi*) between the main clause verb ὤρνυτο and the subordinating conjunction ἵνα.

[95] Or whatever exactly Kirk (1985: 19) means by "a reflection of sentence-articulation as predisposed by a permanent rhythmical pattern."

[96] The dangers of relying on intuition alone are easily illustrated. Take Kirk's example of a prototypical *rising threefold verse*, in which a line is split into three cola of increasing size (Kirk 1985: 20). The verse he discusses is διογενὲς Λαερτιάδη πολυμήχαν' Ὀδυσσεῦ "O divine Odysseus of the many schemes, son of Laertes" (*Il.* 2.173), which he parses as διογενές + Λαερτιάδη + πολυμήχαν' Ὀδυσσεῦ. But nothing suggests that we could not parse the verse as διογενὲς Λαερτιάδη + πολυμήχαν' Ὀδυσσεῦ instead, which would more closely follow the syntactic (and thus prosodic) structure of the clause, which is made up of two noun phrases in asyndeton (i.e., coordinated without an overt conjunction), each formed by an adjective and a proper noun. In fact, if we split διογενές + Λαερτιάδη, there is no reason not to split πολυμήχαν' + Ὀδυσσεῦ as well (since *elisio non officit caesurae*, and thus elisions should not be used to establish line-internal prosodic divisions). This is not to say that archaic hexameters following a tripartite structure do not exist (in fact, such a structure is marked by the interpuncts of Nestor's cup). But it should go to show that in the absence of clear, linguistically grounded reasons for segmenting verses one way or another, attempts at colometry can quickly turn into speculative endeavors.

2.2.5 Homeric Enjambement from a Prosodic Perspective

There is a vast literature on the typology of *enjambement* in Homer.[97] This goes back at least to Parry (1929, 1971: 251–65), who distinguished between *periodic* (necessary, or violent) and *unperiodic* (unnecessary) enjambement, and argued that oral style is rich in the latter, but poor in the former. The difference between the two types of enjambement is easily illustrated by the first two lines of the *Iliad* and the *Odyssey* respectively:

(21)   Μῆνιν ἄειδε θεὰ Πηληϊάδεω Ἀχιλῆος
       οὐλομένην, ἣ μυρί' Ἀχαιοῖς ἄλγε' ἔθηκε, (*Il.* 1.1–2)

   The wrath sing, o goddess, of Peleus' son, Achilles,
   ruinous, which brought countless sufferings upon the Achaeans

(22)   Ἄνδρα μοι ἔννεπε, Μοῦσα, πολύτροπον, ὃς μάλα πολλὰ
       πλάγχθη, ἐπεὶ Τροίης ἱερὸν πτολίεθρον ἔπερσε· (*Od.* 1.1–2)

   The man sing, o Muse, of many turns, who far and wide
   wandered, after he sacked the sacred city of Troy

At the end of *Iliad* 1.1, the poet had a syntactically complete clause, so that adding the enjambed adjective οὐλομένην "ruinous" was not grammatically necessary (thus *unnecessary* enjambement). *Odyssey* 1.1, on the other hand, ends with an incomplete clause (one that lacks a finite verb!), such that the poet *had* to continue it in the next line (thus *necessary* enjambement). Parry argued that oral poets have an easier time managing composition if each line ends with some level of syntactic completion:

> Oral versemaking by its speed must be chiefly carried on in an adding style. The singer has not time for the nice balances and contrasts of unhurried thought: he must order his words in such a way that they leave him much freedom to end the sentence or draw it out as the story and the needs of the verse demand. (Parry 1971: 262)

Significant literature has followed, debating Parry's findings and definitions (Parry, for instance, uses the term "word group" to talk about enjambement), all using different concepts of what counts as a sentence or clause, as well as stipulating different levels of "violence" or intensity of the break, by compiling a typology of clause and conjunction types. As we shall see, a prosodic approach to meter allows us to address this area of

---

[97] See Dugan (2012: 5–14) for a concise review of some of the literature. Important contributions are Parry (1929), Kirk (1966, 1976), Barnes (1979), Cantilena (1980), Higbie (1990), Bakker (1990) (whose approach is in many ways similar to the one espoused here, only using the concept of *intonation unit*), and Friedrich (2000).

study much more simply than a syntactic one, be it formally defined or not.⁹⁸

As mentioned above, each particular meter involves a set of rules for matching prosodic domains with given metrical domains (or the edges thereof). For instance, verses must usually start with the beginning of a word, and end with the end of one. In the Homeric hexameter, as we have just seen, the edges of phonological phrases are encouraged in specific positions within the line (the main incisions), and avoided in others (bridges). The end of the line comes with its specific rules as well, and what we call enjambement phenomena have to do specifically with which prosodic boundaries are allowed at the end of the line.

Different meters and different poets can have different preferences. In surveying English poetry, Hayes (1989: 241) reports that "line boundaries normally coincide with relatively high-level breaks in the prosodic hierarchy, such as that between utterances or intonational phrases." But there is individual variation. Alexander Pope (1688–1744), for instance, likes to begin and end his lines with the edges of intonational phrases and utterances, and only occasionally will end a line with the end of a phonological phrase. John Milton's (1608–74) mature verse, on the other hand, has several run-ons that split a phonological phrase, such as the following:

(23)   Now in loose Garlands thick thrown off, [the bright
       Pavement]$_\varphi$ that like a Sea of Jasper shone (*Paradise Lost* 3.363–64)

These would all strike us as cases of rather "violent" enjambement. Milton doesn't, however, split clitic groups. Shakespeare (1564–1616), finally, usually requires a line to end at least with a phonological-phrase boundary, but he will occasionally split some clitics from their hosts, thus allowing a line to end with a clitic word, as in the two consecutive verses:

(24)   How much you were my conqueror, and [**that**
       My sword]$_C$, made weak by my affection, [**would**
       Obey]$_C$ it on all cause … (*Anthony and Cleopatra* 3.11.66–68)

One important insight from Hayes' survey is that enjambement preferences can be a feature of the personal style of different writing poets, and not necessarily something dictated by the nature of the medium (oral vs. written).

---

⁹⁸ This, in particular, is the weakness of Dugan's (2012) approach, which uses the generative theory of minimalist syntax to reevaluate alleged cases of Homeric enjambement (and comes to the conclusion that, in fact, very little *syntactic* enjambement occurs in Homer). While Dugan's approach has the virtue of relying on a well-established theory of syntax, it still focuses on the wrong level of analysis for poetic meter (i.e., syntax instead of prosody).

It is also not a simple matter of chronology or "evolution" of style, since Shakespere (the earliest poet in Hayes' sample) seems to have the "wildest" enjambement of all. Of course, the fact that writing poets might have the freedom to choose among different types of enjambement does not mean that operating within a traditional oral style might not push a poet towards preferring some types of enjambement over others (which might, after all, be easier or harder to process during composition).

So what are Homer's preferences? It is not a requirement for a hexametric line to correspond to the syntactic unit of the sentence (the first sentence of *Iliad* I, for instance, occupies seven lines), or even to that of the clause (*Il.* 1.1–7, for instance, contains five clauses, three of which stretch over a line end). Rather, Homer is similar to Pope: the ends of lines prototypically correspond to the ends of intonational phrases (as we have just discussed above), or even utterances (such as the end of an episode or book). This is congruent with the observation that over 50 percent of the punctuation in Homer occurs at the end of the line (this is reported, for instance, in Fränkel 1955: 104).

The tendency for the edges of utterances to coincide with line edges is particularly apparent in dialogue, where each piece of direct speech (i.e., a separate utterance) starts at the beginning of a line and ends at the end of one. There is, in other words, no *hemistichomythia* in Homer, where a single line is split between two interlocutors. But there are also no cases of a speech ending in the middle of the line. The after-speech formula ὣς φάτο "thus s/he spoke," for instance, is invariably localized in the beginning of the line, after a speech has ended at the end of the previous verse.

Most cases of unperiodic/unnecessary enjambement in Homer occur when we have a sentence made up of several consecutive intonational phrases, and a new line begins with a new intonational phrase that belongs to an ongoing sentence. Lines starting with nonrestrictive relative clauses are a clear example of this, since we know that these clauses are likely to form their own intonational phrase.[99] See, for instance, the many examples of the relative pronoun used line-initially, as in these passages from *Iliad* 1.

(25) ἢ καὶ ὀνειροπόλον, καὶ γάρ τ' ὄναρ ἐκ Διός ἐστιν,
 ὅς κ' εἴποι ὅ τι τόσσον ἐχώσατο Φοῖβος Ἀπόλλων (*Il.* 1.63–64)

 or even an interpreter of dreams (since dreams also come from Zeus),
 who might tell us why Phoîbos Apollo is so angry.

---

[99] This is true for the whole category of *parentheticals*, which, beyond non-restrictive relative clauses, includes vocatives, tag questions, interjections, expletives, sentence adverbials like *obviously*, epistemic verbs such as *I wonder*, direct quotation verbs such as *he said*, etc. See Devine and Stephens (1994: 417) and Nespor and Vogel (1986[2007]: 188).

(26) οὐδ' ἢν Ἀγαμέμνονα εἴπῃς,
ὃς νῦν πολλὸν ἄριστος Ἀχαιῶν εὔχεται εἶναι. (*Il.* 1.90–91)

not even if you mean Agamemnon,
who now claims to be by far the best of the Achaeans.

The cases that we label as violent (necessary, periodic) enjambement usually involve ending the line with the edge of a phonological phrase instead. The clause ὃς μάλα πολλά / πλάγχθη is one such example, arguably reflecting the prosodic constituency: ((ὃς μάλα πολλά)_φ (πλάγχθη)_φ)_ι. This and many other cases of violent enjambement in Homer (such as those collected by Dugan 2012: 34–45) seem to involve the presence of focus-attracting lexemes (such as ἄλλος "other," αὐτός "he/himself," πᾶς "all," πολύς "much, many," ἕκαστος "each," negations, comparatives, superlatives, numerals, and possessive pronouns), which by their nature force the formation of prosodic domains that are smaller than those not containing any focused materials (see discussion in Devine and Stephens 1994: 478).[100] In other words, while under normal circumstances the relative clause ὃς μάλα πολλά πλάγχθη would likely have formed a single prosodic phrase, the presence of a focus-attracting lexeme like πολλά "very much" created the opportunity for splitting the clause into smaller prosodic constituents, which were then distributed over two lines.

What is not allowed in Homer is to end the line in the middle of a phonological phrase, or to split clitics from their hosts. Thus we have no lines, for instance, ending in a proclitic like καί, or with a preposition separated from its complement. In other words, Homer seems more similar to Pope than to Shakespeare or Milton.

Any further syntactic description of the possibilities for line breaks in Homer (such as those covered in much of the literature on Homeric enjambement) is not a matter of metrics per se, but of style, and thus goes beyond the scope of this chapter. This, for instance, is the case for Bakker's (1997: 151–55) concept of *antimetry* – that is, "a secondary rhythm that is temporarily set up against the movement of the hexametric period," which describes cases in which several consecutive verses show violent enjambement, in a context of "increased semantic salience." None of these individual verses is particularly notable in prosodic terms (the

---

[100] I owe this observation to Rutger Allan, who kindly shared with me the slides from his talk "From Fränkel to Functional: A functional-cognitive approach to Enjambment and Caesura" (Allan 2021). His term for this phenomenon is *emphatic chunking* (and it deserves a monographic treatment). For more details on how prosodic phrases are built in Ancient Greek, see Devine and Stephens (1994: 390–97).

edge of the line is aligned with the end of either an intonational phrase or a phonological phrase, often containing a focus-attracting lexeme), but a consecutive cluster of them can be recognized as an interesting stylistic feature of Homeric composition.[101]

2.3 Historical Approaches to the Hexameter

A chapter on the Homeric hexameter would be incomplete without mention of some of the most recent theories about the possible origin of this verse. These theories are of course closely tied to theories of the origin of the epic tradition in itself, and with the history of the Bronze Age Aegean.

2.3.1 The Antiquity of the Tradition

There are reasons to believe that the epic tradition to which the Homeric poems belong goes back (in one form or another) to at least several centuries before the textualization of the poems themselves. First, the epics themselves seem to reflect a late Bronze Age setting (with, of course, more recent elements mixed in), and perhaps even memories of actual events: this, in a way, is the insight that put Heinrich Schliemann on the hunt for Homeric places and artifacts, and in turn led to the rediscovery of Mycenaean Greece. External evidence can be mustered too: the palace of Pylos preserves the famous Lyre Player and Bird Fresco (ca. 1300 BCE), and it is tempting to see this as a representation of an epic performance at court, just like the ones we witness in the *Odyssey*. The decipherment of Linear B has yielded interesting comparanda for Homer's language, and so have Hittite documents (Hajnal 2003a).[102] The field of Homeric archaeology is dedicated to finding traces of Homeric costumes and objects in the archaeological record, often pointing to a rather deep prehistory.[103] But these are all circumstantial pieces of evidence for the existence of an epic tradition, and do not rule out alternative channels of transmission (the knowledge about some places and types of artifacts need not have been transmitted through epic tradition alone; the same goes for personal names, story patterns, folklore elements, or even the memory of historical events).

---

[101] For other similar observations on Homeric style and the arrangement of discourse over meter, see Edwards (1966).
[102] Bachvarova (2016) is a survey of potential connections between the epic tradition of the *Iliad* and preexisting poetic traditions in ancient Anatolia. Though exciting, many of these connections should be seen as speculative (Metcalf 2016).
[103] For an introduction, see Bennett (1997), with references.

There are, however, more direct pieces of evidence, preserved in Homer's language and meter, that point to the antiquity of the oral epic tradition itself. Several lines in Homer, for instance, scan better when we reconstruct a slightly earlier stage of Greek, undoing some of the most recent sound changes that affected first-millennium Ionic.[104] When Helen addresses Priam in *Iliad* 3, she uses a line that would have scanned better a few centuries earlier:[105]

(27)   αἰδοῖός τέ μοί ἐσσι φίλε *[sw]εκυρὲ δ*[w]εινός τε. (*Il.* 3.172)

You are venerable to me, father-in-law, and held in awe.

It makes sense to believe that Homer's epic tradition goes at least as far back as a time when this line would have scanned regularly (in this case, before Ionic lost the sound [w], which is needed in this line to obtain a heavy syllable in 4a and 5a).

But how far back in time can we actually go? Particular Homeric expressions, which appear to scan better if we restore *syllabic sonorants*,[106] have been argued to point to a time before Mycenaean as we have it (thus *seven hundred years or so before the composition of our poems!*). This is the case, most famously, for the expression ³ᶜλιποῦσ' ἀνδροτῆτα καὶ ἥβην "leaving behind manliness and youth" (*Il.* 16.857, 22.363), which would scan better if ἀνδροτῆτα (⁴ᵇ– ⌣ – ⌣) were restored to a preform *anr̥tāta (⁴ᵇ⌣ ⌣ – ⌣).[107] Following this type of argumentation, we assume that the hexameter as we have it goes back several centuries, and that some expressions that are metrically unhappy in Homer go back to a time when the language was different.[108]

---

[104] Some of these changes have already been discussed above among the special "metrical licenses." More will be discussed in Chapter 3. A systematic treatment of how recent language change in Ionic impacted Homeric phraseology is Hoekstra (1964).

[105] For the traditionality of these types of vocative formulas (arguably associated with the genre of funerary lament), see Bozzone (2016a: 18).

[106] By syllabic sonorants (or resonants) we mean the sounds */l/, */r/, */m/, and */n/ working as syllable nuclei. Syllabic sonorants are reconstructed for Proto-Greek (as well as for PIE), but they are already lost in Mycenaean (cf. Rau 2010: 177). In IE linguistics, syllabic sonorants are indicated through an *underring* (e.g., r̥, l̥). In IPA transcription, they are indicated through an *understroke* (e.g., [r̩], [l̩]). A recent systematic study of the Greek reflexes of syllabic liquids specifically is Van Beek (2022), who argues that these segments had special and separate developments within the Greek epic tradition.

[107] See West (1997: 229) and Watkins (1995: 499) with references. In Bozzone (2022), I use constructional evidence to suggest that this expression is not as old as it appears, and that its original form (preserved in some ancient *testimonia*) was likely λιποῦσ' ἁδρότητα καὶ ἥβην "leaving ripeness and youth behind."

[108] Another line of reasoning, as we shall see, is to explain some irregularities in Homer's hexameter as reflecting a different and more archaic meter (a proto-hexameter of sorts). This is the Tichy–Berg theory of the proto-hexameter, which we shall discuss below.

Table 2.7 *Comparing Vedic and Greek lyric meters: the eleven-syllable line*

Vedic Hymn to Indra (*Rigveda* 1.32.1a–b)	Sappho's Hymn to Aphrodite (fr. 1 Voigt, 1–2)
Indrasya nu vīriyāni pra vōcam	ποικιλόθρον' ἀθανάτ' Ἀφρόδιτα,
– – ⏑⏑ – ⏑ – – – ⏑ – ×|	– ⏑ – ⏑ – ⏑⏑ – ⏑ – ×|
yāni cakāra prathamāni vajrī	παῖ Δίος δολόπλοκε, λίσσομαί σε
– ⏑⏑ – – ⏑⏑ – ⏑ – ×|	– ⏑ – ⏑ – ⏑⏑ – ⏑ – ×|
I shall now proclaim the heroic deeds of Indra which he did first, he who wields the *vajra*	Immortal Aphrodite of the colorful throne, child of Zeus, weaver of plots, I beg you

How far back can the Homeric hexameter itself go? Can we reconstruct it all the way to PIE? The answer here seems to be clearly "no." While Antoine Meillet (the founder, in many ways, of comparative IE metrics) showed that we can successfully reconstruct some Greek and Vedic lyric meters back to a shared source, he was also convinced that the hexameter must have had a different origin entirely.

Observe, for instance, the eerie similarities between the first two lines of a Vedic *Hymn to Indra* (*Rigveda* 1.32) and of Sappho's *Hymn to Aphrodite*, given in Table 2.7. It is not just that the meters are superficially similar: they are built according to the same principles. In both cases, we have a syllable-counting meter (eleven syllables), in which words are scanned in *synapheia*, and which categorizes syllables as heavy vs. light (defined according to the same criteria). In both cases, the beginning of the line is relatively freer (in Greek metrics, we call this the Aeolic base, notated as ××),[109] and the clausula is more fixed (– ⏑ – ×). Inside each line, hiatus is tendentially avoided, and the mitigating strategies of *synekphonesis* and *vocalis ante vocalem corripitur* are in place.[110] In both cases, groups of lines (which, in this case, are of different lengths) are joined together in stanzas, and a complete poem is made up of several stanzaic iterations. Even the context of usage is similar: in both cases, we are looking at sung hymns which

---

[109] Recent scholarship on Greek and Vedic meter suggests that the metrical freedom at the beginning of lines is not as absolute as once thought (see Kiparsky 2018: 4–5, with references). Maas (1923) already notated the Aeolic base as ∘∘: two positions of which at least one must be heavy, given that the tendency is for the first syllable to be heavy more often than not.

[110] For hiatus and prevocalic shortening in the *Rigveda*, see Gunkel and Ryan (2011). For a general introduction to Vedic meter, see Arnold (1905). Interestingly, elision (which is common in later Vedic) does not seem to occur in Rigvedic meter (Macdonell 1916 [1993]: 23).

address the gods, enlisting their help and benevolence (this is more personal and specific in Sappho's case, and more generic in the *Rigveda*).

The hexameter appears, in comparison, quite distinct. Firstly, it's a stichic, not a strophic meter.[111] It is more strict, in that it doesn't have a "free" start. It is not syllable-counting: rather, as we have seen above, it allows for contraction, whereby, in some metrical positions, a single heavy syllable can stand in for two light ones. It is, also, a rather long meter (15 syllables on average). While these features convinced Meillet (1923), as well as Meister (1921: 227), that an IE origin should be ruled out, more recent scholarship has tried to sketch out scenarios by which the hexameter, a new, inner-Greek creation, could emerge from inherited IE components.

There are two reasons why this route is appealing. First, metrical sequences that are found in the hexameter appear in Greek lyric compositions, in a way that might suggest that these units predated the hexameter as we have it.[112] Second, we have a good typological parallel for a long epic verse emerging from a sequence of smaller lyric verses.

Again, Indic provides a useful comparison. In the history of Sanskrit, the lyric meter known as *anuṣṭubh* (a four-line stanza of eight-syllable lines) quite transparently gave rise to the *śloka*,[113] the meter used in much of the post-Vedic oral tradition (including the *Mahābhārata*, the *Rāmāyana*, and the *Purāṇa*) and often considered the Classical Sanskrit verse *par excellence*. Descriptively, one talks of the *śloka* as comprising two hemistichs,[114] each consisting of what originally were two separate eight-syllable lines (in this context, the four original eight-syllable lines are called *pāda*s "feet"). Incisions (more precisely, diaereses) still mark the places where the *pāda*s were conjoined. Each *śloka* forms a complete linguistic unit, and

---

[111] A *stichic meter* (from Gr. στίχος "line") is a meter consisting of repeating identical lines; a *strophic meter* (from Gr. στροφή "strophe" – i.e., turn of the chorus in performances) is made up of repeating groups (stanzas) of potentially diverse lines.

[112] This is the case, for instance, for the metron that Maas (1923), followed by West (1982) and others, labels as D (– ⏑ ⏑ – ⏑ ⏑ –), also called the *hemiepes* or "half epic," since it mirrors the shape of the first half of the hexameter, up to 3a), which is frequent (together with a few more dactylic metra) in Bacchylides and Pindar, where it is combined with nondactylic sequences called *epitrites*.

[113] The noun *śloka*, derived from the root *śru* "hear" (the alternation between /l/ and /r/ is dialectal), is a good idiomatic match for Ancient Greek ἔπος, in that it can mean "any verse or stanza; a proverb, saying" (Monier-Williams 1899 s.v.). For a very short introduction to Classical Sanskrit meters, see Macdonell (1926 [1989]: 232–35).

[114] The two hemistichs are usually printed as separate lines, though some texts might print the *śloka* as a four-line stanza of eight-syllable verses instead, preserving the original *anuṣṭubh* arrangement.

there are no enjambement phenomena between *śloka*s. An example is given below:

(28) *āsīd rājā Nălŏ nāmă | Vīrăsēnăsŭtŏ bălī |*
      ŭpăpannŏ gŭṇair iṣṭai | rūpăvān aśvăkŏvĭdăḥ || (*Mahābhārata* 3.52.1)

   There was a King called Nala, the son of Virasena,
   strong and endowed with desirable qualities, handsome and skilled with horses.

Overall, the *śloka* is more tightly regulated than the Vedic *anuṣṭubh*, with specific variants codified for each *pāda* (and with the choice of variants in a given *pāda* limiting the options for the remaining ones).

2.3.2 *The Tichy–Berg Theory of the Proto-hexameter*

The derivation of the Greek hexameter is not nearly as straightforward, and requires many more intermediate steps and assumptions.[115] Many scholars work with a combination of an eight-syllable verse and a seven-syllable one, using the caesura at 4a as the main seam holding the line together.[116] Thus, for instance, West (1973: 179) suggests "a pherecratean + an expanded reizianum." Berg's (1978) theory, which has been particularly influential in the German-speaking realm (especially as supplemented by Tichy (1981; see now Haug and Welo 2001), starts with the combination of an inherited eight-syllable verse and its catalectic seven-syllable variant (Berg 1978: 23):[117]

(29) xxxx ⌣ – ⌣ – | +   xxxx ⌣ – – |

From there, the theory envisions four intermediate steps of development. The first step involves the creation of some new verse types

---

[115] These are helpfully and clearly summarized by Hajnal (2003b), who provides a history of the problem within the field of IE linguistics. Magnelli (1995) provides a brief appraisal of several more recent theories. For older theories, see Witte (1913: 2241–47).

[116] One could note that using the hephthemimeral caesura as the main seam in the verse is already a step away from the Indic parallel, since it leaves the two most frequent incisions in the Homeric corpus (3b and 4c, which occur in over 50 percent of verses) unexplained, and focuses on one incision (4a) which is just as frequent as those in 2a, 3a, and 5b, occurring in ca. 35 percent of verses. We could add, moreover, that, as reported by Kiparsky (2018: 30), strong syntactic (thus prosodic) breaks only occur at 4a in 7 percent of lines. The actual colometry of the Homeric hexameter, in other words, would remain largely unexplained.

[117] For attested (though not identical) parallels to this combination, Berg points to a fragment of epic content by Corinna and a verse used by Aristophanes in *The Clouds* (Berg 1978: 24–25).

by specifying part of the ×××× sequences, which Berg names a, b, and c (these now contain metra that exist elsewhere in Greek meter):

(30)   a) ××–⏑⏑–⏑–| + ××–⏑⏑––| (glyconean + pherecratean)

   b) –⏑⏑–××××| + ××–⏑⏑––| (inverted choriambic dimeter + pherecratean)

   c) ××××–⏑⏑–| + ××–⏑⏑––| (choriambic dimeter + pherecratean)

After that, the remaining × sequences are further specified: the ones in the second half of the verse come to prefer a dactylic realization, the ones in the beginning of the verse a spondaic one. In the final stage, dactyls are also allowed in the first two metra.

Not all of these intermediate steps are easy to justify (for a critique, see Kiparsky 2018: 23). What this approach claims to explain is four sets of facts:

1. The presence of Hermann's bridge at 4b (and one might add of Varro's bridge at 3c, since the presence of a main incision at 4a makes word ends at 3c unlikely) (Berg 1978: 30).
2. The presence of irregular scansions in the first (1a, 1b) and fourth feet (4b, 4c), which would reflect the original presence of an Aeolic base (××). The fourth foot has played a special role in the scholarship (though not in Berg's original article), with much discussion focusing on the expression ἀνδροτῆτα καὶ ἥβην (Tichy 1981) as reflecting a stage where the scansion (^{4b}– ⏑ – ⏑) would actually have been acceptable.[118]
3. The slightly greater presence of spondees in the first and second feet (Berg 1978: 29), which would reflect the 4-syllable count of the initial sequence ×××× (seen in variant c).
4. The preference for dactyls in the fourth and fifth feet (see discussion in Hackstein 2010: 413–14). In the fifth foot (where the preference is at over 90 percent), this would reflect the original form of variants a, b, and c (i.e., the pherecratean). In the fourth foot (where the preference is only a little over 50 percent), this would reflect the initial preference for the Aeolic base in 4b and 4c to be realized as a sequence of two

---

[118] What would be desirable here is a statistical appraisal of whether the first and fourth feet in the Homeric hexameter truly are exceptionally rich in metrical irregularities. This is sometimes presented as an established fact in the literature, but I have never been able to find statistical support for it.

lights, thus ⏑⏑, which would have remained somewhat ingrained (this, of course, is not what we see in the supposedly archaic scansion of ἀνδροτῆτα καὶ ἥβην).

2.3.3 *Kiparsky (2018) on the Indo-European Origin of the Hexameter*

A more recent approach, grounded in generative metrics and a more systematic comparison with other IE traditions, is that of Kiparsky (2018), who similarly argues for an IE origin of the components of the hexameter, including (and this is the main methodological advantage) the IE origin of the metrical mechanism by which the hexameter would develop from its predecessor: namely *syncopation*, which he documents in the Vedic, Iranian, and Greek traditions.

Kiparsky starts from an inherited IE eight-syllable line built from two metra, each consisting of binary iambic feet. He calls this an iambic dimeter: x–⏑–, ⏑–⏑– |. This line could be combined in distichs (couplets). From these iambic forms, the process of *syncopation*[119] gives rise to a number of attested Greek meters, including our hexameter.

Kiparsky defines syncopation as a type of metrical license,[120] by which "a light syllable in strong position is licensed by a heavy syllable in weak position within the same colon" (Kiparsky 2018: 7). A simple description of syncopation is that two adjacent metrical positions are allowed to "switch" their weights under some conditions (mostly, they have to belong to the same colon). Thus, starting from an iambic metron like (31.a) below, several new sequences can be generated via syncopation (these are discussed in more detail in Kiparsky (2018: 7–8)):

(31) a. ⏑ – ⏑ –

b. – ⏑ ⏑ –

c. ⏑ ⏑ – –

d. ⏑ – – ⏑

The main insight is that syncopations of the type (31.b) and (31.c), when applied to the first and second metron of an iambic dimeter respectively,

---

[119] In Greek metrics, a particular version of this phenomenon is labeled *anaclasis* (Kiparsky 2018: 17).
[120] In Kiparsky's terms, this is an optional *correspondence rule* that holds between the verse design and a specific verse instance.

could give rise to something that is rather similar to the first half of the hexameter (the last syllable can be left out by *catalexis*). Thus:

(32) Stage 1: × – ⏑ –, ⏑ – ⏑ – | iambic dimeter
      Stage 2: – ⏑ ⏑ –, ⏑ ⏑ – – | (b) + (c) syncopation

If we combine this syncopated iambic dimeter with another iambic dimeter (with no syncopation), we obtain a sequence that is actually attested in early Ionic verse, such as Archilochus (Kiparsky 2018: 24–25).

(33) ἀλλά μ' ὁ λυσιμελής, ὦταῖρε, δάμναται πόθος (Archilochus, *Fragmenta* 196, Gerber 1999: 210–11)

      but, my friend, limb-loosening desire overwhelms me
      – ⏑ ⏑ – ⏑ ⏑ – | × – ⏑ – ⏑ – ‖

The combination of the two types of meter (dactylic and iambic) would confirm their genetic affiliation.[121] Most strikingly, type (b) syncopation (in the first foot) can be observed in the first line of Nestor's cup, an iambic line which accompanies (as mentioned above) two recognizable hexameters. The scheme for the entire inscription, as given by Kiparsky (2018: 25), is as follows:

(34) – ⏑ ⏑ –, ⏑ – ⏑ ⏑ –, ⏑ – ⏑ – ‖
      – –, – ⏑ ⏑, – ⏑ ⏑, – –, – ⏑ ⏑, – ⏑ ‖
      – ⏑ ⏑, – –, – –, – ⏑ ⏑, – ⏑ ⏑, – – ‖

For Kiparsky, then, the hexameter originates as an iambic tetrameter in which syncopation has created dactylic sequences. Kiparsky (2018: 29–30) argues that the main caesuras and bridges of the hexameter can handily be derived from those of the iambic tetrameter (he uses statistics from West (1982) on sense pauses in both verse types; the frequencies of the sense pauses do not align, but their positions arguably do), and he also provides accounts of metrical imperfections in the first and fourth feet which are more precise than Berg's (see Kiparsky 2018: 31–32).

All in all, while its technical formulation might prove a barrier for its wide acceptance, and while perhaps not all of the details are yet worked out to the satisfaction of classical metricists, Kiparsky's theory has much to offer: it is derived from an established set of principles of metrical theory, it can provide evidence for its intermediate stages, and it has explanatory

---

[121] In the Italian tradition of Greek metrics, this is the principle of *Dimmi con chi vai e ti dirò chi sei* "tell me who you are going with and I will tell you who you are" (or "you will know a meter by the company it keeps") associated with Giorgio Pasquali.

power not just regarding some peculiarities of the hexameter itself, but regarding the origins and interrelations of other Archaic Greek meters.

2.4 Meter and Cognition

2.4.1 Meter and Language

So far, we have taken a descriptive approach to the Homeric hexameter: we have discussed its building blocks and its features, its rules and tendencies. We have examined theories on how the hexameter could emerge from inherited IE meters. But we haven't asked a more radical, perhaps simpler question: why should oral epics (and oral traditions in general) have meter at all?

In most of the modern literature on Homer's language, meter appears as an inflexible tyrant that forces the language and the poets into uncomfortable situations. To satisfy its needs, archaic forms need to be retained or adapted, dialectal forms need to be borrowed, paradigms need to be reshaped, and not even all personal names can survive unscathed (like poor, metrically unwieldy Patroclus, who does not get a noun-epithet formula in the nominative, but only in the vocative). The picture evoked in this literature is that of a war between meter and language, in which language is always the one yielding ground.[122] Meter, to use another image, is a procrustean bed in which language is made to lie.

Why do poets and oral traditions put up with this? Why are they willing to pay such a high price? Perhaps some oral traditions prefer meter because they perceive metered language to be more aesthetically pleasing than unmetered language. Perhaps they like how meter sets poetic language apart from its everyday usage. Additionally, we know from psycholinguistic research that meter improves the ability to recall a linguistic sequence (Rubin 1995: 85–88). We might, then, see meter as a sort of expedient, yet another way poets might boost their recall of the complex matters of song.[123] But is this enough? And why do all sorts of unrelated human languages and cultures continue devising some sort of poetic meter?

There is an old idea within linguistics that meter *emerges* from language. As Edward Sapir (himself a linguist and a poet) put it: "[Style] is merely the

---

[122] This approach might in fact overstate the inviolability of meter, especially in the face of the many imperfect hexameters that we encounter in our corpus.
[123] For a discussion of other such strategies, see Minchin (2001).

language itself, running in its natural grooves" (Sapir 1921).[124] With respect to Homer, a similar view had been advocated by Nagy (1974, 2004) in describing the origin of the hexameter as it relates to formularity:

> At first [...], traditional phraseology simply contains built-in rhythms. Later, the factor of tradition leads to the preference of phrases with some rhythms over phrases with other rhythms. Still later, the preferred rhythms have their own dynamics and become regulators of any incoming phraseology. (Nagy 1974: 145)

Under such a view, there is no need to derive the hexameter from a PIE proto-verse, since the mechanisms by which traditional phraseology can crystallize into a loose (and then increasingly regulated) type of meter are present at any stage of the language.[125] The most recent incarnation of such an approach to the origin of the Homeric hexameter is found in Bakker (1997: 146), who also argued that the regularization of epic meter was a process which continued (and was amplified by) the textualization of our poems:

> Meter is not something superimposed on language, a form that exists independently of it; meter emerges from language as part of the process by which special speech emerges from speech. (Bakker 1997: 146)

What these accounts leave rather vague, however, is the precise process by which nonmetrical speech would gradually evolve into neatly regulated meter. Why exactly does this happen? What preexisting features of the language does this process leverage and recruit? Are there any immediate causes or facilitating factors? And what is there to gain as a result?

In this section, we will explore the idea that the emergence of meter from language might have something to do with the high cognitive price involved in oral performance. More specifically, we will look at how the speech of exceptionally fluent speakers shows significant *prosodic regularization*, which can be understood as a rudimentary kind of meter. In the cases we will discuss, this prosodic regularization goes hand in hand with an increased employment of formulaic language. "Meter," in other words, much like formularity, would emerge as a strategy to narrow down a performer's choices and streamline language production under conditions of high cognitive strain.

---

[124] This has been called the *development hypothesis* for the origin of poetic form. For a short history of the literature, see Fabb 2015: 58–62.

[125] In the specific case of the hexameter, Nagy proposes a link with an Aeolic meter attested in Alcaeus, and points to shared phraseology between the Homeric hexameter and Aeolic lyric meters as well as dactylo-epitrite meters (see summary in Nagy 2004: 153–55).

This is not to say that "emergence from formulaic sequences" is necessarily the way by which all meter originates. It is also not to say that this is the precise way Homeric hexameter originated. It is quite unlikely (in my view) that first-millennium BCE Greeks would have had to invent a new epic meter from scratch; after all, they had known metered poetry for at least a thousand years.[126] Rather, the purpose of this section is to explore how prosodic regularization (i.e., "meter") can benefit an oral performer in terms of cognitive processing, much in the way I have argued that reliance on formularity sequences can.

2.4.2   Prosodic Regularization in Hyperfluent Speech

A few hints as to how poetic meter (or a rough version thereof) might arise from speech come from a markedly nonpoetic context: the speech of sportscasters – that is, professionals (one might say oral performers) trained in the art of describing events quickly as they unfold. These and other *smooth talkers* have been studied by Koenraad Kuiper in his eponymous 1996 book, which brought to light the extent to which such extraordinary feats of fluency are sustained by an increased reliance on formulaic speech.[127]

Interestingly, formularity is not all that happens when speakers attempt major feats of fluency: Kuiper observed that there are clear *audible* correlates to formulaic behaviors while performing a cognitively demanding task. Specifically, various prosodic aspects of speech (which we shall see below) become regularized. These regularizing effects appear more clearly and reliably where the cognitive task at hand is more difficult – and therefore the need to relieve the speaker's working memory of unnecessary choices is greater. When comparing play-by-play commentary of a slow-moving sport, like cricket, to play-by-play commentary of a fast-moving sport, like horse racing, the differences are stark. Among cricket commentators (a famously slow-moving sport), Kuiper was able to detect formulaic behaviors in the form of discourse structure rules as well as the reliance on some formulas, but while the speech was fluent, it still contained pauses, had an uneven articulation rate, and followed a variety of natural intonational patterns – that is, it sounded like normal speech.

---

[126] As seen in section 2.3.1, some Greek and Vedic lyric meters clearly descend from a common source, which (if we accept the standard chronology for the reconstruction of PIE) must lie sometime in the third millennium BCE at the latest.

[127] Kuiper was the first to point out the similarity between the smooth talkers he was studying and the oral performers studied by Parry and Lord: "It is my contention that race callers (and other speakers still to pass through the pages of this book) are oral performers like the Serbo-Croatian poets who were the focus of Parry and Lord's work" (Kuiper 1996: 21).

Horse-racing commentators (Kuiper 1996: 10–21) present a very different picture: as soon as the race-calling portion of their comment starts, they follow strict discourse structure rules and rely almost exclusively on formulas; they display abnormal levels of fluency, with no hesitations and shorter pauses, and an even articulation rate. Moreover, their intonation becomes droned or chanted (i.e., articulated in a monotone, as opposed to the varied intonational patterns of natural speech). Their speech, in other words, is a lot more "metrical" (i.e., prosodically regulated) than that of cricket commentators. If we imagine operating a dial that can increase or decrease cognitive load during speech, then prosodic regulation ("meter") is something that seems to naturally start to appear when cognitive load has reached a critical point (and perhaps when other circumstances, like extensive training in the task at hand, are in place).

Kuiper hypothesized that the appearance of what he called *formulaic features* in speech (i.e., discourse rules, formulas, droned or chanted intonation, and consequent abnormal fluency) resulted from increased processing pressures on the speakers: "the greater those pressures are, the more in evidence features of formulaic speech will be" (Kuiper 1996: 73). In confirmation of this hypothesis, Kuiper found similar phenomena of combined usage of formularity and prosodic regulation in the speech of antiques auctions conducted by general auctioneers (Kuiper 1996: 56–63), and livestock auctioneers (Kuiper 1996: 63–72), but not in types of auctioneering where cognitive pressure was either higher or lower (because of different sale speed and complexity).[128] In other words, a particular "sweet spot" (not too easy, but not too cognitively taxing) needs to be reached in order for this particular type of hyperfluency (as sustained by formularity and prosodic regulation) to emerge. In situations where the cognitive load is too heavy (e.g., very fast-moving wool auctions in Christchurch, New Zealand, as described in Kuiper 1996: 51–53), the speech of auctioneers is reduced to single words.

Kuiper described a "droned or chanted intonation" as the main prosodic feature of this type of hyperfluent speech. I believe, however, that we can push Kuiper's data further, and particularly that we can argue that several different types of prosodic regulation are happening in the speech of these oral performers, amounting to a type of *metrical regularization*. But how, one might ask, is the speech of horse-racing commentators akin to poetic meter? In what follows, I describe the prosodic regularization observable in

---

[128] In what follows, I discuss extensively only data from horse-race calling, since Kuiper provides the most extensive transcripts for it. But a similar analysis of the speech of auctioneers would be profitable as well.

race calling along four dimensions – length, rhythm, intonation, and pauses – and explain how each of these aspects are relevant for English meter. Finally, I suggest how these findings can translate to meter (i.e., prosodic regularization) in Ancient Greek.

Length
As mentioned above, sportscasters during race-calling portions of their commentaries display an even articulation rate, and produce intonational phrases that are more regular in length.[129] In English, which is a stress-timed language,[130] this regularization will likely result in restrictions on the number of main word stresses within an intonational phrase. This can be seen in Kuiper's data, where we observe multiline stretches showing the same (or almost the same) number of main word stresses per line:[131]

(35) and El-Red the leader by two lengths   (4)
      from Speedy Cheval and Race Ruler   (4)
      On the rails to Twilight Time   (4)
      Belvedere is going up three wide   (4)
      Florlis Fella in the center.   (3 or 4)
      False Image attacking around three wide.   (4)
      In between them is Little River   (4)
      Lone Eagle is up three wide   (4)

Even a cursory examination of Kuiper's transcript suggests that several areas have undergone this type of regularization, and that this regularization precisely does not happen in the non-race-calling portions of the

---

[129] While this effect is not remarked upon by Kuiper, it is observable in the transcript he provides (Kuiper 1996: 11–15). While not all intonational phrases in the race-calling portion of the commentary are of identical duration, there are several stretches in which consecutive intonation units form "blocks" of relatively homogeneous length. Note that, since Kuiper does not provide time measures for his transcript, the relative length of intonational phrases here has to be inferred based on general facts of English prosody (and the crucial piece of information, provided by Kuiper, that articulation rate is even).

[130] In stress-timed languages, stressed syllables (which may in themselves be of different duration) are produced at approximately regular intervals, and unstressed syllables adapt to fit in between those intervals (cf. Nespor, Shukla, and Mehler 2011 on the typology of prosodic timing). In these languages, then, counting main word stresses is a good way to estimate the length of an utterance (for a more precise measurement, the duration of each stressed syllable should also be taken into account).

[131] The text is from Kuiper (1996: 12). I have added solid underlining to signal words carrying a main stress; broken underlining indicates that the stress status of the word is uncertain. The number in parentheses represents the number of main stresses in each intonation unit. Since I don't have audio recordings of Kuiper's data, I relied on the judgment of a native speaker of North American English to reconstruct the likely placement of stresses in each line, as well as to reconstruct the likely parsing in prosodic domains used for examples (36–39) below. While this procedure might fall short of perfectly recreating the original prosody, it should provide an acceptable approximation for the purposes of the current discussion.

commentary (i.e., the introduction, before the horses go off, and the end, after the winner is announced).

In terms of meter, this regularization can be seen as analogous to the creation of *metrical cola* or *lines* of a specific length; in English meter, length is usually specified in terms of how many stressed words (or ictic syllables) each line can contain.

Rhythm

A closer look at Kuiper's data reveals not just that word stresses are being regularized, but that several lines display recurring rhythmic patterns. Perhaps the most frequent of these patterns is a line (i.e., an intonational phrase) consisting of two prosodic phrases, each consisting of two prosodic words, each prosodic word carrying a main stress, and each corresponding to at least one bimoraic foot (i.e., either a heavy syllable or two lights). In this pattern, the odd-numbered stresses appear to be the stronger ones, yielding a trochaic rhythm:[132]

(36)
```
         /              \            /         \
   [and  El-Red  the  leader]φ  [by  two   lengths]φ        ✓
         /              \            /         \
   [from Speedy     Cheval]φ [and  Race   Ruler]φ           ✓
         /        \           /         \
   [On   the    rails]φ  [to  Twilight   Time]φ             ✓
         /              \            /    \
   [Belvedere is   going   up]φ  [three  wide]φ             ✓
         /      \            /
   [Florlis  Fella]φ  [in the  center]φ.
                  /           \          /           \
   [False   Image,  attacking]φ  [around  three   wide]φ.   ✓
         /        \              /       \
   [In    between them]φ [is   Little  River]φ              ✓
         /       \            /     \
   [Lone  Eagle]φ  [is up  three  wide]φ                    ✓ (1.53–60)
```

---

[132] In the text below, above each line, a "/" is used to mark strong main-word stresses (experienced as beats) and a "\" is used to mark weak main-word stresses (experienced as offbeats). Lines conforming to the trochaic pattern just described are marked with a checkmark.

Beyond appearing in consecutive blocks of lines, this pattern is encoded in clearly formulaic lines such as:

(37)

    /   \   / \
  [Twilight Time]$_φ$ [is up against the rail]$_φ$ (I.46)

    /   \   / \
  [Speedy Cheval's]$_φ$ [up against the rail]$_φ$ (I.67)

as well as:

(38)

     / \   / \
   [followed then]$_φ$ [by Twilight Time]$_φ$ (I.34)

     / \   / \
   [followed then]$_φ$ [by Lone Eagle]$_φ$ (I.37)

What looks like a permutation of the scheme just described can be found in a few longer lines consisting of three phonological phrases, in which the first two phonological phrases are grouped in a larger phonological phrase (max φ), and set against the third phonological phrase. Again, a trochaic rhythm results. This pattern too can involve some formulaic material, like in examples I.77 and I.87 below:

(39)

    /   \   / \
  [[Twilight Time]$_φ$ [on the inside]$_φ$]$_{maxφ}$ [of Florlis Fella]$_φ$ (I.69)

     / \   / \
  [[and False Image]$_φ$ [has gone round]$_φ$]$_{maxφ}$ [In a couple of strides]$_φ$ (I.77)

    / \   / \
  [[False Image]$_φ$ [scampers clear]$_φ$]$_{maxφ}$ [by a couple of lengths]$_φ$ (I.87)

What is interesting for our purposes is that by combining prosodic regulations affecting length and rhythm, we obtain something that resembles an English meter, which typically specifies (a) how many stressed syllables (*ictic syllables*) there should be within a line, and (b) which types of metrical feet (e.g., *iambs* vs. *trochees*) should be employed to build the line (e.g., an *iambic pentameter* builds lines out of five iambic feet, allowing for five ictic syllables).[133] Our pattern here, while certainly not as regulated

---

[133] For a generative analysis of some metrical structures of English, see Hayes (1989: 221–44).

(in that it does not specify rules for unstressed words or syllables), nonetheless specifies: (a) how many stressed words there should be within a line, and (b) that these stressed words should be arranged in a trochaic rhythm (effectively forming two trochees).

Intonation

Kuiper (1996: 19) reports that racing commentaries in play-by-play mode display a significantly narrower pitch range than natural speech: they are "basically articulated in a monotone," and they are either spoken (which Kuiper labels *drone*) or sung (which Kuiper labels *chant*). The choice between the two modes of delivery seems to depend on the particular tradition to which each performer belongs.[134]

Kuiper also observes a tendency for the absolute pitch to increase stepwise as horses near the end of the race, likely as a way to convey urgency and emphasis: "The intonational note usually rises in semitones to a high point at the finishing post and then gradually comes down as the commentator moves through the last cycle" (Kuiper 1996: 19).

But there might be some further regularization happening, which Kuiper describes only cursorily. As mentioned in section 2.2.4 above, in intonation languages like English, each intonational phrase is assigned a specific intonational pattern (or *tune*), which conveys some abstract meaning, often related to the information structure of the utterance. It appears that some of Kuiper's commentators have developed specific tunes that they use to mark particular moments in their performance – that is, meanings tailored to the task at hand:

> Commentators also have intonational ornaments of various kinds. For example, Reon Murtha uses a fall tune, that is, a slight drop in pitch on the last stressed syllable of formulae which are in turn at the end of particular sections of the discourse, for instance, the completion of a cycle. (Kuiper 1996: 21)[135]

The adoption of a droned or chanted intonation, with less variation in pitch than is found in natural speech, is something we know from our modern experience of poetry. Fabb (2015: 44–45) reports:

---

[134] "Reon Murtha says that Keith Haub from Auckland [who drones] has modeled himself on the call of Bill Collins who calls races in Melbourne, Australia. It seems, on listening to both of them, that there is a close resemblance in their calling styles. Those callers who follow in the tradition of the great Dave Clarkson, such as Reon Murtha and Peter Kelly, chant because Dave Clarkson chanted" (Kuiper 1996: 20).

[135] Incidentally, this seems similar to the function of the particle οὖν in Homer as described by Bakker (1997: 115): "οὖν frequently signals the moment in which the goal is reached."

> In the recorded performances of English poetry that I have examined, the intonation contour is often more limited in pitch range and variation, a type of what Ladd 1978 calls *stylized intonation* [...] Byers (1979: 371) similarly notes that poetry is generally spoken at a lower pitch and with a narrower pitch range than conversation or prose, and with relatively little variation from line to line.

It might be the case that poets reading their poetry out loud using the same intonational contour (i.e., *tune*) for each line might simply have gone further in the process of prosodic regularization that Kuiper observed for sportscasters (i.e., they are relying on a stereotyped "poetry" tune, just as the sportscasters are relying on stereotyped "race-calling" tunes).

Pauses

Natural speech is rich in pauses and usually peppered with hesitations, false starts, and disfluencies (as seen, for instance, in the Pear Story in Table 2.5). This is thought to reflect the real-time processing of language in the mind, as speakers juggle the cognitive cost of activating and verbalizing sequences of ideas. In the Pear Story, for instance, longer pauses typically precede the speaker's transitioning to a new point in the story, or introducing a new discourse referent that was not already active in their working memory: more than the mere necessity to breathe, pauses and hesitations reflect how the cognitive load is being negotiated by the speaker (Chafe 1994: 57).

It is, then, particularly impressive when, in race-calling commentary (as well as in oral-traditional poetry, or in some of the auctioneering traditions studied by Kuiper), as the complexity of the task arguably increases, hesitations and disfluencies disappear, and pauses are either shortened or eliminated. Both phenomena can be taken as an indication that speakers are finding some effective strategies for planning their utterances, reducing their cognitive load (despite the objective challenge of describing the events of a fast-moving sport in real time), and effectively breaking free of the usual processing concerns.

We have discussed before how relying on automated behaviors (like chunks) is one effective strategy for reducing cognitive load. Thus, one way the speakers are achieving this hyperfluency is by relying on more formulaic (i.e., automated) behaviors. This strategy is clearly visible in Kuiper's data, where the race-calling portions show a high formulaic density. Kuiper's data suggests that a reduction of cognitive load might be achieved through a second strategy: reducing the options normally available to a speaker for the prosodic realization of their speech, and committing to a predictable (and simplified) pattern instead.

The resulting *regulated speech* is not unlike poetry, where everyday units of speech production (e.g., syntactic or intonational phrases) become subordinate to the artificial unit that is the poetic line (see Fabb 2015: 1). In other words, the pace and rhythm of delivery are no longer dictated by fluctuating processing demands, but a preestablished pattern takes over.

Drawing a clear line between the two strategies above (formularity and prosodic regulation) proves a little complicated in practice, since much of the prosodic regularization discussed so far appears in formulaic sequences to begin with. Lin (2010, 2012), for instance, reports that formulaic sequences used in everyday speech tend to display fixed stress placement, intonation, and tempo (as opposed to similar, but nonconventionalized sequences). Moreover, formulaic sequences are typically produced without pauses or disfluencies (even when the surrounding discourse is not), and they tend to align with prosodic boundaries (Lin 2010: 180).[136]

This information is compatible with Nagy's theory, where the prosodic regularization that emerges in the traditional phraseology gradually "spills over" from the more formulaic sequences to the less formulaic ones. But, at present, establishing a clear direction of development (formulas → prosodic regularization vs. prosodic regularization → formulas) seems premature.

What we can conclude, for now, is that the difference between prosodic regularization in formulaic sequences in everyday speech and the "extreme" prosodic regularization in hyperfluent speech just appears to be one of degree: tasks that require performers to rely on an unusually high level of formulaic sequences are also likely to result in an unusually high level of prosodic regularization. At an extreme, this prosodic regularization may be described as a kind of meter.

2.4.3 *Prosodic Regularization in Ancient Greek*

In our discussion so far, we have seen how the same prosodic features that have become more regulated in (English-language) race calling are the features that English meter regulates. But how do our findings translate into Ancient Greek? A reasonable assumption, here, is that the specific

---

[136] Lin in fact suggests that these phonological properties should be taken as an important defining feature of formulaic language, and one that has been largely ignored so far.

prosodic features of a given language should largely determine what type of prosodic regularization takes place. As Sapir (1921: 246) puts it:

> Study carefully the phonetic system of a language, above all its dynamic features, and you can tell what kind of a verse it has developed – or, if history has played pranks with its psychology, what kind of verse it should have developed and some day will.

The regularization of word stresses makes sense for a language like English, which is a stress-timed, stress-accent language.[137] Ancient Greek, according to some analyses (e.g., Devine and Stephens 1994: 213–15), is more similar to Japanese, which is often described as a mora-timed language in which the primary acoustic correlate of accent is pitch:[138] the prediction here is that the regularization would affect *in primis* moras (as is the case for Japanese meter, which counts moras per line),[139] though pitch might also be involved.

The first part of the prediction seems to hold true for Ancient Greek: the meter cares about heavy vs. light syllables, and the hexameter can be described as a meter which must contain twenty-three to twenty-four moras per line.[140] This second part of the prediction seems to hold true as well: while intonational features are not usually part of how we describe Greek meters, the case can be made that standardized tunes also belonged to the poet's metrical grammar. In section 2.2.4 above, for instance, we discussed how Hagel (1994) has reconstructed an average melodic contour for the hexameter (and argued that this contour reflects the colometric organization of the line). Beyond that, we can easily imagine that standardized tunes might have been employed for particular contexts, in particular types of formulas, or by particular singers, just like Kuiper's race-calling commentators developed particular intonational ornaments for particular moments in their performances.

---

[137] Nespor, Shukla, and Mehler (2011: 1149) talk about *stress-timed languages* (like English), *syllable-timed languages* (like French), and *mora-timed languages* (like Japanese). This distinction, while widely used, remains the object of much debate.

[138] For this reason, Ancient Greek is often described as a "pitch accent" language (e.g., Probert 2003: 3, Gunkel 2014: 7), but the appropriateness of this designation in general (see Hyman 2009), and in the case of Ancient Greek in particular (see Sandell 2019), has been questioned. For a review of the evidence for mora-timing in Japanese, see Warner and Arai (2001).

[139] This, for instance, is the case for the *haiku*, consisting of a five-mora line, a seven-mora line, and a five-mora line (Devine and Stephens 1996: 214). For more on Japanese mora-counting meters, see Fabb (2015: 99–100).

[140] For this count, we ignore the difference between a heavy syllable and a superheavy syllable, and we compute both as having 2 μ (that is to say, we care about categorical weight, and count syllables as either heavy or light).

The creation of regular cola, the regulation of pauses, and the attainment of increased fluency are all part of this story as well. What we find in the Greek hexameter is that pauses are allowed only at the end of lines, and that those lines are made up of regularized phonological phrases (cola), and that poets employ formulaic sequences that fit those cola exactly. In other words, usage of automated (i.e., formulaic) sequences, regulation of rhythm, intonational patterns, and prosodic phrasing all converge to support the poet's performance.

2.5 Conclusion: Meter as Prosodic Optimization and the Poet's Freedom

Throughout this chapter, I have highlighted the parallels between the prosodic organization of ordinary speech and poetic meter (and Homer's meter in particular), starting from the smallest units of the prosodic hierarchy, such as syllables, feet, and words (section 2.1), and moving all the way to larger units, such as phonological phrases, intonational phrases, and utterances (section 2.2). In the process, I have touched upon many topics in the field of Homeric metrics (from the practicalities of scanning the hexametric line, to the debates on the colometry of the hexameter and enjambement in Homer). Section 2.3 provided a short excursus on current theories on the historical origin of the Greek hexameter. Finally, in section 2.4, I asked how meter (i.e., prosodic regularization) might arise in the context of some types of oral performance, and how it might support the performer's task.

In particular, building upon the work of Koenraad Kuiper, I have explored the hypothesis that prosodic regularization (along with reliance on formulaic sequences) emerges in the speech of oral performers when a given critical point of cognitive load is reached, as an adaptive response to the high cognitive strain. While prosodic regularization is only incipient in Kuiper's data, and does not form the sophisticated and entrenched patterns that we have discussed for Homeric poetry, the type of regularization that takes place (along the four parameters of length, rhythm, intonation, and pauses discussed above) is remarkably similar to the type of regularization that we find in English poetic meter.

Following Kuiper's reasoning,[141] I have argued that, in situations where the working memory could become overwhelmed, formularity and meter-like

---

[141] "A reduction of linguistic resources in the form of discourse rules, formulae, and stylized prosodics is necessary when speakers are under particular kinds of processing and working memory pressure. Oral formulaic performance provides these *reduced linguistic resources* and thus allows speakers to deal with processing pressure" (Kuiper 1996: 90, emphasis mine).

qualities help speakers sustain their language production by artificially *narrowing down their choices*. Paradoxically, these pared down choices are typically not perceived as language that is unnatural or impoverished. Rather, the language comes across as more stylized and skillful (i.e., more eloquent) than everyday speech. Arguably, the predictability of the patterns (whether phraseological or prosodic) creates a bond with the audience, allowing for the formation and fulfillment of expectations.[142] As a result, this type of language can be perceived as more engaging and entertaining, even though it originates from an attention-saving strategy.

Of course, these "emergency" technologies (i.e., meter and formularity) come at a price (one might argue, a heavy one): they require extensive, likely years-long training in order to be mastered. They might require a speaker to modify their speech to a high degree. They are not available to the casual user or the novice (even though the basic principles that make them up are available to every speaker). Once, however, these technologies are put into place, speakers can achieve (and maintain) an abnormal level of fluency, with relatively little effort, for extended amounts of time.

If this parallel is appropriate, then, at least for an oral poet, we can start to understand how meter is not a straitjacket to fight against: it is a powerful technology which streamlines language production by paring down the poet's choices, and that maximizes cognitive resources. In combination with formularity (with which it can be inextricably linked), it can support exceptional levels of fluency, such as those necessary to entertain an audience with a heroic tale for hours on end.

The view of meter as something directly related to cognition (and the limitations of working memory specifically) has been championed recently by Fabb (2015). In particular, Fabb has argued that the units of texts that are relevant for all types of poetic form (i.e., the units of text over which phenomena like meter, rhyme, alliteration, and parallelism operate) are always relatively short, and specifically short enough to fit comfortably within working memory, where they are likely to be processed. In Chapter 4, I will further argue that technologies like meter and formularity not only prevent a poet's working memory from becoming overwhelmed during an oral performance, but also actively support the poet's creativity.

In closing, a few more words should be said on the topic of metrical necessity (Gk. μετρική ἀνάγκη). For us Homerists, letting go of the idea of the absolute tyranny of meter over a poet's choices (rather than seeing meter as one of the many means to a given poetic end) is particularly hard.

---

[142] For this idea, see the discussion of US folk preachers in Bakker (1997: 134–35).

After all, entire books have been filled with detailed descriptions of how the poet's phonology, morphology, and lexicon are shaped by metrical constraints. It is easy to see meter everywhere in Homer, because, well, meter *is* everywhere: an invisible extension of the phonological environment, providing conditions for all sorts of linguistic alterations (for a compact overview, see Hackstein (2010), with references).

And yet, we might be overstating our case. For one thing, the rules are not unbreakable. As mentioned above, many lines in Homer are metrically imperfect, and have still made their way into the written tradition (whether orthographically patched up or not). It does not appear, in other words, that Homer's main goal was to win a metrics championship: meter was just another tool, another technology, that helped poets tell their stories. Often, meter bent language to its demands, and yet sometimes it did not.

It is also easy to overstate metrical necessity after the fact, by assuming that the way a poet decided to do something (or usually did something) was the only way that was available to them. Sure, once most of a given line is "filled out," only a given form of a word or a formula will fit best in the "remaining space." But that specific configuration of a line is the result of a long (and largely invisible) chain of decisions, which the poet could in many cases have altered, had they had a strong reason to do so: in Chapter 1, we discussed how one does not have to describe, for instance, the killing of a warrior, or the consumption of a meal, in a single line; one can choose between different discourse configurations and different levels of ornamentation; one can decide to use more or less traditional phraseology, all based on the circumstances of performance. And we should not always assume that we know in what order the poet's decisions were taken: did they use a given form of a noun-epithet formula because they wanted to use a given verb, or did they use a given verb because they wanted to use a given noun-epithet formula? The linear order of elements in a line might not always reflect the subconscious order of composition (as also seen in Chapter 1). This is not to say that metrical necessity is never the reason we find a given phenomenon in a given line, but that establishing metrical necessity should be a multistep process in which other potential factors are controlled for.[143]

The purpose of these observations, of course, is not to deny the importance of the findings of Witte, Parry, and many others (see fn. 1 above). In many ways, these discoveries are crucial to understanding the

---

[143] For an example involving evaluating the impact of metrical constraints on constituent order in battle scenes, see Bozzone (2014: 198–201).

complexity and sophistication of Homer's oral and traditional art. Rather, my goal is to carve out some space for appreciating the additional (and sometimes more interesting) reasons *beyond meter* that poets might rely on linguistic forms that are archaic, artificial, and dialectal for telling their stories, and attempting to recover the effect that these forms might have had on their audiences. It is to these tasks precisely that we will turn in the next chapter.

CHAPTER 3

Dialect

This sort of thing – the building up of a poetic language out of words and forms archaic and dialectal or used in special senses – may be regretted or disliked. There is nonetheless a case for it: the development of a form of language familiar in meaning and yet free from trivial associations, and filled with the memory of good and evil, is an achievement, and its possessors are richer than those who have no such tradition.

(Tolkien 2006: 55)

I'm an American guy faking an English accent faking an American accent.

(Green Day lead singer Billie Joe Armstrong, in a 1994 *Rolling Stone* interview)

3.1 Introduction: Words and Forms Archaic and Dialectal

In the absence of an explicit authorial presence, what holds epic poetry together, what identifies it clearly as epic poetry, is the poet's style. The most visible aspect of the poet's style, beyond meter and formularity, is dialect. One cannot read a single line of Homer without encountering the distinctive and intricate mix of archaic, artificial, and dialectal forms that we (and the Greeks) have come to associate with elevated epic poetry. Any passage will do as an example:

(1) Ἦ ῥα καὶ ἄλλον ὀϊστὸν ἀπὸ νευρῆ**φιν** ἴαλλεν
 Ἕκτορος ἀντικρύ, βαλ**έειν** δέ ἑ ἵετο θυμός·
 καὶ **τοῦ** μέν ῥ' ἀφάμαρθ', ὃ δ' ἀμύμονα Γοργυθίωνα
 υἱὸν ἐῢν Πριάμ**οιο** κατὰ στῆθος βάλεν ἰῷ,
 τόν ῥ' ἐξ Αἰσύμη**θεν** ὀπυιομένη τέκε μήτηρ
 καλὴ Καστιάνειρα δέμας ἐϊκυῖα **θεῇσι**.
 μήκων δ' ὡς ἑτέρωσε κάρη βάλεν, ἥ τ' **ἐνὶ** κήπῳ

καρπῷ βριθομένη νοτίῃσί τε εἰαρινῇσιν,
ὡς ἑτέρωσ᾽ ἤμυσε κάρη πήληκι βαρυνθέν. (*Il.* 8.300–8)

> Thus he spoke, and he shot another arrow from his bowstring
> aiming for Hector, for his *thūmós* desired to hit him:
> but he missed him, and instead he hit the blameless Gorguthíōn,
> a strong son of Priam, in the chest, with his arrow;
> he was the son of Priam's bride from Aisúmē,
> the beautiful Kastiáneira, with the form of a goddess.
> Like a poppy his head fell sideways, a garden poppy
> made heavy by its yields and the rains of the summertime,
> so his head bent sideways, made heavy by his helm.

In just a few lines, we can see how frequently Homer departs from standard Attic and the vernaculars in general, and opts instead for forms that are either archaic, dialectal, or artificial.[1] A quick survey will suffice:

- νευρῆ**φιν**: the Proto-Indo-European (PIE) morpheme *-$b^h i$ (cf. Hitt. *kuwa-pi* "where," and the Vedic athematic instrumental plural *-bhis*),[2] survived as a functioning case (one could argue postposition) in Mycenaean Greek but disappeared from all attested first-millennium vernaculars. In Homer, it survives for its metrical utility and archaizing color, even when extended beyond the athematic inflection, as in δακρυόφι "tears" (7x in Homer) and κοτυληδονόφιν "suckers (of an octopus)" (*Od.* 5.433), and covering functions spanning from instrumental, ablative, and locative, to (rarely) genitive and dative (Palmer 1962: 107). Note here its combination with the preposition ἀπό, which elsewhere selects for the genitive case of a bow or similar weapon (cf. *Il.* 8.279, *Il.* 24.605 and examples in Palmer 1962: 107). The application of the -ν *ephelkustikón*[3] to this form is, moreover, secondary, and usually recognized as an Attic–Ionic trait (Passa 2016a: 171).
- The artificial aorist infinitive form in βαλέειν "to hit" (with an extra -ε- preceding the infinitival ending) contrasts with Attic–Ionic βαλεῖν as well as with the Aeolic forms βαλεμεν (found in Thessalian and

---

[1] The most visible dialectal components of Homer's diction are commonly recognized as Ionic and Aeolic; see extensive discussion in sections 3.2 and 3.3 below.
[2] For a brief discussion, see Lundquist and Yates 2018: 7. On Mycenaean *-pi* and Homeric -φι, see Thompson 1999. On the usage and grammatical function in Homer, see now Goldstein 2020.
[3] Literally "attracted -ν," also known as "movable -ν". In Attic–Ionic, this segment can be added to the end of a closed class of vowel-final (specifically -ι- or -ε- final) nouns, verbs, numerals, and adverbs in order to prevent hiatus (though it is occasionally attested before consonant or interpunction). See Devine and Stephens 1994: 251–53, Agazzi and Vilardo 2002: 27.

Boeotian) and βαλην (found in Asiatic Aeolic). This is arguably an innovation of Homer's *Kunstsprache* (Nikolaev 2013), which remarkably has no counterpart in Hesiod's diction.[4]

- The absence of the augment in past indicative forms (as in ἴαλλεν "he shot," ἀφάμαρτε "he missed," τέκε "she gave birth to," and βάλεν "he hit"), vs. its occasional presence (as in ἤμυσε "it bent") is one of the most distinctive features of the Homeric verbal system. A similar alternation between augmented and unaugmented forms is found in the *Rigveda*, and many have been the attempts to explain the distributions.[5] Since the augment is considered an innovation in the Indo-European (IE) daughter languages (Fortson 2010: 101), augmentless forms (traditionally labeled as *injunctives* in the IE literature) can be regarded as archaic, or archaizing, variants.

- Another syntactic feature that sets the language of Homer clearly apart from other first-millennium Greek dialects is the usage of ὁ ἡ τό as demonstrative (anaphoric) and a relative pronoun but not as a definite article.[6] While some "article-like" adnominal usages of ὁ ἡ τό can be occasionally found in the poems,[7] the poets seem to steer away from this feature of their spoken vernacular when performing in the language of epic (Wackernagel 1924: xvi). Since the definite article is an innovation of first-millennium dialects (it is absent from Mycenaean), this feature too can be recognized as archaic or archaizing.[8]

- Πριάμοιο: the genitive singular of thematic nouns knows many shapes in Homer, from Attic -ου, to uncontracted *-οο, to this more archaic

---

[4] Note, however, that there are many ways to get to -εε-, and not all of them point towards a *Kunstsprache*-internal innovation. A good analogical base for such creations (i.e., uncontracted -εο- verbs) is present in all dialects except Attic. In fact, uncontracted forms of *verba vocalia* are commonly attested in Classical-era inscriptions, and remain common in the Greek of the Septuagint, cf. ἐδέετο "he prayed" and δέεσθαι "to pray."

[5] Some influential treatments of the augment are Kiparsky 2005 for Vedic and Bakker 2005 for Greek. Recent studies (taking into account both Vedic and Greek) are Willi 2018 and Hollenbaugh 2020 and 2021. In particular, Hollenbaugh argues that the augment did not originally mark past tense or perfective aspect (two popular proposals), but functioned as a marker of *certainty*, "functioning to exclude the modal uses available to the injunctive in discourse contexts other than past narration" (Hollenbaugh 2020: 3).

[6] Note that Attic uses ὁ ἡ τό as anaphoric, but not as relative; many other dialects use it as relative, including that of Herodotus, as well as Lesbian, Thessalian, Arcado-Cypriot, Boeotian, Heraclean, and Cyrenaean (Buck 1955: 101).

[7] These usages are often concentrated in stretches of text that have been suspected of late textualization, such as *Iliad* 10, or some passages in *Iliad* 1 (e.g., *Il.* 1.11, which West (1998: 4) considers corrupt on account of the article); they are also more likely in specific syntactic functions, like accompanying substantivized adjectives (γέρων "old man," ξεῖνος "stranger, guest"). It is impossible, however, to expunge our text of every adnominal usage of ὁ ἡ τό in such a way (Bozzone and Guardiano 2015).

[8] For the diachrony of the Greek definite article, see Guardiano 2013.

form which comes closest to the reconstructed PIE genitive ending *-osi̯o (cf. Ved. -asya, Old Lat. VALESIOSIO "of Valerius," and Myc. i-qo-jo "of the horse"). For Homer's audiences, -oιo forms may or may not have had a specific dialectal affiliation (see example (4) and section 3.2 below).

- Αἰσύμηθεν: another of the "extra" cases (or postpositions) surviving in Homer, -θεν has ablatival (like in example (1) above, where it means "from Aisū́mē") and sometimes genitival function. Limited traces survive in other dialects (including Attic: see Buck 1955: section 133.1).
- θεῇσι, νοτίῃσί, εἰαρινῇσιν: these dative plural endings for the first declension depart from Classical Attic -αις (reshaped by analogy to the second declension -οις) and literary Aeolic -αισι, as well as from Old Attic -ᾱ/ῃσι and Cretan -ᾱσι, which represent the expected outcome of inherited Proto-Greek *-eh₂-si (here, *-si replaces the PIE locative plural ending *-su). It is likely that the *iota subscript* in our -ῃσι is an innovation of the medieval tradition, on the model of -αις (Cassio 2016a: 85). In Homer, the more numerous datives in -ῃσι coexist with forms in -αις and -ῃς (a "camouflaged" form of the latter, according to Cassio 2016a: 85).
- ἐνί: a metrical variant for ἔν.

Remarkably, the mixing of diachronic and diatopic variants (i.e., linguistic variants coming from different places and different times) in Homer is so thorough that the poet will sometimes use two different variants of the same feature *within the same line* (examples from Hackstein 2010: 407–8):

(2) Τυδεΐδη μήτ' ἄρ με μάλ' **αἴνεε** μήτέ τι **νείκει**. (*Il.* 10.249)

   Son of Tūdeús, you should neither praise me so much, nor blame me

(3) δαίνυνταί τε παρ' **ἄμμι** καθήμενοι ἔνθα περ **ἡμεῖς**. (*Od.* 7.203)

   they dine among us, sitting alongside us

(4) **τοῖου** γὰρ κλέος ἐσθλὸν ἀπώλεσαν **ἡνιόχοιο** (*Il.* 23.280)

   of such a charioteer the great fame they have lost

In (2), the poet combines two diachronic variants: the (conservative) uncontracted allomorph of the second person singular present imperative ending -εε with its (later) contracted counterpart -ει.[9] In (3), we have two

---

[9] Admittedly, αἴνεε could also be an analogical re-creation that happens to look like an archaism.

diatopic variants: the Aeolic and Ionic forms respectively of the first person plural personal pronoun (in the dative and nominative case respectively). Example (4) represents a possible case of combined diachronic and diatopic variation: while the variant -οιο for the genitive singular of the thematic declension is etymologically older than the contracted -ου common in Attic, it is also taken as a distinctly continental Aeolic feature by some (see Haug 2002: 106, 146, 160).

Artificial languages (or artistic languages) of this kind are familiar to the student of traditional epic: Tolkien's aforementioned quote, from a famous essay on translating *Beowulf*, makes a forceful case for their value.[10] Because such languages are most often observed in poetry, a common assumption is that meter (i.e., the necessity to satisfy different metrical constraints in different positions in the line) is a determinant factor in their development. Examples (2) and (4) above seem to confirm this intuition: in both cases, the variants yield different metrical shapes. In (4), switching the two genitive endings would result in a wholly unmetrical line. In (2), an uncontracted νείκεε would be unmetrical at the line end. However, meter is not all that is at stake here, since at least some of our variants are isometric: if used at the line end, the first person plural dative personal pronoun ἄμμι in (3) would scan in exactly the same way as its Ionic counterparts ἥμιν and ἦμιν;[11] in (2), the contracted form αἴνει would be a tolerable substitute for uncontracted αἴνεε in the fourth foot.[12] Examples of this kind could be multiplied, which indicates that poets must have had some additional reason to alternate between different variants.[13]

---

[10] Tolkien goes on to admonish translators who wish to "modernize" such poetic languages: "Personally you may not like an archaic vocabulary, and word-order, artificially maintained as an elevated literary language. You may prefer the brand-new, the lively and the snappy. But whatever may be the case with poets of other ages (with Homer, for instance), the author of *Beowulf* did not share this preference. If you wish to translate, not re-write, *Beowulf*, your language must be literary and traditional: not because it is now long since the poem was made, or because it speaks of things that have since become ancient; but because the diction of *Beowulf* was poetical, archaic, artificial (if you will), in the day that the poem was made." (Tolkien 2006: 54). Despite Tolkien's caution about Homer, this admonishment applies very fittingly to the Archaic Greek epic corpus.

[11] The only difference is that for Aeolic ἄμμι(ν) the final nasal is optional, while in Ionic ἥμιν and ἦμιν it is obligatory. More precisely, then, one might say that the three forms are metrically equivalent *before vowel*, or, like here, at line end.

[12] Even though (as seen in Chapter 2) in this position, before the bucolic diaeresis, a sequence of two light syllables is generally preferred.

[13] As we shall see below, one influential theory that aims to explain the coexistence of Ionic and Aeolic forms in Homer argues that the presence of Aeolisms in the diction is predicated on their metrical utility (that is, Aeolic forms exist in Homer on a needs-only basis). This position, most recently formulated by Nagy (2011), can be referred to succinctly as the *Aeolic default*: "Homeric diction defaults to Aeolic forms when it has no metrically equivalent forms in Ionic" (Nagy 2011: 144).

Introduction: Words and Forms Archaic and Dialectal

Hackstein (2002: Chapter 3) investigated parallels to Homer's mixed dialect in literary prose, particularly with reference to the coexistence of diachronic variants. As it turns out, this type of variability is well documented in the history of many IE languages, from Standard German (whether in Martin Luther or in Standard New High German), to eighteenth-century Russian, to Tocharian.[14] Crucially, variation can occur in the complete absence of metrical concerns. Hackstein traces this phenomenon to the interplay of two opposing forces in the development of a literary language (whether in prose or poetry): the tendency to seek the prestige of archaic forms, as well as the inevitable seeping of high-frequency forms of daily speech into the literary medium. We can see this coexistence in Homer, where the more archaic second person singular present indicative form of "be," ἐσσι "you are," is found alongside the younger "*umgangssprachlich*" Ionic form εἶς (Hackstein 2002: 103–4).

Yet the emphasis on the elevated and the literary may lead us astray here, and make us miss some of the most striking parallels to Homer's language that surround us nowadays. Focusing on the literary aspect may even make us miss part of what these languages achieve – which is not simply to transport us to a mythical past, but has a lot to do with negotiating the poet's identity within the stream of one (or more) poetic traditions. What this rich dialectal mix does, almost without us noticing, is to construct the poet's voice, telling the audience who they are and where they are from (at least for the purposes of this performance), what models they are trying to evoke, and where in the tradition their affiliation lies. In section 3.6, we shall explore some (perhaps unexpected) contemporary parallels for these types of mixed performance languages, and see whether they can shed light on our own thinking about Homer and the Homeric question altogether. First, though, we will look more closely at the role that Greek dialects play with respect to literary *Kunstsprachen* in general, and Homer's *Kunstsprache* more specifically.

Exceptions to this rule, which one can call *unnecessary* or *optional Aeolisms*, require special handling within this theory (Nagy 2011: 149–51). See further discussion in section 3.4.2 below.

[14] According to Hackstein (2002: 57), some phases in the formation and development of literary languages are more prone to variation than others: this is because the work of prescriptive grammarians often curtails (if only partially) the proliferation of variants. Hackstein identifies three phases in the development of a literary language: (1) Constitution (*Konstituierungsphase*), (2) Consolidation (*Konsolidierungsphase*), and (3) Destabilization (*Destabilisierungsphase*). Phases (1) and (3) are the most vulnerable to variation, though no phase is immune to it.

3.2 Archaic and Dialectal Features in Homer

Before stepping more deeply into this debate, it might be useful to lay out an overview of dialectal and archaic features in Homer, which may serve as references in our further discussion.[15] Many longer and fuller treatments of such topics exist in the literature. In order of increasing scale and detail, the reader might consult the short-sized overview in Hackstein (2010), the medium-sized Horrocks (1997) and Passa (2016a), and the longer (though slightly older) Palmer (1962), which is still the best compact but comprehensive treatment of Homeric grammar in English. Finally, the two volumes of Chantraine (1948, 1953) are the classic reference work on Homer's phonology, morphology, and morphosyntax.[16] Miller (2014: Chapters 24 and 25) offers extensive discussion of Homer's dialect and its origin, but is often idiosyncratic. For Greek dialects in general, the most accessible introduction continues to be Buck (1955); a fuller treatment is Thumb and Kiekers (1932) and Thumb and Scherer (1959).

A short list of archaic and dialectal features attested in the language of Homer is provided here. For clarity, the list is sorted from conservative features (i.e., features that preserve the Proto-Greek situation) to innovative features,[17] which in turn are sorted by the first-millennium dialects that attest them, namely the Aeolic and Ionic dialects that most contemporary scholarship has deemed relevant for the language of Homer: these are Asiatic and Continental Aeolic, East and West Ionic, and Attic (see discussion in section 3.4 below).[18] Just like in the stemmatic method of textual criticism, the distinction between conservative and innovative features is crucial, in that only *nontrivial shared innovations* can be used to group items into families (in this case, create dialectal groupings). All of

---

[15] The artificial features would be too many to list here, especially those which are metrically driven; for an overview, see Hackstein (2010: 408–13). A classic treatment is Witte (1913).

[16] Sadly, these predate the decipherment of Mycenaean and the development of laryngeal theory, for which reason a new, updated Homeric Grammar has been a desideratum in the scholarship for decades.

[17] For a compact overview of the changes and relative chronology going from PIE, to Proto-Greek, to the first-millennium dialects, see Rau (2010). An authoritative and linguistically up-to-date medium-sized treatment is Cassio (2016a). The classic book-length reference for the historical grammar of Greek is Rix (1976).

[18] Asiatic Aeolic was spoken on the island of Lesbos (where one can speak more specifically of Lesbian) and on the facing coast of Asia Minor, roughly between the Hellespont and Smyrna (see Figure 3.1). Continental Aeolic indicates the two non-adjacent varieties of Aeolic spoken in Thessaly and Boeotia (i.e., Thessalian and Boeotian). East Ionic was spoken on the central coast of Asia Minor (roughly between Smyrna and Halicarnassus). West Ionic was spoken in Euboea. A third variety of Ionic, not listed here, is Island Ionic (sometimes referred to as Central Ionic), spoken on the Cycladic islands. With colonization, these dialects spread to further locations around the Mediterranean.

the sound changes discussed below are notated as changes affecting *sounds* (e.g., [s]), not *phonemes* (e.g., /s/).[19] When relevant, Classical Attic forms are given as comparison.

1. Conservative features, which continue the Proto-Greek situation. Dialects that preserve each feature are also given in parentheses.
    a. Phonology:
        i. Alleged metrical preservation of PIE *[r̥], as in λιποῦσ' ἀνδροτῆτα καὶ ἥβην "leaving behind manliness and youth" (*Il.* 16.857, 22.363) (already discussed in section 2.3.1).[20]
        ii. Metrical preservation of PIE *[w] (actually preserved in Mycenaean, West Greek, Boeotian, and Thessalian), as in πρῶτος *[w]ἴδεν (*Il.* 22.25).
        iii. Preservation of word-initial [pt] sequences (Mycenaean, Arcado-Cypriot, Continental Aeolic), as in πτόλις "city," πτόλεμος "battle" (cf. Attic πόλις, πόλεμος).
        iv. Preservation of *[ti] (Continental Aeolic, West Greek), as in βωτιάνειρα "nurse of men" (epithet of Phthia, Thessaly in *Il.* 1.155). The change of *[ti] > [si] is common in many other dialects (including Attic–Ionic and Asiatic Aeolic).[21]
        v. Preservation of vowel sequences without contraction (Mycenaean, Aeolic, etc.),[22] as in neuter nom./acc.pl. φάρεα "cloths" (cf. Mycenaean *pa-we-a₂* "cloths"), 2.sg. pres.act.imp. αἴνεε "praise!" (see fn. 4), nom.sg. φάος "light" (cf. Attic φῶς).
        vi. Preservation of vowel sequences without quantitative metathesis (all dialects but Attic–Ionic), as in gen.sg. βασιλῆος "of the king," gen.sg. νηός "of the ship" (cf. Attic βασιλέως, νεώς).

---

[19] For the difference between *sound changes* or *sound laws* (i.e., diachronic changes that hold between two moments in time in our historical record, written as [sm] > [mm]) and *phonological rules* (i.e., synchronic rules in the grammar of a speaker, which operate between an *underlying representation* and a *surface realization*, written as /sm/ → [mm]), see Hayes (2009a: Chapter 10).

[20] Another form which is often mentioned in relation to the potential preservation of [r̥] in Homer is the epithet ἀνδρειφόντης, usually translated as "killer of men," contained in the repeated verse Μηριόνης (τ') ἀτάλαντος Ἐνυαλίῳ ἀνδρειφόντῃ "(and) Mēriónēs, who is equal in heft to Enuálios, the killer of men" (*Il.* 2.651, 7.166, 8.264, 17.259) for which see now Höfler (2019), with references.

[21] See discussion in Buck (1955: 57–58).

[22] Some vowel contractions occur in most dialects, though in different ways and to different extents (for an overview, see Buck 1955: 36–43). Attic–Ionic tends to contract more (and earlier) than other dialects, and Attic more so than Ionic.

vii. Heterosyllabic scansion of *muta cum liquida* sequences (East Ionic), as in πατ.ρός (*Od.* 1.94).
b. Morphology
   i. Preservation of the "instrumental" ending in *-phi* (Mycenaean), discussed above (interestingly, these were considered an Aeolic trait by the ancient grammarians, see Meillet 1920: 127).
   ii. Preservation of the dual (Attic until fourth century BCE, West Greek), as in nom. dual ὄσσε "the two eyes."
   iii. Optionality of the augment (see above in the discussion of example (1)).
   iv. Patronymic adjective in -ιος (Mycenaean, Aeolic), as in Τελαμώνιος "son of Telamōn."
   v. Thematic genitives in -οιο (Mycenaean, Continental Aeolic), as in θεοῖο "of the god," Οὐλύμποιο "of Olympus," etc.
   vi. Preservation of various archaisms in the verbal system (for a list, see Passa 2016a: 156–57).
c. Syntax
   i. *Tmesis* (i.e., the optional splitting of compound verbs, i.e., verbs including a prepositional prefix), as in πρότερος πρὸς μῦθον ἔειπε "first he replied" (*Il.* 13.306) vs. προσέειπε.[23]
   ii. Lack of definite article (Mycenaean).
2. Innovative features, sorted by the first-millennium dialects that attest them.[24]
   a. Aeolic innovations
      i. Pan-Aeolic
         (1) *[r̥] > [or/ro], as in βροτός "mortal" (*Il.* 3.223, lexeme 116x).
         (2) *[kʷ], *[gʷ], *[gʷʰ] > [p], [b], [pʰ] before [e], as in 3.sg. pres.mid.ind. πέλεται "becomes" (*Il.* 1.284, lexeme 109x)[25] (<*PIE *k^wel- "to turn").[26]

---

[23] See Haug (2012), who argues that *tmesis* came to be preferred by poets in later stages of the tradition, even though it had become by then a fully artificial feature.

[24] An effort has been made to provide attestations and counts for each Homeric form, so that the reader can easily look up examples for the forms discussed, as well as get an idea of how common such forms are. Examples give either one representative attestation (if more than five attestations occur) or list all of the attestations (if fewer than five occur). The counts given here for Homer were obtained by selecting the texts of the *Iliad* and *Odyssey* in the TLG, then using the "Search by Lemma" and/or "Word Index" functions.

[25] The Attic–Ionic outcome of this verbal root, τέλλω "to accomplish," is attested 7x in Homer (e.g., κρατερὸν δ᾽ ἐπὶ μῦθον ἔτελλε "he gave a harsh command," *Il.* 1.25).

[26] Another oft-cited example is πεμπώβολα "five-pronged fork" (*Il.* 1.463) (<*PIE *$penk^w$- "five"), which was taken as an Aeolic trait by the author of the *Vita Herodotea* (see section 3.4.1). For a

(3) Extension of the -*ont*- suffix to perfect active participles, as in κεκλήγοντες "having shouted" (*Il.* 12.125, 16.430, 17.756, 17.759, *Od.* 14.30), cf. Attic κεκληγότες, with the suffix -*ot*- (< post-Mycenaean *-*wot*-).

(4) Usage of the modal particle κε(ν) (1184x) vs. Attic–Ionic ἄν (308x).

(5) Monosyllabic prepositions, such as πάρ (104x, also before consonants, as in *Od.* 1.132), κάτ (*Od.* 17.246, *Od.* 22.291), ἄν (also before consonants, as in *Il.* 1.143, *Od.* 2.416), vs. Attic–Ionic παρά, κατά, ἀνά. In Aeolic, the last consonant of prepositions also assimilated to a following consonant. This usage is well represented in Homer, in sequences like ἄμ πεδίον "on the plain" (*Il.* 5.96, ἄμ 14x) κάκ κεφαλῆς "down the head" (*Il.* 18.24, κάκ 10x), or the very frequent κάδ δέ (*Il.* 2.160, κάδ 55x).[27]

(6) Extension of dative plurals in -εσσι to consonant stems beyond -*s*- stems,[28] as in ἄνδρεσσι(ν) "to men" (*Il.* 5.546, 20x), vs. Attic–Ionic ἀνδράσι(ν) "id." (*Il.* 1.151, 67x).

ii. Continental Aeolic

(1) -μεν ending in thematic and athematic infinitives, as in ἔμμεν "to be" (5x in Homer), ἴμεν "to go" (57x in Homer), εἰπέμεν "to say" (6x in Homer).

iii. Asiatic Aeolic

(1) Proto-Greek *[sm], *[sn], *[sl], *[sr] (these are the same sequences that are involved in the *first compensatory lengthening* in other dialects) > [mm], [nn], [ll], and [rr], as in ἐρεβεννή "dark" (*Il.* 5.659, lexeme 8x, <*-sn-*), ἄμμι(ν) "to us" (*Il.* 1.384, 20x, Proto-Greek *asm*- < PIE *n̥sm-*).[29] This geminate outcome with regressive assimilation is also found in Thessalian.[30]

---

different interpretation, see Cassio (2016a: 49), who argues that the form is simply an archaism without a specific dialectal affiliation.

[27] Examples are also found among compound verbs, such as κάππεσον "I fell down" (*Il.* 1.593, 12.23, 16.662, 23.731), vs. Attic κατέπεσον "id.".

[28] This ending is expected for *s*-stem nouns and adjectives, where -εσ- is part of the stem.

[29] This change can be notated more economically as Proto-Greek *[sR] > [RR], where R stands for "any resonant."

[30] By *regressive assimilation* we mean an assimilatory phenomenon whereby the first segment in a sequence becomes more articulatorily similar to the following segment; assimilation can be *partial*, whereby only some articulatory features are copied, or *complete*, where the first segment becomes

(2) Geminate outcome of intervocalic [kʷ], as in the indefinite/interrogative conjunction ὅππως "in which way" (19x in our poems), and in the indefinite/interrogative pronoun/adjective ὁππότερος, -α, -ον "who/which of the two" (13x in our poems) (<PIE *-kʷo-tero-, cf. Skt. *katará*) vs. Attic ὅπως (55x in our poems), ὁπότερος, -α, -ον (which would not fit into the hexameter).

(3) Geminate outcome [ss] for the Proto-Greek sequences *[tj] and *[tʰj], as in the correlative pronoun PIE *tot-i̯o- > τόσσος, η, -ον (lexeme 79x), vs. Attic–Ionic τόσος, η, -ον (lexeme 46x) and in the adjective PIE *medʰ-i̯os "middle" > Proto-Greek *metʰ-i̯os > μέσσος, -η, -ον (lexeme 83x), Attic–Ionic μέσος, -η, -ον (lexeme 62x).

(4) Geminate outcome [ss] for original sequences of two [s] at a morpheme boundary, as in PIE transponat *h₁es-so- > Proto-Greek *es-so-mai "I will be" > ἔσσομαι (*Il.* 4.267, 10.324, 16.499, 17.180), Attic–Ionic ἔσομαι (*Il.* 6.409, *Od.* 13.129, 16.171, 21.131).³¹

(5) A geminate outcome [ss] is also found for sequences of [t] + [s] at a morpheme boundary, as in the aorist form Proto-Greek *dat-sa-nto "they distributed" > δάσσαντο (*Il.* 1.368, *Od.* 19.423) vs. Attic–Ionic ἐδάσαντο (*Od.* 14.208).

(6) *Barytonesis*, i.e., retraction of the accent,³² as in some forms of the word for "son," which is oxytone in Attic–Ionic

---

identical to the second (in the examples under discussion, a sibilant segment [s] has become completely assimilated to the following nasal or liquid segment). The opposite phenomenon, *progressive assimilation*, happens when a segment becomes more articulatorily similar to the preceding segment. In ancient IE languages, regressive assimilation seems to be more frequent overall than progressive assimilation.

³¹ These geminate forms are innovative, as PIE did not allow for two identical consonants to surface at a morpheme boundary (see discussion in Sandell (2015: 4–6), with references), so PIE */h₁es-si/ "you are" was realized as *[h₁esi], and is reflected in Sanskrit *ási*: from this point of view, Hom. ἐσσι should be seen as an innovation, and not an archaism, even though it reflects the PIE underlying form more closely.

³² While the term *barytonesis* originally referred to the retraction of an acute accent from the final syllable of a word (in this sense, *barytone words* are words that are not accented on the final syllable, as opposed to *oxytone words*, which are), this phenomenon is part of a more general pattern in Asiatic Aeolic (i.e., Lesbian), whereby all words receive the *recessive accent*, which in Attic–Ionic is limited to only some lexical items, including, most notably, almost all finite verbs. On the recessive accent in Greek, see Probert 2003: 34–35. It has been argued that Thessalian, too, retracted its accent (Probert 2003: 164). Boeotian, on the other hand, does not appear to share this innovation (Probert 2003: 162–63).

(nom. sg. υἱός, 216x in our poems). These forms are: genitive singular υἷος "of the son" (*Il.* 13.522, 14x in our poems, vs. Attic–Ionic υἱοῦ, which occurs only once at *Od.* 22.238), dative singular υἷι "to the son" (*Il.* 2.20, 11x, vs. Attic–Ionic υἱῷ), accusative singular υἷα "son" (*Il.* 2.129, 7x, vs. Attic–Ionic υἱόν), nominative and accusative dual υἷε "the two sons" (*Il.* 2.679, 10x, vs. Attic–Ionic υἱεῖ), nominative plural υἷες "sons" (*Il.* 1.162, 10x, vs. Attic–Ionic υἱεῖς).[33]

(7) *Psilosis*, i.e., loss of word-initial [h], as in the specifically Aeolic acc.pl. forms ἄμμε "us" (*Od.* 9.404, 14x), ὔμμε "you guys" (*Il.* 23.412, 9x). These forms also show the regressive assimilation just discussed. Note that East Ionic is responsible for some other psilotic forms in Homer (see below).

(8) Prefix ζα- for δια-, as in ζάθεος "sacred" (epithet of towns or islands, 7x in the *Iliad*).[34]

(9) -μεναι ending in thematic and athematic infinitives, as in ἔμμεναι "to be" (*Il.* 1.117, 85x), ἴμεναι "to go" (*Il.* 6.393, 20.32, 20.365, 16x in *Od.*), εἰπέμεναι "to say" (*Il.* 7.375, 14.501, *Od.* 4.682).

b. Attic–Ionic innovations
  i. Pan-Attic–Ionic
  (1) *[r̥] >[ar/ra], as in τέταρτον "fourth" (*Od.* 2.89, 8x) vs. τέτρατον "id." (*Od.* 2.107, 7x).

---

[33] This word has a complex paradigm in Homer (and elsewhere in Greek: see Chantraine (1968–80 [2009]) s.v.), since it can inflect both as a thematic stem (*o-* stem, likely a secondary development) and as a *u-* stem noun (where the suffix can show up in the full grade -*eu-* or in the zero-grade -*u-*), and the -*i-* can be lost between vowels. The familiar Attic forms given here for comparison are all *o-*stems, while the Homeric forms under discussion are *u-* stems with zero-grade of the suffix (in which the -*u-*, being intervocalic, and thus realized as [w], has been lost). What interests us here, however, is not the difference in inflectional class, but the retraction of the accent, which is traditionally recognized as an Aeolic feature. More examples of retracted accentuation in Homer, arguably due to Asiatic Aeolic, are given in Chantraine (1948: 190–91).

[34] Arguably, this type of *διά + adjective compound (where *διά- has intensive semantics) could be regarded as a *morphological* Pan-Aeolic innovation, which was unknown to Attic–Ionic. For Hom. ζάθεος, no equivalent "Attic–Ionic" *διάθεος is attested, while we have a Boeotian form δάθιος attested in Corinna 654 (a) 13 (showing the regular continental Aeolic development for the sequence). Many similar *διά- compounds are found in the works of the Lesbian poets, showing the regular Asiatic Aeolic development *διά- > ζα- (cf. Buck 1955: 26). Similarly, Hom. ζατρεφής "well-fed (of animals)" (ix *Il.*, 3x *Od.*) exists apparently next to the Attic verb διατρέφω "to feed, support" (attested from Thucydides onwards), but the verb does not have the same intensive semantics as the adjective, and the two appear to be entirely independent creations.

(2) *[aː] >[εː], as in the Ionic gen.sg. νηός "of the ship" < Proto-Greek *nāw-ós < PIE *neh₂ w-ós (note that Attic gen.sg. νεώς shows quantitative metathesis – see section 3.4.2 below).³⁵

(3) Degemination of */ss/ > [s], as in μέσος, -η, -ον "middle" (lexeme 62x) vs. μέσσος, -η, -ον (lexeme 83x); τελέσαι "to finish" (*Od.* 2.272, 12x) vs. τελέσσαι "to finish" (*Od.* 23.250, 5x); ἔσομαι "I will be" (*Il.* 6.409, *Od.* 13.129, 16.171, 21.131) vs. ἔσσομαι "I will be" (*Il.* 4.267, 10.324, 16.499, 17.180). As already mentioned, the geminated variants are usually recognized as Aeolic.³⁶

(4) *[kʷ], *[gʷ], *[gʷʰ] > [t], [d], [tʰ] before [e], as in πέντε "five" (<PIE *penkʷ-).

(5) *[ti] > *[si], as in εἴκοσι "twenty" (<PIE *wīkm̥tī).³⁷

(6) First compensatory lengthening: long vowel outcome with loss of [s]: *[VsR] > [VːR], as in the stem of the 1.pl.acc. personal pronoun ἡμέας "us" ([εːme-] < *[aːme]- <Proto-Greek *[asme-] <PIE *n̥sme-).

(7) Contraction of vowels, as in κοιμῶντο "they were sleeping" (*Il.* 6.246, 6.250), cf. the uncontracted form *κοιμάοντο.³⁸

(8) Quantitative metathesis, as in Ἀτρεΐδεω "of the son of Atreus" (*Il.* 2.185, 7x) vs. Aeolic Ἀτρεΐδαο "id." (*Il.* 1.203, 27x), < *-āo. See discussion in section 3.4.2.

---

³⁵ Many forms derived from the zero-grade of this root show, as expected, short [a] in Greek, such as the form ναυσι- in Homeric ναυσίκλυτος "famous for his ship" (lexeme 6x, an epithet for the Phaeacians and the Phoenicians) or the agent noun ναύτης "sailor" (lexeme 12x).
³⁶ As discussed above, these forms come from a variety of sources: some result from sequences of Proto-Greek [t] or [tʰ] + [j], as in PIE *medʰ-jos "middle" > Proto-Greek *metʰ-ios > Aeolic μέσσος, Attic–Ionic μέσος. Some result from a sequence of two [s] at a morpheme boundary, as in PIE transponat *h₁es-so- > Proto-Greek *es-so-mai "I will be" > Aeolic ἔσσομαι, Attic–Ionic ἔσομαι. Some yet come from a sequence of [t] and [s], also at a morpheme boundary, as in Proto-Greek *dat-sa-nto "they distributed" > Aeolic δάσσαντο (*Il.* 1.368, *Od.* 19.423), Attic–Ionic ἐδάσαντο (*Od.* 14.208).
³⁷ This process is called *assibilation*. Sibilants (such as [s]) are a subset of fricative sounds which are produced by directing a stream of air to the upper teeth, thus creating a noisy turbulent flow (Hayes 2009a: 7).
³⁸ The phenomenon known as *epic distraction* (Gk. διέκτασις "stretching") famously "repairs" some of these contractions (which change the metrical shape of the word involved, thus potentially disrupting the meter) by creating artificial forms. This pattern is well established for verbal forms, especially verbs in -αω. See, e.g., the *distracted form* κερόωντο "they poured" in *Od.* 8.470, 20.253 vs. the corresponding contracted form κερῶντο "id." in *Od.* 15.500; the correct historical form would have been *κεράοντο. For more examples of distraction, see Chantraine (1948: Chapter 5).

(9) Earlier thematic genitive singular in *-oo (which scans as two light syllables in isolation), as in Ἰλίου προπάροιθε "before Ilion" (*Il.* 15.66), which must be read as *Ἰλίοο προπάροιθε.[39] Note that this stage could also be reconstructed for Aeolic.[40]

(10) Later, contracted thematic genitive singular in -ου (which scans as a single heavy syllable in isolation), as in νόστου "of the return" (*Od.* 5.344), ὀφθαλμοῦ "of the eye" (*Od.* 1.69).

(11) Third person plural active ending in -σαν, as in (ἔ)θεσαν "they put" (*Il.* 1.290, 35x, vs. Proto-Greek *-the-n < PIE *$d^h h_1$-nt), τάνυσσαν "they stretched" (4x).[41]

(12) -ν *ephelkustikón* (see fn. 3) on verbal forms, as in προσέειπεν "he said." In some cases, the -ν arguably covers an older [w], as in the expression ἴδεν ἄστεα "he saw cities" (*Od.* 1.3) < *ϝίδε ϝάστεα (cf. Mycenaean *wa-tu* "town").[42]

ii. East Ionic

(1) Psilosis, as in οὖλος "whole" (vs. Attic ὅλος "whole"), ἐπ-ίστιον "shed for a ship" in *Od.* 6.265 (vs. Attic ἵστιον "sail").[43]

(2) *[kʷ] > [k] before [o], as in the adverbial form κως "in any way," and in the pronominal form κοῖος, -η, -ον "of what kind" (these forms are not attested in Homer, but they are attested in Herodotus).

(3) Third compensatory lengthening, as in ξεῖνος "guest" (<ξένϝος, a form still attested in Corinth) vs. Attic ξένος "guest." Note that the forms *with* compensatory

---

[39] The expression scans –⏑⏑–⏑⏑–⏑, with the following syllable division: Ἰ.λί.ο.ο π.ρο.πά.ροι.θε.
[40] Note that *-oo forms are not actually attested in our manuscript tradition: they are (relatively safe) conjectures based on metrical considerations (cf. West 1998: xxxiii–iv, with references).
[41] The original PIE ending expected here would have been *-nt, which is very well preserved (as -ν, with regular loss of word-final *-t) in other verbal forms in Homer, and overall more frequent than -σαν (cf. Chantraine 1948: 471–72). For the verb τίθημι "I put" specifically, Homer has another aorist third person plural active form, ἔθηκαν/θῆκαν "they put" (*Il.* 6.300, 10x), which is also an innovation of Attic–Ionic, and a particularly recent one at that (cf. Chantraine 1948: 379).
[42] See recently Hämmig (2013). [43] Examples from Passa (2016a: 164).

lengthening are overwhelmingly predominant in our poems.[44]

   iii. West Ionic[45]
      (1) Reversion of [ɛː] (<η>) to [aː] after [e], [i], and [r], as in the voc.sg. θεά "O goddess" (*Il.* 1.1).
      (2) *[kʷ] > [p] before [o], as in the interrogative form πῶς "in what way" (21x in Homer), and in the pronoun ποῖος, -η, -ον "of what kind" (28x in Homer). The East Ionic forms κῶς and κοῖος, -η, -ον are attested in Herodotus.
   iv. Attic
      (1) Reversion of [ɛː] to [aː] (after [e], [i], and [r]), as in θεά "O goddess" (*Il.* 1.1). Same as West Ionic.[46]
      (2) *[kʷ] > [p] before [o], as in the interrogative form πῶς "in what way" (21x in Homer), and in the pronoun ποῖος, -η, -ον "of what kind" (28x in Homer). Same as West Ionic.
      (3) *Correptio attica*, as in the second syllable of Πάτ.ρο.κλε (*Il.* 19.287). Note that this treatment is unique for this lexical item (cf. the standard treatment Πάτ.ροκ.λε in *Il.* 18.333).
      (4) Further vowel contractions.

Now that we have covered these features, we can step back into our discussion.

---

[44] For instance, the root ξειν- is attested 240x in the *Odyssey* and 25x in the *Iliad* (either in the word for "guest," or in compounds like φιλόξεινος, -η, -ον "who welcomes guests"), while the root ξεν- is only attested 7x in the *Odyssey* (and never in the *Iliad*). Similarly, the root μουν- "only" (<*μονϝ-) is attested 41x in our poems, while the root μον- "id." is effectively a *hapax* (μονωθείς "having been left alone," *Il.* 11.470). While this specific vocalic outcome for the third compensatory lengthening is East Ionic, the phenomenon in itself is attested in other dialects (with the exception of Attic), and it maintains the syllable weight of the pre-form (e.g., ξέν.ϝος). From this point of view, one could arguably see the East-Ionic outcome as conservative (with respect to the meter), and the Attic outcome, with light scansion of the first syllable (e.g., ξέ.νος), as innovative. See forms in Buck (1955: 49–50), and discussion in Cassio (2016a: 69–70).

[45] West Ionic is included here for the sake of completeness, but note that all the innovations listed here are also listed under Attic. We thus have no compelling reason, at this level, to postulate a specifically West Ionic (vs. Attic) component in the language of Homer. See discussion in section 3.4.2 below.

[46] Reversion had stopped operating before post-consonantal [w] was lost, as one can see in the Attic form κόρη "girl" (and not κόρα), < Common Attic–Ionic *[korwɛː] < Proto-Greek *korwā. Note that, for this lexeme, Homer only has East-Ionic forms, with the third compensatory lengthening, as in the nom.sg. κούρη (*Il.* 2.872, 36x, lexeme 112x). The acc.sg. Attic form κόρην appears once in *Homeric Hymn to Demeter* 439, which has an Attic setting (note that the East-Ionic lexeme κούρη, with the third compensatory lengthening, occurs 9x in the same hymn).

3.3 Greek Dialects and Identity

3.3.1 The Maiden Choir at Delos, and Faking Others' Dialects

Our epigraphic and literary record of Ancient Greece reveals a great amount of dialectal variation from very early on.[47] But to what extent, we might ask, were the Greeks of Homer's time themselves aware of such variation (in speech and song), and how did they perceive it? In what follows, we will look at evidence for dialectal diversity (and dialectal imitation) in Archaic Greek literature.

The Homeric hymn to Delian Apollo culminates in a show-stopping scene, which reads like an advertisement for the famous sanctuary: a choir of maidens, servants of the god, give a performance in which they are able to imitate in song the accents and speech patterns (φωνάς καὶ βαμβαλιαστύν[48]) of all men.

(5) πρὸς δὲ τόδε μέγα θαῦμα, ὅου κλέος οὔποτ' ὀλεῖται,
κοῦραι Δηλιάδες, ἑκατηβελέταο θεράπναι·
αἵ τ' ἐπεὶ ἄρ πρῶτον μὲν Ἀπόλλων' ὑμνήσωσιν,
αὖτις δ' αὖ Λητώ τε καὶ Ἄρτεμιν ἰοχέαιραν,
μνησάμεναι ἀνδρῶν τε παλαιῶν ἠδὲ γυναικῶν
ὕμνον ἀείδουσιν, θέλγουσι δὲ φῦλ' ἀνθρώπων.
πάντων δ' ἀνθρώπων φωνὰς καὶ βαμβαλιαστὺν
μιμεῖσθ' ἴσασιν· φαίη δέ κεν αὐτὸς ἕκαστος
φθέγγεσθ'· οὕτω σφιν καλὴ συνάρηρεν ἀοιδή. (*Homeric Hymn to Apollo*, 3.156–64)

> And beyond that a great marvel, whose fame will never perish,
> the Delian maidens, servants of the far-shooter:
> they first sing a hymn to Apollo,
> and then to Leto and Artemis the archer,
> and remembering the men and women of old,
> they sing a hymn and delight the races of men.
> Of all men they can imitate the accents and chatter:

---

[47] Evidence for various dialects of first-millennium Greek is, of course, extensive. It is very likely that dialectal variation was also found in second-millennium Greek, though our evidence from the Mycenaean texts is limited. For variation in Mycenaean Greek, see Milani (2013), with references.

[48] It is reasonable here to interpret φωνάς as "accents" rather than "voices," because it seems unlikely that the musical performance described in the hymn would consist of imitating "the voice quality (i.e., high, low, clear, raspy or the like) of all men." On the other hand, as we shall see, imitating "foreign" dialectal features is a well-attested practice in Greek literature. Note that βαμβαλιαστύν is a (well-supported) *varia lectio* for the dispreferred κρεμβαλιαστύν "sound or rhythm of castanets." See Cassola (1975: 497) with references. For a different interpretation, see Martin (2003: 136) with references.

> Each would say that they themselves were speaking:
> So well their beautiful song matches each accent.

Their singing is hailed as a μέγα θαῦμα "great marvel," whose fame won't perish. It is likely that the tour-de-force performance comprised Greek as well as non-Greek portions: on the one hand, it is said that members of the audience (one imagines, mostly Ionian festival-goers)[49] would be able to recognize their own speech (i.e., dialect); on the other, the onomatopoetic term βαμβαλιαστύν (here translated as "chatter") might suggest foreign tongues unintelligible to the Greeks.

A similar mimetic skill is credited to Helen in *Odyssey* 4.277–79. Here, Menelaus recounts how, back at Troy, Helen walked around the Achaeans' wooden horse at night, calling the best of the Greeks by name and imitating their wives' voices (only thanks to Odysseus' leadership were the Greeks able to resist this test).

(6) τρὶς δὲ περίστειξας κοῖλον λόχον ἀμφαφόωσα,
ἐκ δ' ὀνομακλήδην Δαναῶν ὀνόμαζες ἀρίστους,
πάντων Ἀργείων φωνὴν ἴσκουσ' ἀλόχοισιν. (*Od.* 4.277–79)

> Three times you walked around the hollow trap, touching it,
> Calling by name the best of the Danaans,
> Imitating the voice (accent) of the wives of all Argives.

Unless we want to deem Helen a professional impersonator (and one with perfect command over the idiosyncrasies of each warrior's wife's speech), what she might be more likely to be doing is imitating the women's *accents*, based on their provenance. After all, the Greek expedition to Troy is heterogeneous enough to contain multiple dialects (even if those match the imagination of a first-millennium audience, rather than a second-millennium reality), and Helen may be switching to the appropriate one when addressing each hero. It is unclear whether Helen's performance here is in speech or song,[50] but Martin (2003: 121–23) suggests that she may in fact be intoning a lament here – an even more excruciating test for the Greeks, hearing their wives lament them as if they were dead.

A further famous example of somebody temporarily concealing their native dialect (this time, as a form of disguise) is found in

---

[49] These are mentioned by Thucydides 3.104.3.
[50] In *Od.* 4.281, Menelaus describes her activity using ἐβόησας "you shouted," which only specifies the volume.

Aeschylus, where Orestes (accompanied by Pylades) plans to address the doorkeepers of his palace in the dialect of Phocis, so as to not be recognized: ἄμφω δὲ φωνὴν ἥσομεν Παρνησσίδα/γλώσσης αὐτὴν Φωκίδος μιμουμένω (*Choephoroe* 563–64) "we shall both use a Parnassian accent, imitating the speech of Phocis."

3.3.2 Dialect and Identity

The passages above convey that the Greeks of the Archaic period knew well that accents could be faked, and that they could be faked when speaking as well as when singing. The implications of this fact are not trivial. The Greeks' ideas about ethnicity were complex and ever evolving,[51] but language, dialect, and accent[52] were certainly perceived as an important signifier of provenance and identity.[53] On a large scale, language was a delimiter of Hellenic identity (with the *Héllēnes* contrasted with the *bárbaroi*); on a smaller scale, dialect could be used to delineate subdivisions within ethnic groups. Herodotus (1.142) famously divides the Ionians into four groups based on linguistic criteria.[54] In fourth-century Athens, a father's "foreign" accent (ξενίζειν "to sound foreign") could constitute an obstacle to a son's claim to Athenian citizenship (Demosthenes, *Against Eubulides* 18).[55]

There is, to an extent, continuity between the Greeks' ethnic divisions of Aeolians, Dorians, and Ionians (which were sanctioned in myth)[56] and our modern dialectal designations. Only some adjustments are necessary: first, the term *West Greek* is now commonly used for Doric (with Doric

---

[51] A book-length treatment is Hall (2000).
[52] There is frequently confusion about the usage of these three terms. A simple definition (used in introductory linguistics handbooks), is that a *language* is a grouping of dialects, and *dialects* are "mutually intelligible forms of a language that differ in systematic ways" (Fromkin, Rodman, and Hyams 2014: 279). In practice, sociopolitical and historical factors often determine whether we call a given linguistic variety a language or a dialect (consider the oft-quoted adage, traced to sociolinguist Max Weinreich, that "a language is a dialect with a navy and an army"). By *accent*, one usually means the phonological and phonetic features in somebody's speech that make them recognizable either as a speaker of a given dialect (e.g., a Greek speaker with an Athenian accent), or as a native speaker of another language (e.g., a non-native speaker of English with a Greek accent).
[53] For a recent discussion, see Anson (2009). For a recent survey of the Greek and Byzantine conception of dialect (Gk. διάλεκτος), see Van Rooy (2016).
[54] Interestingly, this partition finds no confirmation in our epigraphic data.
[55] See discussion in Morpurgo Davies (2002).
[56] This is, of course, the myth of the three sons of Héllēn (Aíolos, Dóros, and Xoûthos), first mentioned in Hesiod's *Catalogue of Women*, fragm. 9: Ἕλληνος δ' ἐγένοντο φιλοπτολέμου βασιλῆος/ Δῶρός τε Ξοῦθός τε καὶ Αἴολος ἱππιοχάρμης "And from Héllēn, the war-loving king, were born/ Dóros and Xoûthos and Aíolos who delighted in the battle-chariot." Xoûthos in turn is the father of Íōn (originator of the Ionians), and Akhaiós (originator of the Achaeans). A longer account is found in Strabo, *Geographica* 8.7.1.

being a subgroup thereof). Second, during the first millennium BCE, the Achaeans (i.e., the Greeks of the region of Achaea) spoke Doric, not Achaean;[57] the term *Achaean* is now sometimes used to indicate the second-millennium variety of Greek spoken by the Mycenaeans (whose written version is attested in our Linear B tablets), which is in turn believed to be related to the Arcado-Cypriot group of the first millennium (an addition of modern dialectology, along with the enigmatic Pamphylian[58]).

A modern picture of (mid-)first-millennium Greek dialects is given in Figure 3.1. In broad strokes,[59] starting from the left, we can see the West Greek dialects (including Northwest Greek and the Doric dialects) spoken over a vast expanse stretching from Epirus in the north to the Peloponnese in the south. Continuing to the right, in a semi-circular shape, we find Doric dialects also in Crete, Rhodes, and on the southern coast of Asia Minor, as well as on the southernmost Cycladic islands, such as Thera. These West Greek dialects likely replaced other forms of Greek that were spoken in these regions during Mycenaean times: we can tell this by observing the position of Arcadian, holed up in the mountains of Arcadia, and whose closest relative is to be found much further east on the island of Cyprus: both locations look very much like *relic areas*,[60] where speakers of Arcado-Cypriot (usually seen as the closest surviving relative of Mycenaean) could preserve their dialect after the post-Mycenaean expansion of West Greek. Moving towards the center of the map, we find the Aeolic dialects spoken on both sides of the Aegean Sea (Thessalian and Boeotian on the continent, and Asiatic Aeolic on the island of Lesbos and the adjacent northern coast of Asia Minor). Finally, looking south, and again on both sides of the Aegean Sea, we find the dialects belonging to the Attic–Ionic group: Attic spoken in Attica, and Ionic stretching all the way from Euboea (Euboean or West Ionic), to (most of) the Cyclades (Central Ionic or Island Ionic), to the central coast of Asia Minor (East Ionic).[61]

---

[57] This is an evolution which the Greeks explained through the myth of the "return of the Heraclids," and some modern scholars with the theory of the Dorian invasions. For an introduction to the problem, see Hall (2013: 44–56).

[58] Pamphylian is usually left unclassified, and it is regarded as the likely result of extensive language contact with neighboring Anatolian languages (Skelton 2017).

[59] For a more detailed description, see Cassio (2016a: 14–17).

[60] In terms of dialectology, one often talks about *focal areas* (areas where given linguistic innovations have spread more regularly) vs. *relic areas* (areas where given linguistic innovations haven't spread yet). Geographically (and sociolinguistically), focal areas tend to be central, while relic areas tend to be outlying or remote. See discussion in Hock (2021: 593–94).

[61] A schematic way of remembering this distribution is thinking of superimposing the shape of the letter E over a map of Greece: the two top horizontal strokes represent Aeolic and Attic–Ionic, and the remaining strokes represent West Greek.

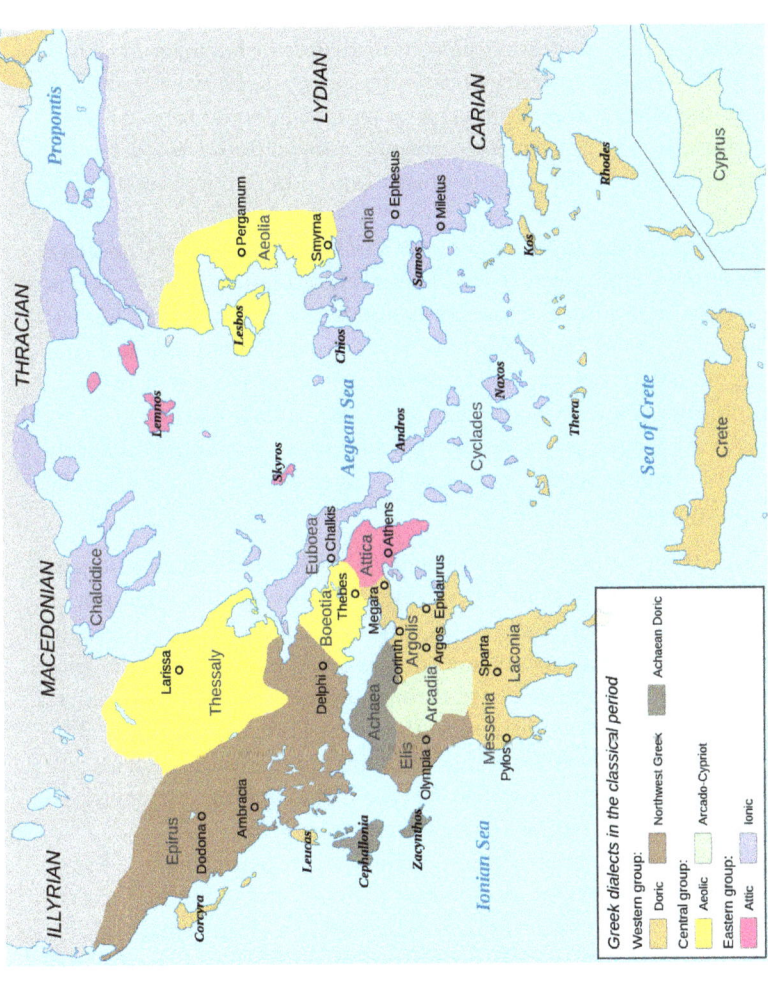

Figure 3.1 Greek dialects in the first millennium[62]

[62] Map created by Wikipedia user Future Perfect at Sunrise (https://commons.wikimedia.org/wiki/User:Future_Perfect_at_Sunrise), based on Woodard (2008: 50).

3.3.3 Dialects in Performance

The area of literature and poetic performance adds an interesting wrinkle to these distinctions. Here, given dialectal features were associated with different genres, and used independently of an author's geographic origin. As noted by Morpurgo Davies (2002: 157, numbering and emphasis mine):

1. There is [...] an interesting pattern of dialect or language switching tied to *the view that some linguistic forms are more suitable than others for certain linguistic genres*. Epic verse is written in some form of Ionic. Attic tragedy is written in Attic except for the choruses which are in a modified form of Doric. Lyric poetry can be in Aeolic; literary prose cannot.
2. In a number of instances *the choice of dialect is independent of the origin of the author*; Pindar was from Thebes but did not write in Boeotian. Hesiod was also from Boeotia but composed in epic language, i.e., in a composite form of Ionic. We have Ionic prose, Doric prose and Attic prose, but, for instance, the Hippocratic corpus is written in Ionic, though Hippocrates himself was from Cos, a Doric place.
3. *The literary dialects are no perfect match for the epigraphical dialects*: the Doric of Attic choruses is far less Doric than that of, for example, Peloponnesian inscriptions.

So, while for an ordinary Greek the choice of spoken dialect would have been one of the clearest signifiers of one's identity, and faking another accent would be a matter of deceit (as with Helen and Orestes), literature and performance were an area where authors could play by different rules: here, authenticity could be achieved through mimesis, and the performer's linguistic identity could be adapted to the needs of the performance. This μέγα θαῦμα of routinely embodying other linguistic selves is perhaps part of the endowment of lies that appear like the truth (ψεύδεα [...] ἐτύμοισιν ὁμοῖα, *Theogony* 27), which are part of the Muses' gifts.

The origin of these linguistic conventions is, in many cases, debated. Quite reasonably, one might assume that the choice of dialect reflects the geographic area of first origin (or establishment) of a given genre, and that later authors within that tradition simply imitated their models. Yet, this "founder effect" finds counterexamples even in the short list of examples provided above (e.g., with Hippocrates).

Moreover, as Morpurgo Davies observes, these literary dialects are at best a distant match for the epigraphic evidence, in that they very often (as illustrated above for Homer) display mixed diatopic and diachronic features, so that tracing them back to a real spoken dialect seems like no easy feat. We will see how critics ancient and modern have tried to solve this challenge in section 3.4. In section 3.6, we'll find that similar mixed features can be found in contemporary performance languages as well.

3.4 Interpreting Homer's Dialect

3.4.1 Ancient Critics

Despite the difficulties just sketched, critics and audiences have been interested in identifying Homer's provenance ever since antiquity, and dialect has always played a fundamental role in this quest. Many options have emerged, with the coastal cities of Asia Minor (like Colophon, Smyrna, as well as the islands of Ios and Chios) having some of the strongest claims. The following epigram, which is attributed to an Antipater of Thessalonica (first century BCE–first century CE), summarizes some of the most popular options:[63]

(7) οἱ μέν σευ Κολοφῶνα τιθηνήτειραν, Ὅμηρε,
οἱ δὲ καλὰν Σμύρναν, οἱ δ' ἐνέπουσι Χίον,
οἱ δ' Ἴον, οἱ δ' ἐβόασαν εὔκλαρον Σαλαμῖνα,
οἱ δέ νυ τὰν Λαπιθᾶν ματέρα Θεσσαλίαν,
ἄλλοι δ' ἄλλο μέλαθρον ἀνίαχον· εἰ δέ με Φοίβου
χρὴ λέξαι πινυτὰν ἀμφαδὰ μαντοσύναν,
πάτρα τοι τελέθει μέγας οὐρανός, ἐκ δὲ γυναικός
οὐ θνατᾶς, ματρὸς δ' ἔπλεο Καλλιόπας. (Antipater of Thessalonica *Epigr.* 72 G-P = *Anthologia Graeca* 12.296)

Some say Colophon was your nurse, Homer,
and some fair Smyrna, and others Chios,
some Ios, some proclaim it prosperous Salamis,
and some again the mother of the Lapíthai, Thessaly,
and others other homesteads. But if I should
openly broadcast Phoîbos' wise oracle,
the broad sky is your homeland, for you were born
of no mortal mother, but of Kalliópē.

The privileged claim that Asia Minor had on Homer (especially in Ionian areas that bordered on Aeolian ones) undoubtedly found support

---

[63] Translation after West (2003). This epigram stands at the end of the first Pseudo-Plutarchean life of Homer (*Plutarchi Vita I*, end of the second century CE). An extensive review of the ancient evidence on Homer's life and whereabouts (including early mentions of Homer's name, direct and indirect literary citations, and the biographic tradition) is available in Latacz (2011).

in the poems' dialect, which appears to mix some broad (East) Ionic features with the occasional Aeolism.

This ancient debate, which certainly had an important ideological and political component, is reflected in our small collection of *Lives of Homer*, which relay several different versions of the Homer myth.[64] These are works that, in their current form, span from the first century CE onwards, and have come to us under various authorial personae (e.g., Pseudo-Herodotus, Pseudo-Plutarch, etc.), though they likely reflect some older traditions. While usually arguing for a specific ethnicity for Homer (Ionic or Aeolic), these stories either make an attempt to seek a location that could naturally combine Ionic and Aeolic dialectal features, or weave a life story that has room for both. For instance, the fact that the city of Smyrna was founded as Aeolian, and was later incorporated in the Ionian league (Herodotus 1.143.3), makes it a particularly suitable candidate for either the "Homer as Ionian" or "Homer as Aeolian" story. So the *Herodotean Vita* presents Homer as born in Aeolian Smyrna, while the *Contest of Homer and Hesiod*[65] presents him as born in *Ionian* Smyrna, after the Ionian migration.[66]

These accounts frequently use explicit linguistic evidence to pinpoint Homer's ethnicity: the *Contest of Homer and Hesiod* states that Homer's name itself (*hómēros*) is an Aeolic dialectal term for "blind."[67]

---

[64] An attempt to contextualize the contradicting accounts has been made by Nagy (2009/2010, summarized in Nagy 2011), who sees them as reflecting the gradual Athenian appropriation of Homer (under the Ionic flag), and the reflex of an even earlier power struggle between the Ionian and Aeolian *dōdekapóleis*. In Nagy's analysis, Athens' imperial desire to present itself as leader (and historical "mother city") of the Ionians underlies the narrative that Homeric poetry is an Ionian matter (cf. Plato's *Ion*; Thucydides 3.104.4 quoting the *Hymn to Apollo* – whose author self-identifies as Chian – as a work of Homer). Nagy also accepts the thesis of Frame (2009) that, before coming to Athens, the *Iliad* and the *Odyssey* went through a formative period during the late eighth and early seventh centuries BCE, when they were performed at a Pan-Ionic festival (the *Paniōnia*) sponsored by the Ionian *dōdekápolis*. Another book-length study of the evidence from the *Lives of Homer* is Graziosi (2002).

[65] Our present version of this narrative dates to the second century CE (it mentions the emperor Hadrian), though fragmentary evidence from papyri suggests that it goes back to the work of the sophist Alcidamas of Elaea (fourth century BCE) (Koniaris 1971, Renehan 1971, Mandilaras 1992). Friedrich Nietzsche (1870) had in fact proposed this theory early in his career as a philologist, and his argument was later confirmed by twentieth-century finds.

[66] See Nagy (2011: 153–54). Intriguingly, the dispute for Smyrna goes even further: according to Pseudo-Plutarch, it was once a Lydian city: this claim is folded into the report of Aristotle's *On Poets*, which fancifully marries Homer's mother off to the Lydian king. It was only afterwards, the account continues, that the Lydians abandoned the city under Aeolian pressure, and Homer decided to accompany them (*homēreîn*).

[67] This information is also reported by Ephorus (*Fragmente der griechischen Historiker* 70 F 1). Modern opinions differ: Chantraine (1968–80[2009], s.v.) gives ὅμηρος as an Ionic word for "hostage, pledge," with the personal name Ὅμηρος presumably derived from the substantive. In Crete, we

The *Herodotean Vita* identifies Homer as Aeolian based on the name of a particular piece of cutlery (πεμπώβολα "five-pronged fork") appearing in *Iliad* 1.463. This not only displays a seemingly obvious Aeolic feature in the root for "five," rendered as *pémpe-*,[68] but it also indicates cultural knowledge of what the author claims to be an exclusively Aeolian custom: using a five-pronged instead of a three-pronged fork during sacrifice, as well as not sacrificing the loin (apparently another exclusively Aeolian feature).[69] Homer, suggests the author, reverts to Aeolian language and customs when talking about regular life, thus betraying his own origin.

Remarkably, these dialect-based lines of reasoning were not applied, even in antiquity, to all poets. Nobody questioned Hesiod's Boeotian provenance (although his family had recently immigrated from Aeolic Cyme in Asia Minor) based on the Ionic "epic" flavor of his language, and nobody doubted Pindar's affiliation with Thebes, though clear Boeotian features do not come to the fore in his choral lyrics. This, of course, is because both Pindar and Hesiod speak about their geographic affiliation in their work. It is entirely reasonable to assume that dialectal considerations took center stage for Homer precisely because of the lack of other types of concrete authorial information in the *Iliad* and *Odyssey*.[70]

3.4.2 Modern Critics

Modern critics have often resorted to very similar ways of thinking, and attempted to pinpoint Homer's location (or at least the location for the composition of the poems) based on linguistic considerations. And while some modern critics, following the ancients, have attempted to apply these linguistic considerations to a single author, others have applied them to the concept of tradition as a whole. So while some will have an individual Homer invent his own mixed dialect while operating within an Aeolic/Ionic area, others will have the epic tradition as a whole follow a similar path – only taking a few hundred years to do so. This division seems to roughly correspond to that of "individualists" (i.e., those who see the epic

---

find a non-Ionic version of the personal name, Ὅμᾱρος. Most etymological attempts point to a combination of ὁμο- and the root of ἀραρίσκω, yielding the meaning "to accompany" (for a semantically parallel evolution, Chantraine points to Lat. *obses* "hostage," from *ob-* and *sedeo* "sit").

[68] But, as mentioned in fn. 26 above, see Cassio (2016a: 49–50), who regards this as an archaism.
[69] Note that, to my knowledge, modern archaeology has not been able to confirm this information.
[70] Famously, the *Homeric Hymn to Apollo* (171–76), a work which was attributed to Homer in antiquity (see information in Dyer 1975), identifies its author as "a blind man, who lives in rocky Chios." But modern scholarship sees this hymn as a later composition, though still relatively early among the hymns (for an introduction to the *Homeric Hymns*, see Cassola 1975).

language as the personal creation of a single exceptional author) vs. "traditionalists" (i.e., those who see the epic language as the end product of a long oral tradition).

The Kunstsprache *as the Creation of an Individual Poet*
Among the former group, a recent contribution is Wachter (2007), who argues that the roots of Homer's *Kunstsprache* are to be found in first-millennium Smyrna, a linguistically Ionian city which was exposed to Aeolian influences. According to Wachter, it was the familiarity of Smyrnean audiences with both Ionian and Aeolian features that allowed Homer to felicitously employ this particular mix of linguistic features (the implication is that other locations would not have been so open to linguistic mixing). Specifically, Homer combined his own native Ionic dialect with some pre-existing Aeolic epic traditions to create his unique brand of epic poetry.

Of course, this type of argument depends crucially on establishing Homer himself as the originator (and, in a way, codifier) of the epic *Kunstsprache* as we know it, and not simply as somebody (like Hesiod) who operates within an existing tradition.[71] The exceptionality of Homer (and presumably his sudden rise to fame, accompanied by a possible stint as a teacher of his own "school of epic") is then used by Wachter to explain why all the works of epic poetry that came after him (such as Hesiod) decided to follow Homer's example and adopt the curious mix of Ionic and Aeolic which he patented, instead of preserving locally colored variants of epic diction, such as the ones evidenced in our earliest hexameter inscriptions (Wachter 2007: 322–23), or devising their own trademark mixture.

Such a theory, moreover, relies on one's willingness (against all oralist warnings) to assume that a single individual poet could invent, within a lifetime, a poetic language and a formulaic system exhibiting extension and economy, even if partially relying on an existing Aeolic poetic tradition. Wachter's thesis, in fact, has a long list of previous incarnations (addressed in Parry 1971: 362, fn. 3), against which the criticisms of Parry are, I believe, still valid:

> The gravest fault of such a theory, however, is that it supposes that one man could all by himself create a poetic language. Such a thing has been seen nowhere. No single poet could even have such powers; and a poetic

---

[71] As evidence that Hesiod's Ionic was artificial (unlike Homer's), Wachter (2007: 321) reports three cases of missing third compensatory lengthening in the first syllables of καλός "beautiful" (< earlier *kalwos) and ἴσος "equal" (< *wiswos) (*Op.* 63, *Th.* 585, and *Op.* 752), and identifies them (following West) as a "slip of the tongue," possibly due to Hesiod's paternal Aeolic dialect (note that the feature could be Attic as well).

language, it is clear, is poetic only by convention shared by the poet and his hearers, so that the growth of a poetic language must be gradual. (Parry 1971: 326).

The Kunstsprache *as the Product of a Long Oral Tradition: Phase Theory*
Scholars operating with the concept of a poetic tradition, on the other hand, have a longer time span with which to play, and can entertain longer scenarios for the formation of the epic diction, if not for the poems themselves as we have them.

The idea that a long (pre)history looms behind Homer's language was first bolstered in the 1700s by Bentley's discovery of metrical traces of the sound [w] (often referred to as *digamma*)[72] in some Homeric verses;[73] as discussed above, [w], still preserved in Mycenaean, had been lost early in some first-millennium dialects (such as Attic–Ionic) but was preserved for longer in other dialectal areas, including Aeolic and, notably, Doric, where it still survives today in the Tsakonian dialect; epic singers seem to preserve a memory of the sound, even though they would not have pronounced it in their daily lives (examples of verses bearing metrical traces of [w] have been discussed in Chapter 2).

Ritschl (1838: 59–60) was the first to propose a *phase theory* for the formation of the Homeric language *and* Homeric myths alike: in his account, the tradition started in the Peloponnese with an Achaean/Aeolic phase; then moved to the northern coast of Asia Minor for a second Aeolic phase; and finally relocated just south along the coast, for a final Ionic phase. Instead of a "traveling Homer," going from one dialectal area to another, we have a "traveling tradition," planting roots in different areas of the Greek world. A phase of "Aeolian enthusiasm" followed at the end of the nineteenth century, with famous attempts (Fick 1883, 1886) to clear both poems of their "Ionian superstrate," and convert them back to their "original" Aeolian.[74] While such extremes fell into disfavor, the idea that

---

[72] More properly, *digamma* is the name for the letter <ϝ>, used to write [w] (as well as the numeral "6") in some Greek alphabetic scripts. When the Romans borrowed a western Greek alphabet from the Etruscans, <ϝ> (initially in combination with <h>) was used to write down Latin [f] (a sound that Greek did not possess at the time, as Greek. /pʰ/ was still an aspirated stop, see Allen 1968: 16), eventually giving rise to the Roman <f>. For a short introduction to the Greek alphabet (and its local variants), see Woodard (2010). The classic book-length treatment is Jeffery (1990).
[73] Bentley, however, had a *written* tradition in mind.
[74] Attempts of this kind still exist today: see Tichy's *Ilias diachronica* project, which aims to identify the older vs. younger verses in each book of the *Iliad* by converting our text to an older form of Greek. Thus, the reconstructed version of *Iliad* 1.1 reads: |Μῆνιν ἄϝει|δε, \Μοῦσα, Πηληϝἱ|δα· */ Ἀχιλῆ|ϝος (see Tichy 2022: 9).

the language of Homer was like a layered cake, preserving materials of varying time-depths, found further support.

Parry (1932) reformulated phase theory, which became informed by his discoveries about the oral-formulaic nature of Homeric poetry and his understanding of how the language of traditional poetry preserves and renews itself. Parry (1971: 340) saw the following origin for the mixed nature of Homer's diction: on the one hand, poets tend to use their native dialect when composing; on the other, they may preserve archaic, foreign, or artificial features in their diction if they have acquired those forms from other poets and if they find them metrically useful and hard to substitute with local and contemporary equivalents. In other words, poets opt for foreign features when they have no other choice. This theory has now been reformulated by Nagy (2011) as the principle of *Aeolic default*.[75]

As Parry saw it, the layer cake of Homer's diction was structured as follows (not too unlike Ritschl's original proposal): at a deeper stage, Arcado-Cypriot elements (mostly lexical in nature) stood next to Aeolic elements (the large majority of these had literary associations, finding close parallels in the language of Sappho and Alcaeus rather than in mainland Aeolic). These two epic traditions, along with their phraseology, had been taken over by Ionian singers, who aimed to systematically convert the diction into their own vernacular, sparing only those few foreign or archaic elements that just could not be substituted (as they were metrically indispensable). Ionic thus constituted the top layer.

The decipherment of Mycenaean led to a further revision of phase theory, one that added more time depth to the cake: the so-called Arcado-Cypriot elements (e.g., words starting in ππ- for Attic–Ionic π-, the preposition *ἀπύ, etc.) were now reinterpreted as Mycenaean, and therefore old, and through them the tradition could stretch even further into the second millennium.[76] Further findings within the field of historical linguistics and comparative IE poetics isolated potentially even older elements in the language of epic: an oft-cited candidate is the alleged preservation of the syllabic liquid sonorant [r̥] (a feature of Proto-Greek) in the Iliadic formula λιποῦσ' ἀνδροτῆτα καὶ ἥβην "leaving behind

---

[75] "In Homeric diction, if an Ionic form is available to fit into a metrical position that is already occupied by an Aeolic form, then the Aeolic form is replaced by the corresponding Ionic form, but the Aeolic form is preserved wherever no metrically equivalent Ionic form is available. Homeric diction defaults to Aeolic forms when it has no metrically equivalent forms in Ionic" (Nagy 2011: 144).

[76] For a discussion of the (relatively low) likelihood of Homeric diction preserving Mycenaean elements, see Hainsworth (1962).

manliness and youth" (*Il.* 16.857, 22.363) already discussed in section 2.3.1. Since this formula is used in connection with the death of Hector (and the foreshadowing of Achilles' own death), scholars have been excited by the possibility that the formula for the death of an important hero may be of considerable antiquity (in this direction, see Barnes 2011; for a recent re-evaluation of the evidence, see Bozzone 2014: 94–113; 2022), but no stable consensus around this matter has yet been reached.

Modern Twists: Gap Theory, Diffusion Model, and Euboea
While the idea that Homer may preserve Mycenaean or even older elements is generally accepted, within recent years the idea of an Aeolic phase has come under close scrutiny. In the first place, several scholars have criticized the idea of Aeolic as a unitary dialect group, both on linguistic and archaeological grounds.[77] Even before then, scholars had argued that what counts as Aeolic in Homer should simply be interpreted either as "archaic" (the classic treatment in this sense is Strunk 1957), or as trivial parallel innovations in the language of epic (e.g., the third declension dative plurals in -εσσι could be analogical to the *-s* stems; the extension of the -οντ- formant to the perfect active participle could be an independent innovation, etc.). A recent attempt to advocate for the legitimacy of the Aeolic traits in Homer is Nagy (2011), which contains a discussion of all of the features just mentioned. For an opposite view, see Miller (2014: Chapter 25).

For those who still believe in some form of the Aeolic phase, the argumentation has curdled around the interpretation of a handful of vigorously debated forms, which are supposed to reveal a chronological gap in the Ionic tradition – thus disproving the thesis that we simply had an Ionic tradition going back all the way to prehistory, and proving the necessity of an Aeolic phase.[78]

The reasoning for what we shall call the *gap theory* is tied with the Attic-Ionic development known as *quantitative metathesis* (already mentioned in section 3.2 above), which is well represented in Homer, even though the poets (whose spoken language likely contained it already) arguably dis-preferred it, perhaps because they perceived it as a modernism. That quantitative metathesis had nonetheless become part of the poetic

---

[77] See Parker (2008) and Rose (2008). For a new account of the development of Aeolic, using phylogenetic systematics, see Scarborough (2016).
[78] For a short discussion, see Horrocks (1997). A more recent (and extensive) discussion is in Nagy (2011).

technique is demonstrated by some formulas that contain it, such as this noun-epithet formula for Zeus:

(8) ³ᶜΚρόνου πάϊς ἀγκυλομήτεω (*Il.* 8x, *Od.* 21.415)

son of Krónos of the crooked counsel

Here, the genitive singular ending of the epithet ἀγκυλομήτης "crooked of counsel," showing a metrically guaranteed example of quantitative metathesis, occupies the last position in the line (an earlier Ionic form without quantitative metathesis would be *ἀγκυλομήτηο).

More specifically, quantitative metathesis targeted a disyllabic sequence of a long non-back non-high vowel (Attic–Ionic <η> [ɛː] < Proto-Greek *[aː], *[eː]) plus a short [a] or [o] vowel, and resulted in the two vowels descriptively "switching" their length feature (V:V > VV:). Thus the sequences <ηο> [ɛːo] and <ηα> [ɛːa] became <εω> [eɔː] and <εᾱ> [eaː], as in Hom. acc.sg. βασιλῆα "the king" > Attic βασιλέα "id." and Hom. gen. sg. πόληος "of the city" > Attic πόλεως "id."[79] The resulting sequence normally scans as a single heavy syllable for metrical and accentual purposes – i.e., the two vowels are in synizesis (as already shown in example (8) above). This situation (as already mentioned in Chapter 2) is visible in the very first line of the *Iliad*, where the gen.sg. Πηληϊάδεω "of the son of Peleus" (monosyllabic – i.e., with synizesis, and with quantitative metathesis) occurs next to the gen.sg. Ἀχιλῆος "of Achilles" (disyllabic – i.e., without synizesis, and without quantitative metathesis):[80]

(9)   Μῆνιν ἄειδε θεὰ Πηληϊάδεω Ἀχιλῆος (*Il.* 1.1)

The wrath, sing, o goddess, of Peleus' son, Achilles

In later Greek (as well as very rarely in Homer), disyllabic scansions of sequences showing quantitative metathesis (⏑–) are also found.[81]

The so-called "gap" in gap theory can be observed for some of the sequences that underwent quantitative metathesis in Ionic, and specifically for those that reflect the Proto-Greek sequence *-āo. Starting from

---

[79] Méndez Dosuna (1993) has proposed to explain the phenomenon of quantitative metathesis as a loss of syllabicity of the first vowel (which likely reduced to a kind of central glide), combined with a compensatory lengthening of the second vowel. While Méndez Dosuna's thesis adduces credible typological parallels, several questions remain open (especially concerning the relative chronology: see Cota 2006). For a recent discussion, see Miller (2014: 66–68, with references), and Brown (2018).

[80] Cf. Attic Ἀχιλλέως "id.," not attested in Homer, with quantitative metathesis.

[81] Three occurrences are listed in Chantraine (1948: 64). In Homer, these are arguably artificial attempts to undo the synizesis which quantitative metathesis presupposes – and they should thus be interpreted as a kind of metrical license.

Proto-Greek, these sequences likely went through three chronological stages, namely:

1. Proto-Greek (and first-millennium Aeolic): -āo, with disyllabic scansion >
2. Archaic Ionic: -ēo, also with disyllabic scansion >
3. Later Ionic: -eō, with monosyllabic scansion.

The core observation around which gap theory is built is that the text of Homer shows steps (1) and (3), but not (2). In other words, the tradition does not seem to have traces of an "Archaic Ionic Phase." Ergo, proponents of an Aeolic phase suggest, Ionian poets must have taken over the diction from Aeolic poets after step (3) had already happened in spoken Ionic; having forgotten that Ionic too once contained step (2) (which would have been metrically equivalent to the Aeolic forms), Ionian poets had to resort to contemporary Aeolic forms as in (1), since the meter would not allow them to use their *umgangssprachlich* forms in (3).

Scholars are split as to whether this is incontrovertible evidence for an Aeolic phase or not: the scenario could also be explained by synchronic spread (a theory to which we shall come back later), in which, in some specific morphological contexts, a contemporary variant (Aeolic -āo) would be preferred to an archaic one (Ionic -ēo) that had no counterpart in the spoken language (this solution is already suggested in Cassio 1998: section 10).[82]

At present, many proponents of an Aeolic phase in fact favor a *diffusion model*, founded on more contemporary dialectological ideas. Rather than assuming that the epic tradition was transplanted as a whole from Aeolia to Ionia, scholars now assume that multiple oral epic traditions (at minimum, an Aeolic one and an Ionic one) coexisted on the coast of Asia Minor, and that borrowing of linguistic materials between the two happened naturally over a long period of contact. Our epic texts simply seem to witness the "Ionic" side of such exchange. In this perspective, one can talk about an Aeolic vs. Ionic "component" in the diction, without implying a strict chronological sequencing.

---

[82] Albio Cesare Cassio has shared with me the important observation that the conditions under which a genitive singular in -āo is licensed in the language of epic (and beyond) are much more restricted than usually acknowledged: -āo genitives only seem to appear with personal names, patronymics, and -της agent nouns (often used as epithets). In other words, we are not dealing with a purely phonological phenomenon, but one that is strictly morphologically defined. An article is in preparation. See also Cassio (2009: 195–96).

While Homer's Ionic is usually connected to the Eastern domain (principally on account of the many psilotic forms, the presence of the third compensatory lengthening, and the coexistence with the Asiatic Aeolic tradition), some scholars have pointed to West Ionic features in the diction, pointing specifically to Euboea, a region whose Dark Ages have been conveniently illuminated by the stunning archaeological discoveries at Lefkandi.[83]

Perhaps the most influential supporter of a West Ionic phase is West (1988),[84] who traces the genealogy of Greek epic (both the mythical themes and the linguistic features) from the depths of IE praise poetry (though postulating that post-IE long-distance contact could explain many shared features between, say, Greek and Indo-Iranian epic), to Early and Late Mycenaean epic (the latter located in Thessaly), to Aeolic epic (in Asia Minor – this step guaranteed by the *gap theory* discussed above), to, finally, a *West* Ionic epic (Euboea), which would have been open to absorbing many of the "oriental" features that are traceable in the poems (some of which, West conjectures, may have already penetrated in Mycenaean times).[85] The individual poets to whom West attributes our *Odyssey* and *Iliad* respectively stand at the end of this millennia-long chain of events, when the epic idiom had already acquired its Panhellenic status ("from the mid eighth century the new epic became Panhellenic, its dialect and conventions now fixed and available for imitation by poets everywhere" – West 1988: 172). West locates the poet of the *Iliad* not far from the Troad (see recently West 2011), based on geographic and landscape knowledge rather than linguistic cues. The poet of the *Odyssey*, on the other hand, might be Euboean (West 2014).[86]

West's Euboean phase has mostly come under criticism from the linguistic viewpoint (see Cassio 1998, Passa 2016a: 165–66). The features employed to identify the diction as Western Ionic specifically include: (1) the very occasional lack of third compensatory lengthening (e.g., two occurrences of the noun ξενίη "hospitality"[87] and five occurrences of the

---

[83] In this, one may invoke the dangers of the so-called *streetlight effect*, or the tendency to seek answers where it is easiest to look. Because the discoveries at Lefkandi provide a light in the Greek Dark Ages, it is tempting (though possibly misleading) to look for Homer under that same light.

[84] See also Peters (1986) and Cassio (1998) (for a critical evaluation of the evidence).

[85] These steps are very close to those laid out by Passa (2016), who presents a fuller list of linguistic features for each step. Passa, however, is skeptical about a Euboean phase, at least as far as the linguistic evidence can tell us.

[86] This reflects the old idea that the adventures of Odysseus are a mythological echo of the West Greek colonization of the Western Mediterranean.

[87] Interestingly, these both occur in *Odyssey* 24, just a few verses apart from each other (*Od.* 24.286 and *Od.* 24.314 respectively).

adjective ξένιος "hospitable" in the *Odyssey*, vs. the extremely frequent word ξεῖνος "guest");[88] (2) the non-East Ionic outcome of some labiovelars (whereby in Homer we find π-forms instead of κ-forms, such as πως and not κως, which would be standard in Herodotus); and (3) the fact that many Homeric forms seem to have maintained their initial [h]'s, contrary to East Ionic psilosis (see also the list of features in section 3.2). Critics of a Euboean phase suggest that none of these features points to Euboea (let alone tenth-century Euboea) specifically: (3) could easily have made its way through editorial meddling in the Attic written tradition; (2) may not have been West Ionic exclusively;[89] and (1) is Panhellenic in general, and can thus simply reflect a more "international" phase in the epic tradition.[90]

This is not to say that Euboean features might be completely absent from Homer's text: Cassio (1998: sections 42–44) speaks of a few continental features (from the areas of Boeotia, Phocis, Euboea, and Attica) that seem to have made their way into Homer's diction in a relatively late phase of the tradition (which Cassio puts from the late ninth century BCE onwards). Among these, the forms 2.pl.pres.mid.ind. βόλεσθε "you guys want" (*Od.* 16.387, cf. Attic–Ionic βούλεσθ(ε), *Il.* 24.39), 3.sg.pres.mid.ind. βόλεται "he wants" (*Il.* 11.319, cf. Attic–Ionic βούλεται, *Il.* 1.67, 5x), and 3. pl.impf.mid.ind. ἐβόλοντο "they wanted" (*Od.* 1.234, cf. Attic–Ionic (ἐ) βούλοντο, *Od.* 4.353, 9.96) could be specifically Euboean.[91]

---

[88] For a complete treatment of the evidence for a lack of third compensatory lengthening in Homer, see Wathelet (1981).

[89] As Chadwick (1990: 175) reports, this feature, at one time only attested for Eretria (a Euboean city), is now also reported for Phocaean colonies in the West (and thus for Phocaea, an East Ionian city). Miller (2014: 180) suggests that the spread of these *k*-forms was a literary fashion (their presence in literary texts far outstrips their epigraphic currency), one that came to stereotypically characterize the Ionic lyric genre as practiced by poets such as Callinus, Anacreon, and Hipponax, and thence "made [its] way to the manuscripts of Herodotus" (Miller 2014: 180).

[90] While the text and language of Homer as we have it shows an unmistakable (East) Ionic coloring, we have famous epigraphic evidence of hexametric inscriptions displaying "Homeric phraseology" adapted to different dialectal contexts (some examples are discussed in Hackstein 2010: 421; see also Passa 2016b: 277–78). The current consensus is to treat these examples as "localizations" of a recognizably Homeric (i.e., Ionic) tradition, and thus as a confirmation of its widespread and early diffusion, as opposed to witnesses of separate local traditions of oral epic poetry. That several local traditions of epic song existed in Archaic Greece (and perhaps thrived before being taken over by the prestige of the Ionic tradition) is still typologically likely, and an unsuccessful attempt was made in the 1970s and 1980s to find traces of a "continental" epic tradition which would explain some linguistic similarities between Hesiod and the language of choral lyric (Pavese 1972; see criticism in Passa 2016a: 176–79). For dialect mixture in the Archaic Greek epigram (a genre which includes early hexametric inscriptions, as well as inscriptions in elegiac couplets starting in the fifth century BCE), see Kaczko (2018).

[91] Following Peters (1986: 310).

3.5 Interlude: Open Questions and Big-Picture Questions

To sum up, there are many aspects of Homer's *Kunstsprache* that still remain under discussion. Some open questions in this domain are: Can we really recognize elements that are older than Mycenaean in the language of Homer? Was there really an Aeolic phase? Should we understand the relationship between the Aeolic and Ionic phases as chronological, or as synchronic diffusion? When we talk about Ionic features in Homer, what variety of Ionic are we talking about? Is the influence of Attic only traceable in the written tradition, or was it a vital part of the last portion of the oral transmission of the texts (for those who embrace this model of textualization)?

But before we can address these questions, there are some even more general questions that have not been addressed (neither for Homer nor for other Ancient Greek *Kunstsprachen*), and that may shed considerable light on the problems at hand. Are there any contemporary parallels for these types of *Kunstsprachen*, or mixed performance languages? How can we make sense of these odd objects from a linguistic point of view, and what do we know of the reasons and conditions under which people may construct and employ such languages? Are we correct in seeing meter as a major motivation for the existence of such languages?

As mentioned above, there are indeed many such parallels in the contemporary world, even though they are not found in places where literary scholars thought to look previously. These parallels can provide us with further instruments to conceptualize and articulate the questions above. Specifically, they can help us understand:

a. why poets use these languages, and what role the meter plays in these choices;
b. whether these languages can be used to assess the geographic provenance of a poet;
c. how linguistic innovation plays out in these artificial varieties;
d. whether there are any known parallels for the Homeric phase theory.

3.6 *Kunstsprachen* in Popular Music Today

3.6.1 *Adele and the Motivation of the Singer*

In February 2012, when Adele won six Grammy Awards, *The Telegraph* ran a story titled "Grammy Awards: Americans baffled by Adele's accent"

(Allen 2012). The reason for the bafflement is clear: Adele was born and raised in Tottenham, England, and is a native speaker of Cockney English, as one can easily notice in interviews, as well as in award acceptance speeches. Yet, notable Cockney features are largely absent from her singing style:

a. Cockney has intervocalic /t/ → [ʔ],[92] but Adele has [ɾ] in her singing, as in be*tt*er.
b. Cockney is non-rhotic (meaning /r/[93] segments in syllable codas are dropped), but Adele's singing is largely r-ful, as in powe*r*.
c. Cockney has *me* for the possessive first person pronoun *my*, but in her singing Adele uses *my* exclusively, often with *ay*-ungliding and compensatory lengthening [maː], which is not a regular feature of Cockney (Wells 1982: 308–10, Mott 2012: 76).

Moreover, Adele shows the same type of dialect mixing that we have observed for Homer in section 3.1 above:

(10) But **it don't** matter, **it** clearly **doesn't** tear you apart anymore ("Hello," 25, 2015).

Here, in the same line, we see a nonstandard English variant for the third singular verbal agreement, "it don't," immediately followed by the standard variant "it [...] doesn't." What is peculiar here is that the nonstandard variant does not seem to come from Adele's own spoken dialect, but rather (as we shall see), from much further afield.[94] Why does this happen?

As it turns out, Adele is not alone in this type of linguistic shift. She is actually part of a long tradition of British singers who seem to almost completely lose their accents during performance. The phenomenon was first studied in a classic paper by the sociolinguist Peter Trudgill (1983), who coined the term *Brit Pop pronunciation* to capture this behavior in

---

[92] The more specific environment for this phonological change in Cockney English is that intervocalic /t/ after a stressed vowel is realized as the glottal stop [ʔ]. In other dialects of English, /t/ in this same environment is pronounced as the voiced alveolar tap [ɾ].
[93] Here and elsewhere in this book, I conventionally use the symbol [r] for the English post-alveolar approximant. The standard IPA symbol for this sound would be [ɹ] (in IPA, [r] represents an alveolar trill instead).
[94] We might indeed want to see the expression "it don't matter" as a chunk (or collocation) borrowed wholesale from another dialect of English (we shall see which one in a moment). Adele's borrowings, however, are not confined to fixed phraseology, but impact the areas of phonology, morphology, and the lexicon.

popular music in the 1960s and 1970s.⁹⁵ Some of the most notable features of this pronunciation are as follows:⁹⁶

a. intervocalic /t/ pronounced as the *voiced alveolar tap* [ɾ]; /t/ → [ɾ], as in be*t*ter;
b. /aː/ pronounced as [æ]; /aː/ → [æ], as in d*a*nce;
c. retention of coda /r/, as in powe*r*;
d. "*ay*-ungliding," as in m*y* [maː].

In fact, these changes are not limited to pronunciation (phonology) alone, but spread to grammatical and lexical choices (this is the case with Adele's nonstandard agreement choice in example (10) above). For instance, Brit Pop singers tend to avoid lexical items that are stereotypically British, like *mate* and *fancy*, and tend to opt for the more neutral *friend* and *like*. Of these and the features above, Trudgill observed:

> No single British variety has all these features, and the vast majority of singers who use these forms do not do so when speaking. There can be no doubt that the singers are modifying their linguistic behavior for the purposes of singing. (Trudgill 1983 [1997: 252])

But why would these singers feel the need to carry out such modification? It seems like the main goal of the Brit Pop pronunciation was for British singers to sound more American in their performances. Since most of the popular music up to the 1960s and 1970s was produced in the US, British singers who wished to insert themselves into that tradition were modifying their dialect to conform to what they perceived was the standard dialect of the genre. They were trying, in other words, to pass themselves off as legitimate members of that performance tradition.⁹⁷

To an extent, their linguistic modification was successful: while the features listed above are largely uncommon in British dialects, they are

---

⁹⁵ The field of sociolinguistics has long concerned itself with studies of dialect, though the study of particular (artificial) forms of dialect employed in music performance specifically is much more recent. For an introduction to sociolinguistics, see Coupland and Jarowski (1997) and Holmes and Wilson (2017). For different varieties of spoken English, see Kortmann and Lunkenheimer (2012, with additional online materials available at: www.ewave-atlas.org). A map of the dialects of American English can be found at www.ling.upenn.edu/phono_atlas/NationalMap/National Map.html; this is based on Labov, Ash, and Boberg (2006). For the sociolinguistics of (music) performance, see Bell and Gibson (2011), with references.

⁹⁶ An updated list of distinctively "American" features adopted by British pop and rock singers is provided by Simpson (1999: 345). These and additional features are discussed in Morrissey (2008), who covers British pop, rock, and folk singing, with copious examples.

⁹⁷ For the more general question as to whether media consumption can induce language change in a population (the topic here specifically is whether British speakers are becoming "Americanized" through watching television programs featuring American English), see Stuart-Smith (2017).

indeed present in different varieties of the English spoken in North America. Adele's American fans would have readily accepted her as a speaker of North American English, and were surprised to find out that she was not.

What is fascinating, however, is that no single, clearly identifiable American dialect actually encompasses all of the features above. While (a) is a systematic trait in North America, (d) is typical of dialects spoken in the Southern US, which, however, normally (and at least up until the 1960s and 1970s) do not preserve coda /r/ as in (c). Similarly, (b) represents a common trait in North America, but the vowel /æ/ is subject to diphthongization to [eə] before a nasal consonant in many areas of the US and Canada (e.g., somewhat simplifying, New Jersey, Florida, Canada, New England). In southern dialects, the same sequence is often realized with the triphthong [æjə]. So, while a speaker of Boston English would pronounce the word *dance* as [deə̃ns] (while dropping coda /r/, much like speakers of British English or from the South of the US), a speaker from the South could say [dæjə̃ns]. British singers, in other words, were adopting an odd, artificial mix of dialectal features for the purposes of singing.

If this sounds familiar, that's because it is indeed very similar to what we have seen in section 3.3.3 above concerning Ancient Greek *Kunstsprachen*:

(1) Some musical genres are associated with a specific dialect (e.g., it would be markedly odd to perform a country music song in a British accent, etc.).
(2) Singers operating within each genre will use the appropriate dialect regardless of their dialect of origin.
(3) This special performance dialect will not be exactly identical to any existing local dialect, but it will show mixed features and a general dialectal "coloring."

We might ask why this phenomenon is apparently so common, and how we might explain it. Following Trudgill, we can seek some answers in the realm of sociolinguistics. First, this is not simply linguistic *accommodation* (Giles and Smith 1979), whereby speakers (consciously or unconsciously) try to match the linguistic features of their audience. After all, these British singers use these features regardless of whether they are performing for a domestic or international audience. As Trudgill suggests, a more appropriate model is Le Page's theory of linguistic behavior (Le Page 1978, Le Page and Tabouret-Keller 1985), originally developed to describe individual linguistic choices in multilingual communities and the creation of Creoles:

> The individual creates for himself the patterns of his linguistic behavior so as to resemble those of the groups with which from time to time he wishes to be identified or so as to be unlike those from whom he wishes to be distinguished. (Le Page and Tabouret-Keller 1985: 181)

In other words, the singers are not trying to adopt the language of their audience; rather, they are trying to adopt the language typical of the performance tradition in which they want to fit. For Adele, this would be the performance dialect of rhythm and blues, which uses features of the English spoken in the South of the US – this, for instance, is where the nonstandard agreement in (10) comes from. This linguistic shift has, then, to do with *self-presentation*,[98] and it can also be impacted by the topic of discourse and other situational considerations.[99]

What is even more fascinating, is that in some cases the motivation to identify with a specific group or tradition seems to override the need to be understood: this is true of genres like opera, where singers perform in a language which is often not entirely mastered by most of their audience, as well as in the extreme cases of songs performed entirely in gibberish.[100]

But if the goal of these singers is to adopt the dialect of another existing group of performers within their genre, why does their shift result in a mixed, "artificial" dialect, and not simply in a consistent adhesion to the linguistic rules of the model group? As many of us might have experienced firsthand, when it comes to adult speakers trying to imitate another linguistic variety (just like adult speakers trying to learn a second language), the results are rarely perfect. As Trudgill remarked (1983 [1997]: 254]), "The end-product of this language modification [...] is by no means entirely

---

[98] For an introduction to the concept of *style* (i.e., how speakers employ language variation to express social meanings), see Coupland (2007).

[99] For instance, Simpson (1999: 353) analyzes the unusual density of specifically New York English features in the song "Money for Nothing" by the British band Dire Straits, who otherwise do not use conspicuously New York English features in their repertoire. Here the *topic* of the song itself is the reason for the linguistic shift: the singer is voicing a character heard speaking at a New York bar, and he is thus picking up some of the character's most notable dialectal features (in this case, they happen to be largely lexical). In Greek poetry (especially monodic lyric), we can think of several situations where the poet is effectively lending his or her voice to a character, and thus potentially facing a similar motivation for a linguistic shift.

[100] An example is the gibberish English song "*Prisencolinensinainciusol*" by the Italian singer Adriano Celentano, which was designed to sound, to an Italian audience, like American English, while comprising a sequence of meaningless syllables. Thus Celentano managed to successfully (if humorously) present himself as a member of the English-language rock music tradition he wanted to embody, even though he (and his audience) did not actually command the language.

successful." Many variables are at play here, but in practice many factors (riders) limit the capacity of speakers to perfectly approximate another linguistic variety, including (after Le Page 1978):

i. the extent to which they are able to identify their model group;
ii. the extent to which they have access to their model group and sufficient analytical ability to work out the rules of their behavior;
iii. the ability to modify one's behavior;
iv. (perhaps most importantly) the strength of one's motivation towards one model and towards maintaining one's linguistic identity.

These riders give rise to the linguistic variation (or dialect mixing) discussed above. As for (i) and (ii), British singers only had partial access to their model group (defined vaguely as "American singers"), and ended up not identifying it clearly: as a result, they selected features from different dialectal groups within North America.[101] Moreover, singers are not always consistent in their linguistic choices, either because they are unable to always make the necessary changes in their behavior (iii), or because (as we shall see in section 3.6.3 below) they do not always feel equally motivated to make those changes (iv).

In Adele's specific case, all of these factors conspire to create a hybrid mixture, whereby features of her native dialect that are notable and stigmatized are systematically substituted with "American" ones, while subtle, less-noticeable Cockney features are allowed to emerge occasionally (most likely because she is not aware that they should be altered). This is visible in the first few verses of her song "Someone Like You" (2011), which combines clear "American features" ([aː] for "I," [sɛrəld] for "settled," [mærid] for "married," and [nɛvər] for "never"), together with two more subtle Cockney features: [freənd] for "friend" (where the vowel is diphthongized), and [bɛk] for "back" (where the vowel is raised):

(11) I [aː] heard that you're **settled** [sɛrəld] down
that you found a girl
and you are **married** [mærid] now
[...]
Old **friend** [freənd] why are you so shy
ain't like you to hold **back** [bɛk]
or to hide from the light
[...]

---

[101] In this direction, most British singers choose to restore coda /r/ in their singing, since the trait sounds generally "American" to them, even though coda /r/ is actually dropped in many sociolects of the South of the US (just like it is in Britain), and specifically in those dialects associated with rhythm and blues and country music.

> **Never** [nɛvər] mind I'll find
> someone like you
> ("Someone Like You," *21*, 2011)

What seems to play no role, at least in contemporary music, in driving the singers' choice of dialect, is what has been hailed as Homer's main motivation for keeping extraneous dialectal material in his performance language: namely, meter. These singers decide to adopt "foreign" linguistic features in order to convey a sociolinguistic message, not out of metrical necessity. And while some contemporary genres have rhyme (and singers can be shown to use dialectal variants opportunistically when it comes to satisfying the rhyme scheme),[102] purely formal considerations of this sort seem to be neither necessary nor sufficient to explain the existence of mixed performance languages.[103]

Should we see the adoption of performance languages in antiquity as cases of abased imitation of existing models? Here (much like in the debate over formulas) we should not let contemporary concerns regarding originality and authenticity lead us astray. Performers adopting a given linguistic model are essentially trying to play by the rules of the genre in which they operate. By doing so, they are not just attempting to "sound the part" (not that we should see anything wrong with that *a priori*) – they are displaying competence with the tradition, declaring affiliation with particular models within, and (perhaps most importantly) exploiting the potential for traditional referentiality that the traditional modes of expression provide. Just like with formulas, their art is made more resonant, not more dull, through the use of traditional resources.

---

[102] For instance, the British band Arctic Monkeys, usually known for the abundance of local phonological features (Sheffield English) in their performance dialect, appear to default to the received/international pronunciation of the sequence [aʊ], instead of local [aː], for the words "around" and "ground," which carry the rhyme, in their song "Mardy Bum" (Beal 2009: 11–12).

[103] Morrissey (2008: 211–14) suggests that some choices within sung performance languages might be affected by phonetic considerations as well, such as the sonority of the segments in question and how that might have an impact on "singability." For instance, leaving out coda /r/ might be an easier option for singers, especially in monosyllabic words and on sustained notes: "A postvocalic /r/ represents a closure in comparison to the position of tongue and mouth during the pronunciation of the vowel. For the singer this creates two problems: firstly, the closure reduces the opening for the air flow, thus reducing sonority, and, secondly, it requires a decision as to when the tongue should begin to move from the vowel constellation towards the alveolar approximation of the [ɹ]. For a singer, non-rhoticity may therefore be preferable, particular in sustained notes" (Morrissey 2008: 213). Considerations of sonority alone, however, cannot explain all of the dialectal variation found in performance languages or, with regard to coda /r/ specifically, the fact that many British singers choose to realize it *despite* their native dialect and *despite* its supposed inferior singability.

3.6.2 Bob Dylan and the Biographic Temptation

British singers are not the only ones who modify their accent for the purposes of singing: Americans do it too, and possibly just as much as their British counterparts. Bob Dylan comes from Minnesota, and has /aɪ/ = [aɪ] and preserved coda /r/ in his speech. When he sings, however, he often displays different features (Trudgill 1983 [1997: 255]):

(12)   You may be an **ambassador** [æmbæsədə]
       To England **or** [ə] France
       You may **like** [laːk] to gamble
       You **might** [maːt] **like** [laːk] to dance
       ("Gotta Serve Somebody," *Slow Train Coming*, 1979)

At a superficial level, the model here seems to be the English spoken in the South of the US. This variety, sharing many features with African American English (AAE), is used in blues, rhythm and blues, and folk music.

In Dylan's case, however, the result of linguistic modification is sometimes so odd and striking that listeners have often wondered as to the origin of his dialect, as they failed to trace it to a specific geographic area. Anecdotally, listeners are more ready to identify what Dylan's dialect is not (e.g., standard Minnesota accent, standard Southern US accent) than to pinpoint what exactly it is. Testifying to this curiosity, in 2009 journalist Graeme Wood traveled as far as Hibbing, Minnesota, the mining town where Dylan was raised, in an attempt to find the origins of Dylan's mysterious idiom. After approaching some locals and observing that nobody really sounded like Dylan, the journalist sought out an old schoolmate of Dylan, Leroy Hoikkala, and declared that his supposed Finno-American accent (Finnish immigrants being one of the many components of the varied ethnic background of Hibbing) was somewhat of a match for that of the young Dylan – though not completely:

> He sounded a little like Bob Dylan, or at least the early Dylan, before he started to sound like a bitter taunter in the 1970s, and a coy jokester in the last decade. (Wood 2009)

Wood pinned some of his difficulties in finding the source of Dylan's accent on the mixed settlement and population movements that characterized the region:

> But accents are tricky, especially in diversely settled regions like northern Minnesota. Hibbing was an iron town, and the mining jobs had attracted immigrants from at least fifty different known ethnic stocks. (Wood 2009)

Although the attempt is undercut by the journalist's lack of linguistic training (one has to take his word for whether somebody sounds like Dylan or not, and no transcriptions or recordings are provided), the episode is quite instructive, because it reminds us of our attempts as philologists (ancient and modern) to locate Homer's dialect on a purely geographical basis. Here, too, scholars opt for mixed settlement (e.g., Aeolians and the Ionians in some city on the Asiatic coast) and archaism (mirroring the choice of an older speaker in Wood's investigation) as a way to explain Homer's peculiarities. What is amusing in Dylan's case is that these types of misguided attempts are happening while the author is still alive, and when facts about his life are readily known and available (we have a birth certificate, and even a family tree for Dylan, unlike for Homer).

Of course, Wood's expedition was doomed from the start: Minnesota is the (partial) source of Dylan's *speaking* style, but not of his *singing* style. And even within his spoken style Dylan shows some chameleonic qualities: if one listens to his Nobel acceptance speech (Dylan 2016), which was recorded over musical accompaniment, and shows some qualities of rhythmical prose, one can spot many artificial features that betray a concerted effort towards stylization.

For Dylan's singing specifically, beyond the general "South US" coloring mentioned above, a significant model seems to come from the US folk music tradition, in which Dylan himself claims to have sought and acquired extensive training early in his career. He talks about this training at length in his Nobel acceptance speech, in terms that very much remind one of Lord's account of the *guslar*'s training (Lord 1960: Chapter 2):

> By listening to all the early folk artists and singing the songs yourself, you pick up the vernacular. You internalize it. You sing it in the ragtime blues, work songs, Georgia sea shanties, Appalachian ballads and cowboy songs. You hear all the finer points, and you learn the details.
> [...]
> I had all the vernacular down. I knew the rhetoric. None of it went over my head – the devices, the techniques, the secrets, the mysteries – and I knew all the deserted roads that it traveled on, too. I could make it all connect and move with the current of the day. When I started writing my own songs, the folk lingo was the only vocabulary that I knew, and I used it. (Dylan 2016)

While in his speech Dylan mostly focuses on acquiring the *themes* (in Lord's terms) and melodies of these folk genres, his training certainly (and perhaps unconsciously) included acquiring the *language* of his models too.

And it is only by tracing Dylan's models that we can make sense of his performance dialect.

One model that seems to have been particularly influential for young Dylan is Roscoe Holcomb, a semiprofessional singer from Daisy, in the Appalachian region of Kentucky. Holcomb was discovered in 1958 by the musicologist and musician John Cohen, who coined the expression "high lonesome sound" to describe his striking singing style.[104] Holcomb had been a miner, a farmer, and a laborer for most of his life, and only started performing professionally after being "discovered," recording three LP albums (in 1962, 1965, and 1975) before retiring from the scene in 1978.

Between the 1940s and the 1960s, during the so-called *American Folk Music Revival*, interest in the traditional folk music genres spiked on the US music scene. Amateur scholars and musicians traveled from New York City to record performers sitting on their front porches in Virginia and Kentucky. Groups like the Weavers and the New Lost City Ramblers (in which Cohen himself performed) interpreted those songs for an urban audience. Dylan was attracted by this circle, and he eagerly absorbed different strands of folk music that were available therein, trying to insert himself into this tradition. In interviews, Dylan repeatedly mentions his admiration for Holcomb specifically, observing that his style possessed "an untamed sense of control."

Dylan was not the only one to idolize Holcomb, and to see him as a symbol of the "pure spirit" of American folk tradition; to this aspiring new generation of urban folk singers, Holcomb represented something archetypical and authentic:

> There is no grain in Holcomb's voice and banjo style; his voice is the grain, the American Grain in all its rough-hewn glory and grace and desolation. It is majestic in its rediness and singular in its power. (Jurek 2003)[105]

That this admiration resulted in imitation can be observed in Dylan's rendition of the song "Man of Constant Sorrow," a folk ballad originally composed in 1913 by the blind singer Dick Burnett,[106] and which knew

---

[104] *The High Lonesome Sound* is also the title of a documentary produced by Cohen in 1962, chronicling the living folk singing tradition in Appalachia, and prominently featuring Holcomb's performances.

[105] Jurek 2003 is a review of the anthology album *An Untamed Sense of Control* by music journalist Thom Jurek.

[106] Dick Burnett (1883–1977) was an influential folk singer and songwriter from Kentucky who was active in the first half of the twentieth century. He had lost his eyesight from a gunshot explosion when trying to fight off a mugger in 1907. Though his musical training had started long before the

many versions throughout the twentieth century.[107] Perhaps the most famous rendition (in terms of commercial success) was that of the Stanley Brothers, a bluegrass duo from Virginia, dating to 1951. Holcomb made a recording of the same song in 1961. If we compare all three versions (the Stanley Brothers', Holcomb's, and Dylan's), it is clear that Dylan is modeling his performance specifically on Holcomb's, and that this is true in terms of both linguistic features and vocal style, as shown in Table 3.1.

Holcomb's influence on Dylan is evident in the marked pronunciation of the word *trouble*, with diphthongization and fronting of /ʌ/, which is entirely absent from the earlier Stanley Brothers recording. The fronting of [ʌ] to [ɜ] (which Dylan approximates as [ə]) is registered as a feature of Midland American English (which includes the Appalachian Regions of Kentucky); it is described as a feature of younger speakers by Thomas (2004) and Labov, Ash, and Boberg (2006), though Holcomb seems to already be showing a development in that direction.

We can see that the end product of Dylan's language modification is not perfect in other features as well: he fails to capture the variation that Holcomb shows between [aɪ] (prevocalic) and [aː] (preconsonantal) for *I*, as well as the nonstandard morphological variant *borned* for *born*, which (interestingly for Homerists) displays *formulaic modification*.[108]

Table 3.1 *Three versions of "Man of Constant Sorrow"*

The Stanley Brothers (1951)	Roscoe Holcomb (1961)	Bob Dylan (1960s)
I [aː] am a man of constant sorrow	**I** [aɪ] am a man of constant sorrow	**I** [aː] am a man of constant sorrow
I've seen **tr**ou**ble** [ʌ] all my days	I've seen **tr**ou**ble** [ɜə] all my days	I've seen **tr**ou**ble** [əɵ] all my days
I [aː] bid farewell to old Kentucky	**I** [aː] bid farewell to old Kentucky	**I** [aː] say goodbye to Colorado
The place where **I** [aɪ] was **borned** and raised	The place where **I** [aː] was **borned** and raised	Where **I** [aː] was **born** and partly raised

accident, he turned to performing professionally as a traveling musician as a way to support his family despite his disability (Wolfe 1982: 19–24).

[107] Some readers will recognize this song from the soundtrack of the Coen brothers' movie *O Brother Where Art Thou?* (2000), as performed by the fictional folk/bluegrass group The Soggy Bottom Boys.

[108] This is the type of formulaic modification that Hoekstra (1964) would have recognized, whereby an "updated" version of an older formulaic prototype displays more recent linguistic features.

As a coda, one might mention that, when Bob Dylan was awarded the Nobel Prize in Literature in 2016 (a first for an author whose main medium of expression is song rather than prose or poetry), commenters and critics readily likened him to Homer and Sappho, two poets who performed orally.[109] It is now clear that the parallel does not end with the mode of delivery of his work: a perhaps even closer similarity is to be found in his "bardic" training and in his mixed performance dialect, whose roots, as we have seen, are not in Dylan's personal geography – rather, they reflect the geography of American folk music as a genre, Dylan's desire to fit within a given lineage of music performance, and the singer's specific choice of models within that lineage.

As classicists, of course, we face a greater challenge in identifying the models for our poets and their performance languages: the task is already complex for contemporary artists for whom we have interviews and live recordings (as well as recordings of their precursors), combined with a good understanding of their sociolinguistic environment. We may never be able to reconstruct such a detailed model for Homer or Sappho, or fully recover the original choices of the poets beneath the blanket of the written tradition. Still, much remains to be done in this direction, and the comparison with contemporary singers can help us to sharpen our analytic tools.

3.6.3 *The Beatles: Between Synchronic and Diachronic Variation*

Performance dialects can change over time, and sometimes they change even within the career of a single artist. The Beatles provide us with an ideal case study for this phenomenon, since their linguistic preferences (i.e., their motivation towards different linguistic models) seemed to shift over the years and with their artistic development.

In general, the Beatles adhere to Trudgill's Brit Pop pronunciation, as can be seen from a short analysis of the 1968 album recording of their song "Hey Jude" (see Table 3.2). Here, they show an extensive use of the "American" variant [ɾ] for intervocalic /t/ in *better*, as well as the "American" vocalism [oʊ] for standard British [əʊ] in the word *go*. Here too, however, we can find clear synchronic variation (i.e., dialect mixing) both within a single performance and across different performances.

---

[109] "Sara Danius, a literary scholar and permanent secretary of the 18-member academy, [...] called Mr. Dylan 'a great poet in the English-speaking tradition' and compared him to Homer and Sappho, whose work was delivered orally" (Sisario, Alter, and Chan 2013).

Table 3.2 *Two versions of "Hey Jude"*

Album version (1968)	White House version (2010)
Hey Jude, don't be afraid	Hey Jude, don't be afraid
You were made to **go** [gou] out and **get her** [gɛt hə]	You were made to **go** [gʉː] out and **get her** [gɛɾə]
The minute you **let her** [lɛɾər] under your skin	The minute you **let her** [lɛt hər] under your skin
Then you begin to make it **better** [bɛɾə]	Then you begin to make it **better** [bɛɾə]
[...]	[...]
Hey Jude, don't let me down	Hey Jude, don't let me down
You have found her, now go and **get her** [gɛt hə]	You have found her, now go and **get her** [gɛɾə]
Remember to **let her** [lɛɾər] into your **heart** [hɑːt]	Remember to **let her** [lɛɾər] into your **heart** [hɑːt]
Then you can **start** [stɑːt] to make it **better** [bɛɾə]	Then you can **start** [stɑːt] to make it **better** [bɛɾə]
[...]	[...]
Remember to let her under your skin	Remember to let her under your skin
Then you'll begin to make it	Then you'll begin to make it
Better [bɛtʰə], **better** [bɛɾə] **better** [bɛɾə] **better** [bɛɾə] **better** [bɛɾə] **better** [bɛɾə], oh	**Better** [bɛɾə], **better** [bɛɾə] **better** [bɛɾə] **better** [bɛɾə] **better** [bɛɾə] **better** [bɛɾə], oh

For instance, the 1968 album version of "Hey Jude" shows two different pronunciations for the word *better* in the same line, the British [bɛtʰə], as well as the "American" [bɛɾə]. Similarly, the phrases *get her* and *let her*, which contain the same phonological sequence with an intervocalic /t/, oscillate between the "American" rendering in [lɛɾər] and the "British" rendering in [gɛt hə]. At the same time, the pronunciation of the words *heart* [hɑːt] and *start* [stɑːt] is markedly British, with [ɑ] vocalism and loss of coda /r/.[110]

It is interesting to compare the 1968 album version with the much more recent live recording of Paul McCartney performing at the White House in 2010.[111] Here, beyond a different distribution of the variants for *let her* [lɛt hər] (apparently a British–American hybrid) and *get her* [gɛɾə], and the disappearance of the "British" variant for *better* in the last verse, we see the conspicuous appearance of the pronunciation [gʉː] for *go*. This effectively

---

[110] Standard American English would have [hɑrt] and [stɑrt] here, and even non-rhotic dialects of American English would display a vowel different from British [ɑː].
[111] A video recording of the performance is available at https://www.youtube.com/watch?v=2RFcd7PqYVU.

replaces the American pronunciation [goʊ] in the original version with a feature of McCartney's native Liverpool dialect (a lower-prestige option than the standard British [gəʊ]).[112]

In other words, McCartney seems to have "let slip" a variant of a high-frequency lexical item typical of his native dialect into his performance.[113] One could say his motivation towards the American model has become somewhat weaker (or, vice versa, his motivation towards his native dialect has become stronger).

This shift away from the "American" model does not seem to be an isolated incident in the Beatles' career trajectory: it is part of a trend already observed by Trudgill (1983) with regard to coda /r/. At the beginning of their career, it seems like the Beatles were trying harder to approximate an "American" pronunciation, and they were making an effort to reintroduce coda [r] in their performance dialect: for their 1963 album *Please Please Me*, Trudgill finds that 48 percent of all instances of coda /r/ are realized on the surface. Their following album, *With the Beatles* (1963), shows an only slightly lower percentage. As the Beatles became more successful, however (and thus more prominent within the pop music tradition, so that they could "be" the model instead of following a model),[114] the need to assimilate to the American model weakened, and they started to retain more features of their own vernacular in their singing: as a result, one can see the sharp decline in the frequency of coda [r] as the 1960s progress. By *A Hard Day's Night* (1964) and *Beatles for Sale* (1964), the percentage of restored coda [r] has dropped to 20 percent (it briefly goes up again close to 24 percent with *Help!* in 1965). By *Sgt. Pepper's Lonely Hearts Club Band* (1967), it has fallen below 10 percent, before hitting its lowest point (less than 5 percent) with *Abbey Road* (1969).

---

[112] An interesting wrinkle: the [ɾ] realization of intervocalic /t/, while stereotypically part of the "Americanized" Brit Pop pronunciation (as per Trudgill), also seems to be a (conditioned) possibility for the urban dialect of Liverpool, sharply distinguished from other prestige British dialects (Watson 2007). In the 1968 Album version of "Hey Jude," it makes most sense to identify this variant as "American" (since other clearly Liverpool features are missing from this and other performances of that period); this identification is probably correct also for the more recent White House performance, though formally both interpretations are available.

[113] This "slipping-in" of a high-frequency, *umgangssprachlich* lexical item into a performance language is precisely what Hackstein (2002) has observed for literary languages (cf. section 3.1 above). Morrissey (2008) remarks that the Beatles rarely include features of their native dialects in their performances: "Lennon's pronunciation of *git* [gɛt] in 'I'm So Tired' (*White Album*), the Liverpudlian style in 'Polythene Pam' or the Scouse /r/ in 'spinal cracker' on 'Come Together' (*Abbey Road*) are relatively rare exceptions" (Morrissey 2008: 216).

[114] Morrissey (2008: 207–9) discusses how the band The Monkees, formed in 1965 as an "American answer" to the Beatles, employed distinctive British features (mixed with US ones) in their singing.

What is particularly interesting (and ought to be thought-provoking) for us as Homerists is the particular nature of loss of coda [r], which could easily be interpreted (from the outside) as diachronic language change. From the point of view of historical linguistics, loss of coda [r] is an *innovation* (which took place in many dialects of English), while retention of coda [r] is an *archaism*. An Ancient Greek parallel to this type of change could be the loss of [w] (see section 3.2 above), or the loss of intervocalic [j] (resulting in the difference between the thematic genitive ending -oιo and the uncontracted -oo).

Now, if we didn't know anything about the sociolinguistic situation of the Beatles, and we only had their corpus to work from, we could easily argue that we are witnessing a clear case of language change taking place before our eyes: namely, that coda [r] was being lost in the language during the 1960s.[115] This reasonable conclusion, of course, would be incorrect: what we are witnessing is not "natural" language change or "modernization" of the singer's dialect, but the result of a competition between two synchronic models: the "American" one (with maintenance of [r]) and the "British" one (with loss of [r]). Similarly, no regular speaker of English would recognize the *r*-ful variants as "archaic," and the *r*-less variants as "innovative."[116] We are simply looking at two synchronic variants, with different geographic and sociolinguistic affiliations.[117]

We could call this the *synchronic bias* or *synchronic default* of the audience, which can be formulated as follows:

> *Synchronic bias*: When possible, speakers will tend to interpret a given linguistic variant as synchronic (i.e., belonging to a different dialect) rather than diachronic (i.e., belonging to an older variety of their own dialect), especially if they have more access to other synchronic dialects than they would have to recognizably archaic versions of their own dialect (e.g., in the form of older speakers who still preserve the features in question in their speech).

---

[115] This would be akin to Janko's (1982, 2012) counts of "archaic" phonological and morphological features in the Greek of epic, and how their numbers dwindle over time.

[116] If anything, the *r*-less variants may be perceived as more "old-timey" by some American speakers because of the general cultural association between Britishness and "tradition."

[117] Anecdotally, while most speakers of English are aware of dialectal variants, they find it hard to identify a given variant as archaic or innovative, especially when it comes to phonological features. For American speakers, the lone exception seems to be the pronunciation of the sequence <wh> as a voiceless labio-velar fricative [ʍ], as in *what, whale*, which has both the connotation of being old-fashioned and (for at least some speakers) that of being associated with dialects of the Mountain West (i.e., "cowboy" speech). Arguably, [ʍ] can be recognized as an archaism because it is largely *older people* who tend to produce it.

Arguably, the synchronic bias would be even sharper in a culture that lacks devices for faithfully preserving older varieties of speech (e.g., widespread writing or audio recording); in such a culture, a feature could be clearly recognized as archaic only as long as two or more of the conditions below apply:

a. It does not immediately match a known synchronic dialect.
b. It can still be observed in the speech of older speakers.
c. It is embedded in a clearly archaizing and conservative medium (e.g., an old prayer or the like).

When we look at Homeric variants, then, we should consider the effect that they may have had on the audience in a similar way: a genitive in -οιο, or a patronymic adjective in -ιος, could arguably have sounded more Aeolic to them than archaic (especially if audiences were familiar with Aeolic dialects showing that feature), and quite possibly this might have been the case for other traits that can be described as conservative in the language (e.g., uncontracted vs. contracted vocalic sequences, as in example (2) above). A similar explanation could also very well hold for the "gap" in the attestation of Archaic Ionic -έο (<Proto-Greek *-āo) discussed in section 3.4.2 above. Speakers are not historical linguists, and a synchronically recognizable dialectal variant (such as Aeolic -āo) would have been more available and sociolinguistically meaningful to them than an isolated and Archaic Ionic -έο (which nobody in the audience might have recognized as Ionic in the first place, especially if it had disappeared from the language more than a generation earlier). And of course, different audiences (or different members of the audience) may have interpreted the same features differently based on their own linguistic experience. Again, speakers are neither historical linguists nor dialectologists: but their conceptions and experiences of language and linguistic diversity can color their perception of a linguistic performance, and contribute to the creation of meaning. We can talk, from this point of view, of a sort of linguistic (more specifically dialectal) reception.

As oral performances give rise to written texts, and as those texts pass through the hands of philologists and grammarians, another layer of linguistic reception can be added: now the ideas that later scholars hold about the requisite dialectal mix for each genre of poetry (or prose, for that matter) can come to impact the way the text is edited or emended. Cassio (2007) is a study of how ancient theories of dialect were applied to the text of Alcman, resulting in significant linguistic alterations. Nineteenth-century editors of Homer engaged in the same type of linguistic reception when they tried to reconstruct an original Aeolic text, cleansed of Ionic forms (e.g., Fick 1883, 1886). And we still (perhaps inescapably) engage in these practices today, every time, for instance, we "restore" a supposedly more archaic form in the text of Homer on the basis of our modern historical linguistic knowledge and our theories as to when and how the text came to be written down.[118]

3.6.4 Green Day and the Punk Rock Phase Theory

There is yet another contemporary musical genre that seems to provide an intriguing parallel to the classic phase theory within epic language. This is the performance dialect employed by punk rock singers (sometimes described as the *punk rock voice*).[119] In this genre, too, audiences have long been intrigued and puzzled by the apparent oddness of the singers' linguistic choices:

> The very specific accent used in the mega-hits of the genre seems to still have a hold over anyone who was a teenager between 1993 and 2003. On Twitter you'll see jokes made about the "pop punk voice" used by bands like the *Offspring*, *New Found Glory*, *Avril Lavigne*, and, especially, *Blink-182*. Their accents are a relic as strong as the Valley Girl voice. There's a whole Tumblr called *Tom DeLonge Lyrics*, dedicated to transliterating the spectacularly strange and exaggerated accent used by DeLonge, one of the singers of pop-punk band Blink-182. (Nosowitz 2015)

To pinpoint the origin of all this strangeness, we need to once again turn to the history of the genre. Punk rock first emerged in the US (with centers both in New York City and on the West Coast), where it was spearheaded by bands like Television (formed in New York in 1973) and

---

[118] Linguistic (or grammatical) reception is tied to another important debate: that of whether the text of Homer should reflect a single, perfectly coherent grammar, or whether it should admit of linguistic variation that might be unclear to us. Van Thiel (1991: xxiv–xxviii), in the introduction of his critical edition of the *Odyssey*, makes a case against following the principle of *linguistic uniformity* when editing the text of Homer (i.e., assuming that only one correct version for each linguistic form should exist in the language of Homer, and that thus one should print the "correct" form everywhere despite the variation manuscripts might show in every specific passage). This opinion is not shared by the other most recent editor of Homer, Martin West (1998, 2017), who instead follows uniform orthographic practices established in his *Praefatio* (see West 1998: xvi–xxxvii).

[119] This dialect has not yet, to my knowledge, been the subject of extensive academic study (except a short analysis of its development in the 1970s in Britain by Trudgill, quoted below), but many facts about it have been reported by journalist Dan Nosowitz (2015) in an *Atlas Obscura* article, who also interviewed sociolinguist Penelope Eckert on the topic.

the Ramones (formed in New York in 1974). Very soon afterwards, the genre was imported into the UK, where it was adopted by bands such as the Sex Pistols (formed in London in 1975), and The Clash (formed in London in 1976). Punk as a genre embraced a strong antiestablishment stance, and one of the vehicles for the expression of this stance was, unsurprisingly, dialect. So, while UK-based bands had inherited some general "American" features from their US predecessors, they also introduced into their songs many features associated with low-prestige (working-class) Southern English accents.[120] This was both in line with the social message of the genre, and (possibly) in conscious polemic with major rock bands from Britain (like Led Zeppelin), who had embraced the Brit Pop pronunciation (Nosowitz 2015).[121] These newly introduced features include (Trudgill 1983 [1997: 262]):

1. the use of wide diphthongs, e.g., /ei/ = [æɪ] as in *face*, and /ou/ = [æʉ] as in *go*;
2. the pronunciation of /ai/ as [ɑɪ], as in *sky*, and of /au/ as [æu~ɛu], as in *out*;
3. the vocalization of /l/, as in *milk* [mɪʊk];
4. the (occasional) deletion of /h/;
5. the use of [ʔ] realizations of /t/, not only finally, as in *get*, but also intervocalically, where it is most socially stigmatized and conspicuous, as in *better*.

---

[120] An additional component in the dialect mixture of punk rock, which I have not found discussed in the sociolinguistic literature so far, is Jamaican English. In the 1960s and 1970s, England was home to a large community of Jamaican immigrants, who lived mostly in the same London working-class districts where punk rock was being adopted. The influence of ska and reggae music on punk rock is universally acknowledged (for a history, see Kroubo 2010 and Letts 2008). One famous example is the song "The Guns of Brixton" (1979) by The Clash, whose musical form is heavily influenced by reggae, and whose lyrics channel the views of a Brixton-born son of Jamaican immigrants. Here, the lack of verb agreement in the verses: *When the law break in/ How you gonna go?* can be seen as a feature of Jamaican English (see Jantos 2009); note that regular verb agreement appears just a few lines later in the verse *The money feels good*, thus confirming this song as another example of dialect mixture. The same lack of verb agreement (this time consistent through the entire song) can be seen in The Clash's "Police and Thieves" (1977), a cover of the reggae song "Police and Thief" (1976) by Junior Murvin, in the line *And all the crime come in, day by day/ No one stop it in any way*. Further linguistic research on the topic is desirable. For Jamaican Creole (not Jamaican English) in popular music today, see Gerfer (2018) and Jansen and Westphal (2017) (on Rihanna's singing style).

[121] These working-class features are evident, for instance, in the singing style of Joe Strummer (real name John Graham Mellor), the co-lead vocalist of The Clash, who was himself from an upper-middle class background (his father was a diplomat), and thus had arguably adopted these features as part of the construction of his musical persona. See Thornhill (2014).

What is interesting for us, however, is that the new linguistic model did not result in a complete elimination of "American" features from the genre's dialect. As Trudgill observes (1983 [1997: 262]):

> The old motivation of sounding American has not been replaced by the new motivation, but remains in competition with it.

And, most importantly for our ends:

> At points when the two pronunciation models are in direct conflict, such as the realization of /ai/, forms like [aː] and [ɑɪ] alternate, even in the same song. (Trudgill 1983 [1997: 262])

In a way, then, we have a genre which moved between different geographical centers, collecting dialectal features at every stop – just like Greek epic is supposed to have done according to phase theory.

While punk rock (in its various currents) continued to be developed in the US, UK, and Australia through the 1980s, the 1990s marked a time where the genre officially crossed over into major mainstream success (sometimes dubbed as the *punk rock revival*, or *pop punk*), as its geographic base shifted once again, this time to the West Coast of the US (first in the Bay Area, then in Southern California). This is the period marked by the MTV-propelled ascent of bands mentioned by Nosowitz in the quote above, such as Green Day (formed in 1986 in Berkeley, California, but first signed by a major record company in 1993), The Offspring (formed in 1984 in Garden Grove, California, and first reaching commercial success in 1994), and Blink-182 (formed in Poway, California, in 1992, and reaching major commercial success in 1999).

Again, these singers preserved some of the linguistic features that already belonged to the genre, while adding their own to the mix, and often in different amounts as their motivation towards different models shifted:

> As an ode to the *Clash*, a lot of their singers adopted a sort of faux-British accent. [...] Tim Armstrong, the [...] lead singer of fellow Bay Area band *Rancid*, sings with an accent that varies song by song; sometimes it's nearly featureless, other times it's a Strummer-esque Brit inflection, other times it sounds nearly New York. (Nosowitz 2015)

What is even more fascinating is that at least some singers within this genre seem to be perfectly aware of what they are doing, and of the historical origins of their *Kunstsprache*: when asked about his performance accent in a

Rolling Stone interview from 1994, Green Day lead singer Billie Joe Armstrong openly explained:

> I'm an American guy faking an English accent faking an American accent. (Foege 1994)

As Homerists, we may ask whether our epic poets had a similar awareness of the composite nature and origin of their *Kunstsprache*. Was "Homer" (following some modern theories) a Euboean guy faking an East Ionic accent, faking an Asiatic Aeolic accent?

What seems most relevant to our discussion is that these phenomena of dialectal stratification (one may say "phase" models) seem common in well-documented contemporary musical genres, even when clear metrical necessities are entirely missing. And while Parry's account of a phase theory (as discussed in section 3.4.2 above) argued that poets adopting a foreign literary idiom only maintained foreign linguistic features out of metrical need, preferring whenever possible to substitute their own vernacular for the inherited language,[122] these contemporary phenomena clarify that these foreign elements, far from being a nuisance, can actually play an important role in the poet's negotiation and signaling of their own position within the stream of tradition. Singers seek to maintain these features, far from rushing to replace them with their own vernacular right away. At the individual level, they feel that, through linguistic shift, they are paying homage to their models.

Of course, one can imagine a sociolinguistic situation where complete purging of foreign elements from a performance dialect may be desirable for a series of reasons (e.g., strong enmity between two communities, which are divided along perceptible linguistic lines). But these are also unlikely to be situations in which cultural borrowing at large scale may occur in the first place. We will see an interesting case in this direction in section 3.6.5 below.

To sum up, "words and forms archaic and dialectal" let singers channel previous performances and famous models, and are key to their self-presentation and the construction of their poetic identity. While it is impossible to deny the ever-present imprint of the meter on Homer's language, when it comes to performance languages in general, it is clear that meter is neither a necessary nor a sufficient condition to explain dialect mixing, and focusing on meter alone may prevent us from seeing the more

---

[122] "They [the poets] make the foreign poetry fit their spoken language in so far as they can do so without any great loss. The new poems thus take on straightaway a local color" (Parry 1971: 337–38).

complex cultural picture that is conveyed when singers choose to stray from their spoken dialect for the purposes of performance.

3.6.5 Alesha Dixon and the Conflict between Topic and Genre

Of course, different musical genres (and different performance situations and topics therein) may prove to be more or less susceptible to language modification. As we have observed above, punk is particularly conducive to incorporating local, low-prestige dialectal features because of its antiestablishment stance and political message. Similarly, we can think of comedy or satire in Rome as more conducive to representing different sociolects than other genres of literature.[123] Not all genres, however, are this way, and sometimes curious mismatches between genres, dialects, and even topic and occasion can arise as a result. Consider a short illustrative example from the present day.

In 2016, the British singer Alesha Dixon was reportedly heckled after her performance of "God Save the Queen" at the British Grand Prix at Silverstone.[124] The reason for the heckling was the "American" accent which she employed in her performance. Viewers commented on Twitter that "Alesha Dixon appears to think Gad should save the Queen instead" (Brown 2015).[125] In the context of the British national anthem, many felt that the adoption of an American pronunciation was inappropriate and unpatriotic.

The source of Dixon's performance accent is, of course, no mystery: she operates within the rhythm and blues tradition (just like Adele), where the adoption of American features is the standard choice. And British audiences (patriotic or not) are apparently otherwise fine with these features in her singing. It is just the particular topic of the national anthem which exposes a conflict in motivation: audiences feel that the motivation towards "sounding British" should take precedence in this context over personal musical style, while Dixon's (likely unconscious) choices reflected a stronger motivation towards the American model.[126]

---

[123] For an overview of sources for sociolects in Ancient Rome, see Clackson (2011). For Greek comedy, see Willi (2002, 2006).

[124] "Alesha Dixon heckled for singing British national anthem in American accent" (Brown 2015).

[125] The specific feature under discussion here is the rounded (British) pronunciation of the vowel in [gɒd], as opposed to the unrounded (American) pronunciation in [gɑd]. The American pronunciation is due to the so-called *father–bother merger*, which took place after the eighteenth century (Labov, Ash, and Boberg 2006: 169).

[126] The fact that Dixon is a woman of color (she is of Jamaican descent on her father's side) may have helped trigger even more suspicions about her loyalty to the flag on the part of more nationalist and conservative segments in the audience.

We can see the national anthem as belonging to a "high" genre of music, where the introduction of certain dialectal or innovative features may be seen as inappropriate. The goal of these genres, in a way, is not to communicate closeness to the audience, but separation. Epic poetry in Ancient Greece seems to have been one such elevated genre, where part of the goal of the language was to construct, to quote Tolkien again, "a form of language familiar in meaning and yet free from trivial associations, and filled with the memory of good and evil." As such (and in the absence of other factors strengthening the motivation towards a specific "local" model), the epic *Kunstsprache* might have been less permeable to the penetration of everyday features – and the local dialectal features of an individual poet specifically – than other genres.

If this is true, then the likelihood of Homer's geographic origin being revealed (or betrayed) by the poet's linguistic choices seems even smaller for epic than for other types of poetry. At the same time, it is reasonable to assume that Homer's language overall must have sounded, to audiences, somewhat timeless and elevated (as opposed to informal, modern, and "down-to-earth") – just like the long chiton of the Ionian rhapsodes must have looked elegant and perhaps old-fashioned to Athenian festival-goers.

3.6.6 *Arctic Monkeys, Stage Persona, and the Perception of Dialect*

Another interesting case study on the theme of conflicting motivations comes from a report on a live performance by the British band Arctic Monkeys at Glastonbury Festival in 2013. Here, lead singer Alex Turner was criticized for apparently sounding "American" during his set. We will remember (see fn. 102 above) that Arctic Monkeys are otherwise famous for preserving several features of their local Sheffield dialect in their singing. Their commitment to their dialectal identity is not just implicit: it's programmatic. Their song "Fake Tales of San Francisco" (2006), for instance, pokes fun at bands attempting to project an American identity:

(13)　He talks of San Francisco, he's from Hunter's Bar[127]
　　　I don't quite know the distance
　　　But I'm sure that's far

---

[127] Hunter's Bar is a location in southwest Sheffield, England.

and

(14)   you're not from New York City, you're from Rotherham
        ("Fake Tales of San Francisco," *Whatever People Say I Am, That's What I'm Not*, 2006)

From this point of view, an accusation of "Americanizing" would be quite damaging to the ethos of the band.

Turner's reply to the criticism is interesting, in that it gives us a window into a singer's perception of their own shifting motivations (or lack thereof), and into the role of a poet's on-stage appearance and behavior in changing the perception of accent. After the show, Turner commented that the apparent shift (which was accompanied by marked hand-gesturing) was "not intentional," and that the audience's perception of his accent might have been influenced by his recent change in look (specifically his new, Elvis-style slicked-back hairstyle):

> I've been pointing my hands for ages though! Maybe it's just the quiff [hairstyle] confusing people? Jo Whiley [an English radio DJ] just said I was channeling my inner Elvis, but I dunno man. It's not intentional! (Stevens 2013)

When it comes to the audience's perspective, the apparent shift was attributed to the adhesion to a particular *personal* model (Elvis Presley), with whom Turner seemed to share appearance, gestures, and accent, as opposed to a more generic model ("sounding American").

The issue of Turner's accent was taken up in a 2016 article by journalist Dan Wilkinson, who interviewed linguist Marina Tyndall on the topic ("We Asked a Linguist Why Alex Turner Now Sounds Like an Old Cowboy").[128] Here, Tyndall seems to agree with Turner's self-assessment: while she is aware that speakers can subconsciously, and very effectively, *code-switch* when motivated to do so (she couches this in accommodation theory, which, as we have seen above, is not sufficient to explain performance dialect phenomena), she does not single out any clearly "American" features in Turner's spoken or performance dialect, and she argues that a multitude of factors (among which is simply using a more "staged," careful

---

[128] https://noisey.vice.com/en_us/article/6x89zn/we-asked-a-linguist-why-alex-turner-now-sounds-like-he-was-born-in-california. The web address here shows an alternative title for the article, which characterizes Turner as sounding "like he was born in California." Of course, for American speakers these would be two radically different dialects. For the British readership, both are stereotypes for "having an American accent."

diction) could result in a weakening of Turner's Sheffield features during performance:

> Listen to "Four Horsemen in a One-Horse Race": He's not even pronouncing his rs before a vowel. If I were coaching him for a US acting role, with this as our starting point, we'd still have a very long way to go. (Wilkinson 2016)

Tyndall's assessment appears to be off here, though it reflects the general British perception of what constitutes an "American" accent: Elvis *spoke* a rhotic dialect, but *sang* in a non-rhotic one (Trudgill 1983 [1997: 256]). If Turner is indeed trying to channel Elvis here, he's making the right choice. In closing, while Tyndall admits that Turner may have picked up some non-Sheffield features in his performance dialect, she doubts the intentionality of the shift.

> I doubt very much it was part of his Dr. Evil-esque public relations master plan, conceived in a ten-point strategy meeting held by his record label, "Adopt Weird Hybrid Accent: Break America." Code-switching is something everyone does, nearly all of the time. (Wilkinson 2016)

Again, Tyndall's assessment seems partially off. As we have seen above, different singers may bring different levels of awareness to their dialectal choices. Turner might be experiencing an unconscious shift in his motivation towards the Sheffield English model, and the audience might be picking up on something after all – only a deeper longitudinal study could give us an answer. And, as Trudgill has demonstrated, a "Dr. Evil-esque public relations master plan," consisting in a strategy to "Adopt Weird Hybrid Accent: Break America," is not too far from what the Brit Pop accent is all about.

Coming back to Homer, this case study suggests that looking at other features (e.g., gestures, voice quality, dress, etc.) in the performance of Homeric epic can give us indications as to how the audience was likely to interpret the poet's *Kunstsprache*. When it comes to fifth-century Attica, it seems that all visual cues in a rhapsode's stage appearance would point to East Ionia specifically (as opposed to, say, Euboea). This is perhaps most visible in Plato's construction of the character of Ion (to which we'll return in Chapter 4).

3.6.7 *Iggy Azalea, Realness, and Overshooting*

Another interesting complication on the topic of performance languages has to do with the contemporary discourse around cultural appropriation, and specifically regarding the adoption of Black musical and linguistic styles by white performers. A famous recent case study is the white Australian rapper Iggy Azalea, who faced significant backlash in 2014 for what critics labeled "linguistic blackface" or "minstrelsy." In particular, audiences objected to the difference between Azalea's speaking style, which mixes features of her native Australian dialect with some general American features (Wilkinson 2014) and her singing style, which has been described as "a comically exaggerated Southern black twang" (Morris 2015).[129]

What is fascinating in Azalea's case is that the linguistic features she adopts in her singing are not mixed or inaccurate (as is often the case with performance languages): rather, they match very closely the performance of native speakers, both quantitatively and qualitatively speaking (Eberhardt and Freeman 2015: 310–12). Azalea, who moved to Miami as a teenager to pursue a hip-hop career, and worked under the tutelage of the Black rapper T.I., displays native-like competency in Southern African American English (AAE).[130] And therein lies part of the problem.

As has become clear from our discussion so far, Azalea is far from the first white performer to borrow various features (linguistic and not) from Black performers and predominantly Black performance traditions. Extensive work exists on the performance language of hip-hop specifically,[131] showing that the use of AAE is in many ways standard for the genre (though not exclusive):

> Hip-hop artists tend to either use African American Vernacular English (AAVE) features (see Alim, 2002 and Morgan, 2001 for African American hip-hop artists) or local features, such as broad Australian features (O'Hanlon, 2006). Akande (2012) and Lee (2011) show that Korean and Nigerian hip-hoppers "cross" (Rampton, 1995) into AAVE to enhance their international credibility (Akande, 2012, p. 238). (Gerfer 2018: 669)

But given the history of antiblack racism in the US, and the values at the core of the hip-hop genre, white performers who decide to operate within the hip-hop tradition need to work on situating their persona within that

---

[129] The effect is perhaps particularly jarring in the music video for her song "Fancy" (2014), where Azalea impersonates (with remarkable physical likeness) Cher Horowitz, the protagonist of the movie *Clueless* (1995), a stereotypical privileged white girl from Beverly Hills, all the while singing with very prominent Southern AAE features.

[130] See Cutler (2014: 5) for a discussion of the various terms for AAE and their history. African American Vernacular English (AAVE) is another common term in the literature, though (as Cutler explains) it is now dispreferred.

[131] In the field of Homeric studies, Edwards and Sienkwicz (1990) is a rewarding exploration of the parallels between rapping as a contemporary form of oral art and Homer's poetry and technique.

tradition in a way that is respectful of its history and acknowledges their outsider status within it.[132] And it is in this respect that Azalea fell short.

Perhaps above all, hip-hop performers strive to project *realness*, a form of credibility which is usually acquired through the experience of social struggle, and typically by affiliation with the African American urban experience (Hess 2005: 372). At the same time, realness demands that a hip-hop performer stay true to themselves, a requirement which "grows out of black rhetorical traditions such as testifying and bearing witness, in which the authority to speak is negotiated through claims to knowledge gained through lived experience" (Hess 2005: 375). The demand for realness, as we shall see, rather complicates the adoption of a performance style.

For white performers seeking affiliation to the hip-hop world, claiming realness can be tricky. A superficial shortcut is to borrow elements from Black identity by imitating stereotypical Black narratives, fashions, and speech styles. This strategy was taken, unsuccessfully, by the disgraced white rapper Vanilla Ice, who employed a Black vocal style in his performances (Sartwell 1998: 171), claimed an impoverished upbringing (as part of a "rags to riches" story), and played into the "gansta rapper" stereotype by citing criminal involvement and gang affiliation. His career unraveled when these narratives were revealed to be untrue, and his whole persona became perceived as inauthentic and commercially motivated (Hess 2005: 373–75).

In a way, we can see these imitative (one could say inauthentic) practices as symptoms of an "insecure attachment" to the hip-hop world. Cutler (2003), who focuses on how white hip-hoppers negotiate language, race, and authenticity, observes that white hip-hop members who feel secure in their affiliation to the hip-hop community tend to use fewer AAE features in their speech:

> Core WHHs (white hip-hoppers), who are typically involved in hip-hop practices like MCing and Djing, feel secure about their right to be in hip-hop and are quite candid about race and class. Furthermore, they do not feel the need to signal their hip-hop identity in linguistically overt ways. (Cutler 2003: 215)

---

[132] Hess (2005) presents a case study comparing successful vs. unsuccessful attempts by white rappers to perform "realness." Eminem is a successful example, in that he managed to emphasize autobiographical elements – such as his disadvantaged upbringing and his outlier status as a white rapper, not being taken seriously because of his race – as a way to fit within the "rags to riches" narrative of hip-hop. Another important step is for white hip-hoppers to acknowledge the commercial privilege that whiteness can convey for them, as Eminem repeatedly does in his work (Hess 2005: 384): "Look at my sales, let's do the math, if I was black, I would've sold half" ("White America," *The Eminem Show*, 2002). This type of awareness is markedly absent from Azalea's work.

This is in line with the practice of respected white hip-hoppers like the Beastie Boys and Eminem (see discussion in Hess 2005), whose vocal styles avoid AAE features, or, in the case of the Beastie Boys, attempt to sound as white as possible.[133] In so doing, these artists are fulfilling a deeper requirement for realness, and can thus be welcomed into the hip-hop community.[134]

Insecure attachment, on the other hand (or perhaps a misunderstanding of the requirement of realness), was associated in Cutler's data with a bolder linguistic shift:

> The more peripheral WHHs [white hip-hoppers] tend to orient more to the idea that authenticity is rooted in one's connection to the street or the urban ghetto. They feel obliged to establish their credibility by placing themselves semiotically closer to the urban ghetto and by obscuring the racial and class boundaries that separate them from the urban African American community. They are also more inclined to make overt use of speech markers highly associated with AAE, such as *ain't*, habitual *be*, multiple negation, and copula absence, which leaves them open to charges of trying to "sound black." (Cutler 2003: 215–16)

Ironically, this overt linguistic shift exposes these already peripheral members to the accusation of "unrealness" or "fronting."

Azalea's case seems to fall within this latter category: the particular clash between her physical appearance (a conventionally attractive white girl), her personal background, and the extreme nature of her linguistic shift meant that she failed at projecting realness. At the same time, her quick and substantial commercial success, and her lack of reflection on how that success rested on appropriating aspects of African American culture, made her a particularly clear target for widespread criticism. A *Cosmopolitan* timeline of the Iggy Azalea controversy (Iandoli 2015) has the telling title "How did Iggy Azalea become the world's most hated pop star?"[135]

---

[133] "They try to sound extremely white" (Sartwell 1998: 171).

[134] Fix (2010) is a comparison of usages of AAE features by white women "acting black" in the media vs. white women in a real Black community. Fix finds that white women who are genuinely part of an African American community, while displaying native-like command of this variety, do not have high rates of stereotypical AAE features that are common in media portrayals. On the other hand, media portrayals tend to overshoot naturalistic usage: "These TV personalities, while using many of the same AAE features as the community speakers, use a qualitatively narrower set of features, while also making use of many features at higher rates, indicating a linguistic hyper-performance" (Fix 2010: 64).

[135] For a discussion of the problematic nature of Azalea's music, see Eberhardt and Freeman (2015: 317–22).

We might contrast Azalea's downfall with the fate of Keith Urban, a fellow Australian who has established himself as one of the leading country music artists in the US. Urban's speech (Australian English) too is markedly different from his singing style, where he adopts several features of Southern American English, matching the frequency of other country music performers who are native speakers of that variety (Duncan 2017). In Urban's case, Duncan argues that language shift is the main strategy available for an outsider to claim "authenticity," and thus affiliation with the country music performance tradition, since the creation of an authentic "country backstory" is ruled out for a foreign national.[136] The fact that Urban's linguistic performance does not cross racial (or gender) lines[137] is arguably part of the reason why his linguistic shift has not been perceived as problematic, or in breach of the "authenticity" requirement (which, moreover, might be less stringent in country music than realness is in hip-hop).

While the coordinates of this last case study are uniquely modern, we might wonder whether they can teach us something about performance languages in Ancient Greece. I can think of two applications. First, the insight that performers that are "peripheral" to the tradition to which they are claiming affiliation might overshoot in their attempt to style shift is suggestive. Several studies have found, for instance, that Ionic traits are more pronounced in Hesiod than in Homer.[138] Edwards (1971: 139) writes:

> All the features which we have been examining thus lead to the somewhat paradoxical conclusion that the language of the mainlander Hesiod shows a more decided preference for Ionic forms of expression than does that of the Ionian Homer.[139]

The usual interpretation of this fact is diachronic: we are told that the language of epic became more and more Ionic over time, and that Hesiod simply reflects a later stage in that tradition (Hoekstra 1957: 201–2). But while it is certainly the case that the language of Hesiod reflects a later textualization than Homer (Cassio 2009: 192), it might be the case that the "hyperionization" in Hesiod is (at least to some extent) the result of poets who were non-native speakers of Ionic overshooting in order to match the model of an Ionic tradition.

---

[136] Specifically, Duncan (2017) describes authenticity in country music as indexing being white, from the South of the US, and working class.
[137] As the "default" performance identity in country music is white, male, working class, and Southern.
[138] A recent and compact treatment of Hesiod's language is Cassio (2009). A classic study is Edwards (1971). Note that I use the name "Hesiod" here in the same way I use "Homer" (see fn. 3 of the Introduction).
[139] See also Cassio (2009: 198): "It seems certain to me that Hesiod and the poets who composed in his wake decided to a large extent to be more Ionic than Homer."

This interpretation might be particularly likely for the neglect of word-initial *[w] (which occurs at higher rates in Hesiod than it does in Homer), even though we find [w] preserved in mainland inscriptions (including Boeotia) well into the Hellenistic age (Cassio 2009: 192).[140] Word-initial [w] might have been a feature that mainland poets had in their daily speech, and from which they purposefully (and ultimately excessively) shifted away in performance, in the attempt to sound more "Ionic."

The second question we can ask is whether given groups existed in Ancient Greece that would have objected to just any performer attempting to insert themselves in the Homeric tradition of poetry. In other words – did you have to be a member of a given in-group to "believably" put on a Homeric performance? The existence of groups like the *Homeridae* does seem to point to some concerns with authenticity within the tradition.[141] On the other hand, we have abundant evidence (Allen 1907: 139) for working rhapsodes with no affiliation to the *Homeridae*, including Plato's Ion (to which we will return in Chapter 4). Overall, Homeric features are pervasive enough throughout Ancient Greek literature to show that they were able to cross all sorts of boundaries (whether geographic or of genre) without much trouble or resistance.

3.7 Conclusion: Style between Tradition and Identity

Why is Homer's language such a treasure trove of forms that are archaic and dialectal? In this chapter, we have looked at the dialectal make-up of Homer's diction (sections 3.1 and 3.2) and the way audiences ancient and modern have tried to make sense of it, first by surveying conceptions of dialect and identity in Archaic Greece (section 3.3), then by examining ancient and modern narratives about Homer's life and origin (section 3.4), and finally by exploring some case studies on performance dialects in contemporary popular music, to see if they might provide answers to some open questions about Homer's own performance language (as listed

---

[140] Famously, initial [w] is preserved in CEG 326, the Mantiklos inscription (in the dative adjective ϝεκαβόλοι "far-shooting," an epithet of Apollo), found in Thebes and dated to the early seventh century BCE, and was thus not too far removed from the usual datings of Hesiod (see Kõiv 2011 for a recent discussion).

[141] First mentioned by Pindar (*Nemean* 2.1), the Ὁμηρίδαι "descendants of Homer" were a professional clan based on the island of Chios, devoted to the recitation of Homeric poetry, and claiming ancestry from the poet (West 2021). See Allen (1907) for a collection of the ancient testimonies.

in section 3.5). We can now return to those questions, to sum up our findings:

a. Why do singers use performance languages, and what role does meter play in selecting linguistic variants?

The role of meter seems neither necessary, nor sufficient, to explain how performance languages arise, and why contrasting variants coexist within them. The adhesion to a given performance dialect seems to depend mostly on whether singers wish to insert themselves into a given performance tradition. Variation within performance dialects (i.e., the coexistence of different variants) is mostly due to: (a) the poet's failure to imitate their models perfectly (as typical of any adult speaker), or (b) the presence of conflicting linguistic motivations either already within the tradition or for a given poet specifically. In the case of Homer (and specifically the text of Homer as we have it), meter may very well play a more prominent role in deciding among variants – but it should not be seen as the only relevant factor in a poet's choice.

b. Can performance languages be used to assess the geographic provenance of a poet?

Despite the temptation on the part of the audience (ancient and modern) of interpreting performance languages as reflecting a singer's personal provenance, these languages do not appear to be particularly informative in this regard. More specifically, while performance languages *may* incorporate features that are native to the poet's dialect, it would be hard to confidently isolate these features and recognize them as such in the absence of abundant sociolinguistic information on the singer and their environment.

The prominent presence of features native to a singer's dialect in a given performance language is perhaps more likely (but still not guaranteed) in the following cases: (a) The singer stands at the very beginning of a brand-new tradition ("founder effect"), and as such can work as the main model for all singers that follow (I am aware of no precise examples for this phenomenon at the moment, and I suspect that it would likely take more than one person or model to start what we would call a tradition). (b) The singer becomes especially prominent within that tradition, so that they are able to impose their own linguistic habits on the genre as a whole (e.g., The Clash for punk rock, or Roscoe Holcomb for American folk music). (c) The usage of markedly local (and often low-register) features is part of the sociolinguistic make-up of the genre (e.g., punk rock or ancient satire or comedy).

c. How does linguistic innovation (or the appearance of language change) play out in performance languages?
The case study involving the "loss" of coda [r] in the Beatles' corpus in particular has warned us that not everything that looks like *bona fide* language change should be taken as such, *especially* when the diachronic variant under study can conceivably be interpreted as a diatopic variant as well. We have hypothesized that audiences may have a *synchronic bias* in interpreting dialectal features, so that given traits register not as "archaic" or "innovative," but simply as having different geographic or sociolinguistic affiliations (e.g., "American" vs. "British").

As far as singers are concerned, what seems to matter the most is their ability to signal, through their linguistic choices, their affiliation with the desired models, which often are contemporary or at least available within recent memory – otherwise, one may add, the audience would not recognize them as such, especially in the absence of recording devices.

d. Are there any known parallels for the Homeric phase theory?
There seems to exist at least one contemporary parallel for the phenomenon of a performance tradition that migrates from one geographic center to the other, all the while preserving the linguistic traces of such a migration. In the case of punk rock, meter again does not seem to play any role in the elimination or maintenance of "foreign" variants: what matters are the conflicting motivations that characterize each specific genre.

Of course, several factors in the formation of the punk rock *Kunstsprache* are different from a classic phase theory scenario for Homer, and thus complicate our comparison: (a) Differences in time span: punk rock emerged over a few decades, while most scholars assume that oral epic in Greece took a few centuries to "travel" between different locations. (b) Modern technology: with punk rock, the maintenance and layering of "foreign" variants is certainly facilitated by the availability of audio recordings. In a way, all singers in the punk rock tradition are "contemporary" to their models (i.e., they have *heard* them perform, whether live or in a recording). In the absence of audio recordings, one might predict that a tradition's "memory span" for given features might be shorter, in that access to older models would be more limited, though this specific prediction does not seem to bear out in Greek *Kunstsprachen* (for Homer, one can think of the maintenance of archaic features like *tmesis* or the optionality of the augment, which have no parallel in first-millennium vernaculars). In this sense, it is hard to tell whether the punk rock phase model should exactly be viewed as a case of diachronic layering or whether, given the shorter time span, it should be seen as "synchronic" diffusion. Further, more detailed study on the performance language of punk rock (and other contemporary *Kunstsprachen*) is certainly desired.[142]

What I hope to have shown beyond objection is that what we find in Homer, yet again, is not unique and exotic, but has credible comparanda in the contemporary world, and that looking more closely at these comparanda can help enrich and refine our scenarios about Homer's language, its development, and (what I find perhaps most intriguing) the effect it had on its audiences.

---

[142] While some sociolinguistic literature exists on contemporary performance languages, much more work remains to be done in this area. Beyond the seminal 1983 Trudgill study discussed above, we have only a handful of studies on the dialect of individual genres or performers (see, for instance, the above cited Simpson 1999 on rock and pop singing, Morrissey 2008 on British rock, pop, and folk singing, Beal 2009 on Arctic Monkeys, and Duncan 2017 on US country music). Several studies have looked at the language of hip-hop (Alim 2002, Guy and Cutler 2011, Clarke and Hiscock 2009). Recent issues of the *Journal of Sociolinguistics* (2011) and *Language and Communication* (2017) have been dedicated to the sociolinguistics of staged performances (which includes music) and language ideologies in music, but none of this amounts to a large-scale, systematic account of performance languages as a whole. An important recent contribution to the debate is Gibson (2019), which focuses on the English employed by pop singers in New Zealand (which tends to show US features), and combines an annotated corpus of vocal performances (ca. 12 hours between US and New Zealand performers) with some perception experiments. Watts and Morrissey (2019: Chapter 10) focuses on folk music specifically, and looks at how a single song ('Billy Grey') is performed by a series of artists, cataloging their linguistic choices.

CHAPTER 4

Creativity

> ὁ δ' ὄλβιος, ὅντινα Μοῦσαι
> φίλωνται· γλυκερή οἱ ἀπὸ στόματος ῥέει αὐδή.
> (Hesiod, *Theogony* 96–97)
>
> Blessed the one whom the Muses
> love: sweet from his mouth flows his voice.

In Chapters 1 to 3, we explored three formal features of Homer's poetry – formularity, meter, and dialect mixing – and showed how they each contribute to the poet's task. Specifically, I tried to make the case that all of these features should be seen as *adaptive technologies*, emerging from the circumstances of oral epic composition, which support different aspects of the poet's cognition and performance.

The goal of this final chapter is to pull all of these strands together, and to sketch out a theory of Homeric creativity that is informed by both contemporary cognitive studies and ancient ideas about poetic craft and divine inspiration. In this context, we will have the chance to revisit the paradox of Homeric creativity presented in our introduction, and understand how automatic behaviors and "inspiration" might work together in a performer's brain. This chapter will be shorter than the preceding ones, mostly because it reflects a much more recent area of study (the cognitive study of creativity), and it is not concerned with explaining formal facts about Homer's poetic technique.

In what follows, I will first review the competing conceptions of poets as craftsmen vs. vessels of divine inspiration, as seen through the prism of archaic poetry and Plato's *Ion*. Next, I will turn to the cognitive psychology of creativity, exploring how these new frameworks can give us insights into old debates. I will focus in particular on the cognitive study of jazz improvisation, which presents several parallels with Homeric composition. I will argue that both jazz improvisation and oral epic performance are conducive to the psychological state of *flow*, which is correlated with elation as well as heightened creativity, and that it is in the context of flow that the system of belief surrounding poetic inspiration and the Muses in Archaic Greece should be understood. Finally, I will look at the neuroscience of jazz improvisation, and tease out how its findings can shed light on the Ancient Greek concepts of *tékhnē* and *enthousiasmós*.

4.1 The Poet as a Craftsman

A poet, in an etymological sense, is a maker. Thus, in Ancient Greek, the word ποιητής "maker, poet," an agent noun to the generic verb ποιέω "make," is used as early as Herodotus (*Historiae* 2.53) to refer to Homer, Hesiod, and their predecessors specifically.[1] It is in this sense that the Latin word *poēta* was borrowed from the Greek.[2]

This conception of the poet as a craftsman is robustly attested in other Indo-European (IE) traditions as well, and likely goes back to Proto-Indo-European (PIE). Celtic and Sanskrit similarly use forms of common verbs of making (from the PIE roots $*d^h eug^h$- and $*k^w er$-, respectively) to refer to poetic activity, while Balto-Slavic traditions do the same for magic (West 2007: 35–36).[3] Common IE metaphors for poetic activity similarly point towards the concept of poetry as a craft: making poetry is akin to carpentry or weaving (cf. Latin *textus* "text," literally "woven"),[4] and the song itself can be visualized as a ship or a chariot (for examples, see West 2007: 36–43).

While some recent debate has portrayed the early poets of Archaic Greece as aristocratic amateurs, a closer review of the evidence suggests that professionalism was always present in archaic poetic practice (see Stewart 2016, with references). This is certainly the case for the ἀοιδοί "singers" we encounter in the *Iliad* and the *Odyssey*, who are invited to court to entertain guests (or to perform at weddings or funerals),[5] receive compensation for their services (in the form of food and drink), are honored by the people and praised for their skill (*Od.* 8.471–91),[6] and are

---

[1] For an extensive treatment of the lexicon pertaining to poetry in Ancient Greece, see Ford (2002: 131–39).
[2] The more general usage "maker" is found in Plautus, *Asinaria* 748.
[3] These observations are largely due to Durante (1960). For a history of the field of IE poetics, see Watkins (1995: 12–27).
[4] These two metaphors can occasionally be used in a gendered fashion (i.e., weaving for women's songs, and carpentry for men's songs), see discussion in Bozzone (2016a).
[5] For singers entertaining guests at court, see Phemius in Ithaka (*Od.* 1.153–54) and Demodocus at Skheríē (*Od.* 8.43–45). In Sparta, Menelaus has a singer perform at the weddings of his daughter and his son (*Od.* 4.17). At the funeral of Hector, singers are brought in to lead the *thrênos* (*Il.* 24.720–21).
[6] The scene of Odysseus and Demodocus in *Od.* 8 encompasses all of these points: Demodocus is brought in as a respected professional (λαοῖσι τετιμένον "honored among the people," *Od.* 8.472),

sometimes even called in from abroad to perform (*Odyssey* translations here and below are adapted from McCrorie 2005):

(1) τίς γὰρ δὴ ξεῖνον καλεῖ ἄλλοθεν αὐτὸς ἐπελθὼν
ἄλλον γ', εἰ μὴ τῶν, οἳ δημιοεργοὶ ἔασι;
μάντιν ἢ ἰητῆρα κακῶν ἢ τέκτονα δούρων,
ἢ καὶ θέσπιν ἀοιδόν, ὅ κεν τέρπῃσιν ἀείδων.
οὗτοι γὰρ κλητοί γε βροτῶν ἐπ' ἀπείρονα γαῖαν· (*Od.* 17.382–86)

Who would go abroad himself and call a stranger here,
unless that stranger was one of those who are *dēmioergoí* (skilled workmen):
a seer, a healer of ills, a master of woodwork,
or a divine poet, who might please (us) with his singing:
for those are the men in demand on the boundless earth

Similarly, Hesiod lists singers among other paid occupations:

(2) καὶ κεραμεὺς κεραμεῖ κοτέει καὶ τέκτονι τέκτων,
καὶ πτωχὸς πτωχῷ φθονέει καὶ ἀοιδὸς ἀοιδῷ. (*Works and Days*, 24–25)

and the potter competes with the potter, the carpenter with the carpenter, the beggar envies the beggar, and the singer the singer

In this sense, poets could be conceived as possessing a τέχνη "craft" (see discussion in Murray 1981: 98–99).[7] When Phemius pleads for his life with Odysseus, and calls himself αὐτοδίδακτος "self-taught" (*Od.* 22.347), he implies that some training was needed in order to master his skill. When Demodocus is praised for singing the doom of the Achaeans κατὰ κόσμον "in the right way" (*Od.* 8.489) or when Odysseus is praised for telling his own story ὅτ' ἀοιδὸς ἐπισταμένως "with knowing ways like a singer" (*Od.* 11.368), the τέχνη of the poet is once again highlighted.

When at the beginning of *Nemean* 5 Pindar reminds us that he is not a maker of statues, he stresses nonetheless that he is a maker of an even better artifact – a song, which can travel faster and farther.[8]

(3) Οὐκ ἀνδριαντοποιός εἰμ', ὥστ' ἐλινύσοντα ἐργά-
ζεσθαι ἀγάλματ' ἐπ' αὐτᾶς βαθμίδος
ἑσταότ'· (Pindar, *Nemean* 5.1–3)

Odysseus offers him a gift of choice meat (*Od.* 8.474–77), and then praises his skill after listening to his first song (λίην γὰρ κατὰ κόσμον Ἀχαιῶν οἶτον ἀείδεις "You surely sang the doom of the Achaeans in the right way," *Od.* 8.489).

[7] Etymologically, τέχνη contains the PIE root *tek* "make, fashion," which we find in Latin *textus* "what is woven."

[8] Ford (2002: 113–30) offers a detailed treatment of the vocabulary and imagery for poetry as a craft in Pindar and Bacchylides.

I am not a sculptor, who makes beautiful objects
which stand unmoving on their pedestals.

4.2 The Poet as Divinely Inspired

4.2.1 Divine Inspiration Before Plato

The idea of the poet as a skilled craftsman is inextricably intertwined with another, potentially contradictory, conception: that of the poet as a vessel for divine inspiration, as a pupil or protégé of the Muses or Apollo.[9] The very passages we just quoted in Homer illustrate this view. When Demodocus is first mentioned in *Odyssey* 8, it is remarked that his ability to sing is a gift from a god (in *Od.* 8.62–64, we are reminded that this gift was accompanied by the countergift of blindness):

(4) καλέσασθε δὲ θεῖον ἀοιδόν,
Δημόδοκον· τῷ γάρ ῥα θεὸς περὶ δῶκεν ἀοιδὴν
τέρπειν, ὅππῃ θυμὸς ἐποτρύνῃσιν ἀείδειν. (*Od.* 8.43–45)

call the divine singer,
Demodocus: to him a god gave the song
to please, in whatever direction his *thūmós* spurs him to sing.

When Odysseus offers Demodocus some food, he does so because:

(5) πᾶσι γὰρ ἀνθρώποισιν ἐπιχθονίοισιν ἀοιδοὶ
τιμῆς ἔμμοροί εἰσι καὶ αἰδοῦς, οὕνεκ' ἄρα σφέας
οἴμας Μοῦσ' ἐδίδαξε, φίλησε δὲ φῦλον ἀοιδῶν. (*Od.* 8.479–81)

Singers have won the praise and honor of all men
living on earth because the Muse has taught them
the ways of song. She loves the clan of her singers.

Similarly, when Phemius pleads for his life, it is his connection to the divine which he tries to parlay into clemency:[10]

(6) αὐτοδίδακτος δ' εἰμί, θεὸς δέ μοι ἐν φρεσὶν οἴμας
παντοίας ἐνέφυσεν· ἔοικα δέ τοι παραείδειν
ὥς τε θεῷ· τῷ μή με λιλαίεο δειροτομῆσαι. (*Od.* 22.347–49)

---

[9] For a compact introduction to poetic inspiration in antiquity, see Murray (2015), with references.

[10] These words are remarkably similar to those of a Kara-Kyrgiz *akyn* (improvising poet or singer), as reported by Bowra (1952: 41) (this connection is pointed out in Finkelberg 1990: 303): "I can sing every song: for God had planted the gift of song in my heart. He gives me the word on my tongue without me having to seek it. I have not learned any of my songs; everything springs from my inner being, from myself."

> I am self-taught, but a god put in my mind
> all of the ways of song. It is right that I sing these to you
> as to the god. Don't be so anxious to cut my throat.

And finally, when Odysseus praises Demodocus for singing the doom of the Achaeans in the right way, he prefaces it by saying:

(7)   ἢ σέ γε Μοῦσ' ἐδίδαξε, Διὸς πάϊς, ἢ σέ γ' Ἀπόλλων· (*Od.* 8.488)

> A Muse must have taught you, a child of Zeus, or Apollo himself.

The clearest (and perhaps most famous) presentation of the connection between the Muses and the poet is in Hesiod, who begins his *Theogony* by remembering how the Muses taught him his song (ἐνέπνευσαν δέ μοι αὐδὴν θέσπιν "they breathed into me a godly song"), and gave him the laurel staff, symbol of his profession:

(8)   αἵ νύ ποθ' Ἡσίοδον καλὴν ἐδίδαξαν ἀοιδήν,
      ἄρνας ποιμαίνονθ' Ἑλικῶνος ὕπο ζαθέοιο.
      τόνδε δέ με πρώτιστα θεαὶ πρὸς μῦθον ἔειπον,
      Μοῦσαι Ὀλυμπιάδες, κοῦραι Διὸς αἰγιόχοιο· (25)
      "ποιμένες ἄγραυλοι, κάκ' ἐλέγχεα, γαστέρες οἶον,
      ἴδμεν ψεύδεα πολλὰ λέγειν ἐτύμοισιν ὁμοῖα,
      ἴδμεν δ' εὖτ' ἐθέλωμεν ἀληθέα γηρύσασθαι."
      ὣς ἔφασαν κοῦραι μεγάλου Διὸς ἀρτιέπειαι,
      καί μοι σκῆπτρον ἔδον δάφνης ἐριθηλέος ὄζον (30)
      δρέψασαι, θηητόν· ἐνέπνευσαν δέ μοι αὐδὴν
      θέσπιν, ἵνα κλείοιμι τά τ' ἐσσόμενα πρό τ' ἐόντα,
      καί μ' ἐκέλονθ' ὑμνεῖν μακάρων γένος αἰὲν ἐόντων,
      σφᾶς δ' αὐτὰς πρῶτόν τε καὶ ὕστατον αἰὲν ἀείδειν.
      (Hesiod, *Theogony* 22–34)

> They were the first to teach Hesiod the beautiful song,
> as he pastured his lambs at the foothills of god-filled Helicon.
> This first thing the goddesses said to me,
> the Muses of Olympus, daughters of Zeus who carries the *aigís*
> "Field-dwelling shepherds, bad reproaches, nothing but bellies,
> we can say many false things that ring similar to the truth,
> and we can if we want tell the truth as well."
> So spoke the daughters of great Zeus, skilled with their words,
> and they gave me a scepter made of a branch of flowering laurel,
> which they picked—a sight. And they breathed into me a godly
> song, so that I might sing of the things that are to be and those that were before,
> and they ordered me to celebrate with hymns the race of the eternal gods,
> but to always sing of them [the Muses] first and last.

Murray (1981, 2015) makes the convincing claim that these two views (the poet as craftsman vs. the poet as a divine vessel) are not necessarily at odds, and they are at least not portrayed as such in Archaic Greece,[11] where the concept of divine possession or poetic furor does not clearly appear before the fifth century (Tigersted 1970).[12]

Certainly, the Muses can provide assistance of various kinds to poets: they can impart a general poetic ability (as they seem to have done with Hesiod and Demodocus); they can provide fluency or gracefulness in expression (cf. *Theogony* 96–97). And, perhaps most importantly of all, they can provide knowledge on particular topics and aid the poet's recall. It is in this function that we see the primary link between the Muses (daughters of Zeus and Mnemosyne) and the powers of memory.[13] In Hesiod just as much as in Homer, the Muses are the sources of information (the eyewitnesses, we could say) that guarantee that the content of the song is truthful:[14]

(9) Ἔσπετε νῦν μοι Μοῦσαι Ὀλύμπια δώματ' ἔχουσαι·
     ὑμεῖς γὰρ θεαί ἐστε πάρεστέ τε ἴστέ τε πάντα,
     ἡμεῖς δὲ κλέος οἶον ἀκούομεν οὐδέ τι ἴδμεν· (*Il.* 2.484–86)

     Tell me now, Muses, who hold the houses of Olympus:
     for you are goddesses and you are present, and you know everything
     we only hear rumors, and we have no knowledge.

It is in this sense that the epic poet asks the Muse to sing on a given topic (Μῆνιν ἄειδε, θεά, *Il.* 1.1 "The wrath, sing, o goddess"; Ἄνδρα μοι ἔννεπε,

---

[11] See also Brillante (2009: 23–29), Halliwell (2011: 55–57).

[12] This is contrary to Plato's widely accepted assertion, in *Leges* 719c, that there is a παλαιὸς μῦθος "ancient myth" of the poet being possessed, like a Pythia on a tripod.

[13] The etymology of the term Μοῦσα (Aeol. Μοῖσα, showing a different outcome of the second compensatory lengthening, reflecting the Proto-Greek *mont-i̯a) itself is somewhat debated. The best semantic connection is provided by the PIE root *men "think," perhaps in the inherited collocation of the root noun *men(s) "mind" + the verb *dʰeh₁ "put," together meaning "to put in mind." This collocation is seen in Skt. *medhā́* "wisdom, insight," Av. *mazdā* "remembrance," and arguably in Gk. μανθάνω "learn." For a similar connection between goddesses of memory and the root *men-, cf. Latin *Monēta* (the mother of the Muses, as well as an appellative of Juno), derived from *moneō* "to cause to think; to remind," a causative form of *men- (for causative formations in PIE, see Bozzone 2020). The noun Μνημοσύνη, on the other hand, is derived from the root *mneh₂- "remind," seen in Gk. μιμνήσκω "remember, remind" (this root might in turn be related to *men-, but not through any established derivational process).

[14] Finkelberg (1990) argues that, in this regard, Homeric epic and South Slavic epic differ radically, in that the former relies on the authority of the gods (here Muses specifically) to guarantee the truthfulness of its contents, while the latter relies on the authority of the tradition. In this way, Finkelberg suggests, "the idea of the poet's inspiration by the Muse offers an excellent alibi for poetic invention" (Finkelberg 1990: 296).

Μοῦσα, *Od.* 1.1 "The man sing to me, o Muse"), or asks them direct questions about the matter to be covered, such as:

(10) Τίς τάρ σφωε θεῶν ἔριδι ξυνέηκε μάχεσθαι; (*Il.* 1.8)

Who was it among the gods who pushed them to fight in discord?

(11) Ἔσπετε νῦν μοι Μοῦσαι Ὀλύμπια δώματ' ἔχουσαι·
ὅς τις δὴ πρῶτος βροτόεντ' ἀνδράγρι' Ἀχαιῶν
ἤρατ', ἐπεί ῥ' ἔκλινε μάχην κλυτὸς ἐννοσίγαιος (*Il.* 14.508–10)

Tell me now, Muses, who inhabit the houses of Olympus:
who was the first among the Achaeans to take bloody spoils,
after the glorious earth-shaker caused the battle to turn?

But to ensure a successful oral poetic performance, both ingredients had to be present: poetic skill on one hand and divine assistance on the other. We find this combination in Archilochus' self-introduction, which uses the verb ἐπίσταμαι "to be capable or skillful, to know" with regard to poetic practice, all the while stating that this activity is a gift (δῶρον) from the Muses:

(12) εἰμὶ δ' ἐγὼ θεράπων μὲν Ἐνυαλίοιο ἄνακτος
καὶ Μουσέων ἐρατὸν δῶρον ἐπιστάμενος (Archilochus, *Fragmenta* 1)

I am the servant of lord Enūálios,
and I know the lovely gift of the Muses.

This cooperation is also expressed in Pindar's famous fragment:

(13) μαντεύεο, Μοῖσα, προφατεύσω δ' ἐγώ (Pindar, *Fragmenta* 150)

Give your oracle, Muse, and I shall interpret it

which captures the collaboration between the poet and the source of his inspiration, comparing it with the complementary religious roles of the μάντις "seer," who experiences a vision, and the προφήτης "announcer," who interprets that vision for the public.[15]

4.2.2 *Divine Inspiration in Plato's* Ion

It is in Plato, and most clearly in the *Ion*, that craft and divine inspiration are pitted against each other as alternatives that cannot coexist.[16] As we shall see, this is because of Plato's strict definition (for the purposes of this

---

[15] For prophecy in Ancient Greece, see Ustinova (2017: 55–112).
[16] Short introductions to *Ion* can be found in Aguirre and Lavilla de Lera (2018), as well as Murray (1996). Cappuccino (2005) provides a complete text with Italian translation, extensive commentary, and a rich bibliography. On Plato and poetry in general, see Destrée and Herrmann (2011).

dialogue) of what a *tékhnē* can and cannot be, as well as because of Plato's collapsing of different cognitive experiences (from the audience's emotive response to a song, to poetic inspiration proper, to prophetic trance, to religious furor, etc.) under the label of *enthousiasmós* "being possessed, being out of oneself."

Before we dive into the *Ion*, though, it might be useful to provide some additional context for the concepts in question. The term *enthousiasmós* itself is first attested in a fragment of Democritus (fifth to fourth century BCE):

(14) ποιητὴς δὲ ἄσσα μὲν ἂν γράφῃ μετ' ἐνθουσιασμοῦ καὶ ἱεροῦ πνεύματος, καλὰ κάρτα ἐστίν

whatever a poet writes with *enthousiasmós* and divine inspiration, (that) is exceedingly beautiful. (Diels-Kranz 68B18)

Democritus' views are reflected in Latin literature, where they appear even more strongly worded. Cicero (*De Divinatione* 1.38) states *negat enim sine furore Democritus quemquam poetam magnum esse posse* "Democritus denies that a poet could be great without furor"; Horace (*Ars Poetica* 296) similarly remarks that Democritus *excludit sanos Helicone poetas* "bans sane poets from Helicon." Both interpretations are akin to saying that poetic greatness is impossible without *enthousiasmós*, but they do not amount to making divine inspiration and craft mutually exclusive (or to denying the role or existence of poetic craft).[17]

A concept close to *enthousiasmós* is that of divine *manía* "madness, possession," which is extensively explored in Plato's *Phaedrus*. Here, a typology of *manía* is given starting at 244a, which includes the *manía* coming from the Muses (245a).[18] This passage arguably gives a more traditional take on the balance between craft and inspiration in a poet's work:

(15) ὃς δ' ἂν ἄνευ μανίας Μουσῶν ἐπὶ ποιητικὰς θύρας ἀφίκηται, πεισθεὶς ὡς ἄρα ἐκ τέχνης ἱκανὸς ποιητὴς ἐσόμενος, ἀτελὴς αὐτός τε καὶ ἡ ποίησις ὑπὸ τῆς τῶν μαινομένων ἡ τοῦ σωφρονοῦντος ἠφανίσθη. (Plato, *Phaedrus* 245a5–8)

[the poet] who comes to the doors of poetry without the *manía* from the Muses, convinced that he will be a poet out of *tékhnē* alone, will appear unaccomplished, because the poetry of someone who is in their right mind (*sōphronoûntos*) pales in comparison to the poetry of those who are experiencing *manía*.

---

[17] See discussion in Evanson (1989: 15–17) on how Democritus' views likely differed from Plato's.
[18] A recent and accessible introduction to the *Phaedrus* is Yunis (2011).

This passage admits that it is possible to compose poetry entirely out of *tékhnē* (and thus that such a *tékhnē* exists), but that without divine *manía* the results will be far inferior. This could point to the idea of *tékhnē* and *manía* being complementary in some fashion.

Plato, as it is known, has a specific agenda when it comes to poetry. While the *Ion* stops short of finding fault with poetry in general, this criticism is carried out systematically in the *Republic* (starting at 377c5), in which Socrates objects to most existing poetry due to its morally harmful content, and goes on to advocate a strict censorship of literature, and a new system of *paideía* based on philosophy instead of poetry.[19] Poetry, just like other seductions, can end up distracting men from the pursuit of virtue and justice:

(16) Μέγας γάρ, ἔφην, ὁ ἀγών, ὦ φίλε Γλαύκων, μέγας, οὐχ ὅσος δοκεῖ, τὸ χρηστὸν ἢ κακὸν γενέσθαι, ὥστε οὔτε τιμῇ ἐπαρθέντα οὔτε χρήμασιν οὔτε ἀρχῇ οὐδεμιᾷ οὐδέ γε ποιητικῇ ἄξιον ἀμελῆσαι δικαιοσύνης τε καὶ τῆς ἄλλης ἀρετῆς. (Plato, *De Republica* 608b4–7)

Great is the struggle, my dear Glaúkōn, greater than it seems, to become a good man rather than a bad one, as it is not appropriate to neglect justice and the rest of virtue having become distracted by honor, money, or power of any kind, or even by poetry.

The scope of *Ion* is, in many ways, more modest (this is also one of Plato's shortest dialogues): the goal here is to relegate poetry to the camp of the divine and irrational, and deny its status as a legitimate field of knowledge. The dialogue begins with Socrates congratulating Ion, a traveling Homeric rhapsode,[20] on his recent win at the poetic competition during the celebrations for Asclepius in Epidaurus (Ion himself is not shy about claiming to be the best rhapsode among the Greeks, as he does at 541b). But this is really just a pretext for dissecting the practice of being a rhapsode (or a poet) altogether. First, Socrates corners Ion into admitting that he possesses no true *tékhnē* or *epistḗmē* regarding poetry, since, in his reasoning, a *poiētikḗ tékhnē* should be a single entity encompassing all of poetry, while Ion admits to only being an expert on Homer, and not on other poets:

(17) Οὐ χαλεπὸν τοῦτό γε εἰκάσαι, ὦ ἑταῖρε, ἀλλὰ παντὶ δῆλον ὅτι τέχνῃ καὶ ἐπιστήμῃ περὶ Ὁμήρου λέγειν ἀδύνατος εἶ· εἰ γὰρ τέχνῃ οἷός τε ἦσθα,

---

[19] For a compact introduction, see Murray (1996: 19–24), with references.
[20] For a short introduction on rhapsodes, see Aguirre and Lavilla de Lera (2018: 108–12). For more extensive treatments, see Gonzáles (2013), and Ready and Tsagalis (2018).

καὶ περὶ τῶν ἄλλων ποιητῶν ἁπάντων λέγειν οἷός τ' ἂν ἦσθα· ποιητικὴ γάρ πού ἐστιν τὸ ὅλον. ἢ οὔ; (Plato, *Ion* 532c5–9)

> It's not hard to show, my friend, but it's clear to all that you are not able to speak about Homer with either *tékhnē* or *epistḗmē*. For if you were able to do it out of *tékhnē*, you would be able to do it about all other poets too; for the [*tékhnē*] *poiētikḗ* is a whole, isn't it?

Socrates then advances his own theory: that excellence in poetry does not come from the poet's (or rhapsode's) skill, but from a divine force (θεία δύναμις), for which poets (and secondarily rhapsodes, and in third line the audience) function as mere vessels:

(18) ἔστι γὰρ τοῦτο τέχνη μὲν οὐκ ὂν παρὰ σοὶ περὶ Ὁμήρου εὖ λέγειν, ὃ νυνδὴ ἔλεγον, θεία δὲ δύναμις ἥ σε κινεῖ, ὥσπερ ἐν τῇ λίθῳ ἣν Εὐριπίδης μὲν Μαγνῆτιν ὠνόμασεν, οἱ δὲ πολλοὶ Ἡρακλείαν. (Plato, *Ion* 533d1–4)

> It is not a *tékhnē* the reason you can speak well about Homer, as I was just saying, but it is a divine power that moves you, like the stone that Euripides called Magnet, and most others call Hērakleía.

Rather than the collaborative process hinted at in archaic poetry, Socrates equates poetic inspiration to divine possession, in which a god "takes away the mind" of poets (οἷς νοῦς μὴ πάρεστιν "their mind is not there"), and uses them as his servants (ὑπηρέταις) and mouthpieces.

(19) διὰ ταῦτα δὲ ὁ θεὸς ἐξαιρούμενος τούτων τὸν νοῦν τούτοις χρῆται ὑπηρέταις καὶ τοῖς χρησμῳδοῖς καὶ τοῖς μάντεσι τοῖς θείοις, ἵνα ἡμεῖς οἱ ἀκούοντες εἰδῶμεν ὅτι οὐχ οὗτοί εἰσιν οἱ ταῦτα λέγοντες οὕτω πολλοῦ ἄξια, οἷς νοῦς μὴ πάρεστιν, ἀλλ' ὁ θεὸς αὐτός ἐστιν ὁ λέγων, διὰ τούτων δὲ φθέγγεται πρὸς ἡμᾶς. (Plato, *Ion* 534c7–d4)

> For this reason, the god, after taking away their mind, uses them as servants, like those who give oracles or the seers, so that we, when listening, are aware that they are not responsible for the many things of value that are said, since their mind is not there, but the god himself is the one speaking, and through them he speaks out to us.

The proof of this divine possession is, among other things,[21] the fact that, as part of the experience of poetry, the rhapsode (and the audience) are transported into the world of the song, and moved by what happens in it:[22]

---

[21] Like the fact that mediocre poets can sometimes produce excellent songs, such as the one-hit wonder (according to Plato) Túnnikhos from Chalcis (534d5).
[22] Ancient and modern critics have remarked on the particular *vividness* of Homer's poetry (however defined). See Grethlein and Huitink (2017) (with references) for an introduction to the contemporary debate.

(20) Ἔχε δή μοι τόδε εἰπέ, ὦ Ἴων, καὶ μὴ ἀποκρύψῃ ὅτι ἄν σε ἔρωμαι· ὅταν εὖ εἴπῃς ἔπη καὶ ἐκπλήξῃς μάλιστα τοὺς θεωμένους, ἢ τὸν Ὀδυσσέα ὅταν ἐπὶ τὸν οὐδὸν ἐφαλλόμενον ᾄδῃς, ἐκφανῆ γιγνόμενον τοῖς μνηστῆρσι καὶ ἐκχέοντα τοὺς ὀιστοὺς πρὸ τῶν ποδῶν, ἢ Ἀχιλλέα ἐπὶ τὸν Ἕκτορα ὁρμῶντα, ἢ καὶ τῶν περὶ Ἀνδρομάχην ἐλεινῶν τι ἢ περὶ Ἑκάβην ἢ περὶ Πρίαμον, τότε πότερον ἔμφρων εἶ ἢ ἔξω σαυτοῦ γίγνῃ καὶ παρὰ τοῖς πράγμασιν οἴεταί σου εἶναι ἡ ψυχὴ οἷς λέγεις ἐνθουσιάζουσα, ἢ ἐν Ἰθάκῃ οὖσιν ἢ ἐν Τροίᾳ ἢ ὅπως ἂν καὶ τὰ ἔπη ἔχῃ; (Plato, *Ion* 535b–c3)

And tell me, Ion, and don't hide anything as I ask: when you are speaking well, and you make the strongest effect on your viewers, be it Odysseus jumping on the threshold, showing himself to the suitors and pouring arrows at his feet, or Achilles charging at Hector, or the tragic bits about Andromache, Hecabe, and Priam, in that time are you in yourself, or are you outside of yourself, and it seems to you like you are present at those events, and your *psyche* is taken by *enthousiasmós*, whether it's in Troy or in Ithaka or anywhere else the verses hold?

To this question, Ion promptly admits that he has emotive reactions to the matters of the story – his eyes fill with tears when narrating something tragic, and his hairs stand up and his heart races when narrating something scary (535c). In other words, Socrates here equates experiencing an emotive response to art to being ἔξω σαυτοῦ "out of oneself."

Returning to the initial line of reasoning, Socrates then proceeds to prove that Ion is not even a true expert in the topics covered in Homer's poetry, since on matters such as chariot driving, potion making, or fishing, his expertise is surely inferior to that of experts of each specialty (for instance, nobody is willing to employ him as a *stratēgós*, despite his supposed excellence in this field coming from his knowledge of Homer). Ion is then content to be called divine, and specifically a divine praiser of Homer, rather than one who does so out of *tékhnē*:

(21) θεῖον εἶναι καὶ μὴ τεχνικὸν περὶ Ὁμήρου ἐπαινέτην (Plato, *Ion* 542b4)

You are a divine praiser (i.e., a rhapsode) of Homer, and not a technical one.

For the purposes of this dialogue, *tékhnē* and *enthousiasmós* appear indeed mutually exclusive.[23]

Plato's ideas on poetry have been deeply influential, and they seem to be shared in part by Aristotle as well, who casually observes ἔνθεον γὰρ ἡ

---

[23] For a discussion of recent scholarship on the topic, see Ustinova (2017: 268–70), with references.

ποίησις "poetry is a matter of divine inspiration" (*Rhetorics* 1408b19). They pervade later Greek discourse on poetry and the arts, and they have clear continuation in Latin and European literature overall.[24]

The question to which we shall turn next is whether, in terms of cognitive science, there is any way of reconciling the two opposites of inspiration and craft, and thus of vindicating Plato's views (that they are incompatible) as opposed to, say, Homer's or Hesiod's (that they coexist).

4.3 Creative Improvisation

4.3.1 The Cognitive Science of Creativity

From its beginnings in the 1950s, the field of cognitive science (which lies at the intersection of philosophy, psychology, artificial intelligence, linguistics, neuroscience, and anthropology)[25] has had a keen interest in human creativity in all of its forms:[26] this includes, but is not limited to, creativity in the arts, sciences, and industry.[27]

One important assumption of this field of research is that creativity, while highly prized and, in its most famous examples, exceptional, is, nonetheless, based on regular human intelligence and everyday cognitive abilities, such as "conceptual thinking, perception, memory, and reflective self-criticism" (Boden 2004: 1). Creativity, in other words, is not just for poets, artists, and (in a contemporary narrative) CEOs: we are all creative, to a degree, in our everyday lives – and this is in part why we are successful as a species.[28]

But what do we mean by creativity exactly? Several working definitions exist, and most are similar to the following: "Creativity is the ability to come up with ideas or artefacts that are *new, surprising, and valuable*" (Boden 2004: 1).[29] From this perspective, the creative process can be split

---

[24] For a short overview of this legacy, see again Murray (1997: 25–28), with references.
[25] For a history of cognitive science, see Boden (2006); more compact treatments are Bechtel, Abrahamsen, and Graham (2001), and Miller (2003).
[26] The goal was partially to replicate human intelligence in a computational fashion (i.e., through artificial intelligence); many applications of creativity research nowadays have to do with fostering creativity in business and organizations, as well as in the classroom (see Kaufman and Sternberg 2019: Part IV).
[27] For an overview of the field of creativity studies, see Kaufman and Sternberg (2019). In this section, I will focus especially on the models of creativity developed by Margaret Boden (starting with Boden 1990). For a critical review of Boden's work and its place in the scholarly debate, see Pearce (2010).
[28] As creativity scholars have pointed out, this view of creativity (and seeing creativity as a value) is clearly a modern invention, and one that is tied to contemporary concepts of individuality and agency. For a historical perspective on creativity, see Glăveanu and Kaufman (2019).
[29] For the history of this definition, see Runco and Jaeger 2012.

into two components: one part that comes up with new and surprising ideas (children are great at this), and another part that evaluates whether the "new" idea is actually valuable or useful (adults tend to be better at this).[30] We can call these components *ideation* and *selection* respectively (Sawyer 1992: 257), and we will revisit them below.

Boden (1998, 2009) talks about three types of creativity, namely *combinatory*, *exploratory*, and *transformative* creativity. The first type involves novel combinations of familiar ideas. An epic poet striking a particularly apt simile (such as the fallen warrior and the poppy discussed in Chapter 3), or Horace coining a fresh new turn of phrase, are operating within this realm. The latter types of creativity involve exploring or entirely restructuring *a conceptual space*, defined as a structured style of thought which usually already exists in the culture (Boden 2004: 2–5). The rules and conventions for composing an epic poem can be understood as one such conceptual space, and exploratory creativity in this area would mean charting new, untrodden ground for what such a poetic medium can do (an unusual topic, for instance, such as in the *Batrachomyomachia*); transformative creativity would mean subverting and rewriting those rules and conventions entirely – as some critics would argue "Homer" did in composing his monumental poems: Čolaković (2019), for instance, argued that both Homer and Avdo Međedović are "post-traditional singers," in that they employ the rules and conventions of the genre in new and subversive ways (see also Danek 2012).[31]

4.3.2 The Study of Jazz Improvisation

Much work on creativity has focused on the study of *compositional creativity*, in which a creator works for a long time on a given project, revising and tweaking it, until the final product (which can be a poem, a painting, or an academic article) matches the desired requirements. In this process, ideation and selection can occur at separate times, and it can be more difficult to trace the creative process in the finished product. This, of course,

---

[30] The concept of "new" needs elaboration here too. Things can be new to a given subject (Boden (2004: 2) calls this *P-creativity* or *Psychological creativity*) or they can be new to history (*H-creativity*). It is the latter type of new that is usually prized (for scholars of antiquity, it is an all too common experience to come up with a "new" idea, only to discover that a scholar in the nineteenth century already scooped it).

[31] Adam Parry's (1956) famous take on the language of Achilles was an attempt to argue that Achilles was trying to apply transformative creativity to the heroic values as encapsulated by epic language (see Reeve 1973 for a short criticism, and Martin 1989: Chapter 4 for a full treatment).

provides only an imperfect parallel for the study of oral-formulaic poetry, where we believe that much of the composition took place in performance.

Luckily, cognitive scientists have also shown some interest in jazz performance, precisely because it provides an example of *improvisational creativity*, in which the ideation and selection process overlap, and in which "the creative process and the resulting product are co-occurring" (Sawyer 1992: 253). This, of course, is the same kind of creativity that students of oral traditions have come to expect from Homer, as opposed to, say, a Virgil or an Apollonius slowly toiling away at their manuscripts.[32]

Cognitive work on jazz improvisation starts at least with David Sudnow's classic account of how he taught himself (a classically trained pianist) to improvise jazz on the piano (1978, 2001).[33] Almost immediately, cognitive psychologists working on musical improvisation (Sloboda 1986: 141–43; Pressing 1987), as well as professional jazz players (Gillespie 1991), started to point out the parallels between the technique of jazz improvisation and oral-formulaic technique as described by Parry and Lord.[34]

> What gives a performance its jazzy character are the particular types of melodic, rhythmic, and harmonic devices which form the basic building blocks for larger sequences. Such devices are almost exactly analogous to the formulas of epic poetry. They constitute the vocabulary of jazz. (Sloboda 1986: 143)

---

[32] Note that many and perhaps most critics invoke a good deal of compositional creativity for Homer as well. See, for instance, West (1998: iii): "Nec tamen ille omnia a μῆνιν ἄειδε usque ad Hectoris exsequias uno et perpetuo tenore protulit, quasi 'stans pede in uno', sed per multos annos, credo, elaboravit et, quae primum strictius composuit, deinceps novis episodiis insertis mirifice auxit ac dilatavit" (And he didn't produce everything from μῆνιν ἄειδε to Hector's funeral in a single, uninterrupted go, almost "standing on one foot," but, I believe, he worked it out over many years, and what he first composed rather briefly, he later marvelously enlarged and expanded by inserting new episodes.) In fact, West would go as far as denying any amount of improvisational creativity for Homer, and arguing for compositional creativity alone: "oral poets [...] composed rapidly – not actually improvising, as some writers have supposed, but putting verses together quickly in their minds as they prepared for giving recitations" (West 2018: 362). This of course could not be farther from an oralist perspective.
[33] Tellingly, the 2001 edition of this work includes a foreword by the philosopher Hubert L. Dreyfus, who sees jazz improvisation as a prime example of *skilled coping*, a way of being and acting in which one is completely immersed in one's actions to the point that one does not think or reflect (for a review of this concept as applied to music performance, see Høffding 2014). We shall return to *skilled coping* in our discussion of *flow* below.
[34] Note that, for other improvisational genres explored by folklorists, these same kinds of similarities had already been observed. See, for instance, Jones (1961), Friedman (1961) on the ballad tradition, and Barnie (1978) for country blues (for which now see Evans 2007).

In the process, they also emphasized how much of improvisational creativity is not, in fact, fully improvised, but relies on extensive preparation (in the form of training and explicit performance planning):

> Commentators on jazz have emphasized that there is often less improvisation on the concert platform than one might imagine. The musician is often "playing safe" by using improvisatory devices which have worked well in other circumstances, so as to create the best effects he knows how. A so-called improvisation may, in fact, be a carefully planned and rehearsed performance; although there is nothing about the performance as such that would allow us to know this. (Sloboda 1986: 149)

The amount of spur-of-the-moment improvisation in jazz also depends on the performance context. Sawyer (1992: 256), for instance, talks about the difference between an *open (jam) session*, in which visiting musicians are invited to share the stage (and experimenting is encouraged), and a *society gig*, in which musicians are paid to perform at a social function (like a wedding), and the expectation for experimenting is minimal ("you have to play things real [straight]"). In Homeric terms, one wonders whether a public competition would be an occasion in which rhapsodes were expected to "play straight," especially if they had to fit within a relay of singers. This type of performance is also likely to have been carefully planned and rehearsed.

Much as we discussed in Chapters 1 and 2 above for Homer, cognitive psychologists suggested that the highly codified genres within which jazz musicians operate essentially serve to curtail the performer's choices during improvisation, thus saving precious cognitive resources:

> What absolves the improviser from the task of evaluation and long term planning is the relatively rigid formal "frame" within which his improvisation takes place, and which dictates the large scale structure of his performances. (Sloboda 1986: 149)

In attempting to develop an algorithm for jazz improvisation, Philip Johnson-Laird (2002: 422) speaks explicitly of the limitations of working memory as well as the importance of constraints:

> If it is necessary to work rapidly within a framework – typically an artistic genre – with no opportunity for revision, then a sensible procedure is for the principles governing the genre and the individual's style to be used at each point in the process of generating ideas. They will constrain the set of options as tightly as possible. (Johnson-Laird 1988: 209)

According to Johnson-Laird, any improvisational genre will rely on two mental components: a long-term memory set of basic structures (e.g., the chord sequences in jazz, or the formulas and type scenes in oral epic poetry) and "a set of tacit principles that underlies the improvisatory skill" (1988: 210), running quietly and efficiently in the background, and generating, for instance, a suitable bass line starting from a memorized chord sequence ("the principles should place a minimal load on memory": Johnson-Laird 1988: 210). The tacit principles, in other words, are what allow the improviser to go from having a mental library of memorized forms to employing them flexibly in performance.

Another interesting perspective emerging from the cognitive study of jazz is the balance between conscious and non-conscious processing on the part of musicians during performance. This is captured in interviews with the musicians themselves:

> I find what I'm playing is sometimes conscious, sometimes subconscious, sometimes it just comes out and I play it; sometimes I hear it in my head before I play it, and it's like chasing after it [...]. When you start a solo, you are still in thinking mode; it takes a while to get yourself out of thinking mode. (Sawyer 1992: 256–57)

Getting out of "thinking mode" is desirable, since musicians believe that their solos are better when they are minimally conscious (Sawyer 1992: 256–57). Often, this state of unconsciousness is described in quite Platonic terms: for instance, English jazz tenor saxophonist Ronnie Scott reported that:

> One becomes unconscious of playing, you know, it becomes as if something else has taken over and you're just an intermediary between whatever else and the instrument. (Bailey 1992: 52)

Still, both thinking and nonthinking are regarded as important in a performance:

> Musicians realize that some conscious awareness is always essential. The "inner" performance state must be balanced with a simultaneous awareness of the other musicians, or of the song form. (Sawyer 1992: 257)

There are many ways of referring to these two modes of processing: the conscious and the unconscious, the attended and the automatic (Givón 2005: 49); a popular recent characterization of this dichotomy is that of Kahneman (2011), who talks about *fast* vs. *slow thinking* (also referred to as System 1 vs. System 2). In Kahneman's account, System 1 (fast thinking, automatic processing) is responsible for a number of cognitive biases and heuristics that can be observed in human behavior and identified through various experiments.

In many ways, we can see these two ways of processing as the modern-day equivalents of the relationship between *tékhnē* and *enthousiasmós*, and the tension between claiming authorship for one's performance (and taking pride in one's hard-earned skills) and the subjective (and often exhilarating) experience of being outside of oneself.

One important take-home from this work on jazz improvisation is the idea (which we'll return to below) that these two modes of processing should not be seen as entirely mutually exclusive. Even within genres that rely primarily on improvisational creativity, the amount of moment-to-moment improvisation can vary from performance to performance, and even within a performance that is mostly improvised, some amount of conscious control will always be present next to the "unconsciousness" of playing. But when it comes to the heightened cognitive state that many jazz musicians (and arguably some oral poets) experience during performance, there is one more concept from cognitive psychology that we might want to examine: flow.

4.3.3 Improvisation, Creativity, and Flow

Flow and the Psychology of Optimal Experience

While he was studying individuals immersed in the creative process (Getzels and Csikszentmihalyi 1976), cognitive psychologist Mihaly Csikszentmihalyi began to notice an interesting phenomenon:

> When work on a painting was going well, the artist persisted single-mindedly, disregarding hunger, fatigue, and discomfort – yet lost interest in the product once it was completed. (Nakamura and Csikszentmihalyi 2018: 279)

The creative process, in other words, was *autotelic* (self-rewarding): artists were seeking it because they drew deep enjoyment from it in and of itself, and not because of its results. Csikszentmihalyi (1975/2000) dubbed this state of immersed activity and enjoyment *flow*, and hypothesized that regularly experiencing states of flow was a key part of experiencing happiness in daily life (he also referred to flow as *optimal experience*).

By studying a wider category of individuals who reported engaging in complex activities out of personal enjoyment (chess players, rock climbers, dancers, and surgeons), Csikszentmihalyi clarified what conditions had to be present for a flow experience to take place. These conditions include (Nakamura and Csikszentmihalyi 2018: 280):

1. perceived challenges that optimally match (or stretch) existing skills;
2. clear proximal goals;
3. immediate feedback about the progress being made.

When experiencing flow, beyond a deep sense of enjoyment, individuals report intense and focused concentration on the present moment, a loss of reflective self-consciousness, a sense of being in control (in the sense that they trust that they are able to respond to whatever comes next), as well as a loss of sense of time ("time flies"). Athletes refer to this state as "being in the zone."

The correct match between individual skills and challenges afforded by an activity is crucial in order to access the state of flow. In particular, an activity needs to present a level of challenge just above an individual's level of skill for flow to take place. If the challenges are too high with respect to the skills, the individual will experience arousal, anxiety, or worry instead. If they are too low, they will experience control, relaxation, boredom, or apathy (Nakamura and Csikszentmihalyi 2018: 286).

Flow in Music and Oral Traditions

Flow states are widely reported among musicians, be it during rehearsal, performance, or composition, or even while listening to music.[35] Musical improvisation is particularly conducive to flow (Kenny and Gellrich 2002). And flow is especially salient in jazz performance (Hytönen-Ng 2013), where these experiences might be labeled as "being in the groove," "swinging," or "happening."[36] In music composition, flow states have been shown to increase creativity (MacDonald, Byrne, and Carlton 2006).

All of this is at least suggestive that oral epic composition in performance (another kind of activity requiring improvisational creativity) might also be conducive to flow. But we can make the argument more precise. In Bozzone (2016b: 88), I have argued that composition in performance in the framework of oral traditional poetry in general (and for Archaic Greek

---

[35] For a review of the literature on flow and music, see Chirico et al. (2015).
[36] This same type of experience is captured by the title of the book *Effortless Mastery*, by jazz pianist Kenny Werner (1996).

epic poetry specifically) displays all of the structural features of an activity conducive to flow. In particular:

1. Poets spend years developing their technique through training, so that the challenge is a good match for their skills.
2. Oral-traditional poets have the clear goal of telling a given story, in a known sequence and a given length (this can be broken down into a series of proximate subgoals, such as narrating a scene, an episode, or a given theme).
3. During performance, poets constantly receive feedback from the audiences (as well as via self-monitoring) as to how well they are doing.

This is not to say that other kinds of poetic activity would not be conducive to flow (after all, flow is reported today by poets who compose in writing), or that performers of oral epic poetry would experience flow every time they performed (this would likely depend on the specific conditions of the performance and how they fit the skills of the poet). But it does suggest that some of the features of poetic activity in Ancient Greece could be understood in terms of the theory of flow.

Additionally, several of the dimensions of flow can be matched to what we know about oral poetic practice: poets immersed in oral performance show great levels of sustained concentration,[37] and they report enjoyment in their activity. Quote (4) above, in which the singer's *thūmós* prompts him to sing, is essentially a description of an *autotelic* activity.

Flow and Loss of Self-Consciousness

But one specific dimension of flow seems particularly relevant for our discussion so far: this is the loss of reflexive self-consciousness (which we have seen jazz musicians report in their performances as well). The physicist and mathematician Freeman Dyson, one of Csikszentmihalyi's subjects, puts it this way:

> I always find that when I am writing, it is really the fingers that are doing it and not the brain. Somehow the writing takes charge. And the same thing happens of course with equations. You don't really think of what you are going to write. You just scribble, the equations lead the way. (Csikszentmihalyi 1996: 118–19)

---

[37] In Bozzone (2016b: 88), I bring the example of how Tibetan paper singers (discussed in Foley 2002: 1–3) use a white piece of paper to focus their attention. For some performers, closing the eyes might achieve a similar effect (Ritter et al. 2018 report that eye closure increases creativity over a different set of tasks). And one could even imagine a link between eye closure during performance and cultural ideas about blind poets (this is not to say that actual blind poets could not have existed).

Just like jazz musicians, Csikszentmihalyi's subjects believe that this "unthinking state" yields better results:

> You have to have a design in view, in which you design a chapter, or a proof of a theorem, as the case may be. Then you put it together ... but if you don't have a clear architecture in mind then the thing won't end up being any good [...] The original design is somehow accidental and you don't know how it comes into your head. (Csikszentmihalyi 1996: 119)

The idea that the "original design" (which is necessary for the final result to be good) may be accidental and of unknown origin, is similar to the passage of the *Phaedrus* discussed in example (15) above, which states that *manía* makes for better poetry. And, of course, the perception that something external ("a design") has somehow come into one's head is compatible with the concept that an external agent (such as a god or a Muse) might have provided that thought.

If oral epic poets experienced flow during their performances, and if their experience of flow included the dimension of loss of self-consciousness (which is likely based on the comparative evidence), we may have found a cognitive basis for the belief in poetic *manía* and divine inspiration in Ancient Greece. In other words, when Archaic Greek poets talk about poetic *manía* or *enthousiasmós* (Ustinova 2017: 265–93) they are likely describing flow states enabled by the structure of poetic composition in performance. But how does this perception of loss of self-consciousness happen in the brain? In order to uncover this last piece of the puzzle, we need to turn to neuroscience.

4.4 The Neuroscience of Improvisation

4.4.1 The Neural Substrate for Creativity and Flow

While cognitive science has investigated the modes of creative thinking for many decades, it is only more recently that neuroscience has allowed us to take a peek into the activity of the brain as it creates. This is particularly true for naturalistic creative activities (such as jazz improvisation), the study of which demands a rather sophisticated experiment design.

Cognitive neuroscience relies on a number of neuroimaging techniques, which allow us to observe different brain areas "in action" as subjects complete a given task.[38] In particular, cognitive neuroscience has focused

---

[38] For a short introduction, see Sawyer (2011).

on activity patterns in the *neocortex*, the thin layer (ca. 5 mm) of grey matter on the outside of the brain that is responsible for many of our higher-order brain functions, such as sensory perception, cognition, and language.

Three main methodologies exist today for observing changes in brain activity as people think: EEG (Electroencephalography), PET (Positron Emission Tomography), and fMRI (Functional Magnetic Resonance Imaging).[39] Additionally, neuroscientists can observe the effects of localized brain lesions on cognitive abilities and behaviors.[40] The combined results of these methodologies have allowed researchers to map some of the insights of cognitive psychology onto brain activity, and thus come closer to locating where thinking happens in the brain.

In a series of studies, Dietrich (2003, 2004a, 2004b) presents a critical review of the evidence for the neural substrates of creativity, flow, and altered states of consciousness, which I partially summarize here, as a way of introducing the cast of characters that will be relevant for the experiments described below. All of these, as we shall see, are pertinent to our discussion of poetic *manía* and inspiration.[41]

The neocortex, as pictured in Figure 4.1, is divided in four lobes: the frontal lobe (in blue), the temporal lobe (in green), the occipital lobe (in red), and the parietal lobe (in yellow). Among these, the latter three (referred to together as TOP, from their combined initials) appear primarily devoted to perception and long-term memory.[42]

The neocortex in the frontal lobe has an altogether different function: about half of it is made up of the *prefrontal cortex* (PFC), which has been tied to many high-level cognitive functions such as the construction of self, self-reflective consciousness, complex social function, abstract thinking, cognitive flexibility, planning, willed action, source memory, and theory of mind (see Dietrich 2004b: 1013 with references).

The prefrontal cortex hosts three more cognitive functions that allow all of the high-level functions above to be computed: these are working

---

[39] All of these technologies serve to measure neural activity (i.e., which areas in the brain "light up" during which tasks), and each has its own strengths and limits. EEG, for instance, has very good temporal resolution, while fMRI has a superior spatial resolution. For these reasons, different methods can sometimes be combined. In general, in order to obtain precise measurements, tasks are repeated over and over, and results are the averages of several iterations. See Sawyer (2011) for a short overview.

[40] This methodology was, of course, already available many decades before the invention of modern neuroimaging techniques. For its position in neuroscience research today, see Vaidya et al. (2019).

[41] The reader should be advised that this (rudimental) presentation of brain anatomy may age relatively quickly. Still, I believe even a superficial grasp of some of these concepts is important for our discussion.

[42] "TOP is the site of long-term memory storage (Gilbert 2001)" (Dietrich 2004b: 1013).

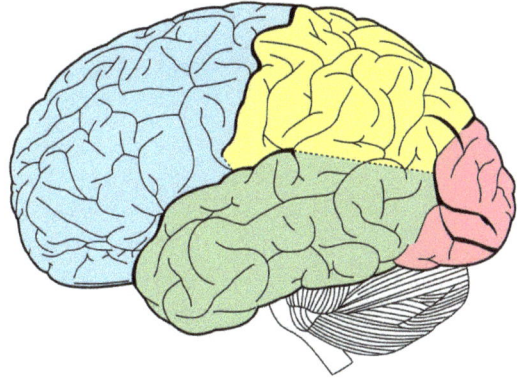

Figure 4.1 The lobes of the brain[43]
From the left: Frontal lobe (blue), Parietal lobe (yellow), Occipital lobe (red), and Temporal lobe (green)

memory, temporal integration, and sustained and directed attention. These functions in particular appear to be tied with the dorsolateral aspect of the prefrontal cortex (*dorsolateral prefrontal cortex* or DLPFC).

The dorsolateral prefrontal cortex (highlighted in blue in Figure 4.2) is strongly connected with the TOP regions (perception and long-term memory), and it can effectively work like a search engine, by pulling relevant pieces of information from the TOP (long-term memory) and temporarily representing them in working memory, where they can be recombined in new and creative ways; the dorsolateral prefrontal cortex is also where new ideas can be operationalized and turned into instructions for the motor system. For this reason, Dietrich (2004b: 1022, 2004a: 759) suggests that the dorsolateral prefrontal cortex must play a prominent role in creative behavior (especially if deliberate and innovative problem solving is required), since any creative insight will need to be attended to and operationalized by this function.

Dietrich (2004a) argues that the neural substrates of flow must be quite separate from those of creativity. He explains that the brain can operate two distinct information-processing systems to acquire, memorize, and represent knowledge (Dietrich 2004a: 749–54): the *explicit system* (which is conscious and rule-based), and the *implicit system* (which is unconscious and skill-based). While the explicit system is operationalized in the

---

[43] Image created by Wikipedia user Mysid based on Gray's *Anatomy of the Human Body* (1918), plate 728.

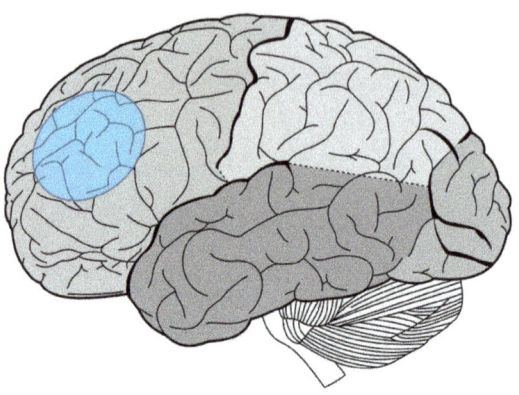

Figure 4.2 The dorsolateral prefrontal cortex

prefrontal cortex (and some of it in the dorsolateral prefrontal cortex specifically), the implicit system runs on (evolutionarily) older structures, such as the *basal ganglia*, which are located well below the neocortex (Dietrich 2004a: 752). When learning a skill (like driving a car), the explicit system (which is conscious and flexible, but attentionally costly) is often employed first, until, through repetition and habituation, the implicit system (which is unconscious and inflexible, but attentionally cheap) can take over (Jenkins et al. 1994). This is exactly the economy of automatization vs. conscious processing that we discussed in Chapter 1 with regard to formularity.

According to Dietrich, flow happens when the implicit system takes over, and the explicit system powers down.[44] In this view, flow is distinct from creativity, because creativity needs the dorsolateral prefrontal cortex, and flow largely does without it.[45] Instead, Dietrich (2004a: 757) suggests that flow is similar to altered states of consciousness (such as those experienced in dreaming, endurance running, meditation, daydreaming, hypnosis, and various drug-induced states), since they involve a condition of *transient hypofrontality* (Dietrich 2003).

It is tempting to see Dietrich's position as a modern form of Plato's conception, in the sense that the two systems (the implicit and the explicit,

---

[44] "A flow experience must occur during a state of transient hypofrontality that can bring about the inhibition of the explicit system" (Dietrich 2004a: 757).
[45] "It is imperative to recognize that flow and creativity recruit different brain circuits" (Dietrich 2004a: 758).

the conscious and the unconscious) are seen as mutually exclusive, and, by definition, "real" creativity is made to reside in only one of them. The only difference is that, for Plato, poetry was the realm of the unconscious system, while, for Dietrich, creativity is the realm of the conscious one.

4.4.2   Experimental Studies of Improvisation

While Dietrich's findings are intriguing, they are still mostly theoretical (i.e., not based on actually studying flow and creativity in real time). Limb and Braun (2008) addressed this gap by carrying out an fMRI study of jazz musicians performing in a relatively naturalistic setting.[46] In this experiment, six professional jazz musicians were brought into the lab and equipped with a special-sized keyboard that could fit into an fMRI scan. They were given two performance conditions: one in which they reproduced a tune that they had memorized (i.e., the control condition), and one in which they had to improvise either alone or accompanying a recorded jazz quartet.[47] The goal was to establish whether performance from memory vs. improvisation triggered the use of different brain regions.

The findings were striking, especially in showing vast patterns of *deactivation* in the dorsolateral prefrontal cortex (precisely the areas that Dietrich had predicted would be crucial for creative endeavors, but not during flow) in the improvisation condition. In particular, for the neocortex, the study observed:

> widespread *deactivation* that included almost all of the lateral prefrontal cortices, extending from lateral orbitofrontal cortex (LOFC), to the superior portions of the dorsolateral prefrontal cortex (DLPFC), as well as dorsal portions of the medial prefrontal cortex (MPFC). (Limb and Braun 2008: 3)

We have already encountered the dorsolateral prefrontal cortex. As for the lateral orbitofrontal cortex (LOFC), Limb and Braun suggest that it "may be involved in assessing whether such behaviors conform to social demands, exerting inhibitory control over inappropriate or maladaptive performance." The deactivation of this area might then leave the artist freer to experiment, feeling less bound by social demands.

---

[46] fMRI can measure blood flow to different areas of the brain, so as to establish which areas become more active in the execution of a given task. In particular: "The fMRI machine uses a magnetic field in order to detect the ratio of oxygenated to deoxygenated blood; each affects the magnetic field differently [...] [This] is referred to as the *BOLD* signal (blood oxygen level dependent). When neuronal activation increases in the neocortex, blood flow increases faster than the neurons can use it, causing the *BOLD* signal to increase" (Sawyer 2011: 3).

[47] The experiment also included two levels of musical complexity: a simple one named *scale* and a more demanding one named *jazz*: they both yielded similar results.

Finally, the medial prefrontal cortex (MPFC) has been linked with instantiations of several aspects of the "self" (Gusnard et al. 2001) – as we shall see below, the deactivation of this area might have something to do with the "self-less" experience of creativity.

But, crucially, not all of the medial prefrontal cortex was "powered down." The pattern of deactivation just described was combined with focal activation of the frontal polar portion of the medial prefrontal cortex:

> The portion of the MPFC that was selectively activated during improvisation, the frontal polar cortex (Brodmann Area 10), remains poorly understood but appears to serve a broad-based integrative function, combining multiple cognitive operations in the pursuit of higher behavioral goals, in particular adopting and utilizing rule sets that guide ongoing behavior and maintaining an overriding set of intentions while executing a series of diverse behavioral subroutines. (Limb and Braun 2008: 4)

All of these functions seem necessary to the task of improvisation, in that they might help a musician keep track of where they are headed (a topic often discussed in interviews with jazz practitioners), as well as following the general rules of the genre. This area has also been linked with internally generated self-expression (López-Gonzáles and Limb 2012: 7).

In other words, Dietrich's predictions were not borne out in the experimental data. Musicians busy in a creative task showed a pattern of *deactivation* of the prefrontal cortex, suggesting some subjective loss of conscious control (which Dietrich would associate with flow, but not with creativity). But the "loss of control" is not total: along with widespread deactivations in the prefrontal cortex, there were focal activations of specific areas in the medial prefrontal cortex, namely Brodmann Area 10, which seem to be involved in regulating behavior in the pursuit of higher goals. One way of understanding this activation might be that improvisers are "keeping an eye" on where they are going, or on the rules of the musical form in which they are operating, or, again – in the case of collaborative performances – on what the other performers are doing.

It is not just musical improvisation that triggers a dissociated pattern of activation in the prefrontal cortex. A separate experiment looking at the neural correlates of lyrical improvisation in freestyle rap found comparable results (Liu et al. 2012). Here, too, fMRI imaging for the improvisation condition revealed:

> a dissociated pattern of activity within the prefrontal cortex: increases in activity throughout the MPFC [...] and simultaneous decreases in the DLPFC (Liu et al. 2012: 4)

In interpreting their findings, the authors take the extra step of tying the deactivation of lateral prefrontal regions with a perceived lack of agency on the part of the performers:

> In the absence of processing by lateral prefrontal regions – where a sense of agency could be constructed post-hoc – ongoing actions, moment to moment decisions and adjustments in performance may be experienced as having occurred outside of conscious awareness. This is not inconsistent with the experience of many artists who describe the creative process as seemingly guided by an outside agency. (Liu et al. 2012: 5)

Intriguingly, deactivation of the lateral prefrontal regions (Dietrich's *hypofrontality*) is regarded as "the primary physiologic change responsible for altered states of consciousness such as hypnosis, meditation or even daydreaming" (Limb and Braun 2008: 5). A similarly dissociated pattern of activation in the prefrontal regions has been observed during rapid eye movement (REM) sleep (Limb and Braun 2008: 5).

In an Ancient Greek context, these are all conditions and activities which were associated with *manía* or communication with the divine. We can see this in the notion that gods might visit people in dreams: this is not only a frequent type scene in Homer (such as Zeus visiting Agamemnon in a dream at the beginning of *Iliad* 2),[48] but is witnessed by the widespread practice of *incubation*.[49] Intoxication as a means of communing with the divine is present in the ancient narrative of the chasm at Delphi emitting an intoxicating vapor (*pneûma*), under whose effects the Pythia would then prophesy.[50]

And, finally, we might recognize a similarly altered state of consciousness in the experience of combat fury (Ustinova 2017: Chapter 4), which is arguably reflected in *Iliad* 5 (when Athena grants Diomedes supernatural strength, fueling his *aristeía*), and which corresponds to the contemporary concept of *combat flow* – that is, the state of extreme focus and heightened mood that soldiers experience in the face of mortal danger (see discussion in Bozzone 2016b: 91–93).

---

[48] For a discussion of all such scenes in Homer, see Morris (1983).
[49] This is the practice, attested in Ancient Greece as well as in the Ancient Near East, of spending the night at a sanctuary in the hope of experiencing a god-sent dream. For a recent book-length treatment, see Renberg (2017).
[50] See Heineman (2010) (with references) for a discussion of the ancient sources. The chasm theory has attracted the attention of modern toxicology, with a widely reported thesis that the ancient sources are compatible with ethylene intoxication specifically (Spiller et al. 2008; for a criticism, see Foster and Lehoux 2007).

In all of these contexts (as well as, of course, in the practice of poetry), we see activities that today are known to cause hypofrontality being culturally tied, in Ancient Greece, to some type of divine intervention.

4.5 Conclusion: Hypofrontality, *Tékhnē*, and *Enthousiasmós*

The goal of this chapter was to reconcile ancient and modern views of creativity as they pertain to the practice of poetry (and improvisational poetry) specifically. In doing so, we have revisited the paradox sketched out in our introduction: how can Homer's poetry be great even though so much in it appears "automatic"?

To answer this question, we have looked at the concepts of *tékhnē* and *enthousiasmós* through the lenses of Archaic Greek poetry and the writings of Plato, and compared them with contemporary findings in the fields of cognitive psychology and neuroscience. While readings of archaic poetry seem to allow for *tékhnē* and *enthousiasmós* to coexist within poetic performance, Plato's *Ion* makes a forceful case that no *tékhnē* is involved in the practice of poetry, and that poets are instead mere vessels for divine inspiration. In contemporary neuroscience, Dietrich has proposed a somewhat Platonic position, whereby creativity proper (which requires conscious control) and a state of flow (a concept close to *enthousiasmós*) are mutually exclusive.

Data from neuroimaging experiments and psychological studies on improvisers, however, suggest a more complex scenario, where both features (control and a lack thereof) can and must coexist as part of the creative endeavor.

So what is the relationship between *tékhnē* and *enthousiasmós*? I would argue that the subjective experience of poetic *enthousiasmós* is likely caused by a state of hypofrontality (i.e., decreased activity in the dorsolateral prefrontal cortex) in the course of improvisation. There are many ways in which hypofrontality can be induced (drugs, hypnosis, endurance sport, REM sleep): one is to take part in activities that are conducive to flow. These are activities that are complex enough to overwhelm the capacity of our working memory (and of our explicit processing system in general), unless we can rely extensively on automatic behaviors (our implicit processing system) to carry them out. They are also highly structured activities with clear goals and feedback built in.

The automatic behaviors necessary to carry out these activities are acquired through extensive training and practice. Ancient Greek *tékhnē* (not in the sense of an explicit system of knowledge, but of a practical, embodied *skill*)⁵¹ can be seen as the sum of these internalized, automatic behaviors. *Tékhnē*, then, opens the door to flow, because, by relying primarily on automatized behaviors, the individual can reduce activation in the dorsolateral prefrontal cortex, which is likely to result in the subjective feeling that "someone else has taken over" – Greek *enthousiasmós*.

This condition is not, however, completely mindless, and it does allow for novel creative insight (and this is where I disagree with Dietrich, and with Socrates' take in the *Ion*). First of all, not all of the prefrontal cortex powers down during improvisational flow.⁵² Brodmann Area 10 (part of the medial prefrontal cortex), in particular, shows focal activation during improvisational tasks, which has been tied to autobiographic self-expression as well as with the pursuit of higher behavioral goals. Second, as Landau and Limb remind us:

> Deactivations of cognitive control regions during improvisation do not indicate an absence of all cognitive control. A relative reduction of DLPFC [dorsolateral prefrontal cortex] during improvisation compared to control conditions only implies that this area is less active during improvisation. For example, one study found that despite overall reductions in DLPFC activity, it showed stronger functional connectivity with other motor areas during improvisation than for memorized performance. This implies that cognitive control is not entirely disengaged during improvisation but used in a frugal and efficient manner and relatively suspended in comparison to memorized control conditions. (Landau and Limb 2017: 28)

Anecdotally, this is what jazz musicians tell us: conscious and unconscious processing are both taking place, perhaps leading the way at different times during a performance, and in different measures depending on the type of performance.

These observations are important as we talk about improvisation in the context of oral-formulaic theory, especially as they might help overcome the reservations of some critics, particularly those who understand improvisation as synonymous with lower-quality outcomes; even within an improvisational genre, not everything is always improvised, and improvisation does not mean mindless cobbling together of preexisting pieces.⁵³ Rather, *improvisational creativity* results from a dynamic balance of unconscious and conscious processes, which, combined, can keep a performer

---

[51] For the distinction between *tékhnē* and *epistḗmē* in Ancient Greek philosophy, see Parry (2020).
[52] This point is also made by philosophers trying to update the concept of *skilled coping* (Brownstein 2014, Høffding 2014).
[53] In the context of oral theory, of course, these points were already emphasized by the work of Finnegan (1977: Chapter 3) among others.

operating right at the edge of the capacities of human cognition, and thus support extreme feats of creativity.

This balance between conscious and unconscious processes might also be what Phemius is hinting at in *Odyssey* 22, again conveying the tension between the gifts of the god and the poet's learning:

(6)   αὐτοδίδακτος δ' εἰμί, θεὸς δέ μοι ἐν φρεσὶν οἴμας
      παντοίας ἐνέφυσεν· (*Od.* 22.347–48)

   I am self-taught, and a god put in my mind
   all of the ways of song.

Admittedly, the causal arrow is reversed here (as opposed to, say, Hesiod's account in the *Theogony* discussed in example (8)): it is not because of an initial gift of the Muses that poets can sing. It is because poets have taught themselves how to sing (likely through that sort of largely unconscious training that Lord (1960) described in the *Singer of Tales*) that the gods can bestow their gifts of song. It is because poets know the paths of song that they can sing ὅππῃ θυμὸς ἐποτρύνῃσιν ἀείδειν "in whatever direction their *thūmós* prompts them to sing."

CONCLUSION

Creativity, Memory, and the Muses

This book has investigated the hypothesis that formularity, meter, and *Kunstsprache* in Homer are adaptive technologies that emerge in response to the challenges of oral-poetic performance. Rather than representing limitations on the poet's creative freedom, I have argued that these features serve to enable Homer's particular kind of *improvisational creativity*, and contribute to the greatness of his art.

In particular, I have tried to bring out how Homer's poetry leverages some of the same mechanisms that we can observe in everyday phenomena all around us (e.g., in language acquisition, popular music, and sports commentary), and how these mechanisms are used for both managing working memory load and creating meaning in performance. Throughout the book, I have compared the process of oral composition in Homer[1] with the process involved in carrying out other cognitively complex tasks (from speaking, to playing chess, to performing jazz music), and I have tried to develop a conversation between existing literature on Homer's poetic technique and insights from modern linguistics and the cognitive sciences.

In Chapter 1, I argued that Homer is like a speaker of any natural language, in that he relies on a vast network of prefabricated expressions in order to speak fluently and idiomatically; these prefabricated expressions (which can be described at different levels of scale, granularity, and abstraction, and go well beyond traditional characterizations of formularity) are learned unconsciously as generalizations over vast amounts of data, and can be adapted creatively. Relying on prefabricated expressions allows poets to bypass the limits of their working memory when composing, as well as (just as importantly) to imbue their poetry with rich traditional associations. What, however, sets Homer apart from other corpora (ancient and modern) is that Homer's prefabricated expressions, as captured through collocational studies, are exceptionally long (and especially

---

[1] In the sense of "any poet operating within the Homeric tradition of oral-formulaic poetry."

numerous, given their length). This, I argue, should be taken as a sign that the poets faced an exceptionally complex challenge when composing (most likely because they were doing so during oral performance), and therefore developed a particularly high level of mastery (i.e., a vast suite of automated behaviors) to be able to meet this challenge. Ancient Greek authors who composed in writing (even hexametric authors like Quintus Smyrnaeus, who otherwise closely imitated Homer's style) never came to rely on such long collocations, arguably because the compositional challenge that they faced did not demand this type of mastery.

In Chapter 2, I compared Homer to the professional auctioneers and horse-race callers described by Kuiper (1996), who rely on thorough prosodic regularization in their speech (paired with extensive formulaic behaviors) in order to maintain a high level of fluency during their performances. This prosodic regularization, I have argued, can be understood as a rudimentary form of meter, and helps performers by narrowing down their choices during language production. In these contexts, "meter" is tied to formularity in the sense that both arise as emergency technologies when a real-time linguistic task becomes particularly complex, and they help speakers to manage their cognitive effort. Together, these technologies enable a performer to achieve and maintain abnormal levels of fluency. The first part of the chapter made the argument, following developments in the field of generative metrics, that we should understand Homer's hexameter as made up of *cola* that are prosodic (and not syntactic or semantic) in nature, and that such prosodic structures can be confirmed by looking at data on the distribution of oxytone words with respect to caesuras and bridges in the line. Adopting a prosodic approach (and, in particular, by paying attention to the larger units in the prosodic hierarchy in Ancient Greek) can help clarify a number of long-debated issues in Homeric poetics, including the problem of enjambement in Homer.

In Chapter 3, I argued that Homer is like many contemporary performers of popular music, in that he shifts away from his spoken dialect for the purposes of performance and adopts instead a mix of dialectal features that serve to signal his affiliation to a given performance tradition (as well as his specific models therein). While Homeric scholarship has seen these mixed linguistic features as motivated primarily by metrical demands, I contend that meter is only one potential factor in the creation of these mixed performance dialects, and one that is neither necessary nor sufficient to explain their development. These dialects arise when performers consciously or unconsciously try to imitate their models (which they can do with different levels of success and consistency) and can (clearly in the case of punk rock, and likely in the case of Homer's dialect) collect different dialectal features as they "travel" from one area to another. Audiences tend to interpret these performance dialects based on their own linguistic knowledge, and they are often more likely to interpret them in synchronic terms (i.e., in terms of other dialects they know) than in diachronic terms (i.e., archaic forms vs. innovative forms). I have also argued that shifts within performance dialects should not immediately be understood as diachronic change, since they might very well reflect changes in the motivation and preferences between different synchronic models. While performance dialects do not exist to help the poet manage the cognitive challenge of performance, they do serve the goal of negotiating the poet's position within a tradition, and, much like formularity, they help poets to create meaning by referring back to a long tradition of performances in the past.

Finally, in Chapter 4, I have made the case that Homer is like jazz musicians and hip-hop performers, in that he sometimes experiences *flow* (a type of hypofrontality) during improvisational tasks. Flow is a mental state that arises during activities when a highly challenging task is matched to sufficiently high skill, and when some other structural conditions are in place, and has been tied to greater creative achievement. Flow can give individuals the impression that their actions are unfolding without effort and coming from a source "outside of themselves" (which reminds us of the Ancient Greek idea that the Muses or the gods are the source of the poet's song). This not only dovetails with contemporary accounts of jazz musicians (who stress the importance of balancing conscious and unconscious processing during their performance), but also with neuroimaging studies of what happens in the brains of musicians when they improvise. These studies reveal a *dissociated pattern* of activation in the prefrontal cortex, with general deactivation of some areas (tied to self-monitoring and the construction of a sense of self), combined with focal activation of some other areas (tied to self-expression and the pursuit of higher behavioral goals). In Ancient Greece this pattern of activation was arguably tied with the cultural construct of the Muses and the concept of divine inspiration. This observation helps us re-evaluate the debate between *tékhnē* and *enthousiasmós* as factors in poetic creation which we can observe from the Archaic to the Classical period: it is arguably because these individuals are highly trained in their craft (which reminds us of the concept of Gk. *tékhnē*), and can rely on a vast suite of automatic behaviors, that they can experience flow (a rough equivalent of the concept of Gk. *enthousiasmós*), as well as the heightened creativity that comes with it, when they face the complex challenges of performance.

Throughout this book, I have argued that Homer's poetic technique leverages some universal features of human memory and cognition in order to sustain the poet's creativity and maximize its effect on the audiences. I see much potential for further research in this direction, both in looking at individual phenomena in Homer in closer detail and in engaging more deeply with the cognitive sciences and further developments therein (which are likely to quickly outpace our own research on Homer). The Greeks regarded the Muses as the daughters of Memory: I believe that by studying language and the human mind more closely we can come to a fuller appreciation of Homer's immortal art.

Glossary of Linguistic Terms

Ablaut: Most morphemes of PIE (i.e., roots, affixes, and endings) possess several variants (i.e., allomorphs), which are identical to each other except for a single variable vowel. The process by which this vowel "alternates" or "changes" between the different allomorphs is called *ablaut*. In PIE terms, this *ablaut vowel* can appear as [e] (*full grade* or *e-grade*), [o] (*o-grade*), or nothing (*zero-grade*). Different ablaut grades are used in different morphological formations, in both the nominal and verbal systems. Many daughter languages have inherited ablaut patterns from PIE, though sound changes affecting vowels have often obscured (or entirely destroyed) the original PIE alternations. Ancient Greek (AG) preserves many original PIE ablaut patterns particularly faithfully. For instance, many AG verbal roots (in the following case, λειπ- "to leave") show different ablaut grades depending on tense: consider the alternation between the present stem λείπ-ω "I leave" (*e-grade*), the perfect stem λέ-λοιπ-α "I have left" (*o-grade*), and the aorist stem ἔ-λιπ-ον "I left" (*zero-grade*). Alternation between *e-grade* and *o-grade* can also be seen in the *thematic vowel*, thus λείπ-ο-μεν "we leave" (*o-grade*) vs. λείπ-ε-τε "you guys leave" (*e-grade*). Less frequently, ablaut vowels can appear in a *lengthened grade* (as [oː] or [eː]). Forms of the word "father" in AG show several ablaut grades of the suffix -τερ- (in PIE terms, this is the *-*ter*- agent suffix), thus nom.sg. πα-τήρ (*lengthened e-grade*), gen.sg. πα-τρ-ός (*zero-grade*), acc. sg. πα-τέρ-α (*e-grade*), nom.sg. εὐπά-τωρ "having a good father" (*lengthened o-grade*), acc.sg. εὐπά-τορ-α (*o-grade*).

Accent (Ancient Greek): AG marked one syllable in each word (with the exception of → **clitics**) as more prominent than the others, and did so primarily through pitch. For this reason, AG has been traditionally labeled a *pitch-accent language*. Several dialects of Greek (including Proto-Greek, Attic–Ionic, and Doric) possessed a so-called *lexical accent system*, whereby speakers had to memorize accentual information about each word/morpheme in order to compute where the accent would fall. Still, some classes of words (such as finite verbs, or neuter nouns in -μα/ματος) contained no listed accentual information, and thus received a default accent that could be assigned based purely on the phonological shape of a word: this is called the *recessive accent*, since it "went back" as far as possible within the permissible *accentable window* in a word. Some AG dialects (such as Asiatic Aeolic) appear to have generalized the recessive accent to all words.

The accentable window within a word can be defined as follows: the accent (as it is notated by *accentual marks* in our texts) can never fall further back than the antepenultimate syllable if the final syllable is light, or further back than the penultimate syllable if the final syllable is heavy (note that some dialects of AG, like Attic–Ionic and Asiatic Aeolic, have *final consonant extrametricality*, whereby the final consonant in each word does not contribute to syllable weight, which means that final syllables containing a short vowel must end in two consonants in order to count as heavy).

Assimilation: A phonological process or historical sound change whereby a sound is made articulatorily more similar to another (usually adjacent) sound, which simplifies pronunciation. The word *assimilation* itself, from Latin *ad* + *similāre*, contains an example of assimilation, whereby the /d/ was made articulatorily more similar to the following /s/ (specifically, the manner of articulation of the /d/ was changed from stop to fricative, matching /s/; the place of articulation was already dental for both sounds). Assimilation can be recessive (the first sound in a sequence becomes more similar to the second sound) or progressive (the second sound in a sequence becomes more similar to the first sound), and it can be partial (only some features of the sound become identical) or total (the two sounds become identical). Latin *ad* + *similāre* > *assimilāre* is a case of total recessive assimilation. Latin *imperfectus* (Engl. *imperfect*), from *in-* + *perfectus*, contains an example of partial regressive assimilation (the sound /n/ was assimilated to the following sound /p/ with respect to its place of articulation only, which was changed from dental to labial).

Asterisk *: In PIE linguistics, forms that are not attested in the historical record, but are reconstructed using the comparative method (i.e., by systematically comparing related forms that are attested in the IE daughter languages), are always prefixed by an asterisk (*). Forms marked by an asterisk can range from universally agreed upon and quite certain in their reconstruction, to debated or resting on uncertain data and interpretation thereof. Reconstructed forms can belong to different chronological stages of a language (or pre-language); thus, an asterisk does not mean that a form is of PIE age, but simply that it is a *pre-form* of some historically attested form (e.g., PIE *h₁es-mi "I am" > Proto-Greek *es-mi). In modern generative linguistics, an asterisk marks words or expressions that are perceived as ungrammatical by native speakers, such as the word *uglity (for *ugliness*) or the phrase **the cat a ball saw* (for *the cat saw a ball*).

Clitic: Clitics are a class of words which do not bear their own accent, and thus have to "lean on" (Gk. κλίνω "I lean") other accented words (i.e., *orthotonic words*) to be pronounced. AG had both *proclitics* (i.e., words that lean on a following word to be pronounced), such as the conjunction καί "and", and *enclitics* (words that lean on a preceding word), such as the particle τε "and" or the unemphatic forms of the personal pronouns με "me," σε "you", etc. Note that several forms that we know were clitic in AG are still written with accents in our medieval manuscripts and modern text editions (such as καί above).

Coda: Within a syllable, the coda is the (optional) part that follows the nucleus. Many cases of compensatory lengthening (→) that happen in AG and other languages involve loss of coda segments and the subsequent lengthening of a nucleus segment.

Compensatory lengthening: A phonological process or historical sound change whereby the segment (typically a vowel) in the nucleus of a syllable is made longer to "make up" for the loss of another weight-bearing segment nearby (→ **Mora (μ)/Phonological Weight**). The goal is to preserve the total phonological weight of a syllable, so that a heavy syllable remains heavy. A very common case crosslinguistically is that of compensatory lengthening of a nucleus vowel after the loss of a coda segment in the same syllable (this loss can happen directly, through deletion of the segment, or, more rarely, indirectly, through resyllabification). The phenomenon of *r-dropping* in some dialects of English (whereby *car* /kɑr/ is pronounced [kɑː]) is an example of coda loss with compensatory lengthening.

In AG linguistics, we talk about *three compensatory lengthenings* (historical sound changes) taking place at different points between Proto-Greek and the first-millennium dialects. Not all dialects take part in all compensatory lengthenings (the first is absent from Aeolic; the second is limited to Attic–Ionic and some Doric dialects; the third is present in some varieties of Ionic and Doric), and different dialects often have different outcomes for the same compensatory lengthening.

The first compensatory lengthening (PIE *h_1es-mi* "I am" > Attic–Ionic εἰμί [eːmí]) occurred after Proto-Greek *[s] was lost in the intervocalic sequences *[sr], *[sl], *[sm], *[sn], *[sw], *[rs], *[ls], *[ns], and *[ws]. Note that in the last four cases the segment that is lost is in the onset of a following syllable; as the resulting sequence is resyllabified (i.e., parsed anew into syllables), the former coda of the first syllable becomes a new onset for the following syllable, and the first syllable has thus "lost its coda" (and thus the vowel is lengthened to preserve the original syllable weight): we can see this development in Proto-Greek *e-stel-sa* [es.tel.sa] "I sent" > Attic–Ionic ἔστειλα [es.teː.la]).

The second compensatory lengthening occurred after [n] was lost in (a) intervocalic [ns] sequences containing a *secondary* [s] (i.e., an [s] generated by post-Proto-Greek processes), and (b) in word-final [ns] sequences: (Proto-Greek feminine nom.sg. *pant-ija* > *pansa* > Attic–Ionic πᾶσα "all"; Proto-Greek thematic acc.pl. *-ons* > Attic–Ionic -ους [oːs]). It is attested in Attic–Ionic and in some Doric dialects. In other dialects, such as Asiatic Aeolic (as well as in the Doric dialects spoken in Thera and Cyrene), the [n] in these sequences was changed to [i], Asiatic Aeolic παῖσα, thematic acc.pl. -οις.

The third compensatory lengthening is attested in Central and East Ionic as well as in a few Doric-speaking areas (Argive, Cretan, Cyrenaean, and East Aegean Doric) and it occurs after [w] is lost in [nw], [rw], and [lw] sequences. Thus Proto-Greek *kor-wā* "girl" > East Ionic κούρη [koːrɛː], but Attic κόρη [korɛ:]. Like with some instances of first compensatory lengthening, the segment "lost" is actually in the onset of the following syllable, and the compensation occurs after the former "coda" segment of the first syllable is resyllabified in the onset of the following one.

Consonant: A sound that is articulated with complete or partial occlusion of the vocal tract. Phonetically, consonants are primarily described with respect to three parameters: glottal state, place of articulation, and manner of articulation (in this order). The *glottal state* indicates what happens in the glottis (i.e., the opening between the vocal folds) while a consonant is produced: it includes voicing, aspiration, and glottalization. Specifically, a voiced consonant (such as [b]) is pronounced with vibration of the vocal folds; a voiceless consonant (such as [p]) is produced without. For an aspirated consonant (such as [pʰ]), the vocal folds are spread wide apart, which allows more air to flow through. A glottalized consonant (these do not occur in AG or Latin) is pronounced with the vocal folds held firmly together, creating a constriction. The *place of articulation* indicates where in the vocal tract the occlusion is produced: [p] and [b] are labial consonants, whereby the occlusion is produced with the lips. The *manner of articulation* indicates how the occlusion is executed: important parameters here include whether the occlusion is complete (as in [p] and [b], which are *stops*) or partial (as in [f], and [v] which are labiodental *fricatives*, or in [w], which is a labiovelar *approximant*), or whether it has some additional properties (such as nasality, as in [m], a voiced labial *nasal*, whereby there is complete occlusion at the lips, but the soft palate (i.e., the velum) is lowered, and air can thus escape through the nose).

Constituent (syntax): A syntactic constituent is a sequence of one or more words that function as a single unit within a syntactic hierarchy. The sentence *the cat saw the bird* can be analyzed into three constituents (or phrases): the noun phrase *the cat*, the verb phrase *saw the bird*, and the noun phrase *the bird*, embedded within the verb phrase. Constituency can be determined by a series of language-specific syntactic tests. In English, some of these tests include whether a given constituent can be moved as a unit within the sentence (e.g., *It was the cat who saw the bird*, where *the cat* has been moved as a whole to the front of the sentence), whether it can be replaced by a stand-in form (*the cat saw it*, in which *the bird* has been replaced by the pronoun *it*), or whether it can stand alone in reply to a question (*Who saw the bird? The cat*).

Contraction (linguistics): A phonological process or historical sound change whereby two adjacent vowels merge, giving rise to a new single vowel. In languages that distinguish between long and short vowels, the new vowels resulting from contraction are usually long. In AG, different dialects have different contraction rules, and some dialects (such as Attic–Ionic) contract earlier and more often than others.

Contraction (meter): A metrical license whereby a metrical position for two light syllables can be optionally filled by a single heavy syllable. In the Homeric hexameter, contraction is dispreferred in the fifth foot, but generally allowed elsewhere.

Diphthong: A sequence of two vowels occupying a syllable nucleus. In AG, the second vowel in a diphthong is always [i] or [u]; originally the first vowel could be either long or short. Any syllable containing a diphthong is a heavy syllable. Note that, in the spelling of AG, the sequences <οι> and <αι> at the word end can stand for either a real diphthong [oi], or a sequence of a vowel [o] + semivowel [j], where the semivowel occupies the coda of the syllable. In dialects with final-consonant extrametricality (such as Attic–Ionic), the former sequence will count as heavy for the purposes of the accent, while the latter will count as light (since the final consonant [j] will be extrametrical).

Monophthong: A single vowel occupying a syllable nucleus.

Spurious diphthongs: This term refers to the digraphs <ει> and <ου> when they are used, in the standard spelling for Classical Attic (i.e., the East Ionic alphabet adopted in Athens and elsewhere in Greece by the fourth century BCE), to write down the long vowels [eː] and [oː] arising from secondary processes (such as compensatory lengthenings and some vowel contractions). The thematic infinitive ending -ειν [eːn] < *e-sen and the thematic genitive singular ending -ου [oː] < *-osyo are examples of such secondary long vowels "spelled like diphthongs." (The primary long vowels, going back to Proto-Greek *$ē$ and *$ō$, had separate treatments, and were spelled as <η> and <ω> respectively. Examples are the first person singular thematic present ending -ω [ɔː] < Proto-Greek -$ō$ < *-oh_2, or the <η> in πατήρ [patɛːr] < Proto-Greek *$patēr$.) This spelling practice arose because the original diphthongs [ei] and [ou] in Attic, also spelled as <ει> and <ου>, had gradually come to be pronounced as the monophthongs [eː] and [oː] respectively (a change completed by the fifth century BCE). During the fourth century BCE, these same sequences developed to [iː] and [uː] respectively. Examples of original [ei] and [ou] diphthongs spelled as such are the words λείπω [leípɔː] "I leave" < PIE *$leik^w$-oh_2 and βου-κόλος [boukólos] "cowherd" < Proto-Greek *$g^w ou$- "cow."

Discourse: The study of discourse is the branch of linguistics that concerns itself with linguistic units larger than the sentence, and with phenomena that become visible at that scale. A major concern in the study of discourse is how information is packaged across clauses and sentences. AG has recently been recognized as a *discourse configurational language* – that is, a language in which the discourse status of a referent (i.e., whether a piece of information is new or given in the discourse) will determine where it will surface in the clause (→ **topic, focus**). See Chapter 1 fn. 27 for more details.

Elision: A phonological process whereby the final vowel of a word is lost before another word starting in a vowel. In AG, elision is an external sandhi phenomenon that operates in the domain of the intonational phrase (in the

Homeric hexameter, this means that elision operates across the whole verse, even if a caesura or punctuation intervenes). AG elision only targets short vowels, most frequently [e], [o], and [a], ([i] only sometimes) and never [u]. The line: οὐλομένην, ἣ μυρί' Ἀχαιοῖς ἄλγε' ἔθηκε (*Il.* 1.2) contains two examples of elision of [a], both marked by an apostrophe in our text.

Epic distraction (Gk. διέκτασις "stretching"): In our text of Homer, some forms which had undergone vowel contraction in spoken Ionic display a "stretched-out" spelling, which represents an artificial compromise between the metrical form of the earlier, uncontracted form and the vocalism of the new, contracted one. This pattern is very well attested for verbs in -αω, but it has been extended further. Thus, in the *Iliad* and *Odyssey* the first person singular of the verb ὁράω "I see" occurs 7x in the distracted form ὁρόω (e.g., *Il.* 5.244) and only once in the contracted form ὁρῶ (*Il.* 3.234). The historically correct, uncontracted form ὁράω never occurs. This arguably means that poets had preserved the memory that this verbal form used to have an extra syllable, but not the memory of what that syllable exactly was.

Final lengthening: A phonological process whereby a vowel is lengthened (i.e., held for longer) at the end of a prosodic domain. Final lengthening is more often observed at the end of larger prosodic domains, such as the *intonational phrase* (this is the case for Modern Greek).

Focus: In the study of discourse (i.e., connected speech above the level of the sentence) and information structure (how information is packaged within sentences), the category of focus indicates information that is (in very general terms) presented as new to the listener, and thus salient. Languages can indicate focus by different means, often either through syntax (e.g., by placing the focused element in a dedicated position in the sentence) or prosody (i.e., through stress or intonation), or a combination of both. In the English sentence *THE CAT, I saw*, a cleft construction (together with stress and intonation) is used to convey focus.

Foot (phonology): In phonology, a foot is a prosodic domain larger than the syllable and smaller than the word. All human languages build feet of some shape (at least according to some accounts), and AG built *moraic trochees* specifically. These are a sequence made up of either one heavy syllable or two light syllables. The effects of footing in AG can be seen in derivational morphology as well as in the assignment of the recessive accent. See Chapter 2 fn. 76 for more detail.

Foot (metrics): In classical metrics, a foot is the smallest possible recurring metrical sequence in a line. Iambs (⌣–), dactyls (–⌣⌣), and spondees (– –) are all types of feet.

Fricative: A type of consonant produced with partial obstruction of the vocal tract, whereby the air is forced through a narrow passage, causing friction and thus turbulence in the air flow. English [f], [v], [s], [z], and [θ] are all fricatives. In the Classical period, Attic Greek only had three fricatives: [s], [z] (an allophone of /s/), and word-initial [h]. <φ> <θ> <χ> were not originally fricatives, but aspirated stops.

Gemination: Some languages allow for geminate consonants, i.e., consonants that are held for longer than a single corresponding consonant. For example, Italian contrasts the words *pappa* [ˈpapːa] "mush" and *Papa* [ˈpapa] "Pope" because the former contains a longer (geminated) consonant, spelled <pp>. English *spells* many geminated consonants (some of which it inherited from Latin, where gemination was allowed), but it does not pronounce them as such (other "double" consonants in English spelling served originally to indicate the quality or length of the preceding vowel, and not a property of the consonant in question).

AG, unlike PIE, allowed for geminate consonants, though some dialects were fonder of them than others. Aeolic, for instance, eliminated many undesired consonantal sequences through gemination, whereas other dialects opted for different solutions (such as consonant loss with or without compensatory lengthening).

Degemination is the process of making a geminate consonant into a singleton.

Hapax legomenon (pl. *hapax legomena*, or *hapaxes* for short): "Said once." A form or expression that occurs only once within a given corpus.

Idiom: A fixed or semi-fixed multiword expression whose meaning is at least partially noncompositional (i.e., cannot be fully or easily derived from its component parts). Examples are English *the elephant in the room*, and Hom. ἔπεα πτερόεντα προσηύδα "s/he spoke winged words."

Liquids: A class of sounds which includes rhotics ([r] sounds) and laterals ([l] sounds). The Lat. term *liquida* translates Gk. ὑγρά "moist" (perhaps in the sense of "slippery"), a term used by Dionysius Thrax in his *Ars Grammatica* (see Chapter 2 fn. 30 for more details). In PIE, liquids could function as syllable nuclei; this property was lost in AG, where syllabic liquids were variously "vocalized" (i.e., turned into sequences of vowel + consonant/consonant + vowel), with different outcomes in different dialects.

Mora (μ)/Phonological weight: An abstract unit of prosodic weight, which is used to explain phenomena like syllable weight (why some syllables count as heavy and some count as light) and compensatory lengthening. In AG, only segments that occur in the nucleus and coda of a syllable can carry moras. Specifically, a short vowel carries one mora, and a long vowel or a diphthong carries two. Every consonant in the coda of a syllable carries one mora as well. When a syllable loses a mora-carrying segment, its mora can sometimes be passed on to an adjacent segment (as to preserve the total prosodic weight of the syllable): when this happens, we talk about compensatory lengthening (→ **compensatory lengthening**).

Moraic trochee (→ **Foot (phonology)**)

Nucleus: Within a syllable, the nucleus is the only obligatory component, which hosts the most sonorous segment(s). Segments that occupy the syllable nucleus are called syllabic. In AG only vowels and diphthongs could be syllabic. In PIE and Proto-Greek, liquids and nasals (i.e., sonorants) could be syllabic as well (see Chapter 2 fn. 106 for more details).

Phoneme: A contrastive sound within the phonological inventory of a language. In English, the sounds [m] and [p] can both be shown to belong to distinct phonemes because they differentiate the otherwise identical words *man* and *pan* (these two words together are called a *minimal pair*). Phonemes are written between slashes (thus /p/ and /m/). Phonemes can have many *allophones*, i.e., different ways of being pronounced, depending on their phonological environment. For instance, English /p/ is pronounced as a [p^h] word initially, as in *pan* [p^hæn], and as plain [p] elsewhere, as in *span* [spæn]. AG alphabetic spelling was largely *phonemic* in nature, meaning each letter was used to write down a single phoneme, and allophonic variation was not notated. An exception to this rule is the use of <γ> to write [ŋ] (a velar nasal), an allophone of the phoneme /n/ before a velar consonant, as in the word ἄγγελος "messenger."

Phonological change (or Phonological rule or Phonological process): A synchronic process that alters the pronunciation of a phoneme based on its surrounding environment. Thus, a phonological change in English that we can call *Word-initial aspiration* changes /p/ to [p^h] in word-initial position, and can be notated as follows: /p/ → [p^h] /#_ (→ **Phoneme**). A phonological change is always a mapping between an *underlying form* (i.e., a sequence of phonemes in the mind of a speaker) and a *surface form* (i.e., a sequence of *pronounced* sounds), and it is meant to describe an active linguistic process in the mind of a speaker. Phonological changes are not the same as historical sound changes (or sound laws), but they can constitute the seeds of historical change.

Plosive → **Stop**

Prosody (linguistics): The study of units of speech above the level of individual segments (i.e., phonemes or sounds). This includes the study of so-called suprasegmental features, such as intonation and stress, as well as the study of *prosodic domains* of increasing size, such as syllables, feet, words, prosodic phrases, intonational phrases, and utterances, which together constitute the *prosodic hierarchy*. For more details on the *prosodic hierarchy* in AG, see section 2.2.3.

Proto-Greek: A reconstructed stage of language development that is the ancestor to all attested varieties of AG, including Mycenaean and the first-millennium dialects. According to most current reconstructions, Proto-Greek would have been spoken around 2000 BCE.

Proto-Indo-European: A reconstructed language that is the ancestor to all attested IE languages. The current consensus is that PIE was spoken around 4000 BCE in the region between the Black Sea and the Caspian Sea. PIE has been reconstructed, since the nineteenth century, by systematically comparing the phonological and morphological systems of the oldest attested IE languages (reconstruction of PIE syntax is relatively underdeveloped). While much of what we know about PIE is relatively secure, PIE reconstructions (marked by *) should always be regarded as hypotheses, which are being continuously revised based on new empirical findings and theoretical advances.

Quantitative metathesis: A sound change that took place in Attic–Ionic, targeting a sequence of a long vowel + a short vowel, and descriptively "switching" their quantities (so that the first vowel became short, and the second long). Specifically, QM operated on the sequences <ηo> [ɛːo] and <ηα> [ɛːa], and resulted in the sequences <εω> [eɔː] and <εᾱ> [eaː] respectively. The resulting sequences normally scan as a single heavy syllable for metrical and accentual purposes (i.e., the two vowels are in *synizesis*). The exact mechanism by which QM operated is still debated, as well as some details of its relative chronology (see section 3.4.2 for an extended discussion).

Referent (discourse): An entity that is referred to by a linguistic expression. The sentence *the black cat saw two birds and ate them* features two discourse referents: "the cat," referred to by the noun phrase *the black cat*, and "the birds," referred to by the noun phrase *two birds*, as well as by the pronoun *them*.

Sonorant (or Resonant): A type of sound produced with neither total occlusion nor turbulence in the vocal tract. Technically, both vowels and non-occlusive consonants (i.e., consonants that are not stops, affricates, or fricatives) are sonorants, though the term is more often used to refer to the consonants that fit this description – that is, the nasals and liquids (and sometimes glides). AG had the nasal sonorants /m/ and /n/ ([ŋ] was an allophone), and the liquid sonorants /r/ and /l/. In IE studies, sonorants are often referred to as *resonants*.

Sound change (or Sound law): A sound change is a diachronic process, which we observe between two chronological stages of a language, and which changes a sound into another sound. Unlike phonological changes, sound changes are historical events, not mental processes, even though they have their roots in synchronic phonological changes. Sound changes can be unconditional (they change all instances of sound A into sound B, everywhere in the language) or conditional (they only change some instances of sound A into sound B, depending on the environment). Sound changes are notated with the sign >, and usually describe the difference between two *surface forms* at two different points in time. Thus, a sound change that we can call *Word-final t deletion* deleted all instances of [t] at the end of a word in Proto-Greek. We can write it as: PIE *[t] > Proto-Greek ø /_# (the PIE sound [t] was changed to zero – i.e., was deleted – at the end of a word in Proto-Greek).

Reversion (Attic): Also known as *Rückverwandlung*. A sound change, operating in Attic and West Ionic, which "undoes" the general Attic–Ionic process that turned all inherited *[aː] into [ɛː] <η> by turning [ɛː] back into [aː] when following the segments [e], [i], or [r]. The Attic word χώρᾱ "land" (vs. East-Ionic χώρη "id.") shows an example of Reversion.

Rhyme (or Rime): The portion of a syllable consisting of the nucleus and the coda, which usually carries the prosodic weight (→ **Mora**).

Sandhi: From the Skt. *sam* + *dhi* "to put together," a class of phonological changes that apply in connected speech, with the general result of making pronunciation easier. Sandhi processes are often assimilatory in nature (i.e., they make nearby segments more articulatorily similar to each other). We can talk of *internal sandhi* (i.e., changes which happen when we put morphemes together inside a word) and *external sandhi* (i.e., changes that happen when we put words together in a larger prosodic unit). See Chapter 2 fn. 71 for more details.

Segment (linguistics): A linguistic segment is the smallest parsable unit of speech; the term can refer to either *sounds* (e.g., [p]) or *phonemes* (e.g., /p/).

Sound: In phonology, when we talk of sounds (as opposed to phonemes), we talk about how a segment is pronounced (as opposed to how it is represented in the mind of a speaker). In *phonetic notation*, sounds are written between brackets, using the IPA (International Phonetic Alphabet). Thus, the English phoneme /n/ can be pronounced as the sounds [n], [m], [ŋ], or [ɱ] depending on its phonological context (see the words i*n*tolerant, i*m*possible, i*n*cautious, and i*ɱ*famous respectively, all of which contain the morpheme /in-/).

Stop (or Plosive): A type of consonant produced with complete occlusion in the vocal tract, and where the air (coming from the lungs) does not escape through the nose (which would make it into a nasal consonant instead). AG had several stops, at the places of articulation: labial ([p], [b], [pʰ]), dental ([t], [d], [tʰ]), and velar ([k], [g], [kʰ]). For each of the places of articulation above, AG had voiceless stops ([p], [t], [k]), voiced stops ([b], [d], [g]), and voiceless aspirated stops ([pʰ], [tʰ], [kʰ]). By the first century BCE to the second century CE, the AG voiceless aspirate stops had developed into the voiceless fricatives [f], [θ], and [x] respectively.

Syllabic: A sound is syllabic when it occupies the nucleus of a syllable. Different languages have different preferences for which sounds can be syllabic, with more sonorous sounds (such as vowels and sonorants) being generally preferred to less sonorous ones (such as stops). For instance, while PIE and Proto-Greek allowed for syllabic sonorants (like many varieties of Present-Day English), such as nasals and liquids, AG dialects did not share this preference, and thus "eliminated" syllabic sonorants by changing them into vowel-containing sequences.

Syllabification: The (language-specific) process by which linguistic segments are grouped into syllables (→ **Syllable**). For the rules of syllabification in the Homeric hexameter, see section 2.1.2.

Syllable: Syllables are prosodic units in which phonemes are grouped (Gk. συλλαμβάνω "take together") for the purposes of pronunciation. Unlike other phonological concepts (such as the phoneme or the foot), syllables are usually psychologically salient for speakers, so that even children can typically divide words into syllables without previous training. Descriptively, syllables are said to be made up of three components: the *onset*, the *nucleus*, and the *coda* (together, these last two components are labelled *rhyme* or *rime*); among these, only the nucleus is indispensable. See extensive discussion in section 2.1.1.

Synizesis: Gk. συνίζησις "falling together," a process by which a sequence of two vowels (or one vowel and a diphthong), originally belonging to two adjacent syllables, is grouped together to form a single syllable. Synizesis can be observed both as a type of metrical license (whereby two adjacent syllables in a word are allowed to occupy the metrical position for a single heavy syllable), as well as a phonological process or sound change.

Thematic vs. Athematic: In the morphology of PIE, Greek, Latin, and many other older IE languages, a distinction is made between *thematic* and *athematic* inflection. This distinction affects verbs (where one speaks of thematic vs. athematic conjugations) as well as nouns and adjectives (where one speaks of thematic vs. athematic declensions). In the thematic inflection, the thematic vowel **e/o* (i.e., a vowel *e* that sometimes alternates with a vowel *o*) is inserted between the stem of a word and its endings. One can then talk about *thematic stems* (i.e., stems that take the thematic vowel) as well as *thematic endings* (i.e., endings that follow or include the thematic vowel). In Greek, substantives of the second declension are thematic (as well as masculine and neuter adjectives in the first adjective class); verbs whose first person singular present active form ends in -ω (often reconstructed as < PIE **oH*, where *o* is the thematic vowel) are also thematic; in fact, based on the present stem alone, one can talk of a first conjugation of Greek verbs containing all thematic presents (-ω verbs) and a second conjugation containing all athematic presents (-μι verbs). Outside of the present stem, Greek futures in -σο- (where the *o* is a thematic vowel), as well as aorists such as ἔλιπον "I left" (where the *o* is a thematic vowel) are thematic formations. In the verb, the (→ **Ablaut**) variant *e* of the thematic vowel is found in the third person singular and dual and in the second person singular, dual, and plural (e.g., ἔλιπεν "s/he left" and λείπετε "you guys are leaving"); in the nominal declension, it is found in the vocative ἄδελφε "O brother." In IE linguistics, it is common practice (perhaps confusingly) to give the thematic vowel both when listing thematic stems in isolation and when listing thematic endings in isolation. Thus, I might give the stem for Priam's name as Πριαμο- (where *o* is the thematic vowel), and the ending for its genitive singular form as -οιο (where the first *o* from the left is also the thematic vowel).

Tokens vs. Types: This distinction, important in the field of corpus linguistics, refers to the difference between counting how many separate instances (i.e., tokens) of the same phenomenon occur in a corpus and counting how many different phenomena (i.e., types) occur in that corpus. Thus, if I have five black cats and four orange cats, I will have two cat types (the black type and the orange type), and a total of nine cat tokens (five tokens belonging to the black type, and four tokens belonging to the orange type). See Chapter 1 fn. 57 for more details.

Topic: In the study of discourse (i.e., continuous speech above the level of the sentence) and information structure (how information is packaged within sentences), the category of topic indicates information that is (in very general terms) assumed to be known to the listener, and that provides the background or context against which new information can be added. Languages can indicate topic by different means, often either through syntax (e.g., by placing the topic in a dedicated position in the sentence) or prosody (i.e., through stress or intonation), or a combination of both. In the sentence *As for cats, I prefer the black ones*, the phrase *As for cats* expresses the topic, as realized in English through *left dislocation* as well as a dedicated intonational tune.

Transponat: In PIE reconstruction, a *transponat* (from the 3.sg.act. subjunctive of Lat. *transponere* "to transfer, transpose") is a reconstructed form that is unlikely to have existed in PIE times, but that is a sound-by-sound back-projection of a form attested in one or more daughter languages.

Vowel: A sound produced with no obstruction whatsoever in the vocal tract. Vowels are the most sonorous class of sounds, and they occupy the nuclei of syllables (i.e., they are syllabic). AG had long and short vowels.

References

Adger, David. 2003. *Core Syntax: A Minimalist Approach*. Oxford: Oxford University Press.
Agazzi, Pierangelo and Vilardo, Massimo. 2002. Ἑλληνιστί: *Grammatica della lingua greca*. Bologna: Zanichelli.
Aguirre, Javier and Lavilla de Lera, Jonathan. 2018. 'The philosopher against the rhapsodist: Socrates and Ion as characters in Plato's *Ion*', *Filozofia* 73: 108–18.
Akande, Akinmade T. 2012. 'The appropriation of African American vernacular English and Jamaican patois by Nigerian hip hop artists', *Zeitschrift für Anglistik und Amerikanistik*, 60: 237–54.
Albright, Adam and Hayes, Bruce. 2003. 'Rules vs. analogy in English past tenses: A computational/experimental study', *Cognition* 90: 119–61.
Alim, Samy H. 2002. 'Street-conscious copula variation in the hip hop nation', *American Speech* 77: 288–304.
Allan, Rutger. 2021. 'From Fränkel to functional: A functional-cognitive approach to enjambment and caesura'. Paper presented at the 14th Trends in Classics International Conference, March 2021, University of Thessaloniki.
Allen, Nick. 2012. 'Americans baffled by Adele's accent', *The Telegraph*, February 13, 2012. http://www.telegraph.co.uk/culture/music/rockandpopmusic/9079988/Grammy-Awards-Americans-baffled-by-Adeles-accent.html
Allen, Sidney W. 1968. *Vox Graeca: A Guide to the Pronunciation of Classical Greek*. Cambridge: Cambridge University Press.
Allen, Thomas W. 1907. 'The Homeridae', *The Classical Quarterly* 1: 135–43.
Allen, Thomas W. 1931. *Homeri Ilias*. Oxford: Clarendon Press.
Andersen, Øivind and Haug, Dag T. T. (eds.). 2012. *Relative Chronology in Early Greek Epic Poetry*. Cambridge: Cambridge University Press.
Anderson, John R. 1983. 'A spreading activation theory of memory', *Journal of Verbal Learning and Verbal Behavior* 22: 261–95.
Anson, Edward M. 2009. 'Greek ethnicity and the Greek language', *Glotta* 85: 5–30.
Arnold, Eduard Vernon. 1905. *Vedic Metre in its Historical Development*. Cambridge: Cambridge University Press.
Arvaniti, A. and Baltazani, M. 2000. 'GREEK ToBI: a system for the annotation of Greek speech corpora', in M. Gavrilidou, G. Carayannis, S. Markantonatou, S. Piperidis, and G. Stainhauer (eds.), *Proceedings of Second International*

Conference on Language Resources and Evaluation 2, 555–62. Athens: European Language Resources Association.

Baayen, R. Harald and Schreuder, Robert. 1995. 'Modeling morphological processing', in L. B. Feldman (ed.) *Morphological Aspects of Language Processing*, 131–54. Hillsdale, NJ: Erlbaum.

Bachvarova, Mary R. 2016. *From Hittite to Homer: The Anatolian Background of Ancient Greek Epic*. Cambridge: Cambridge University Press.

Baddeley, Alan, Eysenck, Michael W., and Anderson, Michael C. 2009. *Memory*. Hove and New York: Psychology Press.

Bailey, Derek. 1992. *Improvisation, its Nature and Practice in Music*. Boston, MA: Da Capo Press.

Bakker, Egbert J. 1990. 'Homeric discourse and enjambement: A cognitive approach', *Transactions of the American Philological Association* 120: 1–21.

Bakker, Egbert J. 1997. *Poetry in Speech*. Ithaca, NY and London: Cornell University Press.

Bakker, Egbert J. 2005. *Pointing at the Past: From Formula to Performance in Homeric Poetics*. Cambridge, MA: Harvard University Press.

Bakker, Egbert J. 2013. *The Meaning of Meat and the Structure of the Odyssey*. Cambridge: Cambridge University Press.

Bakker, Egbert. 2019. 'Learning the epic formula', in C. Reitz and S. Finkmann (eds.), *Structures of Epic Poetry, Volume I: Foundations*, 81–98. Berlin: De Gruyter.

Barnes, Harry R. 1979. 'Enjambement and oral composition', *Transactions of the American Philological Association* 109: 1–10.

Barnes, Harry R. 1986. 'The colometric structure of Homeric hexameter', *Greek, Roman and Byzantine Studies* 27.2: 125–50.

Barnes, Timothy. 2011. 'Homeric ΑΝΔΡΟΤΗΤΑ ΚΑΙ ΗΒΗΝ', *Journal of Hellenic Studies* 131: 1–13.

Barnie, John. 1978. 'Oral formulas in the country blues', *Southern Folklore Quarterly* 42: 39–52.

Bassett, Samuel Eliot. 1919. 'The theory of the Homeric caesura according to the extant remains of the ancient doctrine', *The American Journal of Philology* 40.4: 343–72.

Bauer, Laurie. 2001. *Morphological Productivity*. Cambridge: Cambridge University Press.

Beal, Joan C. 2009. '"You're not from New York City, you're from Rotherham": Dialect and identity in British indie music', *Journal of English Linguistics* 37.3: 1–18.

Bechtel, W., Abrahamsen, A., and Graham, G. 2001. 'Cognitive science: History' in Neil J. Smelser and Paul B. Baltes (eds.), *International Encyclopedia of the Social and Behavioral Sciences*, 2154–58. Oxford: Pergamon Press.

Beck, Deborah. 2005. *Homeric Conversation*. Washington, DC: Center for Hellenic Studies.

Beck, Deborah. 2012. *Speech Presentation in Homeric Epic*. Austin, TX: University of Texas Press.

Beck, William. 1986. 'Choice and context: Metrical doublets for Hera', *The American Journal of Philology* 107: 480–88.
Beckman, Mary. 1986. *Stress and Non-Stress Accent*. Dordrecht: Foris.
Bell, Allan and Gibson, Andy M. 2011. 'Staging language: An introduction to the sociolinguistics of performance', *Journal of Sociolinguistics* 15: 555–72.
Bennett, John. 1997. 'Homer and the Bronze Age', in Ian Morris and Barry Powell (eds.) *A New Companion to Homer*, 511–34. Leiden: Brill.
Bennett, Ryan. 2012. 'Foot-conditioned phonotactics and prosodic constituency', Ph.D. Dissertation, University of California, Santa Cruz.
Berg, Nils. 1978. 'Parergon metricum: der Ursprung des griechischen Hexameters', *Münchener Studien zur Sprachwissenschaft* 37: 11–36.
Blanc, Alain. 2008. *Les contraintes métriques dans la poésie homérique: L'emploi des thèmes nominaux sigmatiques dans l'hexamètre dactylique*, Louvain-Paris: Editions Peeters.
Bloomfield, Leonard. 1933. *Language*. New York: Henry Holt.
Böckh, August. 1811–1821. *Pindari operae quae supersunt*. Weigel: Leipzig.
Boden, Margaret. 1990. *The Creative Mind: Myths and Mechanisms*. London: George Weidenfeld and Nicolson.
Boden, Margaret. 1998. 'Creativity and artificial intelligence', *Artificial Intelligence* 103: 347–56.
Boden, Margaret. 2004. *The Creative Mind: Myths and Mechanisms*, 2nd edition. London: Routledge.
Boden, Margaret. 2006. *Mind as Machine: A History of Cognitive Science*. Oxford: Oxford University Press.
Boden, Margaret. 2009. 'Computer models of creativity', *AI Magazine* Fall 2009: 23–34.
Bolinger, Dwight. 1976. 'Meaning and memory', *Forum Linguisticum* 1: 1–14.
Bowra, C. Maurice. 1952. *Heroic Poetry*. London: Macmillan.
Bozzone, Chiara. 2010. 'New perspectives on formularity', in Stephanie W. Jamison, H. Craig Melchert, and Brent Vine (eds.), *Proceedings of the 21st Annual UCLA Indo-European Conference*, 27–44. Bremen: Hempen.
Bozzone, Chiara. 2014. 'Constructions: A new approach to formularity, discourse, and syntax in Homer'. Ph.D. Dissertation, University of California, Los Angeles.
Bozzone, Chiara. 2016a. 'Weaving songs for the dead in Indo-European: Women poets, funerary laments, and the ecology of *$kléu̯os$*', in David M. Goldstein, Stephanie W. Jamison, and Brent Vine (eds.), *Proceedings of the 27th Annual UCLA Indo-European Conference*, 1–22. Bremen: Hempen.
Bozzone, Chiara. 2016b. 'The mind of the poet: Linguistic and cognitive perspectives', in Federico Gallo (ed.), *Omero: quaestiones disputatae*, 79–105. Milano: Bulzoni.
Bozzone, Chiara. 2020. 'Reconstructing the PIE causative in cross-linguistic perspective', *Indo-European Linguistics* 8: 1–45.
Bozzone, Chiara. 2022. 'Homeric formulas and their antiquity: A constructional study of ἀνδροτῆτα καὶ ἥβην', *Glotta* 98: 1–35.

Bozzone, Chiara. forthcoming. 'Homeric constructions, their productivity, and the development of Epic Greek', in L. Van Beek (ed.), *Language Change in Epic Greek and Other Oral Traditions*. Leiden: Brill.

Bozzone, Chiara and Guardiano, Cristina. 2015. 'Adnominal ὁ ἡ τό in Homer: Tracking the spread of a syntactic innovation'. Paper presented at the Colloquium on Ancient Greek Linguistics, Rome.

Brillante, Carlo. 2009. *Il cantore e la Musa. Poesia e modelli culturali nella Grecia arcaica*, Pisa: Edizioni ETS.

Brown, Anita. 2018. *Quantitative Metathesis in Ancient Greek*. Unpublished manuscript. https://scholarship.tricolib.brynmawr.edu/bitstream/handle/10066/20029/Brown_thesis_2018.pdf

Brown, Cat. 2015. 'Alesha Dixon heckled for singing British national anthem in American accent', *The Telegraph*, July 6, 2015. http://www.telegraph.co.uk/culture/music/music-news/11719110/Alesha-Dixon-heckled-for-singing-England-national-anthem-in-American-accent.html

Brownstein, Michael. 2014. 'Rationalizing flow: Agency in skilled unreflective action', *Philosophical Studies* 168: 545–68.

Buchner, Giorgio and Russo, Carlo Ferdinando. 1955. 'La coppa di Nestore e un'iscrizione metrica di Pitecussa dell'VIII sec. av. Cr.', *Rendiconti Accademia Lincei* 8.10: 215–34.

Buck, Carl Darling. 1955. *The Greek Dialects*, 2nd edition. Chicago, IL: University of Chicago Press.

Burgess, Jonathan S. 2001. *The Tradition of the Trojan War in Homer and the Epic Cycle*. Baltimore, MD: Johns Hopkins University Press.

Bybee, Joan. 2002. 'Sequentiality as the basis of constituent structure', in Talmy Givón and Bertram F. Malle (eds.), *The Evolution of Language out of Pre-Language*, 109–34. Amsterdam: John Benjamins.

Bybee, Joan. 2010. *Language, Usage, and Cognition*. Cambridge: Cambridge University Press.

Bybee, Joan. 2015. *Language Change*. Cambridge: Cambridge University Press.

Camerotto, Alberto. 1992. 'Analisi formulare della *Batrachomyomachia*', *Lexis* 9–10: 1–54.

Cantilena, Mario. 1980. *Enjambement e poesia esametrica orale: una verifica*. Ferrara: Quaderni del Giornale Filologico Ferrarese.

Cantilena, Mario. 1982. *Ricerche sulla dizione epica I- Per uno studio della formularità degli Inni Omerici*. Rome: Edizioni dell'Ateneo.

Cantilena, Mario. 1995. 'Il ponte di Nicanore', in Marco Fantuzzi and Roberto Pretagostini (eds.), *Struttura e storia dell'esametro greco I*, 9–67. Rome: Gruppo editoriale internazionale.

Cantilena, Mario. 2021. 'Incertezze sull'esametro'. Paper presented at the Seminario Omerico, Università Cattolica del Sacro Cuore, Milan, April 2021.

Cappuccino, Carlotta. 2005. *Filosofi e Rapsodi. Testo, traduzione e commento dello* Ione *platonico*. Bologna: CLUEB.

Carnie, Andrew. 2013. *Syntax: A Generative Introduction*. Malden, MA: Wiley-Blackwell.

Cassio, Albio Cesare. 1998. 'La cultura euboica e lo sviluppo dell'epica greca', in Bruno D'Agostino and Michel Bats (eds.), *Euboica. L'Eubea e la presenza euboica in Calcidica e in Occidente*, 11–22. Naples: Publications du Centre Jean Bérard.
Cassio, Albio Cesare. 2007. 'Alcman's text, spoken Laconian, and Greek study of Greek dialects', in Ivo Hajnal (ed.), *Die altgriechischen Dialekte: Wesen und Werden*, 29–45. Innsbrük: Innsbrucker Beiträgen zur Sprachwissenschaft.
Cassio, Albio Cesare. 2009. 'The language of Hesiod and the Corpus Hesiodeum', in Franco Montanari, Christos Tsagalis, and Antonios Rengakos (eds.), *Brill's Companion to Hesiod*, 179–201. Leiden: Brill.
Cassio, Albio Cesare. 2016a. 'Introduzione Generale', in Albio Cesare Cassio (ed.), *Storia delle lingue letterarie greche*, 2nd edition, 1–136. Firenze: Le Monnier.
Cassio, Albio Cesare. 2016b. 'Overlong syllables in the epic Adonius and the compositional stages of Greek hexameter poetry', in Federico Gallo (ed.), *Omero: quaestiones disputatae*, 31–42. Milano: Bulzoni.
Cassola, Filippo. 1975. *Inni Omerici*. Milano: Arnoldo Mondadori.
Chadwick, John. 1990. 'The descent of the Greek Epic', *Journal of Hellenic Studies* 110: 174–77.
Chafe, Wallace G. (ed.). 1980. *The Pear Stories: Cognitive, Cultural, and Linguistic Aspects of Narrative Production*. Norwood, NJ: Ablex.
Chafe, Wallace G. 1994. *Discourse, Consciousness and Time: The Flow and Displacement of Conscious Experience in Speaking and Writing*. Chicago: University of Chicago Press.
Chantraine, Pierre. 1948. *Grammaire homérique. Tome I: Phonétique et morphologie*. Paris: Klincksieck.
Chantraine, Pierre. 1953. *Grammaire homérique. Tome II. Syntaxe*. Paris: Klincksieck.
Chantraine, Pierre. 1968–1980 [2009]. *Dictionnaire étymologique de la langue grecque: Histoire des mots*, New edition. Paris: Klincksieck.
Chase, W.G. and Simon, H.A. 1973. 'The mind's eye in chess', in W.G. Chase (ed.), *Visual Information Processing*, 215–81. New York: Academic Press.
Chirico, Alice, Serino, Silvia, Cipresso, Pietro, Gaggioli, Andrea, and Riva, Giuseppe. 2015. 'When music "flows". State and trait in musical performance, composition and listening: A systematic review', *Frontiers in Psychology* 6.906: 1–24.
Chomsky, Noam. 1995. *The Minimalist Program*. Boston: The MIT Press.
Clackson, James. 2011. 'The social dialects of Latin', in James Clackson (ed.), *A Companion to the Latin Language*, 505–26. Malden, MA: Wiley-Blackwell.
Clarke, Sandra and Hiscock, Philip. 2009. 'Hip-hop in a post-insular community: Hybridity, local language, and authenticity in an online Newfoundland rap group', *Journal of English Linguistics* 37.3: 241–61.
Čolaković, Zlatan. 2019. 'Avdo Međedović's post-traditional epics and their relevance to Homeric studies', *Journal of Hellenic Studies* 139: 1–48.
Cota, Marta. 2006. *La 'metatesi quantitativa' in Ionico-Attico: alcune recenti teorie*. Tesi di Laurea, Università Cattolica del Sacro Cuore, Milano.

Coupland, Nikolas and Jaworski, Adam (eds.). 1997. *Sociolinguistics: A Reader and Coursebook*. Houndmills: Palgrave Macmillan.

Coupland, Nikolas. 2007. *Style: Language Variation and Identity*. Cambridge: Cambridge University Press.

Cowan, Nelson. 2001. 'The magical number 4 in short-term memory: A reconsideration of mental storage capacity', *Behavioral Brain Science* 24: 84–114.

Croft, William. 1995. 'Intonation units and grammatical structure', *Linguistics* 33: 839–82.

Csikszentmihalyi, Mihaly. 1975/2000. *Beyond Boredom and Anxiety: Experiencing Flow in Work and Play*. San Francisco: Jossey-Bass.

Csikszentmihalyi, Mihaly. 1996. *Creativity: Flow and the Psychology of Discovery and Invention*. New York: Harper Perennial.

Cutler, Cecelia. 2003. '"Keepin' it real": White hip-hoppers' discourses of language, race, and authenticity', *Journal of Linguistic Anthropology* 13: 211–33.

Cutler, Cecelia. 2014. *White Hip-hoppers, Language and Identity in Post-Modern America*. New York: Routledge.

Danek, Georg. 1988. *Epos und Zitat: Studien zu den Quellen der Odyssee*. Vienna: Verlag der Österreichischen Akademie der Wissenschaften [Austrian Academy of Sciences Press].

Danek, Georg and Hagel, Stefan. 2002. 'Homeric singing: An approach to the original performance' [webpage]. Vienna: Verlag der Österreichischen Akademie der Wissenschaften. https://www.oeaw.ac.at/kal/sh/

Danek, Georg. 2012. 'Homer und Avdo Međedović als 'post-traditional singers'?' in Michael Meier Brügger (ed.), *Homer, gedeutet durch ein großes Lexikon*, 27–44. Berlin: De Gruyter.

Dauer, Rebecca M. 1980. 'The reduction of unstressed high vowels in Modern Greek', *Journal of the International Phonetic Association* 10: 17–27.

Destrée, Pierre and Herrmann, Fritz-Gregor (eds.). 2011. *Plato and the Poets*. Leiden: Brill.

Devine, Andrew M., and Stephens, Laurence D. 1978. 'The Greek appositives: Toward a linguistically adequate definition of caesura and bridge', *Classical Philology* 73.4: 314–28.

Devine, Andrew M., and Stephens, Laurence D. 1994. *The Prosody of Greek Speech*. Oxford: Oxford University Press.

Dietrich, Arne. 2003. 'Functional neuroanatomy of altered states of consciousness: The transient hypofrontality hypothesis', *Consciousness and Cognition* 12: 231–56.

Dietrich, Arne. 2004a. 'Neurocognitive mechanisms underlying the experience of flow', *Consciousness and Cognition* 13: 746–61.

Dietrich, Arne. 2004b. 'The cognitive neuroscience of creativity', *Psychonomic Bulletin and Review* 11: 1011–26.

Dik, Helma. 1995. *Word Order in Ancient Greek: A Pragmatic Account of Word Order Variation in Herodotus*. Amsterdam: Gieben.

Dik, Helma. 2007. *Word Order in Greek Tragic Dialogue*. Oxford: Oxford University Press.
Dixon, R. M. W., and Aikhenvald, Alexandra Y. 2007. *Word: A Cross-linguistic Typology*. Cambridge: Cambridge University Press.
Du Bois, John. 1985. 'Competing motivations', in J. Haiman (ed.), *Iconicity in Syntax*, 343–65. Amsterdam: John Benjamins.
Dugan, Kelly Patricia. 2012. 'A generative approach to Homeric enjambment: Benefits and drawbacks'. M.A. Thesis, University of Athens, Georgia.
Duncan, Daniel. 2017. 'Australian singer, American features: Performing authenticity in country music', *Language and Communication* 52: 31–44.
Durante, Marcello. 1960. 'Ricerche sulla preistoria della lingua poetica greca: La terminologia relativa alla creazione poetica', *Rendiconti Lincei* 15: 231–49.
Dyer, Robert. 1975. 'The blind bard of Chios (Hymn. Hom. AP. 171–76)', *Classical Philology* 7: 119–121.
Dylan, Bob. 2016. *Nobel Lecture*. NobelPrize.org. Nobel Prize Outreach. https://www.nobelprize.org/prizes/literature/2016/dylan/lecture/
Eberhardt, Maeve and Freeman, Kara 2015. '"First things first, I'm the realest": Linguistic appropriation, white privilege, and the hip–hop persona of Iggy Azalea', *Journal of Sociolinguistics* 19.3: 303–27.
Edwards, G. Patrick. 1971. *The Language of Hesiod in its Traditional Context*. Oxford: Blackwell.
Edwards, Mark W. 1966. 'Some features of Homeric craftsmanship', *Transactions and Proceedings of the American Philological Association* 97: 115–79.
Edwards, Mark W. 1986. 'Homer and oral tradition: The formula, Part I', *Oral Tradition* 1/2: 171–230.
Edwards, Mark W. 1988. 'Homer and oral tradition: The formula, Part II', *Oral Tradition* 3: 11–60.
Edwards, Viv and Sienkwicz, Thomas J. 1990. *Oral Cultures Past and Present: Rappin' and Homer*. Oxford: Basil Blackwell.
Erman, Britt and Warren, Beatrice. 2000. 'The idiom principle and the open choice principle', *Text* 20: 29–62.
Evans, David. 2007. 'Formulaic composition in the blues: A view from the field', *The Journal of American Folklore* 120: 482–99.
Evanson, Doris Muriel. 1989. *Imitation and Inspiration: Aspects of Literary Theory in Early and Middle-Period Platonic Dialogues*. M.A. Thesis, University of British Columbia, Canada.
Fabb, Nigel. 2015. *What is Poetry? Language and Memory in the Poems of the World*. Cambridge: Cambridge University Press.
Facchinetti, Roberta (ed.). 2007. *Corpus Linguistics 25 Years On*. Amsterdam: Rodopi.
Faraone, Christopher A. 1996. 'Taking the "Nestor's cup inscription" seriously: Erotic magic and conditional curses in the earliest inscribed hexameters', *Classical Antiquity* 15: 77–112.
Fenk-Oczlon, Gertraud and Fenk, August. 2002. 'The clausal structure of linguistic and pre-linguistic behavior', in Talmy Givón and Bertram F. Malle (eds.),

The Evolution of Language out of Pre-Language, 215–32. Amsterdam: John Benjamins.

Féry, Caroline. 2017. *Intonation and Prosodic Structure*. Cambridge: Cambridge University Press.

Fick, August. 1883. *Die homerische Odyssee in der unsprünglichen Sprachform wiederhergestellt*. Göttingen: Peppmüller.

Fick, August. 1886. *Die homerische Ilias*. Göttingen: Vandenhoeck & Ruprecht.

Finkelberg, Margalit. 1990. 'A creative oral poet and the muse', *The American Journal of Philology* 111: 293–303.

Finkelberg, Margalit. 2012. 'Late features in the speeches of the *Iliad*', in Øivind Andersen and Dag T. T. Haug (eds.), *Relative Chronology in Early Greek Epic Poetry*, 80–95. Cambridge: Cambridge University Press.

Finnegan, Ruth. 1977. *Oral Poetry: Its Nature, Significance, and Social Context*. Eugene, OR: Wipf & Stock.

Firth, John Rupert. 1957. *Papers in Linguistics 1934–1951*. Oxford: Oxford University Press.

Fix, Sonya. 2010. 'Representations of blackness by white women: Linguistic practice in the community versus the media', *University of Pennsylvania Working Papers in Linguistics* 16.2: 56–65.

Foege, Alec. 1994. 'Green Day: The kids are alright', *Rolling Stone*, September 22, 1994. http://www.rollingstone.com/music/news/green-day-the-kids-are-alright-19940922

Foer, Joshua. 2011. *Moonwalking with Einstein: The Art and Science of Remembering Everything*. New York: Penguin Books.

Foley, John Miles. 1991. *Immanent Art: From Structure to Meaning in Traditional Oral Epic*. Bloomington, IN: Indiana University Press.

Foley, John Miles. 1999. *Homer's Traditional Art*. University Park, PA: Penn State University Press.

Foley, John Miles. 2002. *How To Read an Oral Poem*. Champaign, IL: Illinois University Press.

Ford, Andrew. 2002. *The Origins of Criticism: Literary Culture and Poetic Theory in Classical Greece*. Princeton, NJ: Princeton University Press.

Forte, Alexander S. W. 2017. 'Tracing Homeric metaphor', Ph.D. Dissertation, Harvard University.

Fortson, Benjamin W. IV. 2010. *Indo-European Language and Culture: An Introduction*, 2nd edition. New York: Blackwell.

Foster, J. and Lehoux, D. 2007. 'The Delphic Oracle and the ethylene-intoxication hypothesis', *Clinical Toxicology* 451: 85–89.

Frame, Douglas. 2009. *Hippota Nestor*. Washington, DC: Center for Hellenic Studies.

Fränkel, Hermann. 1926. 'Der kallimachische und homerische Hexameter', 1st version, *Nachrichten von der Gesellschaft der Wissenschaften zu Göttingen, philologische-historische Klasse* 1–33.

Fränkel, Hermann. 1955. 'Der homerische und kallimachische Hexameter', 2nd version, in F. Tietze (ed.), *Wege und Formen frühgriechischen Denkens: Literarische und philosophiegeschichtliche Studien*, 100–56. Munich: C. H. Beck.

Friedman, Albert B. 1961. 'The formulaic improvisation theory of ballad tradition: A counterstatement', *The Journal of American Folklore* 292: 113–15.

Friedrich, Rainer. 2000. 'Homeric enjambement and orality', *Hermes* 128: 1–19.

Frog and Lamb, William. 2022. *Weathered Words: Formulaic Language and Verbal Art*. Cambridge, MA: Harvard University Press.

Fromkin, Victoria, Rodman, Robert, and Hyams, Nina. 2014. *An Introduction to Language*, 10th edition. Belmont, CA: Thomson Wadsworth.

Gablasova, Dana, Brezina, Vaclav, and McEnery, Tony. 2017. 'Collocations in corpus-based language learning research: Identifying, comparing, and interpreting the evidence', *Language Learning* 67.S1: 155–79.

Gaunt, Jasper. 2017. 'Nestor's cup and its reception', in Niall W. Slater (ed.), *Voice and Voices in Antiquity*, 92–120. Leiden: Brill.

Gerber, Douglas E. 1999. *Greek Iambic Poetry from the Seventh to the Fifth Centuries BC*. Loeb Classical Library 259. Cambridge, MA: Harvard University Press.

Gerfer, Anika. 2018. 'Global reggae and the appropriation of Jamaican Creole', *World Englishes* 37: 668–83.

Getzels, Jacob W. and Csikszentmihalyi, Mihaly. 1976. *The Creative Vision: A Longitudinal Study of Problem Finding in Art*. New York: John Wiley & Sons.

Gibson, Andy M. 2019. 'Sociophonetics of popular music: Insights from corpus analysis and speech perception experiments'. Ph.D. Dissertation, University of Canterbury, New Zealand.

Gilbert, P. F. C. 2001. 'An outline of brain function', *Cognitive Brain Research* 12: 61–74.

Giles, Howard and Smith, Philip. 1979. 'Accommodation theory: Optimal levels of convergence', in Howard Giles and Robert N. St. Clair (eds.), *Language and Social Psychology*, 45–65. Oxford: Basil Blackwell.

Gillespie, Luke O. 1991. 'Literacy, orality, and the Parry-Lord "formula": Improvisation and the Afro-American Jazz tradition', *International Review of the Aesthetics and Sociology of Music* 22: 147–64.

Givón, Talmy. 2005. *Context as Other Minds: The Pragmatics of Sociality, Cognition and Communication*. Amsterdam: John Benjamins.

Glăveanu, Vlad Petre and Kaufman, James C. 2019. 'Creativity: A historical perspective', in James C. Kaufman and Robert J. Sternberg (eds.), *The Cambridge Handbook of Creativity*, 9–26. Cambridge: Cambridge University Press.

Goldberg, Adele E. 2006. *Constructions at Work: The Nature of Generalization in Language*. Oxford: Oxford University Press.

Goldberg, Adele E. 2019. *Explain Me This*. Princeton, NJ: Princeton University Press.

Goldstein, David M. 2014. *Classical Greek Syntax: Wackernagel's Law in Herodotus*. Leiden: Brill.

Goldstein, David M. 2020. 'Homeric *-phi(n)* is an oblique case marker', *Transactions of the Philological Society* 118.343–75.

Golston, Chris and Riad, Tomas. 2000. 'The phonology of Greek meter', *Journal of Linguistics* 38: 99–167.
Golston, Chris and Riad, Tomas. 2005. 'The phonology of Greek lyric meter', *Journal of Linguistics* 41: 77–115.
Golston, Chris. 1990. 'Floating H (and L*) tones in Ancient Greek', in J. Meyers and P. E. Peréz (eds.), *Arizona Phonology Conference iii*, 66–82. Tucson, AZ: University of Arizona Linguistics Department.
Golston, Chris. 1991. 'Both lexicons', Ph.D. Dissertation, University of California, Los Angeles.
González, José M. 2013. *The Epic Rhapsode and His Craft: Homeric Performance in a Diachronic Perspective*. Washington, DC: Center for Hellenic Studies.
Graupe, Daniel. 2013. *Principles of Artificial Neural Networks*, 3rd edition. Singapore: World Scientific.
Gray, D. H. F. 1947. 'Homeric epithets for things', *Classical Quarterly* 61: 109–21.
Graziosi, Barbara. 2002. *Inventing Homer: The Early Reception of Epic*. Cambridge: Cambridge University Press.
Grethlein, Jonas and Huitnik, Luuk. 2017. 'Homer's vividness: An enactive approach', *Journal of Hellenic Studies* 137: 67–91.
Gries, Stefan T. 2005. 'Syntactic priming: A corpus-based approach', *Journal of Psycholinguistic Research* 34: 365–99.
Guardiano, Cristina. 2013. 'The Greek definite article across time', *Studies in Greek Linguistics* 33: 76–91.
Guarducci, Margherita. 2017. *L'epigrafia greca dalle origini al tardo impero*. Rome: Istituto Poligrafico dello Stato.
Gunkel, Dieter C. 2010. 'Studies in Greek and Vedic prosody, morphology, and meter', Ph.D. Dissertation, University of California, Los Angeles.
Gunkel, Dieter C. 2011. 'The emergence of foot structure as a factor in the formation of Greek verbal nouns in -μα(τ)-', *Münchener Studien zur Sprachwissenschaft* 65: 77–103.
Gunkel, Dieter C. 2014. '(Ancient Greek) accentuation', in Georgios K. Giannakis (ed.), *Encyclopedia of Ancient Greek Language and Linguistics*, 7–12. Leiden: Brill.
Gunkel, Dieter C. and Ryan, Kevin M. 2011. 'Hiatus avoidance and metrification in the Rigveda', in Stephanie W. Jamison, H. Craig Melchert, and Brent Vine (eds.), *Proceedings of the 22nd Annual UCLA Indo-European Conference*, 53–68. Bremen: Hempen.
Gusnard, Debra A., Akbudak, Erbil, Shulman, Gordon L., and Raichle, Marcus E. 2001. 'Medial prefrontal cortex and self-referential mental activity: Relation to a default mode of brain function', *Proceedings of the National Academy of Sciences of the United States* 98: 4259–64.
Guy, Gregory R. and Cutler, Cecelia. 2011. 'Speech style and authenticity: Quantitative evidence for the performance of identity', *Language Variation and Change* 23.1: 139–62.

Hackstein, Olav. 2002. *Die sprachform der homerischen Epen. Faktoren morphologischer Variabilität in literarischen Frühformen, Tradition, Sprachwandel, sprachliche Anachronismen*. Wiesbaden: Reichert.
Hackstein, Olav. 2010. 'The Greek of epic', in Egbert Bakker (ed.), *A Companion to the Ancient Greek Language*, 401–23. Malden, MA: Wiley-Blackwell.
Hagel, Stefan. 1994. 'Zu den Konstituenten des griechischen Hexameters', *Wiener Studien* 107/108: 77–108.
Hagel, Stefan. 2004. 'Tables beyond O'Neill', in François Spaltenstein and Olivier Bianchi (eds.), *Autour de la césure*, 135–215. Bern: Peter Lang.
Hainsworth, John Bryan. 1962. 'The Homeric formula and the problem of its transmission', *Bulletin of the London Institute of Classical Studies* 9: 57–68.
Hainsworth, John Bryan. 1968. *The Flexibility of the Homeric Formula*. Oxford: Clarendon Press.
Hainsworth, John Bryan. 1978. 'Good and bad formulae', in Bernard C. Fenik (ed.), *Homer: Tradition and Invention*, 41–50. Leiden: Brill.
Hajnal, Ivo. 2003a. *Troia aus sprachwissenschaftlicher Sicht. Die Struktur einer Argumentation*. Innsbruck: Institut für Sprachen und Literaturen, Abteilung Sprachwissenschaft.
Hajnal, Ivo. 2003b. 'Der epische Hexameter im Rahmen der Homer-Troia-Debatte', in Christoph Ulf (ed.), *Der neue Streit um Troia. Eine Bilanz*, 217–31. Munich: C.H. Beck.
Hall, Jonathan M. 2000. *Ethnic Identity in Greek Antiquity*. Cambridge: Cambridge University Press.
Hall, Jonathan M. 2013. *A History of the Archaic Greek World, ca. 1200-479 BCE*. New York: John Wiley & Sons.
Halle, John and Lerdahl, Fred. 1993. 'A generative textsetting model', *Current Musicology* 55: 3–23.
Halliwell, Stephen. 2011. *Between Ecstasy and Truth: Interpretations of Greek Poetics from Homer to Longinus*. Oxford University Press.
Hämmig, Anna Elisabeth. 2013. *Ny Ephelkystikon. Untersuchung zur Verbreitung und Herkunft des beweglichen Nasals im Griechischen.* Hamburg: Baar.
Hansen, P. A. 1983. *Carmina Epigraphica Graeca saeculorum VIII-V a.Chr.n.* Berlin: De Gruyter.
Haeselin, David. 2019. 'Concordance', *Archbook: Architectures of the Book*. http://drc.usask.ca/projects/archbook/concordance.php
Haug, Dag T. T. 2002. *Les phases de l'évolution de la langue épique: Trois études de linguistique homérique*. Göttingen: Vandenhoeck & Ruprecht.
Haug, Dag T. T. 2012. 'Tmesis in the epic tradition', in Øivind Andersen and Dag T. T. Haug (eds.), *Relative Chronology in Early Greek Epic Poetry*, 96–105. Cambridge: Cambridge University Press.
Haug, Dag T. T. and Welo, Eirik. 2001. 'The proto-hexameter theory: Perspectives for further research', *Symbolae Osloenses* 76: 138–44.
Hayes, Bruce and Kaun, Abigail. 1996. 'The role of phonological phrasing in sung and chanted verse', *The Linguistic Review* 13: 243–303.

Hayes, Bruce. 1989. 'The prosodic hierarchy in meter', in Paul Kiparsky and Gilbert Youmans (eds.), *Rhythm and Meter*, 201–60. Orlando, FL: Academic Press.
Hayes, Bruce. 1995. *Metrical Stress Theory: Principles and Case Studies*. Chicago, IL: University of Chicago Press.
Hayes, Bruce. 2009a. *Introductory Phonology*. New York: Blackwell.
Hayes, Bruce. 2009b. 'Textsetting as constraint conflict', in Jean-Louis Aroui and Andy Arleo (eds.), *Towards a Typology of Poetic Forms*, 43–61. Amsterdam: John Benjamins.
Heineman, Kristin. 2010. 'The chasm at Delphi: A modern perspective', in Neil O'Sullivan (ed.), *Proceedings for the 31st conference of the Australasian Society for Classical Studies*. classics.uwa.edu.au/ascs31
Hengeveld, Kees and Mackenzie, J. Lachlan. 2008. *Functional Discourse Grammar: A Typologically-Based Theory of Language Structure*. Oxford: Oxford University Press.
Hermann, Gottfried. 1816. *Elementa doctrinae metricae*. Glasgow: J. Duncan.
Hess, Mickey. 2005. 'Hip-hop realness and the white performer', *Critical Studies in Media Communication* 22: 372–89.
Higbie, Carolyn. 1990. *Measure and Music. Enjambement and Sentence Structure in the Iliad*. Oxford: Clarendon Press.
Higdon, David Leon. 2003. 'The concordance: Mere index or needful census?' *Text* 15: 51–68.
Hoekstra, Arie. 1957. 'Hésiode et la tradition orale', *Mnemosyne* 10: 193–225.
Hoekstra, Arie. 1964. *Homeric Modifications of Formulaic Prototypes: Studies in the Development of Greek Epic Diction*. Amsterdam and London: North-Holland.
Hoenigswald, Henry M. 1991. 'The prosody of the epic Adonius and its prehistory', *Illinois Classical Studies* 16: 1–15.
Hoey, Michael. 2005. *Lexical Priming: A New Theory of Words and Language*. London, New York: Routledge.
Høffding, Simon. 2014. 'What is skilled coping?: Experts on expertise', *Journal of Consciousness Studies* 21.9–10: 49–73.
Höfler, Stefan. 2019. 'Slaying men, or an etymology? Homeric ἀνδρειφόντης'. Paper presented at the conference Indo-European Religion and Poetics, October 11–12, 2019, University of Copenhagen. https://rootsofeurope.ku.dk/kalender/arrangementer-2019/indo-european-religion-and-poetics/handouts/S3T2_H_fler.pdf
Hollenbaugh, Ian B. 2020. 'Augmented reality: A diachronic pragmatic approach to the development of the IE injunctive and augment'. Paper presented at the 39th East Coast Indo-European Conference in Blacksburg, VA. https://ihollenbaugh.files.wordpress.com/2020/12/augmented_reality_a_diachronic_pragmatic.pdf
Hollenbaugh, Ian B. 2021. 'Tense and aspect in Indo-European: A usage-based approach to the verbal systems of the R̥gveda and Homer'. Ph.D. Dissertation, University of California, Los Angeles.

Holmes, Janet and Wilson, Nick. 2017. *An Introduction to Sociolinguistics*, 5th edition. London: Routledge.
Honko, Lauri. 2000. *Textualization of Oral Epics*. Berlin: De Gruyter.
Hopper, Paul. 1987. 'Emergent grammar', *Proceedings of the Thirteenth Annual Meeting of the Berkeley Linguistics Society*, 139–57.
Horn, Fabian. 2018. 'Dying is hard to describe: Metonymies and metaphors of death in the *Iliad*', *Classical Quarterly* 68: 359–83.
Horrocks, Geoffrey. 1997. 'Homer's dialect', in Ian Morris and Barry Powell (eds.), *A New Companion to Homer*, 193–217. Leiden: Brill.
Hovav, Malka Rappaport and Levin, Beth. 2008. 'The English dative alternation: The case for verb sensitivity', *Journal of Linguistics* 44: 129–67.
Hyman, Larry M. 2009. 'How (not) to do phonological typology: The case of pitch-accent', *Language Sciences* 31: 213–38.
Hytönen-Ng, Elina. 2013. *Experiencing 'Flow' in Jazz Performance*. Farnham: Ashgate.
Iandoli, Kathy. 2015. "How did Iggy Azalea become the world's most hated pop star?", *Cosmopolitan*, June 1, 2015. https://www.cosmopolitan.com/entertainment/celebs/news/a41270/iggy-azalea-timeline/
Ingalls, Wayne B. 1970. 'The structure of the Homeric hexameter: A review', *Phoenix* 24.1: 1–12.
Jakobson, Roman. 1960. 'Linguistics and poetics', in Thomas A. Sebeok (ed.), *Style and Language*. Cambridge, MA: MIT Press.
Janko, Richard. 1982. *Homer, Hesiod, and the Hymns: Diachronic Development in Epic Diction*. Cambridge: Cambridge University Press.
Janko, Richard. 1992. *The Iliad: A Commentary. Volume IV: Books 13–16*. Cambridge: Cambridge University Press.
Janko, Richard. 2012. 'πρῶτόν τε καὶ ὕστατον αἰὲν ἀείδειν: Relative chronology and the literary history of the early Greek epos', in Øivind Andersen and Dag T. T. Haug (eds.), *Relative Chronology in Early Greek Epic Poetry*, 20–43. Cambridge: Cambridge University Press.
Janse, Mark. 2003. 'The metrical schemes of the Hexameter', *Mnemosyne* 56: 343–48.
Janse, Mark. 2021. 'Phrasing Homer: A cognitive-linguistic approach to Homeric versification', *Symbolae Osloenses* 94.1: 2–32.
Jansen, Lina and Westphal, Michael. 2017. 'Rihanna works her multivocal pop persona: A morpho-syntactic and accent analysis of Rihanna's singing style', *English Today* 130: 46–55.
Jantos, Susanne. 2009. 'Agreement in educated Jamaican English: A corpus investigation of ICE-Jamaica'. Ph.D. Dissertation, Albert-Ludwigs-Universität Freiburg.
Jeffery, L. H. 1990. *The Local Scripts of Archaic Greece: A Study of the Origin of the Greek Alphabet and its Development from the Eighth to the Fifth Centuries BC*. Oxford: Clarendon Press.
Jenkins, I. H., Brooks, D. J., Nixon, P. D., Frackowiak R. S., and Passingham, R. E. 1994. 'Motor sequence learning: A study with positron

emission tomography', *Journal of Neuroscience* 14: 3775–90. https://doi.org/10.1523/JNEUROSCI.14-06-03775.1994

Johnson-Laird, P. N. 1988. 'Freedom and constraint in creativity', in R. J. Sternberg (ed.), *The Nature of Creativity: Contemporary Psychological Perspectives*, 202–19. Cambridge: Cambridge University Press.

Johnson-Laird, P. N. 2002. 'How jazz musicians improvise', *Music Perception* 19: 415–42.

Jones, James H. 1961. 'Commonplace and memorization in the oral tradition of the English and Scottish popular ballads', *The Journal of American Folklore* 74: 97–112.

Jurek, Thom. 2003. *An Untamed Sense of Control*. https://www.allmusic.com/album/mw0000019275

Kaczko, Sara. 2018. 'Faraway so close: Epichoric features and "international" aspirations in Archaic Greek epigram', *Revue de philologie, de littérature et d'histoire anciennes* XCII: 27–56.

Kahane, Ahuvia. 1994. *The Interpretation of Order: A Study in the Poetics of Homeric Repetition*. Oxford: Oxford University Press.

Kahneman, Daniel. 2011. *Thinking, Fast and Slow*. Westminster: Penguin.

Kaufman, James C. and Sternberg, Robert J. 2019. *The Cambridge Handbook of Creativity*. Cambridge: Cambridge University Press.

Kenny, B. J. and Gellrich, M. 2002. 'Improvisation', in R. Parncutt and G. E. McPherson (eds.), *The Science and Psychology of Music Performance: Creative Strategies for Teaching and Learning*, 117–34. Oxford: Oxford University Press.

Keuleers, Emmanuel. 2008. 'Memory-based learning of inflectional morphology', Ph.D. Dissertation, University of Antwerp.

Kiparsky, Paul. 1976. 'Oral poetry: Some linguistic and typological considerations', in Benjamin A. Stolz and Richard S. Shannon III, (eds.), *Oral Literature and the Formula*, 73–106. Ann Arbor: Center for Coordination of Ancient and Modern Studies.

Kiparsky, Paul. 2005. 'The Vedic injunctive: Historical and synchronic implications', in Rajendra Singh and Tanmoy Bhattacharya (eds.), *The Yearbook of South Asian Languages and Linguistics (2005)*, 219–36. Berlin: De Gruyter.

Kiparsky, Paul. 2017. 'Formulas and themes', in Frog (ed.), *Formula: Units of Speech, 'Words' of Verbal Art: Working Papers*, 155–63. Folkloristiikan toimite 23. Helsinki: University of Helsinki.

Kiparsky, Paul. 2018. 'Indo-European origins of the Greek hexameter', in Dieter Gunkel and Olav Hackstein (eds.), *Language and Meter*, 77–128. Leiden: Brill.

Kirk, Geoffrey Stephen. 1966. 'Studies in some technical aspects of Homeric style: I. The structure of the Homeric hexameter', *Yale Classical Studies* 20: 74–152.

Kirk, Geoffrey Stephen. 1976. *Homer and the Oral Tradition*. Cambridge: Cambridge University Press.

Kirk, Geoffrey Stephen. 1985. 'The structural elements of Homeric verse', in Geoffrey Stephen Kirk (ed.), *The Iliad. A Commentary. Volume I: Books 1–4*, 17–37. Cambridge: Cambridge University Press.

Kõiv, Mait. 2011. 'A note on the dating of Hesiod', *The Classical Quarterly* 61: 355–77.

Koniaris, George Leonidas. 1971. 'Michigan Papyrus 2754 and the *Certamen*', *Harvard Studies in Classical Philology* 75: 107–29.

Kortmann, Bernd and Lunkenheimer, Kerstin. 2012. *The Mouton World Atlas of Variation in English*. Berlin: De Gruyter Mouton.

Kroubo, Dagnini J. 2010. 'The importance of reggae music in the worldwide cultural universe', *Études caribéennes* 16.4740. https://doi.org/10.4000/etudes caribeennes.4740

Kuiper, Koenraad. 1996. *Smooth Talkers: The Linguistic Performance of Auctioneers and Sportscasters*. Mahwah, NJ: Lawrence Erlbaum Associates.

Labov, William, Ash, Sharon, and Boberg, Charles. 2006. *The Atlas of North American English: Phonetics, Phonology, and Sound Change*. Berlin: De Gruyter.

Ladefoged, Peter. 1972. 'Phonetic prerequisites for a distinctive feature theory', in A. Valdman (ed.), *Papers in Linguistics and Phonetics in Memory of Pierre Delattre*, 273–85. The Hague: Mouton.

Lakoff, George and Johnson, Mark. 1980. *Metaphors We Live By*. University of Chicago Press.

Lakoff, George and Turner, Mark. 1989. *More than Cool Reason: A Field Guide to Poetic Metaphor*. University of Chicago Press.

Landau, Andrew T. and Limb, Charles J. 2017. 'The neuroscience of improvisation', *Music Educators Journal* 103: 27–33.

Langacker, R. W. 1987. *Foundations of Cognitive Grammar, Volume I: Theoretical Prerequisites*. Stanford, CA: Stanford University Press.

Latacz, Joachim. 2011. 'Zu Homers Person', in Antonios Rengakos and Bernhard Zimmermann (eds.), *Homer Handbuch: Leben – Werk – Wirkung*, 1–25. Stuttgart: J. B. Metzler.

Le Page, Robert B. 1978. *Projection, Focussing, Diffusion: Or, Steps towards a Sociolinguistic Theory of Language, Illustrated from the Sociolinguistic Survey of Multilingual Communities*. Trinidad: Society for Caribbean Linguistics.

Le Page, Robert B. and Tabouret-Keller, Andrée. 1985. *Acts of Identity: Creole-Based Approaches to Language and Ethnicity*. Cambridge: Cambridge University Press.

Lee, Jamie Shinhee. 2011. 'Globalization of African American vernacular English in popular culture', *English World-Wide* 32: 1–23.

Legendre, Géraldine, Miyata, Yoshiro, and Smolensky, Paul. 1990. 'Harmonic grammar: A formal multi-level connectionist theory of linguistic well-formedness: Theoretical foundations', in *Proceedings of the Twelfth Annual Conference of the Cognitive Science Society*, 884–891. Cambridge, MA: Erlbaum.

Letts, Don. 2008. *Culture Clash: Dread Meets Punk Rockers*. London: SAF Publishing.

Limb, Charles J. and Braun, Allen R. 2008. 'Neural substrates of spontaneous musical performance: An fMRI Study of jazz improvisation', *PLoS ONE* 32. e1679. https://doi.org/10.1371/journal.pone.0001679

Lin, Phoebe M.S. 2010. 'The phonology of formulaic sequences: A review', in D. Wood (ed.), *Perspectives on Formulaic Language: Acquisition and Communication*, 174–93. New York/London: Continuum.

Lin, Phoebe M.S. 2012. 'Sound evidence: The missing piece in the jigsaw in formulaic language research', *Applied Linguistics* 33: 342–47.

Liu, Siyuan et al. 2012. 'Neural correlates of lyrical improvisation: An fMRI study of freestyle rap', *Scientific Reports* 2: 834. https://doi.org/10.1038/srep00834

López-González, M. and Limb, Charles J. 2012. 'Musical creativity and the brain', *Cerebrum* January 2012. https://www.ncbi.nlm.nih.gov/pmc/articles/PMC3574774

Lord, Albert Bates. 1960. *The Singer of Tales*. Cambridge, MA: Harvard University Press.

Lord, Albert Bates. 1968. 'Homer as oral poet', *Harvard Studies in Classical Philology* 72: 1-46.

Lord, Albert Bates (ed.). 1974. *Serbocroatian Heroic Songs, Volume 3: The Wedding of Smailagić Meho*. Cambridge, MA: Harvard University Press.

Lord, Albert Bates. 1991. *Epic Singers and Oral Tradition*. Ithaca, NY: Cornell University Press.

Lundquist, Jesse and Yates, Anthony. 2018. 'The morphology of Proto-Indo-European', in Matthias Fritz, Jared Klein and Brian Joseph (eds.), *Comparative Indo-European Linguistics: An International Handbook of Language Comparison and the Reconstruction of Indo-European*, Vol. 3, 2079–195. Berlin: De Gruyter.

Lynch, Tosca. 2016. '*Arsis* and *Thesis* in ancient rhythmics and metrics: A new approach', *The Classical Quarterly* 66.2: 491–513.

Maas, Paul. 1923. *Griechische Metrik*. Leipzig: Teubner.

Maas, Paul. 1962. *Greek Metre* (Translated by Hugh Lloyd-Jones). Oxford University Press.

MacDonald, Raymond, Byrne, Charles, and Carlton, Lana. 2006. 'Creativity and flow in musical composition: An empirical investigation', *Psychology of Music* 34: 292–306.

Macdonell, Arthur A. 1916 [1993]. *A Vedic Grammar for Students*. Delhi: Motilal.

Macdonell, Arthur A. 1926 [1989]. *A Sanskrit Grammar for Students*. Delhi: Motilal.

Magnelli, Enrico. 1995. 'Studi recenti sull'origine dell'esametro: un profilo critico', in Marco Fantuzzi and Roberto Petragostini (eds.), *Struttura e storia dell'esametro greco II*, 111–37. Rome: Gruppo editoriale internazionale.

Mandilaras, Basil. 1992. 'A new papyrus fragment of the *Certamen Homeri et Hesiodi*', in Mario Capasso (ed.), *Papiri letterari greci e latini I*, 55–62. Galatina: Congedo.

Martin, Richard P. 1989. *The Language of Heroes: Speech and Performance in the Iliad*. Ithaca: Cornell University Press.

Martin, Richard P. 2003. 'Keens from the absent chorus: Troy to Ulster', *Western Folklore* 62.1–2: 119–42.
Martinelli, Maria Chiara. 2001. 'Da Fränkel a Kahane. Considerazioni sulla divisione in cola dell'esametro omerico', *Gaia* 5: 119–29.
Matić, Dejan. 2003. 'Topic, focus, and discourse structure: Ancient Greek word order', *Studies in Language* 27.3: 573–633.
McCrorie, Edward. 2004. *Homer: The Odyssey.* Baltimore, MD: Johns Hopkins.
Meillet, Antoine. 1920. *Aperçu d'une histoire de la langue grecque*, 2nd edition. Paris: Hachette.
Meillet, Antoine. 1923. *Les origines indo-européennes des mètres grecs.* Paris: Presses Universitaires de France.
Meister, Karl. 1921. *Die homerische Kunstsprache.* Leipzig: Preisschriften der Jablonowskichen Gesellschaft.
Méndez Dosuna, Julián Víctor. 1993. 'Metátesis de cantidad en jónico-ático y heracleota', *Emerita* 61: 95–134.
Metcalf, Christopher. 2016. 'The Homeric epics and the Anatolian context', *The Classical Review* 67.1: 1–3.
Meusel, Eduard. 2020. *Pindarus Indogermanicus: Untersuchungen zum Erbe dichtersprachlicher Phraseologie bei Pindar.* Berlin: De Gruyter.
Milani, Celestina. 2013. 'Variation in Mycenaean Greek', in Georgios K. Giannakis (ed.), *Encyclopedia of Ancient Greek Language and Linguistics.* Leiden: Brill. http://dx.doi.org10.1163/2214-448X_eagll_COM_00000363.
Miller, George A. 1956. 'The magical number seven, plus or minus two: Some limits on our capacity for processing information', *Psychological Review.* 63: 81–97.
Miller, George A. 2003. 'The cognitive revolution: A historical perspective', *Trends in Cognitive Sciences* 7: 141–44.
Minchin, Elizabeth. 2001. *Homer and the Resources of Memory: Some Applications of Cognitive Theory to the* Iliad *and the* Odyssey. Oxford: Oxford University Press.
Minsky, Marvin. 1986. *The Society of Mind.* New York: Simon & Schuster.
Minton, William. 1975. 'The frequency and structuring of traditional formulas in Hesiod's *Theogony*', *Harvard Studies in Classical Philology* 79: 26–54.
Monier-Williams, Monier. 1899. *A Sanskrit-English Dictionary: Etymologically and Philologically Arranged with Special Reference to Cognate Indo-European Languages*, revised by E. Leumann, C. Cappeller, et al. Oxford: Clarendon Press.
Morgan, Marcyliena H. 2001. '"Nuthin but a G thang": Grammar and language ideology in hip-hop identity', in Sonja L. Lanehart (ed.), *Sociocultural and Historical Contexts of African American English*, 187–209. Amsterdam: John Benjamins.
Morpurgo Davies, Anna. 2002. 'The Greek notion of dialect', in Thomas Harrison (ed.), *Greeks and Barbarians*, 153–71. Edinburgh: Edinburgh University Press.

Morris, David Z. 2015. 'Iggy Azalea's minstrel show is imploding', *CL Tampa Bay*, January 9, 2015. https://www.cltampa.com/music/article/20760313/iggy-azaleas-minstrel-show-is-imploding

Morris, J. F. 1983. '"Dream scenes" in Homer, a study in variation', *Transactions of the American Philological Association* 113: 39–54.

Morrissey, Franz Andres. 2008. 'Liverpool to Louisiana in one lyrical line: Style choice in British rock, pop, and folk singing', in M. Locher and J. Strässler (eds.), *Standards and Norms in the English Language*, 195–220. Berlin: De Gruyter.

Mott, Brian. 2012. 'Traditional Cockney and popular London speech', *Dialectologia* 9: 69–94.

Murray, Penelope. 1981. 'Poetic inspiration in Early Greece', *The Journal of Hellenic Studies* 101: 87–100.

Murray, Penelope. 1996. *Plato on Poetry*. Cambridge: Cambridge University Press.

Murray, Penelope. 2015. 'Poetic inspiration', in Pierre Destrée and Penelope Murray (eds.), *A Companion to Ancient Aesthetics, First Edition*, 158–74. New York: John Wiley & Sons.

Nagler, M. N. 1967. 'Towards a generative view of the Homeric formula', *Transactions of the American Philological Association* 98: 269–311.

Nagy, Gregory. 1974. *Comparative Studies in Greek and Indic Meter*. Cambridge, MA: Harvard University Press.

Nagy, Gregory. 2004. *Homer's Text and Language*. Urbana and Chicago: University of Illinois Press.

Nagy, Gregory. 2009/2010. *Homer the Preclassic*. Berkeley and Los Angeles, CA. The 2009 online version is available at http://chs.harvard.edu/publications/. The 2010 print version is published by the University of California Press.

Nagy, Gregory. 2010. *The Homer Multitext Project*. https://chs.harvard.edu/curated-article/gregory-nagy-the-homer-multitext-project/

Nagy, Gregory. 2011. 'The Aeolic component of Homeric diction', in Stephanie W. Jamison, H. Craig Melchert, and Brent Vine (eds.), *Proceedings of the 22nd Annual UCLA Indo-European Conference*, 133–75. Bremen: Hempen Verlag. https://chs.harvard.edu/CHS/article/display/4138.gregory-nagy-the-aeolic-component-of-homeric-diction

Nakamura, Jeanne and Csikszentmihalyi, Mihaly. 2018. 'The experience of flow: Theory and research', in C. R. Snyder, Shane J. Lopez, Lisa M. Edwards, and Susana C. Marques (eds.), *The Oxford Handbook of Positive Psychology*, 279–96. Oxford: Oxford University Press.

Neely, James H. 1977. 'Semantic priming and retrieval from lexical memory: Roles of inhibitionless spreading activation and limited-capacity attention', *Journal of Experimental Psychology: General* 106.3: 226–54.

Neely, James H. 1991. 'Semantic priming effects in visual word recognition: A selective review of current findings and theories', in Derek Besner and Glyn W. Humphreys (eds.), *Basic Processes in Reading: Visual Word Recognition*, 264–336. New York: Routledge.

Nespor, Marina and Vogel, Irene. 1986 [2007]. *Prosodic Phonology*. Berlin: De Gruyter.
Nespor, Marina, Shukla, Mohinish, and Mehler, Jacques. 2011. 'Stress-timed vs. syllable-timed languages', in Marc van Oostendorp et al. (eds.), *The Blackwell Companion to Phonology*, 1147–59. Malden, MA: Blackwell.
Nida, Eugene Albert. 1946. *Morphology: The Descriptive Analysis of Words*. Ann Arbor, MI: University of Michigan Press.
Nietzsche, Friedrich. 1870. 'Der Florentinische Tractat über Homer und Hesiod, ihr Geschlecht und ihren Wettkampf', *Rheinisches Museum Für Philologie* 25: 528–40.
Nikolaev, Alexander. 2013. 'The Aorist infinitives in -εειν in early Greek hexameter poetry', *Journal of Hellenic Studies* 133: 81–92.
Nosowitz, Dan. 2015. 'I made a linguistics professor listen to a Blink-182 song and analyze the accent', *Atlas Obscura*, 18 June 2015. https://www.atlasobscura.com/articles/i-made-a-linguistics-professor-listen-to-a-blink-182-song-and-analyze-the-accent
Notopoulos, James A. 1964. 'Studies in Early Greek Oral Poetry', *Harvard Studies in Classical Philology* 68: 1–77
O'Hanlon, Renae. 2006. 'Australian hip-hop: A sociolinguistic investigation', *Australian Journal of Linguistics* 26: 193–209.
O'Neill, Eugene G., Jr. 1942. 'Localization of metrical word-types in the Greek hexameter', *Yale Classical Studies* 8: 105–78.
Pace-Sigge, Michael. 2013. *Lexical Priming in Spoken English Usage*. New York: Palgrave.
Pagán Cánovas, Cristóbal. 2020. 'Learning formulaic creativity: Chunking in verbal art and speech', *Cognitive Semiotics* 13.1. https://doi.org/10.1515/cogsem-2020-2023
Pagán Cánovas, Cristóbal and Antović, Mihailo. 2016. 'Formulaic creativity: Oral poetics and cognitive grammar', *Language and Communication* 47: 66–74.
Palmer, Leonard R. 1962. 'Homeric grammar', in Alan J.B. Wace and Frank H. Stubbings (eds.), *A Companion to Homer*, 75–178. London: MacMillan.
Parker, Holt. 2008. 'The linguistic case for the Aiolian migration reconsidered', *Hesperia* 77: 431–64.
Parry, Adam. 1956. 'The language of Achilles', *Transactions and Proceedings of the American Philological Association* 87: 1–7.
Parry, Milman. 1929. 'The distinctive character of enjambement in Homeric verse', *Transactions of the American Philological Association* 60: 200–20.
Parry, Milman. 1932. 'The Homeric language as the language of an oral poetry', *Harvard Studies in Classical Philology* 43: 1–50.
Parry, Milman. 1971. *The Making of Homeric Verse: The Collected Papers of Milman Parry*. Oxford: Clarendon Press.
Parry, Richard. 2020. 'Episteme and techne', in Edward N. Zalta (ed.), *The Stanford Encyclopedia of Philosophy*. https://plato.stanford.edu/archives/fall2020/entries/episteme-techne/

Partington, Alan. 1998. *Patterns and Meanings: Using Corpora for English Language Research and Teaching*. Amsterdam: John Benjamins.
Passa, Enzo. 2016a. 'L'epica', in Albio Cesare Cassio (ed.), *Storia delle lingue letterarie greche*, 139–96. Florence: Le Monnier.
Passa, Enzo. 2016b. 'L'elegia e l'epigramma su pietra', in Albio Cesare Cassio (ed.), *Storia delle lingue letterarie greche*, 260–88. Florence: Le Monnier.
Pavese, Carlo Odo. 1972. *Tradizioni e generi poetici della Grecia arcaica*. Rome: Edizioni dell'Ateneo.
Pavese, Carlo Odo 1996. 'La iscrizione sulla kotyle di Nestor da Pithekoussai', *Zeitschrift für Papyrologie und Epigraphik* 114: 1–23.
Pavese, Carlo Odo 2014. *La metrica e l'esecuzione dei generi poetici tradizionali orali nell'Ellade antica*. Trieste: EUT.
Pavese, Carlo Odo and Boschetti, Federico. 2003. *A Complete Formulaic Analysis of the Homeric Poems*. Amsterdam: Adolf M. Hakkert.
Pavese, Carlo Odo and Venti, Paolo. 2000. *A Complete Formular Analysis of the Hesiodic Poems*. Amsterdam: Adolf M. Hakkert.
Pawley, Andrew and Syder, Frances Hodgetts. 1983. 'Two puzzles for linguistic theory: Nativelike selection and nativelike fluency', in Jack C. Richards and Richard W. Schmidt (eds.), *Language and Communication*, 191–225. London: Longman.
Peabody, Berkley. 1975. *The Winged Word: A Study in the Technique of Ancient Greek Oral Composition as Seen Principally through Hesiod's Works and Days*. Albany: State University of New York Press.
Pearce, Marcus. 2010. *Boden and Beyond*: The Creative Mind *and its Reception in the Academic Community*. http://webprojects.eecs.qmul.ac.uk/marcusp/notes/boden.pdf
Peters, Martin. 1986. 'Zur Frage einer "achäischen" Phase des griechischen Epos', in Annemarie Etter (ed.), *O-o-pe-ro-si Festschrift für Ernst Risch zum 75. Geburtstag*, 303–19. Berlin: De Gruyter.
Pinker, Steven. 1994 *The Language Instinct*. New York: William Morrow and Company.
Porter, H. M. 1951. 'The early Greek hexameter', *Yale Classical Studies* 12: 3–63.
Pressing, Jeff. 1987. 'Improvisation: Methods and models', in J. Sloboda (ed.), *Generative Processes in Music: The Psychology of Performance, Improvisation, and Composition*, 129–78. Oxford: Oxford University Press.
Prince, Alan and Smolensky, Paul. 2008. *Optimality Theory: Constraint Interaction in Generative Grammar*. New York: John Wiley & Sons.
Probert, Philomen. 2003. *A New Short Guide to the Accentuation of Ancient Greek*. London: Bristol Classical Press.
Rampton, Ben. 1995. *Crossing: Language and Ethnicity among Adolescents*. London: Longman.
Rau, Jeremy. 2010. 'Greek and Proto-Indo-European', in Egbert J. Bakker (ed.), *A Companion to the Ancient Greek Language*, 171–88. Malden, MA: Wiley-Blackwell.

Read, John and Nation, Paul. 2004. 'Measurement of formulaic sequences', in Norbert Schmitt (ed.), *Formulaic Sequences: Acquisition, Processing and Use*, 23–35. Amsterdam: John Benjamins.
Ready, Jonathan and Tsagalis, Christos. 2018. *Homer in Performance: Rhapsodes, Narrators, and Characters*. Austin: University of Texas Press.
Ready, Jonathan. 2019. *Orality, Textuality, and the Homeric Epics: An Interdisciplinary Study of Oral Texts, Dictated Texts, and Wild Texts*. Oxford: Oxford University Press.
Reeve, Michael David. 1973. 'The language of Achilles', *The Classical Quarterly* 23: 193–95.
Renberg, Gil H. 2017. *Where Dreams May Come: Incubation Sanctuaries in the Greco-Roman World*. Leiden: Brill.
Renehan, Robert. 1971. 'The Michigan Alcidamas-Papyrus: A problem in methodology', *Harvard Studies in Classical Philology* 75: 85–105.
Ritschl, Friedrich. 1838. *Die Alexandrinischen Bibliotheken unter den ersten Ptolemäern und die Sammlung der Homerischen Gedichte durch Pisistratus nach Anleitung eines Plautinischen Scholions. Nebst litterar- historischen Zugaben über die Chronologie der alexandrinischen Bibliothekare, die Stichometrie der Alten, und die Grammatiker Heliodorus*. Breslau: Georg Philipp Aderholz.
Ritter, Simone M., Abbing, Jens, and van Schie, Hein T. 2018. 'Eye-closure enhances creative performance on divergent and convergent creativity tasks', *Frontiers of Psychology* 9: 1315. https://doi.org/10.3389/fpsyg.2018.01315
Rix, Helmut. 1976. *Historische Grammatik des Griechischen: Laut- und Formenlehre*. Darmstadt: Wissenschaftliche Buchgesellschaft.
Rose, C. Brian. 2008. 'Separating fact from fiction in the Aiolian migration', *Hesperia* 77: 399–430.
Rossi, Luigi Enrico. 2020. 'Anceps: vocale, sillaba, elemento', in Giulio Colesanti and Roberto Nicolai (eds.), *Scritti editi e inediti: Vol. 1: Metrica e Musica*, 125–39. Berlin: De Gruyter.
Rubin, David. 1995. *Memory in Oral Traditions: The Cognitive Psychology of Epic, Ballads, and Counting-Out Rhymes*. Oxford: Oxford University Press.
Rumelhart, David E. and McClelland, James L. 1986. *Parallel Distributed Processing. Explorations in the Microstructure of Cognition*. Cambridge, MA: MIT Press.
Runco, Mark and Jaeger, Garrett J. 2012. 'The standard definition of creativity', *Creativity Research Journal* 24: 92–96.
Russo, Joseph. 1966. 'The structural formula in the Homeric verse', *Yale Classical Studies* 20: 217–40.
Ryan, Kevin M. 2011. 'Gradient syllable weight and weight universals in quantitative metrics', *Phonology* 28.3: 413–454.
Ryan, Kevin M. 2013. 'Against final indifference'. Paper presented at M@90: Metrical Structure: Meter, Text-Setting, and Stress, MIT. https://www.youtube.com/watch?v=lHS2J6w4Wwc&t=1477s
Ryan, Kevin M. 2016. 'Phonological weight', *Language & Linguistics Compass* 10: 720–33.

Ryan, Kevin M. 2019. *Prosodic Weight: Categories and Continua*. Oxford: Oxford University Press.
Ryan, Kevin M. 2022. 'Syllable weight and natural duration in textsetting popular music in English', *English Language and Linguistics* 26.3: 559–82 https://www.people.fas.harvard.edu/~kevinryan/Papers/ryan_2021_textsetting_draft.pdf
Sale, Mary Merritt. 1996. 'In defense of Milman Parry: Renewing the oral theory', *Oral Tradition* 11.2: 374–417.
Sandell, Ryan P. 2015. 'Productivity in historical linguistics: Computational perspectives on word-formation in Ancient Greek and Sanskrit', Ph.D. Dissertation, University of California, Los Angeles.
Sandell, Ryan P. 2019. 'The place of Attic-Ionic Greek in word-level prosodic typology'. Paper presented at the conference New Ways of Analyzing Ancient Greek 1, 13–14 December 2019, Göttingen.
Sapir, Edward. 1921. *Language: An Introduction to the Study of Speech*. New York: Harcourt.
Sartwell, Crispin. 1998. *Act Like You Know: African-American Autobiography and White Identity*. Chicago, IL: University of Chicago Press.
Sauzet, Paul. 1989. 'L' accent du grec ancien et les relations entre structure métrique et représentation autosegmentale', *Langages* 24: 81–113.
Sawyer, Keith. 1992. 'Improvisational creativity: An analysis of jazz performance', *Creativity Research Journal* 5: 253–63.
Sawyer, Keith. 2011. 'The cognitive neuroscience of creativity: A critical review', *Creativity Research Journal* 23: 137–54.
Scarborough, Matthew. 2016. 'The Aeolic dialects of Ancient Greek: A study in historical dialectology and linguistic classification', Ph.D. Dissertation, University of Cambridge.
Schmidt, Carl Eduard. 1885. *Parallel- Homer, oder, Index aller homerischen Iterati in lexikalischer Anordnung*. Göttingen : Vandenhoeck und Ruprecht.
Schmitt, Norbert, Grandage, Sarah, and Adolphs, Svenja. 2004. 'Are corpus-derived recurrent clusters psycholinguistically valid?' in Norbert Schmitt (ed.), *Formulaic Sequences: Acquisition, Processing, and Use*, 127–51. Philadelphia, PA: John Benjamins.
Schulze, Wilhelm Emil. 1892. *Quaestiones Epicae*. Gütersloh: C. Bertelsmann.
Selkirk, Elisabeth O. 1980. 'Prosodic domains in phonology: Sanskrit revisited', in Mark Aronoff and Mary-Louise Kean (eds.), *Juncture: A Collection of Original Papers*, 107–30. Saratoga CA: Anma Libri.
Selkirk, Elisabeth O. 2011. 'The syntax-phonology interface', in John Goldsmith, Jason Riggle and Alan Yu (eds.), *The Handbook of Phonological Theory*, 2nd edition, 435–84. Malden, MA: Wiley-Blackwell.
Seuren, Pieter A. M. 2015. 'Prestructuralist and structuralist approaches to syntax', in Tibor Kiss and Artemis Alexiadou (eds.), *Syntax – Theory and Analysis: An International Handbook*, 134–57. Berlin: De Gruyter.

Shipp, George Pelham. 1972. *Studies in the Language of Homer*. Cambridge: Cambridge University Press.
Simons, D.J. and Chabris, C.F. 1999. 'Gorillas in our midst: Sustained inattentional blindness for dynamic events', *Perception* 28.9: 1059–74.
Simpson, Paul. 1999. 'Language, culture and identity: With (another) look at accents in pop and rock singing', *Multilingua* 18.4: 343–67.
Sinclair, John. 1991. *Corpus, Concordance, Collocation*. Oxford: Oxford University Press.
Sisario, Ben, Alter, Alexandra, and Chan, Sewell. 2013. 'Bob Dylan wins Nobel Prize, redefining boundaries of literature', *The New York Times*, October 13, 2013. https://www.nytimes.com/2016/10/14/arts/music/bob-dylan-nobel-prize-literature.html
Skafte Jensen, Minna. 2011. *Writing Homer. A Study Based on Results from Modern Fieldwork*. Copenhagen: Det Kongelige Danske Videnskabernes Selskab.
Skelton, Christina. 2017. 'Greek-Anatolian language contact and the settlement of Pamphylia', *Classical Antiquity* 36.1: 104–29.
Sloboda, John A. 1986. *The Musical Mind: The Cognitive Psychology of Music*. Oxford: Oxford University Press.
Smolensky, Paul and Legendre, Géraldine. 2006. *The Harmonic Mind: From Neural Computation to Optimality-Theoretic Grammar (Cognitive Architecture)*, Vol. 1. Cambridge, MA: MIT Press.
Solmsen, Felix. 1901 [2019]. *Untersuchungen zur griechischen Laut-und-Verslehre*. Berlin: De Gruyter.
Spiller, Henry, de Boer, Jella, Hale, John R., and Chanton, Jeffery. 2008. 'Gaseous emissions at the site of the Delphic Oracle: Assessing the ancient evidence', *Clinical Toxicology* 46.5: 487–88.
Steriade, Donca. 1988. 'Greek accent: A case for preserving structure', *Linguistic Inquiry* 19.2: 271–314.
Stevens, Jenny. 2013. 'Alex Turner reacts to Glastonbury accent comments', *NME*, June 29, 2013. http://www.nme.com/news/music/arctic-monkeys-171-1264151#LeLy8v5OB8uwVcVb.99
Stewart, Edmund. 2016. 'Professionalism and the poetic persona in Archaic Greece', *The Cambridge Classical Journal* 62: 200–23.
Strunk, Klaus. 1957. *Die sogenannten Äolismen der homerischen Sprache*. Inaugural-Dissertation, Universität zu Köln.
Stuart-Smith, Jane. 2017. 'Variationist approaches to the influence of the media on language', in D. Perrin and C. Cotter (eds.), *The Routledge Handbook of Language and Media*. London: Routledge.
Sudnow, David. 1978[1], 2001. *Ways of the Hand*, 2nd edition. Cambridge, MA: MIT Press.
Thomas, Erik R. 2004. 'Rural southern white accents', in Edgar W. Schneider et al. (ed.), *A Handbook of Varieties of English, 1: Phonology*, 300–24. Berlin: De Gruyter.
Thompson, Rupert J. E. 1999. 'Instrumentals, datives, locatives and ablatives: The -φι case form in Mycenaean and Homer', *The Cambridge Classical Journal* 44: 219–250.

Thompson, Stith. 1955–58. *Motif-Index of Folk-Literature: A Classification of Narrative Elements in Folk-Tales, Ballads, Myths, Fables, Mediaeval Romances, Exempla, Fabliaux, Jest-Books, and Local Legends*. Copenhagen: Rosenkilde and Bagger.

Thornhill, Michael T. 2014. 'Strummer, Joe [*real name* John Graham Mellor]', *Oxford Dictionary of National Biography*. Oxford: Oxford University Press. https://doi.org/10.1093/ref:odnb/88710

Thumb, Albert and Kieckers, Ernst. 1932. *Handbuch der griechischen Dialekte I*. Heidelberg: Carl Winter.

Thumb, Albert and Scherer, A. 1959. *Handbuch der griechischen Dialekte II*. Heidelberg: Carl Winter.

Tichy, Eva. 1981. 'Hom. ἀνδροτῆτα und die Vorgeschichte des daktylischen Hexameters', *Glotta* 59: 28–67.

Tichy, Eva. 2022. *Ilias diachronica Alpha*. https://freidok.uni-freiburg.de/fedora/objects/freidok:223894/datastreams/FILE1/content

Tigersted, E. N. 1970. 'Furor Poeticus: Poetic inspiration in Greek literature before Democritus and Plato', *Journal of the History of Ideas* 31: 163–78.

Tolkien, John Ronald Reuel. 2006. *The Monsters and the Critics and Other Essays*. London: Harper Collins.

Tomasello, Michael. 2003. *Constructing a Language: A Usage-Based Theory of Language Acquisition*. Cambridge. MA: Harvard University Press.

Tomasello, Michael. 2009. 'The usage-based theory of language acquisition', in Edith L. Bavin (ed.), *The Cambridge Handbook of Child Language*, 69–87. Cambridge: Cambridge University Press.

Topintzi, Nina. 2010. *Onsets: Suprasegmental and Prosodic Behaviour*. Cambridge: Cambridge University Press.

Trudgill, Peter. 1983. 'Acts of conflicting identity: The sociolinguistics of British pop-song pronunciation', in Peter Trudgill (ed.), *On Dialect: Social and Geographical Perspectives*, 141–60. Oxford: Blackwell. Reprinted as: Trudgill, Peter. 1997. 'Acts of conflicting identity: The sociolinguistics of British pop-song pronunciation', in Nikolas Coupland and Adam Jaworski (eds.), *Sociolinguistics: A Reader and Coursebook*, 251–66. Houndmills: Palgrave Macmillan.

Ustinova, Yulia. 2017. *Divine* Mania: *Alteration of Consciousness in Ancient Greece*. London: Routledge.

Vaidya, Avinash R., Pujara, Maia S., Petrides, Michael, Murray, Elisabeth A., and Fellows, Lesley K. 2019. 'Lesion studies in contemporary neuroscience', *Trends in Cognitive Science* 23: 653–71.

Van Beek, Lucien. 2022. *The Reflexes of Syllabic Liquids in Ancient Greek: Linguistic Prehistory of the Greek Dialects and Homeric* Kunstsprache. Leiden: Brill.

Van Rooy, Raf. 2016. 'What is a "dialect"? Some new perspectives on the history of the term διάλεκτος and its interpretations in ancient Greece and Byzantium', *Glotta* 92: 244–79.

Venti, Paolo. 1991. 'Per un'indagine sulla formularità dello *Scudo di Herakles*', *Lexis* 7/8: 26–71.

Vergados, Athanassios. 2009. 'Penelope's fat hand reconsidered (Odyssey 21,6)', *Wiener Studien* 122: 7–20.
Visser, Edzard. 1987. *Homerische Versifikationstechnik: Versuch einer Rekonstruktion.* Frankfurt: Peter Lang.
Visser, Edzard. 1988. 'Formulae or single words? Towards a new theory of oral verse-making', *Würzburger Jahrbücher für die Altertumswissenschaft* 14: 21–37.
Von der Mühll, Peter. 1962. *Odyssea/Homerus*, 3rd edition. Basel: Helbing and Lichtenhahn.
Wachter, Rudolf. 2007. 'Greek dialects and epic poetry: Did Homer have to be an Ionian?' in Miltiades B. Hatzopoulos and Vassiliki Psilakakou (eds.)· *Actes du Ve Congrès International de Dialectologie Grecque*, 317–28. Paris: Diffusion de Boccard.
Wachter, Rudolf. 2010. 'Inscriptions', in Egbert J. Bakker (ed.), *A Companion to the Ancient Greek Language*, 47–61. Malden, MA: Wiley-Blackwell.
Wackernagel, Jacob. 1924. *Vorlesungen über Syntax mit besonderer Berücksichtigung von Griechisch, Lateinisch und Deutsch.* Basel: Philologisches Seminar der Universität Basel.
Wanta, Wayne and Meggett, Dawn. 1988. '"Hitting playdirt": Capacity theory and sports announcers' use of clichés', *Journal of Communication* 38: 82–89.
Warner, Natasha and Arai, Takayuki. 2001. 'Japanese mora-timing: A review', *Phonetica* 58: 1–25.
Wathelet, Paul. 1981. 'La langue homérique et le rayonnement littéraire de l'Eubée', *L'Antiquité Classique* 50: 819–33.
Watkins, Calvert. 1976. 'Observations on the "Nestor's cup" inscription', *Harvard Studies in Classical Philology* 80: 25–40.
Watkins, Calvert. 1995. *How to Kill a Dragon: Aspects of Indo-European Poetics.* Oxford: Oxford University Press.
Watson, Kevin. 2007. 'Liverpool English', *Journal of the International Phonetic Association* 37: 351–60.
Watts, Richard J. and Morrissey, Franz Andres. 2019. *Language, the Singer and the Song: The Sociolinguistics of Folk Performance.* Cambridge: Cambridge University Press.
Wells, John C. 1982. *Accents of English. Vol. 2: The British Isles.* Cambridge: Cambridge University Press.
Werner, Kenny. 1996. *Effortless Mastery.* New Albany, IN: Jamey Aebersold Jazz.
West, Martin Litchfield. 1973. 'Greek poetry 2000–700 B.C.', *Classical Quarterly* 23: 179–92.
West, Martin Litchfield. 1982. *Greek Metre.* Oxford: Clarendon Press.
West, Martin Litchfield. 1988. 'The rise of the Greek epic', *Journal of Hellenic Studies* 108: 151–72.
West, Martin Litchfield. 1997. 'Homer's meter', in Ian Morris and Barry Powell (eds.), *A New Companion to Homer*, 218–37. Leiden: Brill.
West, Martin Litchfield. 2007. *Indo-European Poetry and Myth.* Oxford: Oxford University Press.

West, Martin Litchfield. 2011. *The Making of the Iliad: Disquisition and Analytical Commentary*. Oxford: Oxford University Press.
West, Martin Litchfield. 2014. *The Making of the Odyssey*. Oxford: Oxford University Press.
West, Martin Litchfield. 2018. 'Unmetrical verses in Homer', in Dieter Gunkel and Olav Hackstein (eds.), *Language and Meter*, 362–79. Leiden: Brill.
West, Martin Litchfield. 2021. 'Homeridae', *Oxford Classical Dictionary*. Oxford: Oxford University Press.
West, Stephanie. 1994. 'Nestor's bewitching cup', *Zeitschrift für Papyrologie und Epigraphik* 101: 9–15.
White, John Williams. 1912. *The Verse of Greek Comedy*. London: Macmillan.
Whitman, Neal. 2010. 'Prime time for "Imma"', *Behind the Dictionary*. https://www.visualthesaurus.com/cm/dictionary/prime-time-for-imma/
Wilkinson, Dan. 2014. 'Why do rappers put on fake accents?' *Vice*, September 9, 2014. https://www.vice.com/en/article/rb9yw6/why-do-rappers-insist-on-putting-on-fake-accents
Wilkinson, Dan. 2016. 'We asked a linguist why Alex Turner now sounds like an old cowboy', *Vice*, April 8, 2016. https://noisey.vice.com/en_us/article/6x89zn/we-asked-a-linguist-why-alex-turner-now-sounds-like-he-was-born-in-california
Willi, Andreas. 2002. *The Language of Greek Comedy*. Oxford: Oxford University Press.
Willi, Andreas. 2006. *The Languages of Aristophanes: Aspects of Linguistic Variation in Classical Attic Greek*. Oxford: Oxford University Press.
Willi, Andreas. 2018. *Origins of the Greek Verb*. Cambridge: Cambridge University Press.
Witte, Kurt. 1913. 'Homeros', in Georg Wissowa and Wilhelm Kroll (eds.), *Paulys Real-Encyclopädie der Classischen Altertumswissenschaft: neue Bearbeitung* VIII, 2188–247. Stuttgart: J. B. Metzler.
Witte, Kurt. 1972. *Zur homerischen Sprache*. Darmstadt: Wissenschaftliche Buchgesellschaft.
Wolfe, Charles. 1982. *Kentucky Country: Folk and Country Music of Kentucky*. Lexington: University Press of Kentucky.
Wood, Graeme. 2009. 'The answer, my Friend . . . Our correspondent makes a pilgrimage to Bob Dylan's hometown in search of the source of his bizarre accent', *The Atlantic*, August 2009. http://www.theatlantic.com/magazine/archive/2009/08/the-answer-my-friend/307647
Woodard, Roger D. 2008. 'Greek dialects', in Roger D. Woodard (ed.), *The Ancient Languages of Europe*, 50–72. Cambridge: Cambridge University Press.
Woodard, Roger D. 2010. 'Phoníkēia Grammata: An alphabet for the Greek language', in Egbert J. Bakker (ed.), *A Companion to the Ancient Greek Language*, 25–46. Malden, MA: Wiley-Blackwell.
Wray, Alison and Perkins, Michael R. 2000. 'The functions of formulaic language: An integrated model', *Language & Communication* 20: 1–28.

Wyatt, W.F. 1978. 'Penelope's fat hand (*Od.* 21.6–7)', *Classical Philology* 73: 343–44.
Yunis, Harvey. 2011. *Plato: Phaedrus*. Cambridge: Cambridge University Press.
Zanker, Andreas T. 2019. *Metaphor in Homer: Time, Speech, and Thought*. Cambridge: Cambridge University Press.

Index Locorum

Antipater of Thessalonica *Epigrammata* 72 G-P = *Anthologia Graeca* 12.296; 151
Archilochus, *Fragmenta* 1; 200
Archilochus, *Fragmenta* 196; 114

Democritus, Diels-Kranz 68B18; 201

Hesiod, *Theogony* 22–34; 198
Hesiod, *Works and Days* 24–25; 196
Homeric Hymn to Apollo, 3.156–64; 145

Il. 1.1–2; 103
Il. 1.1–25; 8
Il. 1.1; 75
Il. 1.2; 85
Il. 1.7; 63; 74, 85
Il. 1.8; 200
Il. 1.10–11; 85
Il. 1.63–64; 105
Il. 1.90–91; 106
Il. 1.148; 53
Il. 1.277; 75
Il. 1.364; 53
Il. 1.517; 53
Il. 2.418; 61
Il. 2.484–86; 199
Il. 3.172; 108
Il. 4.356; 53
Il. 5.114; 8
Il. 7.264; 57
Il. 8.300–8; 131
Il. 10.31; 57
Il. 10.249; 133
Il. 11.89; 56
Il. 11.425; 60
Il. 11.749; 60
Il. 13.508; 59, 60
Il. 13.520; 60
Il. 14.452; 60
Il. 14.508–10; 200
Il. 16.517–22; 96

Il. 17.315; 60
Il. 19.61; 60
Il. 21.403; 57
Il. 22.17; 61
Il. 22.269; 59
Il. 23.280; 133
Il. 24.738; 60

Mahābhārata 3.52.1; 111

Nestor's Cup; 68

Od. 1.1–2; 103
Od. 3.64; 8
Od. 4.277–79; 146
Od. 7.203; 133
Od. 8.43–45; 197
Od. 8.479–80; 197
Od. 8.488; 198
Od. 13.260–1; 54
Od. 17.382–86; 196
Od. 21.6; 57
Od. 22.269; 60
Od. 22.326; 57
Od. 22.347–49; 197
Od. 22.347–48; 222

Pindar, *Fragmenta* 150; 200
Pindar, *Nemean* 5.1–3; 196
Plato, *Ion* 532c5–9; 203
Plato, *Ion* 535b–c3; 204
Plato, *Ion* 533d1–4; 203
Plato, *Ion* 534c7–8, 534d1–4; 203
Plato, *Ion* 542b4–5; 204
Plato, *Phaedrus* 245a5–8; 201
Plato, *De Republica* 608b4–7; 202

Rigveda 1.32.1a–b; 109

Sappho, *Fragmenta* 1.1–2; 109

General Index

accent (stress); 73, 77–78, 82, 92 (fn. 76), 98, 101, 125, 140, 141 (fn. 33), Glossary
accent (way of speaking); 145–47, 163, 169, 179, 182, *see also* English
Adele; 162–68
Aeolic base; 109, 112
Aeolic default (theory of); 134 (fn. 12)
Alcman; 177–78
alliteration; 68, 127
alphabet
    Euboean; 67
    East Ionic; 67, 73 (fn. 25)
Apollonius Rhodius; 9, 39, 207
Arctic Monkeys; 168 (fn. 102), 183–85, 193 (fn. 142)
Aristotle; 152 (fn. 66), 205
arsis and thesis; 69 (fn. 13)
assimilation; 76, 90, Glossary
authenticity; 150, 168, 187–90
ay-ungliding (English); 163–64, 169, 172

Bacchylides; 1, 110 (fn. 112), 196 (fn. 8)
barytonesis; 140–41
biceps (elementum); 69, 78, 80, 99 (fn. 86)
Blink-182; 178, 180
Böckh, August; 86 (fn. 62), 100 (fn. 91)
bound phrases; 15–16
breve (elementum); 69 (fn. 12)
Brit–Pop pronunciation; 163–66, 173, 175 (fn. 112), 179, 185
bucolic diaeresis or 4c; 10, 51, 82, 84

caesura
    definition; 80–83
    bucolic; *see* bucolic diaeresis
    feminine or caesura κατὰ τρίτον τροχαῖον or 3b; 10, 56, 82, 84
    hephthemimeral or 4a; 10, 17, 82, 111
    masculine or penthemimeral or 3a; 56, 82, 84
chunking; 24–25, 27–30, 35, 43–44, 46, 61

clitic; 73, 82–83, 90 (fn. 72), 91, 95, 98 (fn. 88), 104, 106, Glossary
cognitive psychology; 1 (fn. 2), 28, 207, 210, 214, 220
cola; *see* hexameter, colometry of
collocation
    definition; 33–34
    in Homer; 37–39
    in Herodotus; 36–37
    in Quintus Smyrnaeus; 39–40
    in the London–Oslo–Bergen corpus; 34–36
    collocational measures; 33
    short vs. long; 35
    as indirect proof of orality of composition; 43–44
    see Index of Homeric phraseology
compensatory lengthening
    in English; 72 (fn. 23), 163
    first (Greek); 67 (fn. 6), 139, 142
    second (Greek); 199 (fn. 13)
    third (Greek); 143, 144 (fn. 44, 46), 154 (fn. 71), 160–61
    see Glossary
conceptual association (or mini-theme)
    definition; 48
    see Index of Homeric phraseology
concordance; 21–22
connectionism; 44–45, 56, *see* priming
constituent
    order; 18, 128 (fn. 143)
    prosodic; 89, *see* prosodic hierarchy
    syntactic; 88
constructions (in Homer); 51–52, *see* Index of Homeric phraseology
construction grammar; 44, 50–51
creativity; 1–4, 14, 16 (fn. 24), 30, 66, 127, 194–95, 205–7, 223

Democritus; 201
Dire Straits; 166 (fn. 99)
dialect (Greek)
    distribution of; 136, 148–49

dialect (Greek) (cont.)
  imitation of; 145–47
  and ethnicity; 147–48
  mixing; 163
  see also Greek
dialect (English); see English
digamma (the sound [w])
  definition; 155
  metrical traces of; 74, 76, 108, 143, see hiatus
  loss of; 176, 190
Dixon, Alesha; 182–83
Dylan, Bob; 169–73

elision
  elisio non officit caesurae (Hermann's Law); 85, 101–2
  in Ancient Greek; 90
  in the hexameter; 83, 85, 95
  in Vedic; 109 (fn. 110)
  see Glossary
English
  African American; 169, 186–88
  American; 24 (fn. 39), 72 (fn. 23), 164–65, 169, 172, 174, 189, 192
  British; 72 (fn. 23), 90 (fn. 71), 165, 174–75, 192
  English; 163, 167–68
  Jamaican; 179 (fn. 120)
  Liverpool; 175
  Sheffield; 168 (fn. 102), 183–85
enjambement
  in English poetry; 104–5
  in Homer; 103
  periodic or necessary or violent; 103, 106–7
  unperiodic or unnecessary; 103, 105–6
Eminem; 187–88
enthousiasmós; 201–4, 210, 213, 220–21, 225
epic distraction; 142 (fn. 38), see Glossary
epistḗmē; 202–03

features (linguistic, in Homer)
  archaic; 131, 136–38
  artificial; 131–32
  dialectal; 138–44
  mixed; 133–34
fermata; 79–80
final devoicing; 89
flow; 210–20
foot; 68 (fn. 10), 92
formula
  antiquity of; 58
  flexibility of; 14–17, 58
  fossilization of; 15
  in Indo-European; 16
  liveliness of; 61

meaning of; 62–63, see also referentiality
origin of; 15
productivity of; 61
renewal of; 16. 9 (fn. 6), 58, 49
structural; 14, 19
extension and economy of; 9–10
see also formularity
formula (definitions in Homeric scholarship)
  Bakker; 19
  Hainsworth; 15
  Hoekstra; 14
  Kiparsky; 15–16
  Nagler; 17
  Nagy; 19
  Parry; 6–8, 13–14
  Russo; 14, 19
  Visser; 17–18
  Watkins; 16
formula (quantitative analysis)
  history; 1, 12, 33, 43, 5–8, 11–13
  examples; 7–8, 12, 12 (fn. 14)
  limitations; 12–13, 27
formulaic expression; 6, 14, 50
formularity
  as an emergency technology; 127, 224
  as epiphenomenon; 17
  factors affecting; 31–33
  in Homer; 5, see Index of Homeric phraseology
  in Homeric similes; 32
  in natural languages; 20, see idiom principle, bound phrases, prefabricated expressions
  in sports commentary; 117
  frequency; 15, 24–25, 35 (fn. 17), 37–39

gap theory; 157–60, 177
generative grammar; 22
generative metrics; 87–88, 113
grammaticalization; 24–25
Greek
  Aeolic; 136 (fn. 18), 138–41
  Arcado–Cyprian; 132 (fn. 6), 137, 148, 156
  Attic–Ionic; 73 (fn. 27, 28), 131, 137–44, 148, 155, 156, 157–58, 161
  Attic; 136, 137–44, 148, 150, 154 (fn. 71)
  Boeotian; 132, 137, 140 (fn. 32), 141 (fn. 34), 148, 150, 153, 161, 190
  Central Ionic; 136 (fn. 18), 148
  Doric; 147–48, 150, 155
  East Ionic; 136 (fn. 18), 161, 181, 185, 189–90
  Ionic; 136 (fn. 18), 141–44
  Mycenaean; 74 (fn. 29), 108, 131, 132, 136 (fn. 16), 137–39, 143, 145 (fn. 47), 148, 155–57, 160
  Thessalian; 131–32, 136 (fn. 18), 137, 139, 140 (fn. 32), 148
  West Greek; 137–38, 147–48

General Index

West Ionic (or Euboean); 66–7, 148, 160–61, 181
Green Day; 180–81

Hesiod; 12 (fn. 14), 189–90, 195–96, 198–99, 205
hexameter
   antiquity of; 107–11
   colometry of; 86–88, 99–102
   Fränkel's theory of; 87, 102
   incisions and bridges; 81–85
   Kiparsky's theory of; 113–15
   Kirk's theory of; 102
   melody of; 98–99
   mentions in Herodotus; 64
   reading aloud; 77–78, 85–86
   scansion of; 72–73
   schematic notation of; 78–80
   spondaic; 69 (fn. 15)
   structure of; 68–69
   Tichy–Berg Theory of; 111–13
hiatus
   and –v *ephelkustikón* 131 (fn. 3), 143
   at the end of a line; 100–1
   at the juncture of two formulas; 8
   due to loss of [h]; 59
   due to loss of [w]; 76, 108, 143
   in British English; 90 (fn. 71)
   in Homer (general strategies); 74
   in the *Rigveda*; 109
   shortening; *see* metrical errors/licenses
   tolerance; 101
Holcomb, Roscoe; 171–72
Homeric question; 2 (fn. 3), 11
Homeridae; 190
Horace; 1–2, 31, 201, 206
hypofrontality; 215, 219–20, 225

idiom (idiomaticity, idiom principle); 15, 20, 22–27, 26, 48 (fn. 74)
Iggy Azalea; 185–90
improvisation; 32, 194–95, 205–13, 215, 217–22, 223–25
indifferens (elementum); 79
interpuncts; 67, 91, 102 (fn. 96)
intonation unit; 93–97
intonation; *see* tunes
intonational phrase; 90–91, 93–97, 100, 119–20

jazz; 206–10

Kiparsky, Paul; 14–16, 22, 50, 58, 65, 109 (fn. 109), 112 (fn. 116), 112, 113–15, 132 (fn. 5)
Kunstsprache; 3, 130–35, 154–55, 162, 192–93, *see also* performance language

longum (elementum); 68–69, 78, 80
Lord, Albert; 2, 6 (fn. 3), 11–12, 16 (fn. 23), 29 (fn. 51), 32 (fn. 52), 43, 48, 76 (fn. 34), 86, 170, 207, 222
loss of coda [r] (English); 163, 169, 174–76, 192

manía; 201–02, 213
mastery; 29–33, 43, 62, 224
Međedović, Avdo; 11
memory
   long term; 28 (fn. 45, 46), 46–47, 55, 209, 214–15
   working; 27–30, 46–47, 54, 61, 117–18, 123, 126–27, 208–9, 215, 220, 223, *see also* chunking
meter
   "emerges from language"; 115–16
   and cognition; 127
   as prosodic regularization; 116–17, 126–27
   Classical Sanskrit; 110–11
   English; 121–22
   in oral traditions; 115, 127
   in Homer; *see* hexameter
   Vedic; 109
metrical errors/licenses
   at the juncture of formulaic expressions 8–9
   at the line end; 79–80
   brevis in longo; 69 (fn. 12), 108
   correptio Attica; 74, 144
   correptio epica (hiatus shortening, *vocalis ante vocalem corripitur*); 74, 109 (fn. 110)
   in Homer; 76–77
   in oral-traditional poetry; 64, 76
   syncopation (anaclasis); 113
metrical necessity; 115, 127–29, 168
mora; 71–72, *see also* Glossary
motif; 2, 28
Muses; 198–200, 201
muta cum liquida; 74–75, 138

Nagy, Gregory; 19, 116, 124, 134 (fn. 13), 152 (fn. 64), 156, 157
Nestor's cup; 67–68, 73, 114
neuroscience; 205, 213–221

oral-formulaic theory; 5, 11, 17, 156, 207, 221
overshooting; 185–90
oxytone words; 98–101

Parry, Milman; 2, 6–14, 16–18, 21, 43, 48, 50, 53, 56, 62, 86, 103, 128, 154–56, 181, 207
Pear stories; 94–95, 123
performance language; 135, 151, 162, 168, 181, 185–86, 189, 190–93
phoneme; 69 (fn. 16), Glossary

phonological phrase; 89–89, 101, 120–21
Pindar; 86 (fn. 62), 150, 153, 190 (fn. 141), 196, 200, 222
Plato; 152 (fn. 64), 185, 190, 194, 199 (fn. 12), 200–5, 209, 216–17, 200
prefabricated expressions (or prefabs); 5, 12, 20, 25–27, 30, 33–35, 223, *see* idiom principle
priming
  by absolute frequency (long–term memory); 46–47
  by recency (working memory); 46–47, 54
  definition; 45–46
  in Homer; 47, 55–58
  lexical priming; 44, 47
  syntactic priming; 46
productivity; 61
prosodic hierarchy; 88–92, 97
prosodic regularization
  in hyperfluent speech; 116–26
  in formulaic sequences; 124
  in Ancient Greek; 124–26
proto–hexameter, *see* Hexameter, Tichy-Berg Theory of
psilosis; 141, 143, 161
psycholinguistics; 24, 45–46, 115
punk rock; 178–82, 192

quantitative metathesis; 75, 142, 157–59, 177, Glossary
Quintus Smyrnaeus; 9 (fn. 7), 39–44, 62, 224

raddoppiamento fonosintattico; 90
reception (linguistic); 177–78
referentiality
  traditional; 32 (fn.53), 62, 168
  intertextual; 63
rhapsode; 202–04, 208
rhythm and blues; 166, 167 (fn. 101), 169, 182
rhythm; 77, 79–80, 106, 116, 120–22, 124, 126, 207, *see also* arsis and thesis

sandhi
  definition 89 (fn. 71), Glossary
  in Sanskrit; 90
  in British English; 90 (fn. 71)
Sappho; 109–10, 156, 173
sociolinguistics; 148 (fn. 60), 164 (fn. 95), 165, 168, 173, 176–77, 179 (fn. 120), 181, 191–93

sonorant
  syllabic; 108, 156–57
  consonantal; 74, 76
  see Glossary
sonority sequencing; 70–71
sound; 69 (fn. 16)
sports commentary; 31, 117–24, 223
spurious diphthongs; 67 (fn. 6), 73 (fn. 27), Glossary
syllabification; 70–73
syllable
  definition; 69–71
  heavy vs. light; 68–69, 71–73, 80
  superheavy; 72, 73, 79
  weight; 72 (fn. 23), *see* mora
synapheia; 72, 81, 109
synchronic bias; 176–77, 192
synekphonesis; 75, 109
synizesis; 75, 158, Glossary

tapping of /t/ (English); 163–64, 174
tékhnē; 196, 201–4, 210, 220–21
textsetting; 79
textualization; 11 (fn. 9), 107, 116, 132 (fn. 7), 162, 189
The Beatles; 173–76
The Clash; 179
theme; 2, 11 (fn. 11), 16, 48–49, 50, 54, 56, 62, 170, 212
tmesis; 138, 193
Trudgill, Peter; 163–67, 175, 178–180, 185, 193 (fn. 142)
tunes (prosodic)
  in hyperfluent speech; 118, 122
  in intonation languages; 97–98
  in poetic recitation; 123
  in the hexameter; *see* hexameter, melody of
type scene; 48, 54, 209

Urban, Keith; 189

Virgil; 9, 33, 207
vowel contraction; 137, 142, 144

Wernicke's Law; 59
West, Martin; 160–61, 195, 207 (fn. 32)
word
  in oral traditions; 62
  linguistic definitions of; 82
  metrical (*Wortbild*); 82–3, 99

Index of Homeric forms

-θε(ν); 133
-ν *ephelkustikón*; 143
3.pl. in -σαν; 143

augment; 132

dat.pl. in -εσσι; 139
dat.pl. in -ῃσι; 133
definite article; 18, 132, 138

gen.sg. in -οιο; 132–33, 138, 176
gen.sg. in -ου; 143
gen.sg. in *-οο; 143, 176

infinitives in -εειν; 131–32
infinitives in -μεν; 139
infinitives in -μεναι; 141

patronymic adjectives in -ιος; 138, 177

-φι(ν); 131, 138
ἄμμε; 141
ἄμμι; 133–34, 139
ἀνδρειφόντης; 137 (fn. 20)
ἀνδροτῆτα; 108, 137, 156–57
βροτός; 138

δάσσαντο vs. ἐδάσαντο; 140
εἰς vs ἐσσι; 135
ἐνί; 133
ἐπίστιον; 143
ἐρεβεννή; 139
ἔσσομαι vs. ἔσομαι; 140, 142
ζάθεος; 141
ἡμέας; 142
ἡμεῖς; 133–34
κε(ν); 139
κεκλήγοντες; 139
κοιμῶντο vs. *κοιμάοντο; 142
μέσσος vs. μέσος; 140, 142
νηός vs. νεώς; 142
ξεῖνος vs. ξένος; 143–44
ὁππότερος; 140
ὅππως; 140
ὄσσε; 49–50, 138
οὖλος; 143
πέλεται; 138
πεμπώβολα; 138 (fn. 26), 153
τελέσαι vs. τελέσσαι; 142
τέταρτον vs. τέτρατον; 141
τόσος; 140
υἱός, υἱι, υἷα, etc. 141
ὔμμε; 141

Index of PIE forms

*-bhi (instr.pl.); 131
*-nt (3pl.act.); 143
*-osi̯o (gen.sg.); 133
*-su (loc.pl.); 133
*dʰeugʰ- "make"; 195
*dʰh₁-nt "they put"; 143
*h₁e- (augment); 132
*h₁es-mi "I am"; 67 (fn. 6)
*h₁es-si "you are"; 140 (fn. 31)
*h₃ók"-ih₁ "two eyes"; 49
*k"el- "turn"; 138
*k"er- "make"; 195
*medʰi̯os "middle"; 140

*meǵh₂- "big"; 76 (fn. 32)
*men- "think"; 199 (fn. 13)
*nebh- "cloud"; 76 (fn. 32)
*neh₂w-ós "ship"; 142
*n̥sm- "we"; 139
*peh₃- "drink"; 68 (fn. 8)
*penk"- "five"; 138 (fn. 26), 142
*snigʷʰ- "snow"; 76
*sreu- "flow"; 76
*swe (reflexive pronoun); 76
*tek̑- "make"; 195 (fn. 7)
*wīk̑m̥tī "twenty"; 142
*wreh₁ǵ- "break"; 76

Index of Homeric phraseology

Formulas
  ἄλγεα πάσχων; 48
  βαρὺ στενάχων; 53
  βοὴν ἀγαθὸς Διομήδης; 8
  βοὴν ἀγαθὸς Μενέλαος; 8
  βοῶπις πότνια Ἥρη; 59
  εἵλετο (...) χειρὶ παχείῃ; 56–57
  ἕλε γαῖαν ἀγοστῷ; 59
  θεὰ λευκώλενος Ἥρη; 59
  λιποῦσ' ἀνδροτῆτα καὶ ἥβην; 108, 137, 156–57
  ὀδὰξ ἕλον ἄσπετον οὖδας; 59
  Ὀδυσσῆος φίλος υἱός; 8
  πήματα πάσχων; 51
  πόδας ὠκὺς Ἀχιλλεύς; 54
  πολύτλας δῖος Ὀδυσσεύς; 8
  τὸν δὲ κατ' ὀφθαλμῶν ἐρεβεννὴ νὺξ ἐκάλυψε; 49
  ὣς φάτο; 105

Collocations
  ἀλγ- "pain" + παθ- "suffer"; 16, 48
  πηματ- "misery" + παθ- "suffer"; 50
  βαρυ- "deep" + στεναχ- "sigh"; 53–54
  πεδ- "foot" + ὠκυ- "swift"; 54
  πεδ- "foot" + ταχ- "swift"; 54
  γλυκ- "sweet" + ἱμερο- "desire"; 55–56
  χειρ- "hand" + ἑλ- "take" + παχυ- "thick"; 57
  τεύχεα "weapons" + καλά "beautiful"; 16
  ἵμερος "desire" + αἱρέω "seize"; 66 (fn. 2)

Constructions
  ^{3b}⏑⏑ − [⏑⏑ − − ⏑]$_{Subject.Noun\ Phrase}$ αἱρεῖν; 56
  [−]$_{Object.Pronoun}$ δ' [⏑⏑ − ⏑ ⏑ −]$_{Subject.Participial\ Phrase}$ προσέφη [− ⏑ ⏑ − ⏑ ⏑ −]$_{Subject.Noun\ Phrase}$; 53
  ^{5a}[πήματ- + παθ-]^{6b}$_{Verb\ Phrase}$; 52
  ^{5a}[πήματα πάσχ- −]$_{Verb\ Phrase}$; 51
  ^{3c}[ποσὶν ταχέεσσι]$_{Dative.Noun\ Phrase}$ [διώκ- −]$_{Verb\ Phrase}$; 54

Conceptual Associations
  PAIN + SUFFER; 48–49, 50, 55
  DARKNESS (DEATH) + COVER + EYES; 49–50
  SIGH + DEEPLY; 53–54
  FEET + FAST; 54
  TAKE + EARTH + WITH TEETH; 59–61
  TAKE + EARTH + WITH PALM; 59–61
  EMOTION + TAKE OVER; 56

For EU product safety concerns, contact us at Calle de José Abascal, 56–1°,
28003 Madrid, Spain or eugpsr@cambridge.org.

www.ingramcontent.com/pod-product-compliance
Ingram Content Group UK Ltd.
Pitfield, Milton Keynes, MK11 3LW, UK
UKHW020046230326
469195UK00013B/105